KV-050-915

Judging from Experience

Available or forthcoming titles
Judging from Experience: Law, Praxis, Humanities
Jeanne Gaakeer

Schreber's Law: Jurisprudence and Judgment in Transition
Peter Goodrich

Living in Technical Legality: Science Fiction and Law as Technology
Kieran Tranter

edinburghuniversitypress.com/series/ecsllh

Judging from Experience

Law, Praxis, Humanities

Jeanne Gaakeer

EDINBURGH
University Press

Edinburgh University Press is one of the leading university presses in the UK. We publish academic books and journals in our selected subject areas across the humanities and social sciences, combining cutting-edge scholarship with high editorial and production values to produce academic works of lasting importance. For more information visit our website: edinburghuniversitypress.com

Edinburgh University Press Ltd
The Tun – Holyrood Road
12 (2f) Jackson's Entry
Edinburgh EH8 8PJ

Typeset in 11/13pt Adobe Garamond Pro by
Servis Filmsetting Ltd, Stockport, Cheshire
and printed and bound in Great Britain

A CIP record for this book is available from the British Library

ISBN 978 1 4744 4248 0 (hardback)
ISBN 978 1 4744 4250 3 (webready PDF)
ISBN 978 1 4744 4251 0 (epub)

Contents

PART II *IURIS PRUDENTIA* OR INSIGHTFUL KNOWLEDGE
OF LAW

Acknowledgements

This book has gestated over many years, and it carries an intellectual debt both to institutions and to people. My thanks go to Erasmus School of Law and my colleagues Sanne Taekema and Wibren van der Burg in the Department of Sociology, Theory, and Methodology, for providing the opportunity to pursue the scholarly course I have had in mind these past decades. With Marc Loth, I had the pleasure of co-authoring the coursebook *Meesterlijk Recht* (Boom: The Hague, 2001), and this proved formative for my view on jurisprudence. To James Boyd White, I owe what grasp I have of *Law and Literature*. He has been a constant source of inspiration since 1993, and I am deeply grateful for his continued friendship. I am also much indebted to convenors of numerous conferences all over the world, and to their audiences. They have granted me the benefit of their thoughtful comments and critical remarks, all of which helped me reflect on my project. To Daniela Carpi (University of Verona), Greta Olson (University of Giessen) and Arild Linneberg (University of Bergen), I am particularly grateful for their support and encouragement over the years. My thinking was also greatly enriched by conversations with fellow judges participating in the annual summer course 'Language, Literature and the Judiciary', organised by the Dutch Training and Study Centre for the Judiciary, which I co-teach with other *Law and Literature* aficionados. My colleagues at the Court of Appeal in The Hague, with whom I share the beauty and the burden of the judicial shop floor, taught me by experience the importance of narrative in the fact-finding process. For decades of tender loving care, unwavering support and patience, I cannot thank Christan Zantboer enough.

I am grateful to the publishers and editors for permission to publish here materials and sections from:

'Why am I here? Some observations on medical triage in Pat Barker's *Regeneration*', in F. Meulenberg and I. D. de Beaufort (eds), *Science, Fiction, and Science-Fiction: The Role of Fiction in Public Debates on Medical Ethical Issues and in the Medical Education* (Overveen: Belvedère, 2006), pp. 80–8; '"The Word that Coincides with You", the poet Gerrit Achterberg's experience with law and forensic psychiatry', *Revue Interdisciplinaire d'Études Juridiques*, 2008, pp. 49–71; 'The Future of Literary-Legal Jurisprudence: Mere Theory or Just Practice?', 5 *Law and Humanities*, no.1, 2011, pp. 185–96; 'The Genetics of Law and Literature: What is Man?', in D. Carpi (ed.), *Bioethics and Biolaw through Literature* (Berlin: De Gruyter, 2011), pp. 23–67; *'Iudex Translator*: The Reign of Finitude', in P.-G. Monateri (ed.), *Methods of Comparative Law* (Cheltenham and Northampton, MA: Edward Elgar, 2012), pp. 252–69; 'Understanding Fact and Fiction in Robert Musil's *The Man without Qualities*', 7 *Pólemos*, 2013, pp. 15–38; 'Control, Alt, and/or Delete? Some Observations on New Technologies and the Human', in M. Hildebrandt and J. Gaakeer (eds), *Human Law and Computer Law* (Dordrecht: Springer, 2013), pp. 135–57; 'Dignity and Disgrace in Law and Literature', in I. Ward (ed.), *Law, Literature and Human Rights* (Berlin: De Gruyter, 2015), pp. 309–28; 'Futures of Law and Literature: a Jurist's Perspective', in C. Hiebaum et al. (eds), *Recht und Literatur im Zwischenraum/ Law and Literature In-Between, aktuelle inter-und transdisciplinäre Zugänge/contemporary inter- and transdisciplinary approaches* (Bielefeld: Transcript, 2015), pp. 71–103; 'Close Encounters of the "Third" Kind', in D. Carpi and K. Stierstorfer (eds), *Diaspora, Law and Literature* (Berlin: De Gruyter, 2016), pp. 41–67; 'Sua Cuique Persona? A Note on the Fiction of Legal Personhood and a Reflection on Interdisciplinary Consequences', 28 *Law & Literature*, no. 3, 2016, pp. 287–317; 'The Judge's Perplexity is the Scholar's Opportunity', 18 *German Law Journal*, no. 2, 2017, pp. 332–62; 'Configuring Justice', 9 *No Foundations, An Interdisciplinary Journal of Law and Justice*, 2012, pp. 20–44, available at <http://nofoundations.com/NoFo9GAAKEER. htm>; 'Reverent Rites of Legal Theory: unity-diversity-interdisciplinarity', 36 *Australian Feminist Law Journal*, 2012, pp. 19–43, available online <http:// www.tandfonline.com/>, <https://doi.org/10.1080/13200968.2012.108544 66>; 'Practical Wisdom and Judicial Practice: Who's in Narrative Control?', The Online Collection of the Italian Society for Law and Literature, available at <www.lawandliterature.org>.

I wish to thank William MacNeil, Shaun McVeigh, and the team at Edinburgh University Press for the opportunity to publish with them, and for all the work done in order to translate the manuscript into the book. I owe thanks as well to the accomplished Dutch-Canadian translator Pleuke Boyce for her translation of various Achterberg poems in Chapter 5, for which translation permission was obtained from the Willem-Kloos Fonds, The Hague. James Clarke kindly granted me permission to cite his poem 'When He Read' (from: *The Juried Heart* (New York: Pleasure Boat, 2015), p. 21) in Chapter 11. The epigraph to this book is taken from W. G. Sebald, *Austerlitz* (Harmondsworth: Penguin Books, 2002), pp. 174–5, with the permission of Penguin Publishers.

'Language may be regarded as an old city full of streets and squares, nooks and crannies, with some quarters dating from far back in time while others have been torn down, cleaned up and rebuilt, and with suburbs reaching further and further into the surrounding country'

Introduction

Hinterland

The voyage that this book is a reflection of started in the late 1970s when I was studying for an MA in English and American literature. In those days, the teaching staff at Utrecht University, the Netherlands, consisted of a mix of staunch defenders of New Criticism and early adepts of narratology, post-colonialism and deconstruction, a combination that often left us students baffled as we oscillated between memorising metaphysical poetry and excavating texts for hidden, ideological meanings. These methodologies generated in me an acute interest in what people do to and with language. When I began my legal education, I was driven by the idea that law is what people do to one another by means of language. But disappointment awaited. Rule-oriented courses were the main staple. Where were the people to whom the rules applied? What did it mean to apply a rule? What did one actually do when one said one did? What view on language was there behind the notion of rule application? No answers were given, simply because such questions did not matter much. However, when I took courses in legal philosophy and the history of ideas of law – revealingly called, as they still are today, *meta-juridica* – I understood that the reflective methodology of the humanities had its place in law.

This formative moment caused a shift in my academic focus. While searching for a dissertation topic, I came across Richard Posner's *Law and Literature*.[1] The book came as a double shock. The very idea of a bond existing between law and literature was immensely consoling, yet Posner's elaboration seemed restrictive. It reduced the importance of a literary turn of mind for legal practice. As I continued my parallel education in law and literature, I experienced that in the humanities departments the topic met with suspicion.

---

[1] R. A. Posner, *Law and Literature: A Misunderstood Relation* (Cambridge, MA: Harvard University Press, 1988 [rev. eds 1998 and 2009]).

I was, more or less, hounded out as a traitor to the humanities, for we all knew that law had absolutely nothing to do with the postmodern study of literature, did we not? Fortunately, Erasmus School of Law offered me the opportunity to pursue my goal. In the works of James Boyd White and Richard Weisberg, the revitalisation of the two early twentieth-century challenges provoked by John Wigmore and Benjamin Cardozo[2] was both aspirational and critical in nature. To me at least, these two lenses with which to view contemporary law and literature differed in degree rather than in kind. White's thesis on the homology of law and literature resonated,[3] given the earlier unity of law and literature in the European context. And so did his approach to the connection between two disciplines as an integrated product of translation. Weisberg's emphasis on an ethical view with respect to the enterprise of law and literature added to its importance.[4]

When I began to serve as a judge, this occasioned another shift in my thought. Only then did I realise fully the potential of what the fields of *Law and Literature*, or, more broadly, *Law and the Humanities*, have to offer: namely, the reminder that success in practising law depends to a large extent on developing one's imagination, while constantly remaining alert to the pitfalls of our linguistic usages in relation to our own private and professional biases when we read and write the narratives in and of law. This is one of the ideas animating this book.

When as academic jurists we turn to the humanities to further our inter-disciplinary legal projects, I therefore suggest that we reconsider the alliance of theory and practice in law and jurisprudence, lest we run the risk of legal practice remaining unresponsive to interdisciplinary studies, and of students of law dismissing 'Law and' courses as irrelevant for the development of their professional skills. In short, in developing interdisciplinary scholarship, we should not create new academic ghettos. It is only through law in practice that we can learn to speak of justice. This is why the *quid-iuris* question at the heart of legal doctrine and jurisprudence traditionally conceived remains crucial when it comes to investigating the possibilities of the contribution of the humanities on the methodological plane. On the one hand, this speaks for attention to how legal and social relations are established by means of our

[2] J. H. Wigmore, 'A list of legal novels', 2 *Illinois Law Review*, 1908, pp. 574–93; 'A list of one hundred legal novels', 17 *Illinois Law Review*, 1922, pp. 26–41. B. N. Cardozo, 'Law and literature', *Yale Review*, 1925, pp. 489–507.

[3] J. B. White, *When Words Lose Their Meaning: Constitutions and Reconstitutions of Language, Character, and Community* (Chicago: University of Chicago Press, 1984), p. xii.

[4] R. H. Weisberg, *The Failure of the Word: The Protagonist as Lawyer in Modern Fiction* (New Haven: Yale University Press, 1984).

discourse on legal meaning and justice. On the other hand, it ties in with the subject of the methodology of the legal perception of the case at hand. This is important to note, because the view of law as a normative set of propositions that are 'out there' in an unadulterated form, ready for our application, unfortunately remains in need of refutation. Because jurists are obviously trained for the purpose of doing law, the humanistic study of law should be a *praxis*, a merger of reflection with action. Academic research can then also have an impact of the kind desired so highly by its leadership.

This brings me to another issue. I often perceive that my academic colleagues in law and the humanities from common law countries have misconceptions about civil law legal reasoning. It is supposedly a mere syllogistic, deductive rule application, moving from abstract, codified legal norms to the decision in a specific case, all in contradistinction to common law reasoning. The expectation raised by such a conception of rule application seems to be that of an unproblematic existence and use of abstract norms. That notion is oversimplified, to say the least. If we start categorising what is to count as knowledge in the field of law, and begin from the premise that law is a domain of rules only, this simplification can lead to the marginalisation of interdisciplinary ventures based on it. Furthermore, it creates a false opposition between common law and civil law thought on the act of judging – adjudication being the most prominent feature of the intertwinement of theory and practice; namely, it proclaims for civil law jurisdictions a formalist hermeneutics. That is to say, one of 'outside-in' legal reasoning, as Ronald Dworkin called it, from the abstract to the concrete, rather than 'inside-out' reasoning, with a focus on the judicial effort of connecting the facts of the case to the legal norms.[5]

I suggest that it is on the plane sketched above that the humanities can, firstly, help elucidate the problems connected to this type of misunderstanding, and, secondly, contribute to their possible solution. That is why I turn to philosophical hermeneutics, especially as developed by the French philosopher Paul Ricoeur. I aim to draw a blueprint of what the humanities can contribute to the realm of *praxis* by bringing to the fore the resources that can contribute to the judge's development of her professional quality of *phronèsis*: namely, practical wisdom. The view behind my enterprise is that, despite their differences, most legal systems share core values such as judicial impartiality, consistency and integrity, which, not incidentally, are considered virtues in the Aristotelian sense. Methodological reflections on the determination of the facts of a case, the judicial justification of deliberative

[5] R. Dworkin, *Justice in Robes* (Cambridge, MA and London: Belknap Press, 2006), p. 54.

choices made, and the way in which law establishes relations between people are therefore shared tasks.

A Pragmatic Approach

Since the days of Quintilian, law students have been taught to argue both sides of the case, the method of the *controversiae*. My perhaps not so humble proposal therefore is to cherish the old legal adages of interpretation *diversi sed non adversi* (different, but not contrary)[6] and *eadem sed aliter* (the same, but differently) to help *Law and Literature* continue to thrive worldwide. *Law and Literature* offers wonderful opportunities for a methodology that can renew the legal pedagogy of close reading and sharing a text, responding to it with the generosity of an open mind, and engaging in dialogue with those whose perspectives are informed by other notions and experiences. In Europe as well, the humanistic study of law has regained momentum. This inspires me to return to various aspects of text, language, and narrative discussed in *Law and Literature*, in order to investigate new possibilities for contributions to legal practice.

My views are obviously informed and influenced by the context of my legal education, and my work as an academic and a judge in a European civil law system, and within it, the field of criminal law. However, I do not intend to promote forms of parochialism along the lines of continent. Being the nomad that I am, I hope that it is not professional arrogance that compels me to opt for a focus on the judicial perspective.[7] The pragmatic reason for doing so – the ancient Greek word πραγματικος referring to one skilled in law – is why not try to turn to profit what one thinks one knows? Books on the act of judging are not seldom written by academics with no actual, visceral experience of the sublime, or rather the terrible, responsibility of the judge: namely, what it means to have a fellow human being right in front of you across the bench, and being the one assigned the duty to decide about his or her fate.

Firmly rooted as I still am in the notion of law as text, and of language as the profession's software, I look for fundamental commonalities of law and literature. The double premise of this book is that law as an academic discipline belongs to the humanities, given its development since the redis-

---

[6] The term 'different, but not contrary', or its equivalent *diversum sed non contrarium* ('different, but not conflicting') was used in medieval law and theology to show that texts on a subject and their various interpretations need not be in conflict. See G. R. Evans, *Law and Theology in the Middle Ages* (London: Routledge, 2002).

[7] An honorary title bestowed on me by Greta Olson ('De-Americanizing law-and-literature narratives: opening up the story', 22 *Law & Literature*, 2010, pp. 338–64, p. 340).

covery of the Justinian Code that is characterised by a language-oriented, philosophical-hermeneutical perspective, and that, as a consequence, jurists necessarily combine the theoretical and the practical. Practice turns to theory for justification of new arguments, and input from practice is necessary to move doctrinal debates forward. Because hermeneutics is not merely a methodology for interpretation, but rather a philosophical view for a broad mode of inquiry into text and human action, the art of doing law in concrete cases always requires attention to the reciprocal relation between fact and norm.

Given this interaction, the primary object of interpretation is always a combination of the narrative(s) of the facts and the relevant propositions of law. This necessitates attention to the effects of the narrative construction of the facts on the interpretation and application of the legal norm, substantive or procedural, both for scholarly reflection and for legal practice. One way to look at the importance of narrative for law is that the picture of reality that law orders at the moment it tells its tale resembles the literary rendering of a particular moment – how a world is captured in words. Therefore, narrative construction matters, and we should ask in which way does it steer the reader towards interpretation. Equally important is that in each casuistic account of the facts the theoretical knowledge of legal doctrine is necessarily confronted with the narrative knowledge of literature.[8] That makes *Law and Literature* essential for legal practice. It also suggests that jurists should bear in mind the influence of their own interpretive frameworks and unconscious choices or preferences with regard to both facts and norms. To the skeptics whom I hope to convince, I say that the 'and' of *Law and Literature* does not imply a methodologically dangerous liaison of dissimilar disciplines, but a fundamental relatedness.

Another reason to turn to philosophical hermeneutics is that in legal theory as well as in interdisciplinary legal studies the debate continues on whether law is part of the social sciences or firmly rooted in the humanities. Any stand we take here is important when it comes to discussing the future of such broader fields as *Law and the Humanities* or *Law and Culture* and their critical functions. My point is that it will simply not do for law to lump together the empirically inclined 'Law ands' with the language-based varieties. I conceive jurisprudence to be contextual knowledge of law. This requires the ability to enter imaginatively into any given situation. As a practical skill of knowing what a situation amounts to, and what it requires

---

[8] R. Foqué and A. C. 't Hart, *Instrumentaliteit en rechtsbescherming* (Arnhem: Gouda Quint, 1990), p. 369.

in terms of judicial action, it benefits from what the humanities have to offer by way of insight into different aspects of humanity. That is another idea animating this book.

The Roadmap

This book is divided into three parts. Part I takes as its overarching topic the enchantment of knowledge in law. Chapter 1 discusses Gustave Flaubert's eponymous clerks *Bouvard and Pécuchet* to illustrate the result of a process of differentiation of knowledge culminating in the positivist thought of the nineteenth century. It serves as the blueprint for the book as a whole. Chapters 2 and 3 take the return road to the 'nooks and crannies' – as the epigraph to this book calls them – of the language of law, not out of nostalgia for the halcyon days of the unity of law and the humanities, but to show what brought us where we are now. Chapter 2 offers a short overview of the processes of differentiation in law and jurisprudence – from the unity brought about by the rediscovery of the *Corpus Iuris Civilis* in the eleventh century to the rise of national legal systems culminating in the nineteenth century, and from law as an autonomous discipline to 'Law ands' in the twentieth century – in order to provide a small map of the territory from a historical, European perspective. Chapter 3 discusses the limits of language in relation to questions of determinism and volition, and asks what the nineteenth-century epistemological and methodological debate on the disciplinary character of the humanities – the *Erklären-Verstehen* controversy – means for contemporary interdisciplinary legal studies. Discussions of Robert Musil's novel *The Man without Qualities* and the Dutch poet Gerrit Achterberg's *Acid* poems in Chapters 4 and 5 illuminate how the theoretical considerations of Chapters 1 to 3 have literary counterparts.

Against this background, Part II turns to *iuris prudentia*, insightful knowledge of law. It provides the building blocks for a humanistic model for doing law. Chapter 6 elaborates on the importance of practical knowledge, *phronèsis*, when it comes to combining facts and norms. On the basis of the works of Aristotle and Ricoeur, it discusses the distinction between theoretical and practical knowledge, and offers an analysis of *phronèsis* as the disposition that takes its deliberations from the circumstances of things. As such, it forms the basis for a proposal to incorporate philosophical hermeneutics in law, both in theory and in practice. Chapter 7 addresses the uses of metaphor in law. It asks in what way does metaphor help spark new meaning, and in what way can it hold us captive and make us fall into the trap of cognitive dissonance, confirmation bias and belief perseverance. Chapter 8 asks after the requirements of judicial narrative intelligence. It introduces the topic of empathy, and analyses the way in which mimesis as re-presentation of human action works in law and in literature. Finally, it connects these topics to a right discrimination of the equitable. Pat Barker's *Regeneration* illustrates the argument by connecting the topic of voice to (in)justice. The interconnections of law and narrative are the topic of Chapters 9 and 10. They consider the possibility of a legal narratology and the form(s) it could take, firstly by focusing on the topics of probability, coherence, and plot in law and literature and, secondly, by turning to the implications of a narratological approach for criminal law in practice. John Coetzee's *Disgrace* exemplifies the issues that Chapter 10 raises.

Part III deals with what Benjamin Cardozo called the perplexities of judges that become the scholar's opportunity, again a connection of theory and practice in law. With Ian McEwan's *The Children Act*, Chapter 11 returns to the topic of empathy. Because narratives can trigger empathic and emotional responses in various ways, it asks what the cognitive turn in narratology means for the judge who deals with the emotions and narratives of others. By way of conclusion as to why *Law and Literature* matters deeply for legal practice, Part III also goes to 'the suburbs', as the epigraph has it, and to the dystopic effects of technology unbridled by just law. Chapter 12 focuses on DNA biotechnology by means of a reading of Michel Houellebecq's *Atomised*, combined with Martin Heidegger's view on technology. Finally, in Chapter 13, issues of privacy and freedom in connection with the consequences of artificial and ambient intelligence in law are raised by turning to Juli Zeh's *The Method*. Both chapters ask how new technologies affect the constitution of the human self, and consider what influences an instrumental use of technology can have on selfhood, on legal personhood, and on our ability to narrate ourselves, in law and elsewhere.

While in one sense this book reflects my parallel education and career, partisan as that may be, at the same time it hopes to offer some food for thought for a continued discussion on interdisciplinary research, and guidance for judicial self-reflection, or at least suggestions for wonderful reading. Mine is not a grand theory of law and literature, but an attempt – an essay as Montaigne used the term – to show that their combined study in *Law and Literature* is best viewed as the intertwined snakes portrayed on Hermes's *caduceus*, symbolic of the negotiation of meaning: in concord. At the end of this prefatory chapter, this would probably be the place to offer, in truly juridical fashion, a few disclaimers on terminology or on what lies beyond the scope of this book – and that is a great deal. One trigger warning suffices: this book offers perhaps an idealistic view that policy-oriented jurists find hard to swallow. But since Aristotle advised us to start 'by wondering that things are as they are',[9] they, as well as my other readers, who I hope will prove to be the Maecenases of this book, have to find out for themselves.

[9] Aristotle (trans. W. D. Ross), *Metaphysics* (Oxford: Oxford University Press, 1958) 16, 983a14–15.

Part I

The Enchantment of Knowledge:
Fact and Fiction in
Law and Literature

1

The Enchantment of Knowledge and its Apotheosis: Gustave Flaubert's *Bouvard and Pécuchet*

Law, Fact, Fiction

Paris, summer 1838

It is thirty-two degrees Celsius on the deserted Boulevard Bourdon. Deserted? No, not really. Two solitary walkers brave the heat. From the direction of the Bastille, François Denys Bartholomée Bouvard, widower, aged forty-seven, and copy-clerk in a business concern, appears. From the Jardin des Plantes, Juste Romain Cyrille Pécuchet, bachelor, aged forty-seven, and copy-clerk at the Admiralty, comes into view. On making one another's acquaintance – on a seat in that historical Arsenal triangle – they immediately feel 'the charm of affection in its initial stages'.[1] Their conversation soon turns to scientific developments, and 'neither concealed his opinion from the other. Each recognized that it was well-founded' (BP 24, 27–8). Thus opens the novel that, as far as its factual descriptions is concerned, vies only with Robert Musil's novel *The Man without Qualities* (the topic of Chapter 4), and that launches the story of the curious quest for perfect knowledge with which Bouvard and Pécuchet become obsessed. Characterised by the deep-rooted belief in human progress typical of the nineteenth century, their search for knowledge is, on the one hand, a meaningless, pathetic journey through all the available disciplines and their scientific findings, and is, on the other hand, a metaphor for progress itself. But more on that later.`

---

[1] G. Flaubert (trans. A. J. Kreilsheimer), *Bouvard and Pécuchet* (Harmondsworth: Penguin Books, [1881] 1978), p. 23. Hereinafter (BP + page number). All quotations are from this edition unless otherwise stated. My first guideline was G. Flaubert, *Bouvard et Pécuchet* (Paris: Livre de Poche, [1881] 1959).

Why Flaubert?

Oddly, on the now accepted view that literature has an epistemic value for law, Flaubert is an author who has so far received scant attention in *Law and Literature*, both in Anglo-American and continental-European contexts.[2] Admittedly, attention to the trial for literary obscenity following the publication of *Madame Bovary* is not wanting.[3] However, most of the research focuses on the way in which law deals with alleged obscenity or blasphemy in literary works. Flaubert himself was obviously instrumental in this. He hired a stenographer, and had him make a verbatim report of the court proceedings. What is more, this report was added to the first official edition of the novel. It should be noted that Flaubert was accused on the basis of the publication of *Madame Bovary* in six installments in the *Revue de Paris*, from October to December 1856.[4] Therefore, it is time to make amends, not least because in studies of Flaubert attention is directed predominantly towards the socio-political context of his literary works. The fact that Flaubert had studied law is all too often disregarded. The study of law was a constitutive factor when Flaubert turned his hand to authorship, yet he was as much captivated by law as averse to it.

Res ipsa loquitur

In November 1841, on the eve of his twentieth birthday, Flaubert travels to Paris to enroll at the *École de Droit*. Law was a choice that went without saying for the sons of the upper classes, especially those cherishing literary ambitions.[5] From the very start, however, Flaubert lacks enthusiasm for his chosen discipline. He reads poetry rather than the required textbooks. It takes him months before he has ploughed his way through the *Institutes*. Only with

[2] But see R. H. Weisberg, *The Failure of the Word* (New Haven: Yale University Press, 1984), on *L'éducation sentimentale* and *Salammbô*.

[3] See D. LaCapra, *Madame Bovary on Trial* (Ithaca and London: Cornell University Press, 1982); M. Wan, 'Fetishistic reading, intertextual reading: law, literature and androgyny in the *Madame Bovary* Trial', 2 *Law and Humanities*, no. 2, 2008, pp. 233–54.

[4] E. Ladenson, *Dirt for Art's Sake* (Ithaca and London: Cornell University Press, 2007), p. 18.

[5] For biographical data and Flaubert's letters, I draw on: F. Brown, *Flaubert, A Biography* (New York: Little, Brown and Company, 2006); H. Troyat, *Flaubert* (Paris: Flammarion, 1988); G. Flaubert, *Correspondance*, vols I–IV, J. Bruneau (ed.), vol. V, J. Bruneau and Y. Leclerc (eds) (Paris: Gallimard, Bibliothèque de la Pléiade, 1992–2007); F. Steegmuller (trans. and ed.), *The Letters of Gustave Flaubert*, vols I–II, 1830–80 (Basingstoke and Oxford: Picador, 2001); G. Wall (trans. and ed.), *Gustave Flaubert, Selected Letters* (Harmondsworth: Penguin, 1979).

the exams in sight does he really start working.[6] He laments that he spends each morning at the faculty of law, and each afternoon he crams whatever his teachers have preached in the morning.[7]

Why is the study of law such an arduous task? Because it is restricted to an exegesis of codified law. The staple diet is learning by heart the standard texts of Roman law as laid down in the *Corpus Iuris Civilis*, and reproducing literally, in Latin, the relevant passages of the *Institutes* and *Pandects*:

> The *Institutes* are written in Latin and the *code civil* is something even less resembling French. The gentlemen who compiled it didn't offer much of a sacrifice to the Graces. They made it as dry, as hard, as flatly bourgeois as the wooden benches of the Law School, where we go to harden our buttocks while hearing it explained.[8]

In spring 1843, Flaubert writes to Ernest Chevalier that the thought of taking the exams in procedural law horrifies him; to his sister, he confesses that although he still attends the lectures, he no longer pays attention because they are a waste of time.[9] Only the fear of incurring his father's wrath makes him stay on, but he already knows he will never enter legal practice. The life of a student, however, is enjoyable. Even though visits to the opera and to 'the girls' drain his purse, and he can hardly pay the rent and tuition fees, 'it is incredible fun to study law in Paris'.[10] The fun, however, does not last long. In 1844, Flaubert suffers a series of epileptic attacks that force him to break off his studies without having succeeded in any exam, but not without already entertaining the embryonic idea of writing a story depicting the history of two clerks.[11]

Flaubert's disappointment in law comes as no surprise. The legal profession as the *noblesse de robe* was held in high regard, but the legal curriculum was arid, and the dominant methodology was that of teaching doctrine *pur*

---

[6] Steegmuller, *Letters*, pp. 32–3, letter to Ernest Chevalier, 22 July 1842, 'I am so harassed by it all that the other night I *dreamed* of the law! I felt ashamed at having so dishonoured dreaming. I'm sweating blood and tears, but if I can't find somebody's notes on Oudot it's the end – I'll be rejected for next year' (italics in the original).

[7] Flaubert, *Correspondance*, vol. I, p. 112, letter to his sister Caroline, 9 July 1842.

[8] Steegmuller, *Letters*, p. 35; Flaubert, *Correspondance*, vol. I, pp. 134–5.

[9] Flaubert, *Correspondance*, vol. I, pp. 147 and 169.

[10] G. Flaubert (trans. E. Borger), *Haat is een deugd, een keuze uit de correspondentie* (Amsterdam: De Arbeiderspers, 2009), p. 24, letter to Ernest Chevalier, 10 February 1843 (my translation).

[11] See R. Queneau, 'Preface', in G. Flaubert, *Bouvard et Pécuchet* (Paris: Point du Jour, [1881] 1947), for the view that the idea of *Bouvard and Pécuchet* can be traced back to a work of his youth, 'Une leçon d'histoire naturelle', that appeared in *Le Colibri* in 1837.

sang. In the years before 1842, a group of scholars who were associated with the journal *Thémis* had attempted to broaden the study of law from the perspective that jurists should become the humanists they once were: namely, with a sound knowledge of legal theory and philosophy in order to be able to understand law in its specific contexts, and to contribute to the development of law by being responsive to the economic and social reality of modern France.[12] To this end, historiography and political sciences would have to find their place in the curriculum. Alexis de Tocqueville and François Guizot played an important role in this development by establishing, in 1832, the *Académie des sciences morales et politiques*, aptly named precisely by way of reaction to the prohibition of the study of the 'sciences morales et politiques' by law in 1803 within the *Institut national des sciences et des arts* that was founded in 1795. Nevertheless, even though constitutional law was introduced into the curriculum in 1834, no foothold was gained by the idea that one needed a broad humanistic education in order to understand the sources of law and their potential contribution to change.

To me, the life of Flaubert, precisely because it is richly documented – avid letter-writer that he was – provides ample vantage points from which to consider his personal context in relation to an analysis of *Bouvard and Pécuchet*. This is why I offer a reading of *Bouvard and Pécuchet* with reference to what we know of Flaubert's view with respect to this specific novel. There is even more reason to do so, because during the course of his life, Flaubert's desire to complete this novel was as vital as it was obsessive.[13] Hence, I do not fully agree with Flaubert's proposal that – with regard to literary criticism – the objectivity of the written text (and where would that idea come from?) rather than the private life of the author should be the object of our study. The author of that perhaps apocryphal remark 'Madame Bovary, c'est moi' is himself to blame. Thirty-odd years after he had conceived the idea – Bovary also being the source for the name Bouvard – Flaubert began the task of writing the lives of his copy-clerks, and it appears that he identified himself with them.[14]

---

[12] Brown, *Flaubert*, p. 118.

[13] For Flaubert's obsession, see Flaubert, *Correspondance*, vol. V, p. 757, letter to Turgenev, 2 December 1879, and Steegmuller, *Letters*, p. 651, letter to Turgenev, 30 December 1879, 'As for the novel. I am frightened by its three volumes. Three volumes just now, outside my work, is an undertaking', and, p. 624, letter to De Maupassant in August 1878, 'Bouvard and Pécuchet keeps trotting along . . . What a book! As for expecting that the public will read a work like this – what madness!' Flaubert was also inspired by Barthélemy Maurice's 1841 novella *Les Deux Greffiers*.

[14] See Steegmuller, *Letters*, pp. 507 and 565, for the observation that Flaubert derived both names from that of a hotelkeeper in Cairo, Bouvaret, whom he met during his visit to Egypt

Yet I do not read *Bouvard and Pécuchet* mimetically but metaphorically: namely, in the Aristotelian sense that the literary work represents what it illustrates. What it has to say to us is by means of comparison, and it therefore suggests meanings other than the literal. In short, they go beyond the received notions that Flaubert exposed brilliantly in what was to be the final part of the novel – the *Dictionnaire des Idées reçues* that Bouvard and Pécuchet composed in due course – which Flaubert had written before actually starting on the novel.[15] As Owen Barfield suggested, such other meaning obviously has to be of a kind that is worth our while, and the author actually has to have something worth saying to begin with.[16] This is exactly the case with Flaubert. He shows *in* the novel what he wants to demonstrate *with* the novel. Therein lies the epistemological importance of the metaphorical. It demands from us twice the amount of interpretation, as Francis Bacon already explained in *The Advancement of Learning*,

> for that knowledge which is new, and foreign from *opinions received* [italics mine], is to be delivered in another form than that that is . . . familiar; . . . those whose conceits are beyond popular opinions, have double labour: the one to make themselves conceived, and the other to prove and demonstrate. So that it is of necessity with them to have recourse to similitudes and translations to express themselves.[17]

Flaubert literally put in twice the effort by connecting the story of his two copy-clerks to the *Dictionnaire* by means of a series of grotesque citations called 'La Copie': that is, the copy that Bouvard and Pécuchet write down when they return to their old profession at the end of the novel – Flaubert left a detailed scheme for the rest of Chapter 10 – in order to overcome their disappointment regarding the results of their search for *épistème*.

---

in 1849–50. Steegmuller, *Letters*, p. 593, 'Bouvard and Pécuchet occupy me to such point that I have become them. Their stupidity is mine and I'm dying of it. Perhaps that's the explanation'; Flaubert, *Correspondance*, vol. IV, p. 920, letter to Edma Roger des Genettes, 15 April 1875.

[15] Steegmuller, *Letters*, p. 177, translates *Dictionary of Accepted Ideas*; Wall, *Selected Letters*, p. 221, has *Dictionary of Received Ideas*. Flaubert, *Correspondance*, vol. V, p. 599, letter to Edma Roger des Genettes, 7 April 1879, 'Restera le second volume . . . Sans compter le *Dictionnaire des idées reçues*, entièrement fait.'

[16] O. Barfield, 'Poetic diction and legal fiction', in O. Barfield, *The Rediscovery of Meaning and Other Essays* (Middletown, CT: Wesleyan University Press, 1977), pp. 44–64.

[17] F. Bacon, *The Advancement of Learning* (Oxford: Clarendon Press, [1605] 1876), p. 174 (Book II, ch. xvii, par. 1).

The Encyclopedia of Human Stupidity

'Where is the rule then?'

On 19 August 1872, Flaubert writes to Edma Roger des Genettes that he is embarking on a task that will keep him busy for a number of years.[18] It will be the story of two hilarious chaps who copy silly texts for a critical encyclopedia, subtitled 'The encyclopedia of human stupidity'.[19] In order to write it, Flaubert is forced to study all kinds of topics, and, just like his two characters, he takes no chances. He reads 1,500 books, and then complains about the costs he incurs before he has even written one word.[20] Only months before his death, he complains that there is so much to be read.[21] That *Bouvard and Pécuchet* is a risky venture we already know from Flaubert's letter to Jules Deplan dated 2 April 1863, in which he expresses his fear of being chased out of France and Europe.[22] Actually, this is not so strange a complaint if we consider that Flaubert holds up a mirror to his readers, and even more so when we realise that it is not immediately clear whether this mirror will turn out to be a carnival mirror or a mirror for magistrates, or both. If the man who prided himself on always writing with a view to pure objectivity was right when he said that the stupidity that Bouvard and Pécuchet display was his own, then *bouvardisme* is also the mirror of the author as subject: that is to say, the author-reader is as fanatical as his characters.

Onward to our clerks! The very moment that Bouvard and Pécuchet realise how boring their clerical work is, fortune smiles on them in the form of an inheritance from Bouvard's natural father. They retire to the country. The search for a suitable place to settle takes a year and a half, but towards the end of 1840 they finally take up residence on a farm. In order to guarantee success in agriculture 'they took out from their library the four volumes of the

---

[18] Flaubert, *Correspondance*, vol. IV, pp. 558–9.

[19] Steegmuller, *Letters*, pp. 562–3, 'the farcical story of those two characters who copy a kind of critical encyclopedia. I think I gave you some idea of it. I'm going to have to study many things I'm ignorant of . . . One has to be insane – wildly mad – to undertake such a book.'

[20] Steegmuller, *Letters*, p. 650, letter to Edma Roger des Genettes, 24 January 1879, 'Do you know how many volumes I've had to absorb for my two characters? More than fifteen hundred! My pile of notes is eight inches thick. This superabundance of documents has enabled me to be free of pedantry: of that I'm sure.' Flaubert, *Correspondance*, vol. IV, p. 698, letter to his niece Caroline, 11 August 1873, 'Il me tarde de pouvoir me livrer complètement à *Bouvard et Pécuchet*, pour lesquels j'ai fait hier une dépense de 60 francs de livres!'

[21] Flaubert, *Correspondance*, vol. V, p. 855, letter to Turgenev, 4 March 1880. Steegmuller, *Letters*, p. 630, letter to his niece Caroline, 18 January 1879, 'I continue reading for my book – Kant, Hegel, Leibniz. Not much fun.'

[22] Flaubert, *Correspondance*, vol. III, p. 315.

Country Household, sent for Gasparin's course, and took out a subscription to an agricultural journal' (BP 43). Training in theory, however, does not yield a crop. Pécuchet decides to stick to gardening. Despite careful reading of the *Complete Gardener* (BP 46), the successive cultivation of strawberries, tomatoes, melons, and the complete range of flowers available fails miserably. Any insight into *physis* is lacking. But not to worry. Meteorology 'according to Luke-Howard's classification' (BP 48) will undoubtedly bring relief. And indeed it does, albeit in the form of a thunderstorm and a fire in the haystack, caused by overheating. Why listen to the sound advice of your tenant farmer or the village people if you can study method from a book? After the pair get over the initial shock, they turn to fruit farming, or better said, they buy all standard works on the subject. Pécuchet works by the book, but no tree yields any crop. His lament, I suggest, is the crux of the narrative that also illuminates the negative outcome of what Stephen Toulmin called the quest for certainty (a topic of Chapter 2) since early modernity:

> I demand to know why! It is not just that every species requires special treatment, but each individual as well, according to the climate, temperature, lots of things! Where is the rule then, and what hope can we have of success or profit? (BP 56)

Arboriculture being a joke, they turn to winegrowing in order to produce champagne, and when the bottles of chablis diluted with must explode spontaneously, their doubts about success vanish, although obviously one has to know more about chemistry.[23] Again, codified knowledge prevails, and everything they read becomes scripture as code to them. Other than in the humanist tradition – Pico della Mirandola, for example, was as avid a reader and a buyer of books – our copy-clerks do not consider law in the books to be a possible building stone of knowledge that needs critical, hermeneutical testing, but rather as absolute truth reified to dogma, at least as long as it takes for a new book to be published that will provide new incontrovertibly true dicta that will in turn, and so on and so forth.

The combined results of the study of chemistry, anatomy and physiology cost the lives of a flock of pigeons, numerous kittens and a goose, while a stray dog and half the inhabitants of the village fall so seriously ill that they barely survive. Pécuchet, however, eulogises the authoritative codified sources, and tells the village doctor that his practical experience and ability to observe are meaningless. Onward to astronomy then, and to the study of the

---

[23] Steegmuller, *Letters*, p. 523, letter to George Sand, 10 September 1870, 'Our only rational hope is in *chemistry*. Who knows?'

universe according to Buffon, because one wants to gain a clear answer to the central question, 'What is the point of it all?' (BP 85). Geology, archeology and the history of ideas – the two gentlemen's attention span is short – will bring solace and help them fathom the origins of the Revolution of 1793, while Giambattista Vico's *Scienza Nuova* will provide insight into myths. The results are spectacular: 'From carelessness about dates they passed on to contempt for facts' (BP 122), for 'the external facts are not everything. They must be completed by psychology' (BP 129). From this perspective, the genre of the historical novel will guarantee the development of the imagination that historiography lacks, will it not? In a triumph of representation, they read Walter Scott, Alexandre Dumas and George Sand before attempting to become writers themselves by applying Boileau's aesthetic principles. The latter project is doomed to fail now that Boileau does not provide rules on how to imagine an interesting plot and develop a captivating writing style. What a pity that is, especially now that Pécuchet 'wanted to reconcile doctrines with works, critics with poets, grasp the essence of the Beautiful' (BP 145) in a final attempt to chain the facts to the Procrustean bed of theory. Thus they keep adding to their resources. However, as with Emma Bovary, all to no avail.

The announcement of the Paris uproar, February 1848, leads them to plant a liberty tree and to study Rousseau, Saint-Simon and Fourier in order to refute the absolute divine right of kings. But when sound proof of the social contract is nowhere to be found – not even in Locke – and Rousseau disappoints as 'the pontiff of democracy' (BP 167), Bouvard muses, 'Ah, progress, what a farce! . . . And politics, what a filthy mess!' (BP 172). In order to cultivate the body and the soul, they decide to fall in love. Bouvard proposes to the widow Bourdin, but she is only after his farm, while Pécuchet is exasperated when he catches a venereal disease during his courtship of the servant girl Mélie – any idea of causality is totally unfamilar to our literal reader – 'But why did she do that to me?' (BP 181).[24] Written instructions in gymnastics will bring back the sane body to accompany the sane mind necessary for the Platonic wonder required to study philosophy, because 'a preparatory regime is indispensable' (BP 197). Cartesian doctrine does not augment their insight, however, nor do the complete works of Voltaire, La Mettrie, and Aristotle, even though the romantic hermeneutics of psychology

---

[24] Flaubert himself had already caught syphilis before attending university. In the *Dictionary of Received Ideas*, he writes 'SYPHILIS Everybody is more or less infected with it' (BP 327), which is a realistic definition, given that the disease was widely spread in Flaubert's days, and half of the male population suffered from it. See Steegmuller, *Letters*, p. 669, quoting Theodore Zeldin, *France, 1848–1945*.

– emotion, volition, and knowledge – offer opportunities to overcome the disappointment caused by reading Spinoza's *Ethics*.

'LAW (THE) Nobody knows what it is' (BP 314)

Not once do Bouvard and Pécuchet ask themselves why time and again their search for truth founders in its methodological shortcomings. Opposite doctrines are taken for granted. Not once do they attempt to refute or mediate different views and contexts. No wonder then that, battle weary, they see the light during evening mass, and accept the credo as a substitute for the Cartesian *cogito*. *Credo quia absurdum*? The men fall prey to the parish priest whose exegesis of Scripture is based on a metaphorical reading of the six days of creation as six great ages. Pécuchet's hope for a reconciliation of religion and reason is annihilated, with or without Spinoza, for, 'if one sees metaphors everywhere, what will become of the facts?' (BP 238). Full of contempt for a religion that is only an instrument to maintain authority, Bouvard and Pécuchet start a new project: namely, that of educating two orphans on the basis of phrenology and their own Hegelian synthesis of numerous books on pedagogy. Doomed to failure, the undertaking teaches them one thing: society as a whole needs re-educating, and, to this end, new rules for all adults are to be designed. There, abruptly, the kaleidoscopic, eclectic quest of the by then aged protagonists ends with the death of their author.

But the demise is not until they have become acquainted with law, and there too jurists find wonderful starting points for professional reflection. In the revolutionary days of 1848, Pécuchet has already tackled the juridical-political question that has lost none of its importance in contemporary societies: namely, the manner in which words can assault, and how subsequently 'words lead to crimes', because 'how are you going to distinguish between innocent and guilty phrases? Something that is forbidden now may come to be applauded' (BP 159). Only logic can offer a solution to all our errors because they 'almost all come from using words wrongly' (BP 209). From this vantage point, Pécuchet teaches himself to speak according to one of the great dreams of rationalism, that of exact language. He begins to use a Leibnizian language that supposedly represents the world at a level of abstraction, and with a manner of reasoning that would not have been out of place in the nineteenth-century French Exegetical School or the German *Begriffsjurisprudenz*, one that refrains from using any emotive language. Surely this will be the path to truth if we have laws for everything? Such a language-related premise did well during the heyday of legal formalism and legal positivism, and it is still with us if we read some defenders of 'plain speech' interpretation.

Bouvard and Pécuchet immediately get into trouble with the law. When they see the gamekeeper write a report on a poacher whom they think is a good chap, they interfere. They insult the gamekeeper and are summoned to attend the police court. Bouvard pleads innocent, but Pécuchet unwisely persists,

> the words offence, crime and misdemeanour are meaningless. If you take the penalty as a basis for classifying punishable acts then you are taking an arbitrary basis. You might as well tell citizens: 'Do not worry about the moral value of your actions, that is determined solely by the State's punishment.' Besides, the penal code seems to me to be an irrational piece of work, devoid of principles. (BP 278)

Pécuchet's linguistic conviction leads him to treat the judge with derision, for if the text of law is clear, surely judicial interpretation is superfluous. Ergo, the judge does not need intelligence, and therefore 'the law dispenses you from having any' (BP 278). *Voilà*, the cornerstone of a theory of adjudication *à la Pécuchet*.

'METHOD Of no use whatever' or 'On the lack of method in the sciences'[25]

Flaubert left to us the plan for his intended ending of the novel.[26] Utterly disillusioned, Bouvard and Pécuchet simultaneously have the same brilliant idea. Unlike that other clerk, Melville's Bartleby with his 'I would prefer not to', the two men, in a kind of reflex action because they are devoid of any creative imagination, return to their former occupation. They resume copying, seated at a double-sided desk that is the image of their continuous symbiosis. Beyond their former epistemological doubt and despair, they file away as 'Copy' anything that may, at some point in time, somewhere, for someone, serve a useful purpose as a way of providing implicit legitimacy to their quest for absolute knowledge. They close their library, because copying is representation only: that is, it consists in repeating what already exists, with no imagination required.

And so they plod along, and jot down under the random classifications of the section LITERATURE: '*Method*. Philosophy cannot exist without the art of disregarding any objections.'[27] This is exactly what they themselves

---

[25] (BP 316), and the entry 'Method' from the *Dictionary of Received Ideas* and the intended subtitle of the novel, see Steegmuller, *Letters*, p. 649, letter to Mrs Charles Tennant, 16 November 1879, 'What this book is? . . . The subtitle might be: 'On lack of method in sciences.'

[26] The *Bouvard et Pécuchet* manuscripts are stored in the Bibliothèque Municipale of Rouen; they are divided into three parts and contain more than 1,200 pages; the different drafts per chapter not included.

[27] My translation from the Dutch edition, G. Flaubert (trans. E. Borger), *Bouvard en Pécuchet* (Amsterdam: De Arbeiderspers, [1881] 1988), p. 439. The English translation does not include this section.

have done all along. When they embarked on their quest, the first effect was that 'the more ideas they had the more they suffered' (BP 29). Because they exchanged critical reflection for a blind belief in the success that an accumulation of knowledge would bring, the wonderful Enlightenment ideal, their mania for all things 'intellectual' leads to sorrow. Ecclesiastes 1: 18 (AV) is right, 'For in much wisdom is much grief.' Pathetic hermeneuts that they are, Bouvard and Pécuchet remain literal readers who accept everything they read at face value. Their desire for certainties only exposes the shortcomings of the human condition. What sort of world does Flaubert sketch in this novel without a plot, and that is no more than a dry enumeration of episodes in the lives of his characters with companion disciplines?[28] Do we as readers accept this reality, and, if so, what does that mean?

On the one hand, the unity of form and content of the text that is *Bouvard and Pécuchet* shows us the cynical mirror of realism. Significantly, it was not until the nineteenth century that literature became an autonomous discourse, the official task of literature during the Second Empire in France being the edification of the reader. Flaubert experienced the latter, to his disgrace, in the *Madame Bovary* trial. I think it plausible that Flaubert found even more inspiration for *Bouvard and Pécuchet* in what the public prosecutor remarked on the necessity of artistic rules: namely, that art without rules is like a woman who drops all her clothes.[29] On the other hand, the novel exemplifies the failure of the rule as representation and guarantee, also in law, with as a consequence: 'JUSTICE Never worry about it' (BP 313).

This is to say that *Bouvard and Pécuchet* is a novel 'about nothing', in the sense that it is illustrative of the consequences of an ultimate rule orientation that no longer needs a reality in which both the rule and law function. It comes as no surprise that Flaubert wrote about the *Dictionary* that he would carefully construct it in such a way that the law could not get hold of him.[30] Understood counterfactually as the German philosopher Jürgen Habermas suggests,

> a literary text is marked by the fact that it does not come forth with the claim that it documents an occurrence in the world; nonetheless, it does want to draw the reader into the spell of an imagined occurrence step

---

[28] See P. Brooks, *Reading for the Plot* (Cambridge, MA: Harvard University Press, 1984), for the view that we cannot read the episodes, incidents, and actions in a novel without grasping the plot.

[29] As cited in Wan, 'Fetishistic reading', p. 245, 'L'art sans règle n'est plus l'art; c'est comme une femme qui quitterait tout vêtement.'

[30] Flaubert, *Correspondance*, vol. II, p. 208, letter to Louise Colet, 'aucune loi ne pourrait me mordre quoique j'y attaquerais tout.'

by step, until he follows the narrated events *as if* they *were* real. Even the
fabricated reality must be capable of being experienced by the reader as a
reality that is real – otherwise a novel does not accomplish what it is supposed to do.[31]

Viewed this way, the interpretation of *Bouvard and Pécuchet* is inscribed in
the text and it offers the reader an opportunity to claim (another) meaning
for it. In what Italo Calvino calls 'levels of reality in literature',[32] the credibility of the narrative is a precondition of the success of the text, both internally
as far as the possible world that is shown and at the level of what the reader
is ready to accept. Both are criteria for the legitimacy of law in a comparable
way, when jurists 'fabulate' and their imaginations body forth a world by
means of language.

In their passion for classification, Bouvard and Pécuchet hold up a mirror
to us with regard to the idea of referential language and linguistic convention.
To what extent can we maintain the idea that the language of any scientific
field or discipline refers to a truth? The advice hidden in the *Dictionary* in
the lemma 'ENCYCLOPÉDIE – Laugh at it pityingly for being quaint and
old-fashioned, or else thunder against it' (BP 303) is not taken up once by
our copy-clerks. They are impossible fools.[33]

Language Reveals All

Back then to the crucial question. Where is the rule if the number of excep-
tions grows? What is the use of a general rule? Where Aristotle offered the
solution of *epieikeia*, the equitable, Bouvard and Pécuchet are out in the
epistemic cold for lack of *phronèsis* (a topic of Chapter 6). Their encyclopedic
desire is ultimately a sign of insecurity for which 'the rule' offers no solace,
because it is neither self-applying nor absolutely clear beforehand. When
an exasperated Pécuchet asks, 'What is the point of it all?' Bouvard's only
answer is, 'Perhaps there isn't a point' (BP 85). This utterance is the epitome

---

[31] J. Habermas, 'Philosophy and science as literature?', in J. Habermas (trans. W. M.
Hohengarten), *Postmetaphysical Thinking: Philosophical Essays* (Cambridge, MA: MIT Press,
1992), pp. 205–27, p. 211.

[32] I. Calvino, 'Levels of reality in literature', in I. Calvino (trans. P. Creagh), *The Uses of
Literature* (New York: Harvest, 1987), pp. 101–21.

[33] J. B. White, *The Legal Imagination. Studies in the Nature of Legal Thought and Expression*
(Boston: Little, Brown and Company, 1973), p. 863, 'One who believes that everything
can be said in a language of theory and system is an impossible fool.' Cf. M. de Montaigne,
'On Educating Children', Book I, Essay 26, in M. de Montaigne (trans. and ed. M. A.
Screech), *The Complete Essays* (Harmondsworth: Penguin, [1580] 1991), p. 170, 'Only
fools have made up their minds and are certain.'

of the crisis of the belief in progress and the absolute value of taxonomy in whatever field. Turned the other way around, insight into aspects of language and narrative ideally provides an intellectual antenna to help one recognise what is illusory in science or a mere pseudo-erudition, and also to recognise any ordering of the world that is only a process of classification and reduction deteriorating into cliché. This is also why a turn to narrative can help dislocate conventional ideas of rationality.

This brings us to the topic of the meaning and uses of legal concepts and categories, because it is by no means certain, as adherents of the explanatory sciences seem to hope, that 'classificatory schemes provide a science of the concrete'; it is instead a matter of 'narrative schemes [that] may provide a science of the imagination.'[34] Habermas therefore argues that to understand contextually the rootedness of theory in our social environments is to discover truth in metaphoric aspects of storytelling.[35] This is also to say that there is no immediate, unmediated access to truth and reality other than in the dialectics of subject and object that forms the methodology of the humanities. What matters, then, especially for law, is how linguistic usage is part of that truth or untruth. Bouvard's and Pécuchet's naive linguistic and scientific assumptions can, I suggest, also be read as a warning to remain alert to the scope and significance in contemporary debate of such concepts as terrorism, enemy combatant, and hate speech, to name but a few. Linguistic change as a form of subversion of reality as we knew it can be a first sign of pernicious developments leading to totalitarian outgrowths.

A few examples suffice to illustrate the point. In his personal account of the language of Nazi Germany, Victor Klemperer demonstrates how this ideology was able to maintain its position because a special service guarded every linguistic detail, and decided what could and could not be said. In this language web conceived by the minister of propaganda, the first Nazi words were *Strafexpedition*, 'as a kind of punitive expedition against all kinds of despised peoples', and *Staatsakt*, the term for a state occasion – that is, a party rally organised by Goebbels to legitimise any state action aimed at eliminating those deemed unwanted.[36] After Dresden was bombed in February 1945, Klemperer on his flight through Germany found that the Nazi language had spread into all regions of Germany, into all layers of society. Trying to

---

[34] E. M. Bruner, 'Ethnography as narrative', in V. W. Turner and E. M. Bruner (eds), *The Anthropology of Experience* (Urbana: University of Illinois Press, 1986), pp. 139–55, p. 14.

[35] Habermas, 'Philosophy and science', p. 225.

[36] V. Klemperer (trans. M. Brady), *The Language of the Third Reich, LTI-Lingua Tertii Imperii, a Philologist's Notebook* (London and New Brunswick, NJ: Athlone Press, [1957] 2000), p. 43.

further his knowledge of this *Lingua Tertii Imperiii*, Klemperer explains, 'I read whatever I could catch sight of, and everywhere I saw traces of this language. It was truly totalitarian.'[37] He emphasises the immense importance of developing an appreciation of the power of language, because – 'whatever it is that people are determined to hide, be it only from others, or from themselves, even things they carry around unconsciously – language reveals all.'[38] A literary rendering of the same linguistic perversion is given by Jonathan Littell in *The Kindly Ones*. In it we can indeed detect the truth in the metaphors of the narrative. When the main character Max Aue is appointed to the personal staff of the *Reichsführer*, he is told by the *Obersturmbannführer*, 'For your reports, the Reichsführer has issued *Sprachregelungen*, language regulations. Any report that doesn't conform to them will be returned to you.'[39] Behind that is the logic of the *Führerprinzip*,

> It's up to the recipient to recognize the intentions of the one who gives the command, and to act accordingly. The ones who insist on having clear orders or who want legislative measures haven't understood that it's the will of the leader, and not his orders, that counts, and that it's up to the receiver of the orders to know how to decipher and even anticipate that will.[40]

Such a tendency to dehumanise is also captured in Jorge Semprun's comparable language experience during his captivity in the Buchenwald concentration camp, and is one that would perhaps be grotesque if it did not show how atrocities pervaded all Nazi activities. Semprun gives us the example of

> *Gärtnerei*, gardening – a euphemism, because it was probably the worst labor of all. It consisted . . . of carrying in pairs . . . at a run and while being beaten with clubs, poles from which hung heavy wooden tubs filled to the brim with night soil (hence the familiar name of 'shit duty') intended for the vegetable garden of the SS.[41]

And so in the course of time meaning is lost. Or, as Littell writes,

> 'Endlösung' (final solution), 'völlige Lösung' (complete solution) and 'allgemeine Lösung' (general solution), . . . according to the period, . . . meant exclusion from public life or exclusion from economic life or, finally, emigration. Then, little by little, the signification had slid toward the abyss, but without the signifier changing, and it seemed almost as if this final

---

[37] Klemperer, *LTI*, pp. 260–1.
[38] Klemperer, *LTI*, p. 11.
[39] J. Littell (trans. C. Mandell), *The Kindly Ones* (London: Vintage, 2010), p. 546.
[40] Littell, *Kindly Ones*, p. 548.
[41] J. Semprun (trans. L. Coverdale), *Literature or Life* (New York: Viking, 1997), p. 38.

meaning had always lived in the heart of the word . . . and then we had passed the event horizon, beyond which there is no return.[42]

Paradoxically, we are back then in the situation that the poet John Donne described as an anatomy of the world, in his poem of that title written in 1611, in which 'Tis all in pieces, all coherence gone.' This should make us pause as well, to reflect on contemporary phenomena such as the *bouvardian* contempt for facts.

Narrative Intelligence I

To tie the strands of this chapter together and connect them to the main thrust of the argument of this book, I turn to what Bernard Edelman called the twofold meaning of the legal maxim *ex fabula ius oritur*,[43] the counterpart of *ius in causa positum*: namely, that on the one hand, out of the narrative of the facts follows the law, while on the other hand, jurists in practice 'fabulate'.[44] Judges, I would suggest, anticipating my argument on the bond between legal theory and practice in Part II, are like authors in that they select the facts offered in the materials of the case before them with a view to structuring the world in the decisions they take. The epistemological question to be kept in their minds should therefore always be whether there is indeed a chain of circumstance 'out there', or whether (some)one carefully fits together the evidence with other established facts.

This is also to say that in this dialectical and cyclical movement, from facts to legal rules and back, judges are not only – at least in part, given that it is always another human being's act that occasions what happens in court – responsible for the constitution of the facts, but also for the legal and societal order that follows from that choice. As a consequence, it is of crucial importance to guarantee the polyphony of the stories in court as much as that of law's own stories – doctrine and legal theories included – lest any voice be forgotten or silenced. At the same time, it necessarily leads to an appreciation of the fact that neither law nor its narratives can be understood other than within their cultural and normative universe, their *nomos*, as Robert Cover called it, of their origin and existence.[45] In other words, the creation of

---

[42] Littell, *Kindly Ones*, pp. 630–1.

[43] The original maxim *ex facta ius oritur* was coined by the Italian jurists Bartolus de Saxoferrato and Baldus de Ubaldus in the thirteenth century in their *glosses* on the *Digests* (D. 9. 2. 52. 2).

[44] B. Edelman, 'La fabulation juridique', 41 *Droits*, 2005, pp. 199–217, 'Quand le juriste fabule, quand il construit sa propre réalité, . . . il n'a en vue que la régulation sociale concrète.'

[45] R. Cover, '*Nomos* and Narrative', 97 *Harvard Law Review*, 1983, pp. 4–68. See also Chapter 8.

legal meaning cannot be imposed from the outside, but is essentially always the product of a process of cultural mediation. Narratives structure human experience and action, and their cognitive and literary-aesthetical contents and meanings need to be investigated.

The narrative paradigm of fact and fiction therefore deserves our constant attention, especially when we realise that legal professionals, whether they work in academic surroundings or in legal practice, need to rely on their capacity to value the facts and circumstances of any case before them, literally and figuratively. Literary narratives can contribute to the development of our practical wisdom to do what the circumstances require. In doing so, they teach us how to increase our ability to judge wisely and to decide justly. They do so by exploring alternative views on the human condition, by showing us options that we had thus far not even considered. In short, they open up new sources of knowledge and perspectives beyond traditional disciplinary borders that all too often confine rather than facilitate. It is precisely by reading literary narratives that we can begin to understand the world around us and to better appreciate the people in it.

The importance of this insight for law cannot be overestimated. The narratives in legal practice are always the result of different views about what people had expected to happen and what actually happened; they are the start of any dispute. In the sense that these narratives both re-present and constitute reality, or realities, we need to consider in what way narratives operate as instruments of the legal constructs we devise, and what that means for our definition of knowledge and truth. After all, narrative truth cannot, or at least not easily, be judged according to 'received' standards of referentiality and verification. It is measured along lines of probability and plausibility. Is Julian Barnes's novel *Flaubert's Parrot* about the parrot that Flaubert had on loan from the Rouen museum in order to write *Un cœur simple*? Or do we attribute another meaning to this fact given its hermeneutic ambiguity?[46]

From the perspective of legal theory, this is also to say that both showing and observing a concrete experience is the starting point of reflection on the normative dimension of case-bound reasoning. It is essential for an understanding of law in context (as contrasted to a view of law as a set of abstract rules in existence prior to the facts), as the precondition of any constitution of a theoretical foundation of the enterprise that is law. Put differently, not only is the picture of reality offered by law always in narrative form, the bond of law and literature in particular lies in the confrontation of the theoretical knowledge or *épistème* (a topic of Chapter 6) as expressed in legal doctrine

---

[46] J. Barnes, *Flaubert's Parrot* (London: Pan Books, 1985), p. 21.

with narrative knowledge as expressed in the narratives of the legal facts. It is precisely the combination of these insights that make the field of *Law and Literature*, or, more generally, *Law and the Humanities*, indispensable for legal practice. This is also why contemporary law and legal practice need a renewed humanist *res publica litterarum*. Unlike Bouvard and Pécuchet, we do not have the option of withdrawing from our responsibilities and becoming copy-clerks.

So my caveat for interdisciplinarians as well would be not to imitate Bouvard and Pécuchet, who probe the cognitive worth of one discipline after the other when they find that no single methodology suffices to answer all of their questions or to solve all their problems. The gentlemen's quest led them into an epistemological desert for lack of practical wisdom to do what the circumstances required. Pécuchet, finally exasperated, asks 'What is the point of it all?', Bouvard answers, 'Perhaps there isn't a point' (BP 85). This should be our caveat as well. We should not engage in an ongoing (inter)disciplinary diaspora that cannot but lead to methodological shallowness.

2

A Raid on the Inarticulate

Law and Language: 'an old city full of streets and squares, nooks and crannies'

In the first instance, Bouvard and Pécuchet's craze is the apotheosis of the quest for certainty that started in early modernity with the rise of rationalism and empiricism, and culminated in the scientific positivism of the nineteenth century. It resonates in legal positivism and formalism. Important for the context of the history of ideas of law and philosophy, in view of the overarching topic of this book, is the parallel development of a descriptive language view that favours a picture theory of the world in which the idea of full correspondence between the thing and its representation in language dominates. As far as the search for truth is concerned, it is reminiscent of the correspondence theory, or *adequatio rei et intellectus*, as found in Thomas Aquinas, that starts from the premise that in order to understand the world and find the truth, the knower's intellect must be adequate to the thing. It culminated in the idea that, given their explanatory methodology, the natural sciences are superior instruments of knowledge. In the second instance, the craze is the outcome of a long process of disciplinary differentiation that terminated the old unity of law and the humanities, occasioned by the Justinian *Corpus Iuris Civilis* in eleventh-century Bologna.

Cogito *and certainty*

When the goddess Athena in Aeschylus's *Oresteia* decides to 'appoint judges . . . and establish a tribunal'[1] to judge Orestes' case, a narrative of ongoing violence ends in the foundation of an institution that settles disputes between people. From then on, the instrument by means of which law and justice are to be shaped is language: hence the title of this chapter.[2] However, the forma-

---

[1] Aeschylus, *Eumenides* (*Oresteia* part 3), in H. W. Smyth (trans.), *Aeschylus in Two Volumes*, vol. II (Cambridge, MA and London: Harvard University Press, 1971), p. 317.
[2] Derived from T. S. Eliot, 'East Coker', *The Complete Poems of T. S. Eliot* (London: Guild

tive aspect of language as our way of being in the world does not preclude outgrowths of violence and power. Remember the story of the tower of Babel. The Bible's Book of Genesis describes how the people decided to build a tower in order to make a name for themselves, 'lest we be scattered abroad upon the face of the whole earth' (Genesis 11:4 (AV)). God's interpretation of this human action is based on the fear of losing divine authority, because 'now nothing will be restrained from them, which they have imagined to do' (Genesis 11:6 (AV)). The divine reaction is to cause a linguistic diaspora. God confuses the people's language and, as a result, there occurs precisely what they feared would happen. They are scattered abroad – the literal meaning of the Greek root *diasperein* being to sow or to scatter – and the original relation between language and the individual is destroyed. In *Law and Literature*, the ineradicable topic in legal theory of the interconnection of language and violence is highlighted in the opposing views of the late Robert Cover and James Boyd White on the violence of the judicial word versus the view on law as a culture of argument.[3] To me, these views are not mutually exclusive but are instead *diversi sed non adversi* in the sense delineated in the Introduction.

In early modernity, the idea of law as a linguistic-discursive practice finds its theoretical origin in Thomas Hobbes's *Leviathan*. In the twilight zone before the origin of law and civil society founded on the basis of the social contract, Hobbes postulated that there is only a state of war in which everybody takes justice into their own hands, the *bellum omnium contra omnes*, with the *lex talionis* – an eye for an eye, a tooth for a tooth – as the only guiding principle, and, as a consequence, human life, 'solitary, poore, nasty, brutish, and short'.[4] Justice is non-existent in the state of nature. Or, as the Dutch jurist Hugo Grotius wrote, '*ubi iudicia deficiunt incipit bellum*': namely, where judicial decisions fail, war begins.[5] The introduction of the rule of law – a concept of law as a social institution developed by contractarians from Hobbes, Locke, and Rousseau to Rawls – thus constitutes the basis for legitimate expectations and it provides a means to be able to object when expectations are not properly fulfilled, and, subsequently, to ensure

---

Publishing/Faber and Faber, 1986), p. 182: 'Trying to learn to use words, and every attempt . . . a wholly new start, . . . a raid on the inarticulate.'

[3] R. Cover, 'Violence and the Word', 95 *Yale Law Journal*, 1986, pp. 1601–29; J. B. White, 'Law and Literature: no manifesto', 39 *Mercer Law Review*, 1988, pp. 739–51.

[4] T. Hobbes, *Leviathan* (London: J. M. Dent and Sons, Everyman's Library, [1651] 1987), Part I, 'Of Man', ch. XIII, p. 65.

[5] H. Grotius, *De Iure Belli ac Pacis* (Leyden: E. J. Brill, [1625] 1939), Liber II, caput I, par. 2. Andrew Marvell mentioned *De Iure Belli ac Pacis* and *Mare Liberum* in his poem 'The Character of Holland' (1653).

that comparable cases are treated similarly, for all of which the institution and organisation of a proper administration of justice is a prerequisite. This brings us to the systematic reason that law is a culture of argument: namely, it is the product of an exchange of arguments in which no *a priori* right answers are given. Law is always made; it is not given beforehand. The discursive aspect teaches us to respect the principle of *audi et alteram partem* (to hear both sides of the argument), and to realise that law is a work that is never finished. With each case and each new interpretation, a new element of meaning may be introduced.

A short historic recapitulation of the prelude of modernity is in order for the purpose of sketching the background against which my project takes shape. Firstly, it should be noted that I certainly do not intend to project evil onto legal positivism as such, only to mark its possible negative sides, given its long-standing influence on continental-European legal thought. Secondly, as the German philosopher Peter Sloterdijk contends, contemporary Europe is struggling to regain its foothold, geopolitically as well, as far as its intellectual positions are concerned, as it reflects on the causes and consequences of its own historic development.[6] This development shows a movement from an initially strong legal unity brought about in continental Europe by the implementation and subsequent dominance of Roman law after the rediscovery of the *Corpus Iuris Civilis* to diversity, following the rise of nation states and national codifications in the eighteenth century. It then circles back to a new form of unity that came with the European Union in the form of supranational law and overarching international courts, such as the European Human Rights Court in Strasbourg, each by now with its own issues of legitimacy and scope, given recent events such as the Brexit vote in the United Kingdom. To Sloterdijk, since Europe's very being is now questioned, the question is not what the real Europe was or is, but which forces were at work at decisive moments in European history: in other words, what were the ideas and the constitutive narratives that moved Europe forward.[7] Not incidentally, this argument ties in with the topic of what is captured under the umbrella idea of the humanities, based on the view that European countries are the result of the *translatio Imperii*, the transference of empire and the politics of expansion brought about by Saxon emperors since the coronation of Otto I in 962, and that a European is he or she who lives in the geographical zone in which the cultured people understand Latin.[8]

Furthermore, as I am not a trained (legal) historian, much of what follows

---

[6] P. Sloterdijk, *Falls Europa erwacht* (Suhrkamp: Frankfurt am Main, 2002).

[7] Sloterdijk, *Europa*, p. 33.

[8] Sloterdijk, *Europa*, pp. 34–5.

derives from a lifetime of reading and research, my 'mental library', and the guidance provided by others.[9] A broad sweep, however simplified, is nevertheless in order to provide a small map of the territory to those unfamiliar with European history. Suffice it to say, firstly, that the Renaissance world was one of complexity and diversity, accepted as bound up inextricably with the human condition. Renaissance optimism replaced the medieval emphasis on traditional authority with the spirit of tolerance, especially from a religious viewpoint to which the 1598 Edict of Nantes that granted French Protestants certain civil rights bears testimony. (It should at once be noted that religious tolerance did not extend to Jews who were expelled from Spain in 1492 and from Portugal in 1497. And French tolerance was short-lived if we note the scattering of French Huguenots to the Lower Countries, my forefather among them, after the revocation of the Edict of Nantes in 1658.) The reverse side was a desire for more security as Europe became an increasingly destructive battlefield. The period after around 1580 was one of great social unrest and political instability, as well as of dispersion as a result of warfare. Examples abound: for instance, the Dutch Eighty Years War of independence against the Spanish ruler (1568–1648), for which Grotius provided a theoretical foundation and the constitutive narrative of the Batavian Myth in his *Liber de antiquitate reipublicae Batavicae* (*The Antiquity of the Batavian Republic*);[10] the Anglo-Spanish conflicts between 1585 and 1604; and the Thirty Years War or Bohemian War fought on German grounds (1618–48). The latter broke out when the Protestant movement proved to be not only a religious movement but one with political implications that the Catholic League could not tolerate. The Czech Jan Amos Comenius's satire *The Labyrinth of the World and the Paradise of the Heart* captures the spirit of that conflict. In England, the internal strife that culminated in the trial and beheading of Charles I (1649) contributed to a feeling of unrest. The Peace of Westphalia, signed in Münster and Osnabrück in 1648, marked the onset of a new era that aimed at stability and order.

A desire for unity and certainty rather than diversity began to characterise the period, as Stephen Toulmin has extensively argued in *Cosmopolis, The Hidden Agenda of Modernity*.[11] After a prolonged period of wars and concomitant social upheavals, the treaty formed the basis for the rise and consolidation of European nation states. A rapid growth of interest in national legal systems

[9] T. Snyder, 'Foreword', in T. Judt and T. Snyder, *Thinking the Twentieth Century* (London: William Heinemann, 2012), p. 3.

[10] H. Grotius (trans. and ed. J. Waszink), *The Antiquity of the Batavian Republic* (Assen: Van Gorcum, 2000).

[11] S. Toulmin, *Cosmopolis: The Hidden Agenda of Modernity* (New York: The Free Press, 1990).

at the end of the eighteenth century was auxiliary in bringing about nation states that strove for homogeneity, especially after the demise of the Holy Roman Empire, and after the Congress of Vienna (1814–15), which settled the new boundaries in Europe. It also led to concomitant concepts of nationhood that did not always coincide with societal views. The whole process, it should at once be noted, was not completed until after First World War. The unification of the German empire took place in 1871. In Italy, also in 1871, the *Risorgimento* movement and the struggles for independence in the 1860s led to the Kingdom of Italy with Rome as its capital. The Austro-Hungarian Empire and the Ottoman Empire ruled over the Balkan states until 1918. Noteworthy is that the decisions made on the basis of the 1919 Treaty of Versailles continued to affect relationships between the inhabitants of European nations both old and new, and, internally – to mention but one aspect of the flipside of this development – to affect citizens' identities based on forced linguistic homogeneity until well into the 1990s. After the fall of the Iron Curtain, dissension on issues with respect to ethnicity, religion, and identity proved insurmountable, and led to civil war and disaster in the Balkan region.

In science, the quest for certainty started with the elaboration of Francis Bacon's empirical methodology and René Descartes's rationalism based on the method of deduction, the duality of mind and matter, and the principle of fundamental doubt as expressed in his maxim *Cogito, ergo sum* in his *Discourse on Method* (1637). It ended in a mechanistic worldview that placed everything in the perspective of causal relations, the dreams of which Toulmin describes as those of a uniform method aimed at universal application, a perfect language as the ultimate representation of objective reality, and a unitary system of nature.[12] Cultural and other diversities were thought of as interesting only insofar as they elucidated universal principles. What Cartesian rationalism meant for the natural sciences was extended to ethics a century later by Immanuel Kant (1724–1804) in the abstract categorical imperative as the guideline for human action.

Gottfried Wilhelm von Leibniz (1646–1716) elaborated on the idea of unity to prevent war and dissension by means of a uniform language: that is, shared meaning on the plane of linguistics. Leibniz was obsessed by the ideal of the *characteristica universalis*, a universal system of characters not

---

[12] S. Toulmin, *Return to Reason* (Cambridge, MA: Harvard University Press, 2001), ch. 5. I have also benefitted from recent in-depth studies of the Holy Roman Empire and the Habsburg Empire: P. H. Wilson, *The Holy Roman Empire, A Thousand years of Europe's History* (London: Allen Lane, 2016); P. M. Judson, *The Habsburg Empire, A New History* (Cambridge, MA and London: Belknap Press of Harvard University Press, 2016); P. Stein, *Roman Law in European History* (Cambridge: Cambridge University Press, 1999).

only for different peoples to share and communicate by but especially as a neutral medium to convey the results of sensory perceptions and rational thought.[13] The Leibnizian design shattered, however, because it was logically impossible – a people's language cannot be dissociated from its way of life. Furthermore, language itself provides the categories with which we think and perceive, so reciprocity rather than linguistic transparency is the keyword. Philosophically, this development culminated in the twentieth century in Wittgenstein's *Philosophical Investigations* (that put aside as erroneous his earlier (Leibnizian) picture theory of meaning of the *Tractatus Logico-Philosophicus* (1922)). Empirically, it led to linguistic theories such as the Sapir/Whorf hypothesis.

The falling to pieces of the old world view and the subsequent rise of dichotomies such as mind versus matter, and nature versus culture, led to a dualistic worldview that affected law and legal theory. The reception of Roman law throughout continental Europe was a gradual one. Local law became permeated by this *ius commune* as the dominant force, also when it came to interpreting local customary law. Roman law, in short, epitomised the law held in common because of its generally accepted claim for legitimacy, and because it formed the basis for the subsequent development of specific areas of law.[14] The legal humanist philology of the sixteenth century, following Desiderius Erasmus (1469–1536) and Thomas More (1478–1535), had already advocated a return to the sources – in Erasmus's words, *ad fontes* – of the *Corpus Iuris Civilis*, rather than adding to the text as the commentators of the previous centuries had done, and, as a result, had questioned its claim of universal applicability.

Seventeenth-century legal theorists responded to the period's instability by emphasising the human intellect or *recta ratio*. This led to the development of rational natural law initiated by Hugo Grotius as a response to war and strife: for example, in *De iure belli ac pacis* (1625). Grotius's ideal being that of bringing about *pax*, *unitas* and *humanitas*, his contribution lies in his proposal to subject warfare to legal rules. Connected to this is his idea for an integrated view of Christianity and classical views and precepts – the Ciceronian concept of *humanitas* prominently present[15] – with which

---

[13] L. E. Loemker (ed.), *G. W. Leibniz, Philosophical Papers and Letters* (Dordrecht and Boston: D. Reidel Publishing, 1976), p. 9.

[14] See H. Coing, *Die ursprüngliche Einheit der europäischen Rechtswissenschaft* (Wiesbaden: F. Steiner, 1968), p. 12.

[15] Ciceronian *humanitas* is based on the idea that a community of people, precisely because they are endowed with reason and guided by the spirit of human kindness, will gather under a legal order and promote peaceful relations.

Grotius hoped to bring about unity in the diversity of opinions of his times, a way to regulate social conflict, with a view to inspiring later attempts at establishing unity and solidarity in Europe. In Germany, Samuel Pufendorf (1632–94) and Christian Wolff (1679–1754) followed suit, and built a legal system *more geometrico*, that is, by means of a deductive method as propagated by the natural sciences, and implemented already by Thomas Hobbes in his contractarian theory of sovereignty in England where Edward Coke had proclaimed the rationality and origin of common law in natural law in *Calvin's Case* (1608).

The view of law based on human reason contributed to the Enlightenment ideal of rational law in the second half of the eighteenth century, and subsequently to the idea of law as a system of codified rules, as well as to the concept of democracy under the rule of law. Roman law became obsolete with the rise and consolidation of European nation states, which led to a rapid growth of interest in national legal systems. The codifications of national positive law, such as the French Napoleonic *Code Civil* of 1804 and the Austrian codification of 1812, were the result. This development was accompanied by the notion originating in Montesquieu's *The Spirit of the Laws* that the judge is *la bouche de la loi*, the literal spokesperson who tells us what the lawgiver intends, at least in the interpretation that positivist thinkers gave to it, thereby changing the earlier idea that the law is unable to speak unless a judge gives it voice: *iudex lex loquens*. From the positivistic perspective, law and justice coincide. The (Hobbesian-Leibnizian) language view behind this is that the instrument of language can adequately fulfill its task of objectively and comprehensively describing the world as it truly is. This view is connected to the natural sciences paradigm of scientific positivism of philosophers such as Auguste Comte, John Stuart Mill and Herbert Spencer. It culminated in legal positivism in its various guises.

Only in Prussia did Roman law survive a bit longer, but it derailed in formalism. In his fierce struggle notably against the codification project initiated by Frederick the Great (the Prussian General Legal Code of 1794), Friedrich Carl von Savigny (1779–1861) posited the true legislator in the spirit of the people, the *Volksgeist*, a term coined by Johann Gottfried Herder. Because it was ahistorical, Von Savigny rejected the priority of human reason to understand law as advocated by Enlightenment thinkers. Thus, the French Revolution was viewed as a dangerous thing as was the codification ideal of the Napoleontic era.[16] Romantic in its cherishing of tradition as a source of

---

[16] In 1815, Von Savigny warned the German peoples not to follow the example of the French

knowledge, this Historical School aimed to understand law by seeking the meaning of legal concepts in the context of their origin. Hence, from the perspective that the development of the *Volksgeist* could be traced throughout the ages, Roman law was deemed essential because it was thought to have developed from that very same consciousness of the people. In short, German law was the natural synthesis of Roman law. Paradoxically, Von Savigny and his followers of the Historical School then used Roman law, more specifically the *Digests* or *Pandectae*, to build a strict system of legal concepts of a kind totally unknown to original Roman law itself, case-based as Roman law was. This *usus modernus pandectarum* or *Pandektenwissenschaft* resulted in a deductive, formalist jurisprudence of concepts, the *Begriffsjurisprudenz*, a semantic essentialism devoid of any ethical or social notion. But the heaven of legal concepts with its infernal hair-splitting machine and other inhabitants was soon exposed as the realm of fictions – namely, constructs – useful though they may be.[17] Concepts exist only because of the order that law imposes, from the intangibles such as the corporation to the duty of care of the reasonable man, or the division of torts into intentional wrongs, negligence, and strict liability. It should be noted that both the formalists' erroneous notion of self-evident truths in law and the fictional aspect of concepts are epistemologically not that different from the idea, inspired by natural law, that William Blackstone cherished: namely, that the laws of England were an expression of the laws of nature in the sense of the natural order. (Indeed, all of Blackstone's systematisation of the *Commentaries on the Laws of England* was based on that premise: rights are what nature and law allow, order or assign; wrongs are their mirror images.) Rudolf von Ihering (1818–92), who started as a theorist of the jurisprudence of concepts, eventually recognised its dangers. He then developed a sociological jurisprudence on the basis of the interests of individual persons in society, the *Interessenjurisprudenz*, comparable to the Benthamite sociological idea of law as a means to an end.[18]

The long-cherished and generally accepted dominance of a unifying Roman law-oriented thought was forced to give up its territory to the study

---

codification in his *Vom Beruf unserer Zeit für Gesetzgebung und Rechtswissenschaft*, translated by A. Hayward as *Of the Vocation of our Age for Legislation and Jurisprudence* (New York: Argo, 1975).

[17] R. von Ihering (trans. C. L. Levy), *In the Heaven for Legal Concepts: A Fantasy*, 58 *Temple Law Quarterly*, [1884] 1985, pp. 799–842.

[18] R. von Ihering (trans. I. Husik), *Der Zweck im Recht*, 3 vols., 1877-1884, *Law as a Means to an End* (Boston: The Boston Book Co., 1913). It is worth noting that in the United States the movement away from Langdellian legal formalism to sociological jurisprudence and legal realism greatly resembles this European development.

of national jurisdictions. The simultaneous existence of a variety of types of legal systems along the lines of nationhood is also a legacy of Hobbes, given the superiority attached to the state as the sole legislator. In legal interpretation, the idea became dominant that once the facts and the rules are clear, the right answer will necessarily be found by applying syllogistic reasoning. Its hermeneutic insistence on the separation of law and facts, given its tendency to out-of-context reasoning and its focus on the normative component of law, encompasses as large a danger of essentialism as does Platonism. The other separation thesis of positivism only adds to this, because the separation of law and morals in a pure theory of law such as that of the German jurist Hans Kelsen, or the empiricist variety promoted by H. L. A. Hart, is also accompanied by a claim of neutrality.

Unity and Diversity in European Law and Legal Theory

Law and jurisprudence

The second part of my historical account – the same story told from a different viewpoint – presupposes an ordering perspective of the development from unity to diversity in law and legal theory. Its premise is that jurisprudence, legal science, or legal theory – call it what you will – is in two ways the product of a long process of both integration and differentiation. The first way is geographically, when we consider the implementation of Roman law in Europe – the integrative move – and its subsequent demise with the rise of the nation state when the diversification of national codification sets in. The second way is methodologically, when this original formation of law as an autonomous discipline was followed by a long process of differentiation that eventually led to the birth or emancipation of the empirical sciences in the nineteenth century (external differentiation), and to the branching off of law into a variety of subfields, each with its respective subdiscipline of legal theory (internal differentiation, a topic outside the scope of this book). In short, it involved a development from a form of unified European law to a variety of national legal systems, and a parallel development from a unified legal science to a broad range of subdisciplines and auxiliary disciplines, resulting in the growth of specialisation in both the university and the legal profession. Given that since the late twentieth century legal theory has shown an increasing growth of interdisciplinary movements or fields, this speaks for a historical-comparative overview.

The Byzantine emperor Justinian (527–565) ordered the codification of imperial Roman law from the period of the second to the sixth century. The result was the *Codex Justinianus*. He then had a committee of scholars codify Roman case law, the *Digests*, on the basis of which the *Institutes* were written for the purpose of legal education. Together these texts also gained force of law in Italy by papal decree. When copies of these codifications were found, they were brought together as the *Corpus Iuris Civilis* (the corpus of civil law as distinct from canonical law) and used in the *studium generale* in Bologna. Justinian had forbidden any interpretation of his code. Paradoxically, interpretation and commentary became the key words as the philological studies inaugurated at Bologna formed the basis of the new discipline of law. Roman law in its original form had a completely contextual rationality based on case-by-case reasoning. The new learned Roman law and its philological study, however, were the products of scholarship, not of the development of case law. Initially, the scholars who studied the *Corpus* added glosses in the margins of the text, and thus a law school of *glossatori* came into being, in the period from approximately 1100 to 1250. Soon after, the *glossatori* added contemporary legal texts such as Frederick Barbarossa's imperial constitution. Later on, from 1250 to 1400, their successors, the *post-glossatori*, completed this process of harmonisation of texts, with as a result the growth óf a rational methodology aimed at forming law into a well-organised structure. Glosses became independent texts. They formed a first attempt at systemisation: the scholastic method and the birth of jurisprudence in the sense of academic legal scholarship as distinct from *doing* law.[19] Its characteristics are the centrality of the text – the root of legal scholarship as we know it – and its detailed attention to the removal of inconsistencies by means of refining logical distinctions. As glosses grew into legal doctrines that were in turn used in legal arguments in practice, the interaction of theory (*cognitio*, knowledge) and practice (*applicatio*, application) characteristic of the western legal tradition began to take shape. Legal texts became the places in which to search for legal arguments (that is, in contradistinction to the oral legal tradition(s) of local law including custom).

It should be noted here that the historical bond between law and letters in Europe, as found in the original symbiosis of law and literature in legal practice, has undeservedly been neglected in interdisciplinary legal studies. The scholastic method of debate, originating from theology and later prominent throughout academia – as it eventually perfected the dialectic method – also incorporated into law certain elements that were originally part of the oral tradition of law and the poetical tradition of the *trobadores* or *trouveurs,* who found their texts while in the process of constructing them from the materials of their cultures. The ordeal is a case in point. There were

---

[19] See J. M. Kelly, *A Short History of Western Legal Theory* (Oxford: Clarendon Press, 1992), esp. ch. 4; O. F. Robinson et al., *European Legal History: Sources and Institutions* (Butterworths: London, 1994), chs 9 and 10.

also morphological affinities between literary and legal language, for example in the language of poetry in comparison to the wording of legal figures such as the *customal*; given the formulaic aspect of legal language, especially when it came to the accusation in criminal law proceedings, jurists sought refuge in the story in order to give the formula more body.[20]

Legal texts as sources for arguments gained practical relevance. The rhetorical art of debate in legal education, the *disputatio* with reasoning advanced by *opponens* and *respondens* that ended in the *determinatio* or *sententia* – namely, the conclusion on a doctrinal point of law – was reflected in the judicial procedure, geared as it has always been to taking a decision, to giving a sentence. Thus, when in medieval Europe legal texts based on the *Corpus* gained their independence, they outgrew the local situation of their birth as translations of Roman law, and grew into a system that became autonomous and, simultaneously, in still further need of interpretation. The bond of law and literature in rhetoric can also be seen in the French culture of the *basoches* around 1500. These were assemblies or brotherhoods of clerks and young lawyers working in a *Parlement* that held fake trials, referred to as *causes grasses*, in order to satirise those in power, in the *Parlement* and elsewhere. In common law, a comparable development resulted in the rise of legal humanism at the Inns of Court, the rhetorical culture of which 'led jurists to think of legal writing as a cultural rather than a technical exercise, even, in the case of Sir Edward Coke, as a species of nation building'.[21]

Authority was added to textuality and logic when a shift took place from authority granted to the persons issuing decrees, such as kings and popes – fierce struggles for power took place between the kings and popes in the High Middle Ages from 1100 to 1350 – to those able to interpret the legal text in a concrete situation: namely, jurists and, more specifically, judges. They then began to defend their position as being independent of politics. This ultimately resulted in what Nonet and Selznick called the historic bargain of the separation of powers, one that has by now become a contentious area in many nations to the extent that it makes sense to keep the historic root in mind.[22]

---

[20] R. Howard Bloch, *Medieval French Literature and Law* (Berkeley: University of California Press, 1977), p. 5.

[21] See M. Bouhaïk-Gironès, *La Basoche et le théâtre comique: identité sociale, pratiques et culture des clercs de justice (Paris 1420–1550)* (Brussels: De Boeck, 2004); K. Dolin, *A Critical Introduction to Law and Literature* (Cambridge: Cambridge University Press, 2007), ch. 3, 'Renaissance humanism and contract', pp. 80–1.

[22] See P. Nonet and P. Selznick, *Law and Society in Transition: Toward Responsive Law* (New York: Harper and Row, 1978), ch. 3.

Methodologically, medieval legal science was a step forward in that it led to more abstract knowledge that had the advantage of being more easily transferred, literally and figuratively. From a professional-ethical point of view, the tension between the authority of the text itself, on the one hand, and the rationality of the integrative method, on the other, formed the basis for a critical scholarly attitude open to change, at least in principle. Sociologically, all this is connected to the institution of the university.[23] As the scholastic method gained its foothold in law and all other areas of thought, the *studium generale* developed into the *universitas*, a term referring to the alliance of students, the *universitas studiosorum* (and not to what we now consider the university, the whole of the sciences or *universitas scientiarum*), hence also its corporate personality, which offered protection against worldly and clerical intrusions. Its curriculum covered the whole range of subjects important for a general, humanist education. Originally, the term *artes liberales*, or liberal arts, was the common Roman denominator for all those fields of knowledge pertaining to the human. In his defence speech for the poet Archia ('Pro Archia Poeta'), Cicero already wrote that all the arts have a common bond, a *commune vinculum*. With the rise of the university, the *artes liberales* formed the basis for secular studies (and that included law and medicine) as distinguished from theology: namely, the *trivium* (grammar, rhetoric and dialectic) and the *quadrivium* (arithmetic, geometry, astronomy and musicology).

Thus, the jurist was a *litteratus*, one who possessed letters in the sense that he was able to read and write and thus to offer valuable services as *clericus*. Here is another source not only for the original identification of literature with literacy but also for the interrelation of letters and the legal profession. After having obtained their degrees, the new Masters of Laws swarmed across Europe because their knowledge and the simple fact that they could read and write well placed them in great demand. As a result, the new discipline of law experienced a golden age, fulfilling both a political and an economic and social function.[24] Given that local circumstances obviously differed, the reception of Roman law was not identical in all parts of Europe. What happened was a gradual spread of the *Corpus* across Europe, a process in which local law became the *ius speciale* to Roman law as the *ius commune*, the law common to the continental European territories. As a result, local law was interpreted in the light of the rules, principles, and decisions of the *ius commune*. All this is important to note when we think

---

[23] See H. J. Berman, *Law and Revolution: the Formation of the Western Legal Tradition* (Cambridge, MA, and London: Harvard University Press, 1983), pp. 162–3.
[24] See Berman, *Law and Revolution*, ch. 2, and Kelly, *Short History*, ch. 4.

of the growth of supranational European Union legislation and recent developments towards a uniform European private law,[25] as well as when we consider the way in which constitutions work in nations with a federal system.

As an integrated body of knowledge, legal science became paradigmatic for other fields.[26] In due course, however, the scholastic method was taken to its logical extreme, and ended up in an unproductive doctrinal formalism wholly out of touch with the practical and social context of law. With the onset and subsequent expansion of the *studia humanitatis,* now known as humanism, in the fifteenth and sixteenth centuries, the rigid scholastic division between logic (the reign of theoretical or scientific knowledge) and rhetoric (favouring practical knowledge and context-dependent reasoning) dissolved. For law, the result was not only the integration with the *artes liberales* in general but also the unity of theory and practice, as the Italian scholastic method, *mos italicus,* was replaced by the French, more local and case-oriented, *mos gallicus.* Legal humanism thus originated from the growing awareness that the *Corpus Iuris Civilis* had come into being in a specific historic context that no longer existed. As a result, the authority of Roman law declined. Its second, short flourishing was in the seventeenth century in the Dutch Republic, with the jurisprudence of the Hollandic school,[27] and, as noted above, in the German *Pandektenwissenschaft.*

What remained was the attention to the above-mentioned classification of legal concepts, rules and principles. The convenient arrangement of private law along the lines drawn by the *Institutes – personae, res* and *actiones* – gained prominence, and was later also used by Blackstone in his *Commentaries on the Laws of England.* In England, too, theoretically inclined common law jurists had increasingly moved away from common law's somewhat loose medieval form towards the systematisation of case law. This resulted in the desire to rationalise law, and continental humanism provided guidance. The work of the French Peter Ramus was influential in that his challenge of scholastic logic with its firm distinction between invention – namely, the identification of arguments on a certain subject by considering their location, and subsequent judgement based on it – sought to emphasise the importance of rhetoric

[25] See G. C. J. J. van den Bergh, '*Ius commune:* a History with a Future?', in B. de Witte and C. Forder (eds), *The Common Law of Europe and the Future of Legal Education* (Deventer: Kluwer, 1992), pp. 593–607.

[26] See Berman, *Law and Revolution,* pp. 152–3.

[27] Note that it is called Hollandic rather than Dutch, because the first generations of humanists from the sixteenth century and onwards came from Holland, which was then the most important province in the Republic.

in the process.[28] As methods of reasoning came to the fore in legal methodology, hermeneutics and practical reasoning aimed at persuasion gained prominence, and English common law humanists and continental European legal humanists alike began to think in terms of the bond between theory and practice. An integrative approach that lasted well into the eighteenth century was favoured, until the emphasis on the *lex scripta* of the national legislator made a strict distinction between text and application.

From disciplinary unity to differentiation of knowledge: the external differentiation of law

What matters to me here is that the process of the differentiation of knowledge into separate academic disciplines is a relatively recent process, and that this *Ausdifferenzierung*, as Niklas Luhmann coined it, also took place in the form of a process of differentiation of law itself.[29] The origin of this process can be traced back to early eighteenth-century Enlightenment thought, when the concept of law as a science was still governed by the notion that law should be in accordance with humanity and human reason. To start with, it is important to note that the process of disciplinary differentiation is a gradual one. Philosophers such as Giambattista Vico (1668–1744) in *On the Study Methods of Our Time* continued the Renaissance aspiration of the *homo universalis*. Vico is of course best known for his *Scienza Nuova*, which our copy- clerks Bouvard and Pécuchet found so disappointing.[30] He also postulates the primacy of *ingenium* – as opposed to rational thought – as the human capacity to see what must necessarily be done in a given situation. To him, law is discursive in that it is always the provisional result of a process of judging on the basis of *prudentia*. This can be traced back to Aristotle, who distinguished between *épistèmè* and *phronèsis* (the topic of Chapter 6), and makes Vico important for our contemporary literary-legal studies.

Johann Gottfried Herder deserves mention as one who deviated from the path of the rationalist quest for certainty that had been followed by his immediate predecessors such as Leibniz, and who heralded the twentieth-century view on contextualised meaning. Herder had studied briefly under Immanuel Kant's tutelage, but was critical of Kant's Enlightenment stance. He fulminated against the lack of originality of German literature, the cause

---

[28] M. D. Walters, 'Legal humanism and law-as-integrity', 67 *Cambridge Law Journal*, 2008, pp. 352–75.

[29] N. Luhmann, *Ausdifferenzierung des Rechts: Beiträge zur Rechtssoziologie und Rechtstheorie* (Frankfurt am Main: Suhrkamp, 1981).

[30] T. Goddard Bergin and M. H. Fisch (trans. and eds), *The New Science of Giambattista Vico* (Ithaca and London: Cornell University Press, [3rd edn 1744] 1986).

of which he took to be precisely the Romanist influence pervasive in German society.[31] Herder, like Benjamin Cardozo much later, claims that the 'what' and the 'how' of any text are intimately connected. Language is not a mere instrument but formative of thought itself, a cultural and historic storehouse. His is a view on the cultural rootedness of law and language. Herder distances himself from the Enlightenment view on the relation between language and reality, between the word and the idea it aims to express, as found in Hobbes's *Leviathan* and in Locke's *Essay Concerning Human Understanding*. Herder's folk and fairy tales influenced the philologists Jacob and Wilhelm Grimm's research culminating in their 1812 *Kinder- und Hausmärchen*. Herder's general idea of organic growth later served Von Savigny and his assistant Jacob Grimm as jurists when they reconceived the Roman *Pandects* as German law.[32] Grimm's view is especially important, in terms of differentiation in contradistinction to the earlier unity of law and letters, in that like Vico he claimed that originally all jurisprudence was poetic. In his essay 'Von der Poesie im Recht', Grimm offered the observation that law and literature arose from the same bed; he emphasised the importance of the medieval tradition of *Dichterjuristen*, poet-jurists, claiming that *Richter* (judges) are finders of their decisions, just like poets (*Dichter*) are finders of the right words, or *poetai*, the ancient Greek term for makers, here, of texts.[33] Here is another paradox: Grimm wrote this in connection to the advent of the strand of Germanists, a term he coined himself to indicate – in contradistinction to the Romanist *Begriffs*-jurisprude Friedrich Carl von Savigny – the importance for the development of law of the *Volksgeist*, the spirit of the people as exemplified in medieval Germanic rather than Roman law.[34]

The intellectual curiosity of these scholars was not yet limited by specialisation and disciplinary boundaries as we know them. It is often forgotten that the same goes for Beccaria in his *On Crimes and Punishment* (1764), and for Montesquieu, who is chiefly remembered for the concept of *la bouche de la loi* (1748) in its positivist guise. His *The Spirit of the Laws*, however, not

[31] J. G. Herder, 'Die Sprache überhaupt', an essay in the collection entitled *Fragmente über die neuere deutsche Literatur* (1766–7), in J. G. Herder (ed. W. Pross), *Werke, Band I Herder und Sturm und Drang 1764–1774, erste Sammlung, zweite völlig umgearbeite Ausgabe* (Munich: Carl Hanser Verlag, [1768] 1984), pp. 71–90.

[32] I. Berlin, *Vico and Herder, Two Studies in the History of Ideas* (London: Hogarth Press, 1976), p. 147 n.1.

[33] J. Grimm, 'Von der Poesie im Recht', *Zeitschrift für geschichtliche Rechtswissenschaft*, repr. in J. Grimm, 6 *Kleinere Schriften* (Hildesheim: Olms, [1816] 1965), pp. 152–91.

[34] It should be noted that the Herderian premise that ideally *Volk* and language coincide has a dark side. History shows that it can lead to exclusion and expulsion. That is a topic outside the scope of this chapter.

only propounds the foundations of the separation of powers but it does so by including the study of a variety of legal and political orders as well as a focus on the natural and societal circumstances of their development. In short, the study of law long remained part of an all-encompassing study of society. Nevertheless, its focus shifted, and while this broad cultural relevance of law is apparent in the nineteenth-century progress of external differentiation as separate scholarly communities came into existence, each with their own culture in the sense of conceptual frameworks, methodologies, and values, the original rootedness of law in language disappeared into the background. After Blackstone, a writer of verse since boyhood, entered legal practice in 1741, he soon lamented – in the poem 'The Lawyer's Farewell to His Muse' – that he was forced to leave the companion of his youth.[35] The poem not only highlights the bifurcation Blackstone obviously experienced in his life but it is also indicative of the divorce between law and literature's original professional connections.

Pioneers of the empirical social sciences were jurists who emphasised the importance for law of human behaviour and social relations. The first systematic gathering of empirical data took place in the field of what is now called economics. In eighteenth-century Germany, juridical-political science became diversified because of the practical need to rationalise the polity. The *Kameralwissenschaften* (or Cameralism, the term for all fields pertaining to the state's government and administration) provided the means to do so with their study of politics, statistics, and political economy. Theoretically, the economics of the private household and of political economy were distinguished. Legal concepts such as private property were no longer seen as belonging to a system of rules but as part of commercial relations, economic processes, and elements of national welfare. In this view, law's role in society transformed into the precondition of the market, a line of thought initiated in Adam Smith's *An Inquiry into the Nature and the Causes of the Wealth of Nations* (1776). Attention to questions of economics implied the shift from a normative approach to law and ethics towards an empirical one that not only fit in with the development of the natural sciences but also provided a new challenge for those jurists who wanted to move away from the tradition of textual exegesis characteristic of legal methodology. With Karl Marx (1818–83), the new science of economics gained revolutionary force and

---

[35] The poem was first published anonymously in the 1755 *Collection of Poems* edited by Robert Dodsley. For a jurisprudential reading of the poem against the background of Blackstone's *Commentaries on the Laws of England*, see M. Mauger, '"Observe how parts with parts unite/ In one harmonious rule of right": William Blackstone's Verses on the Laws of England', 6 *Law and Humanities*, no. 2, 2012, pp. 179–96.

political influence through *The Communist Manifesto* (1848) and *Capital: Critique of Political Economy* (1867).

Anthropology and sociology also derive from law as the mother discipline. In the Greek cosmological view on natural law as well as in Roman law, the bond between law and human nature was already emphasised, but it was not until the rise of anthropology that attention was paid to collective and cultural patterns of human behaviour. Stimulated by colonial policies and ethnological interests, anthropology became an empirical science. It widened the context of law to religion and to any capacity or custom a person has as a member of a group or society. Henry Maine in his study of *Ancient Law* (1861) laid bare the connection between types of culture and forms of law.[36] With the famous words *from status to contract*, he pointed to the fact that the way in which people live together creates the conditions for the legal concepts with which they regulate their society. Where economics looked upon law as a mechanism of distribution, anthropology viewed law as a cultural artefact.

And 'As anthropologists took "culture"', wrote Kelley, 'so sociologists took "society" as their master abstraction.'[37] Coined by Auguste Comte around 1830, the term 'sociology' was given to the study of society, and its members that evolved as the jurists Emile Durkheim (1858–1917) and Max Weber (1864–1920) took up the task. Durkheim followed Comte, and took social facts as units of research for the new discipline along explanatory lines. Worried as he was by potentially disruptive forces in society that resulted from the industrial revolution (such as class struggle and urbanisation), he developed the notion of social cohesion in his seminal work *The Division of Labor in Society*, on the premise that the way in which labour is divided is the litmus test for any society and its legal system.[38] Weber's methodological starting point was different. He took sociology to be a cultural science of human behaviour, and as a consequence he developed an interpretive methodology aimed at understanding human actions rather than explaining them by using empirical data and statistics. Each discipline developed its own professional language and methodology. The effect of disciplinary differentiation and the combined emphasis on facts and literal meaning that is the heritage of positivism, are beautifully illustrated in a scene from a Dutch literary classic, Multatuli's *Max Havelaar* (1860), where the coffee-broker,

---

[36] H. Maine, *Ancient Law: Its Connection with the Early History of Society and its Relation to Modern Ideas* (Oxford: Oxford University Press [1861] 1950).

[37] D. R. Kelley, *The Human Measure: Social Thought in the Western Legal Tradition* (Cambridge, MA: Harvard University Press, 1990), p. 271. Kelley provides an extensive treatment of disciplinary differentiation.

[38] E. Durkheim, *The Division of Labor in Society* (New York: The Free Press, [1893] 1984).

Batavus Droogstoppel, criticises literature, and especially poetry, for its lack of correspondence with the supposedly real world, saying,

> Mind you, I've no objection to verses themselves. If you want words to form fours, it's all right with me! But don't say anything that isn't true. '*The air is raw, the clock strikes four*' I'll let that pass, if it really *is* raw, and if it really *is* four o'clock. But if it's a quarter to three, then I, who don't range my words in line, will say: '*The air is raw, and it is a quarter to three.*' But the versifier is bound to four o'clock, or else the air mustn't be raw. And so he starts tampering with the truth. Either the weather has to be changed, or the time. And in that case, one of the two is false.[39]

One thing is certain. Since the nineteenth century, differentiation has become the key notion in legal theory. And in a sense, it is typical for our social lives as well, as they first became fragmented following the divisions between labour and leisure, between arts and business, and between our public and private persona. These displacements were accompanied by increasing contemporary developments in the areas of globalisation and digitalisation, which gave rise to the emergence of yet another form of fragmentation; namely, divisions between the public and the private have now begun to blur as a result of our use of new technologies and smart devices.

---

[39] Multatuli (trans. R. Edwards), *Max Havelaar, or the Coffee Auctions of the Dutch Trading Company* (Harmondsworth: Penguin Books, [1860] 1987).

3

Explanation or Understanding:
Language and Interdisciplinarity

The Limits of Language in their Consequences

'It is interesting to compare the multiplicity of the tools in language and the ways they are used, the multiplicity of kinds of word and sentence, with what logicians have said about the structure of language. (Including the author of the Tractatus Logico-Philosophicus),' wrote the later Ludwig Wittgenstein (1889–1951) in his *Philosophical Investigations*.[1] It shows a remarkable shift in linguistic view compared to the *Tractatus Logico-Philosophicus* of his youth, when he wrote 'the limits of my language mean the limits of my world'.[2] In the *Tractatus*, Wittgenstein investigated the possibility of a logical basis for language with unifying principles. His early focus was on uniformity, logicity and transparency. He abandoned this pursuit when he understood that the ambiguity and pluriformity of linguistic usage and claims of meaning should be looked upon as essential characteristics of language rather than flaws. On the relationship between language and reality, the early Wittgenstein has been of decisive importance in forming the positivist programme of objective science, because of the premise that the results of empirical observation can be expressed in language in an objective way. With the later Wittgenstein, attention shifted to the function of linguistic usage in a specific context: 'the meaning of a word is its use in the language'.[3] The key question became what could a language user do with language: in other words, in which way could he or she act by it.[4] In law, this led to a contextual approach. Think, for example, of the conclusion of an agreement through offer and accept-

---

[1] L. Wittgenstein (trans. G. E. M. Anscombe), *Philosophical Investigations* (Oxford: Oxford University Press, 1953), section 23.

[2] L. Wittgenstein (trans. D. F. Pears and B. F. McGuiness), *Tractatus Logico-Philosophicus* (London: Routledge, [1922] 1961), proposition 5.6.

[3] Wittgenstein, *Philosophical Investigations*, section 43.

[4] See J. L. Austin (eds J. O. Urmson and M. Sbisà), *How To Do Things With Words* (Oxford: Oxford University Press, [1962] 1976).

ance. Offer and acceptance were long considered to be utterances that either did or did not give a proper description of the will of the parties. The result was a fairly ineffective search for the parties' supposedly true intention. If offer and acceptance are seen as speech acts, as promises that are under the circumstances considered as binding and enforceable pledges, then the attention shifts from the intention of the parties to the context in which they have acted. This chapter discusses some consequences of a positivist approach to language for law and the humanities, to serve as a backdrop for Chapters 4 and 5, which focus on Robert Musil's novel *The Man without Qualities* and on the Dutch poet Gerrit Achterberg's asylum poetry. Both literary works demonstrate with great force the derailment of its connected view that knowledge is objective.

Determinism and the Limits of Language

The first way in which the importance of Wittgenstein's 'limits' proposition 5.6 shows is in the scientific debate on determinism. Following Julien de La Mettrie's *L'homme machine* (1747), with its mechanistic Enlightenment concept of the human being as a machine understood in physicalist terms, this debate raises the question of the dehumanising effects of scientific rationality in matters concerning the legal and penal treatment of the criminally insane. It also shows how the concept of law as science as it developed in the nineteenth century led to a profound belief in the transparency of objective knowledge, one that Max Weber referred to as the disenchantment of the world.[5] Rationalism's hope of a universal method and a perfect language as a vehicle to communicate exact thoughts are the main components of modernity's framework of unconditional acceptance of causal necessity in the natural world. Its underlying idea of unity is indissolubly connected to modernity's quest for certainty that culminated in scientific positivism. The view of language as a neutral sign system functioning as a vehicle to convey meaning is based on the presupposition that the world of things exists totally apart from language. Hence, the mere function of language is to represent these things in a form that, supposedly, is unambiguously transferable. Descriptive usage of language is characteristic of science, while expressive usage is the domain of literature and poetry, as well as of ethics; moral judgements, for example, were viewed only as emotive expressions.

Modernity's premise regarding the relationship between language and

---

[5] M. Weber, 'Science as a vocation', in P. Lassman et al. (eds), *Max Weber's Science as a Vocation* (London: Unwin Hyman, 1989).

reality, combined with the positivist premise of a clear separation between the observer and the observed, aimed to guarantee the objective expression in words of the results of empirical observation. In law, this ideal of objective scientific knowledge based on logic and on the accumulation of empirical data culminated in legal positivism. Given its understandable theoretical aversion to interpretation, legal positivism restricted itself to the hermeneutic methods of, firstly, the search for authorial intention on the grounds that any text sends its author's message, and, secondly, of the application of the plain meaning of words, or rather the idea that a word always has at least one clear and simple meaning in everyday usage, which is automatically known to all language users. If linguistic usage represents the will of the author, the text of law, and thus law itself, is the concrete manifestation of the lawgiver's will. It works the other way around as well. On the Enlightenment premise that man has free will, his utterances and actions – as the expression of the free will of an autonomous being – are deemed to be purposeful as well as purposely and legally binding. The continued effect of the idea of atomic determinism as found in Newtonian physics is obvious. Legal certainty also collapsed legal causation with scientific causation in the objectification of the concept of contract. The US Supreme Court's decision in *Lochner v. New York*, 198 U.S. 45 (1905) is a case in point. In short, the late nineteenth-century emphasis in law and language was on uniformity and transparency.

However, when at the end of the nineteenth century the classical school of criminal law – which held that each individual is fully responsible for his actions – was forced to define its position on the question of the free will because of the rise of criminal anthropology, it did not take long before a methodological and epistemological battle was in full swing. The focus of the classical school was on the legal qualification of crime as a violation of a given norm, and on the Kantian notion of punishment as retribution. An offender should therefore be deterred, and penalties should be proportioned to the type of crime and the degree of guilt. In contrast, the new criminal anthropology or criminology posited that both natural and social sciences could share a single scientific positivist methodology. Furthermore, it proposed the separation of morality and science, as well as that of morality and law. It did not want to take the subject's inner thoughts into consideration, because self-reflection and subjectivity would create only illusions and not verifiable data. The facts, presumed to be ascertained easily, would be the only starting point. Simultaneously, within the discourse of law, the descriptive and expressive usage of language collapsed precisely because of the dominance of the idea that what one says or writes is a description of one's intention, which in turn is generated by the function of free will.

In law, the concept of free will is the product of a long period of development. Its foundation is the combined classical-philosophical view of the will as an ability in the sense of an attribute of the soul, and of religious views ranging from Saint Augustine to Calvin, who as champions of predestination as far as the afterlife is concerned also thought in terms of the free will to do what is right and to abstain from what is wrong (both the *mala per se* such as murder, and the *mala prohibita*, or what law prohibits). The entries in the Enlightenment *Dictionnaires* of the French philosophers Bayle and Voltaire provide insights. To Pierre Bayle, the subjective philosophical concept of the *liberum arbitrium indifferentiae* is the key. If one has free will, this means, for example, that one is free to decide to go either left or right, even if there is no specific reason to do either. In other words, one has freedom to act if – simply speaking – one is able to do whatever one decides.[6] Or, as Voltaire stated succinctly in his *Dictionnaire Philosophique*, 'Vous êtes libre de faire, quand vous avez le pouvoir de faire': if one can act, one is free to act.[7] Freedom of will consists in the person being free in making the decision to act at all. This is the precursor and precondition of the freedom to act, in that it presupposes the mental ability to decide whether or not to do this, that, or the other.

For jurists, the interesting question involves what it means that a decision is free. What are the necessary and sufficient conditions that enable such a decision? What are its consequences? These are also essential questions when dealing with the topic of the relation between subject and object. From a philosophical point of view, the Cartesian ontological dualism of mind and matter is a necessary presupposition if one wants to assert the working of free will and the freedom of human agency as opposed to an all-encompassing determinism. Even though Immanuel Kant had already discussed guilt and punishment in *Metaphysics of Morals* (1797) in the context of what would nowadays be called diminished responsibility on the basis of a psychiatric diagnosis,[8] the view of absolute indeterminism with no restrictions on the individual's free will – that is to say, not even by his own innate characteristics and/or bodily restrictions – remained dominant. It was not until the further development in the nineteenth century of empirical sciences such as craniology, physiognomy and anthropometry, claiming that we can learn to judge a person's character and disposition from the features of his face and outward appearance of his bodily characteristics, that it became seriously

---

[6] P. Bayle, *Dictionnaire historique et philosophique*, Tome II (Amsterdam: Compagnie des Libraires, 1734), p. 466.

[7] Voltaire (eds J. Benda and R. Naves), *Dictionnaire historique et philosophique* (Paris: Garnier, [1744] 1961), p. 277.

[8] See A. Mooij, 'Kant on criminal law and psychiatry', 21 *International Journal of Law and Psychiatry*, no. 4, 1998, pp. 335–41.

challenged.[9] The new field of criminal anthropology took up the notion of the direct relationship between crime and certain facial features. Its founder, Cesare Lombroso (1835–1909), in his *L'Uomo Delinquente* (1876), emphasised the need for statistical methods as well as social and economic data for the scientific differentiation of criminals.[10] Crime thus came to be viewed as the product of measurable causes that existed more or less independently of a person's free will. In criminal law, the notion that punishment must fit the individual criminal became the new argument. Based on the claim that there are criminal types whose behaviour is determined rather than chosen, treatment rather than punishment became the new trend.

In a nutshell, the conflict between indeterminism and determinism comes down to this: the indeterminist presupposes volition *per se*, and reproaches the determinist for denying the option of attributing the criminal act to the individual. The determinist takes the indeterminist to task for his inability to give reasons for his actions, other than by saying 'I wanted it because I wanted it'. This is the philosophical stalemate of the *tertium non datur*, a topic I turn to in Chapter 4. With it comes the ontological and methodological problem with regard to those fields of knowledge that take the human as both subject and object of inquiry. It results in the debate on their disciplinary positions on the spectrum of the sciences. The deterministic view as espoused by the modern school of criminal law thought of human volition as the combined product of both internal causes, such as the individual's character, and external causes, such as societal circumstances. Where the classical school linked volition to powers of reason and judgement, the deterministic school dealt with questions of whether disturbances of the intellectual powers or a mental disease could provide extenuating factors, both with respect to punishment and to the psychiatric treatment of a defendant.[11]

One Dutch determinist, Hamon, concluded that volition is a meta-

---

[9] Phrenology was developed by the German physician Gall (1758–1828), and physiognomy by the Swiss poet and scientist Lavater (1741–1801). Lavater was the first to identify a relationship between crime and certain facial features.

[10] See J. Gaakeer, 'The art to find the mind's construction in the face: Lombroso's criminal anthropology and literature: the example of Zola, Dostoevsky, and Tolstoy', 26 *Cardozo Law Review*, no. 6, 2004, pp. 2345–77; G. Olson, *Criminals as Animals from Shakespeare to Lombroso* (Berlin: De Gruyter, 2013).

[11] See M. A. Tissaw, 'The person concept and the ontology of persons', in J. Martin and M. H. Bickhard (eds), *The Psychology of Personhood: Philosophical, Historical, Social-Developmental, and Narrative Perspectives* (Cambridge: Cambridge University Press, 2013), pp.19–39; K. Danziger, 'Historical psychology of persons: categories and practice', in J. Martin and M. H. Bickhard (eds), *The Psychology of Personhood, Philosophical, Historical, Social-Developmental, and Narrative Perspectives* (Cambridge: Cambridge University Press, 2013), pp. 59–80.

physical fad, a sophism to be denied by criminologists who necessarily have to accept that criminals could not be held accountable, on the basis that positivistic natural sciences have proved that everything is in one way or another determined.[12] He argued that the only basis for indeterminism is that man is aware of the fact that he has a will, but that is not enough, because being conscious of something is not evidence of its existence. Or rather, consciousness and free will can themselves be the determined product of the human brain and its workings, because, as Locke had already argued earlier on, we do not know the causes that determine our thoughts and actions. This point was well ahead of its time, and it was not until twentieth-century advancements in neurobiology that its value was accepted. Outside the scope of this book are questions concerning the compatibility of volition and determinism with respect to new insights into neuronal processes (for example neuronal Darwinism), the evolution of the idea of volitional impairment, and with it the classification of the mentally insane: that is, the generation of more patients and/or criminally insane with every new edition of the *Diagnostic and Statistical Manual of Mental Disorders* (DSM). Deserving of mention are the results of recent investigations into the relationship of the amygdala and the prefrontal cortex when it comes to determining irrational behaviour, because they suggest that we should acknowledge that the concept of free will is and has always been a rational construct rather than the absolute we took it to be. For those to whom the root of criminal behaviour is to be looked for in the neurobiological set-up of the human, the Lombrosian question returns as to whether the structure of the brain can indeed contain a 'criminal' part. One thing is clear, however; in order to get out of the stalemate of determinism-indeterminism, the topic of (ab)normality was introduced in the course of nineteenth-century legal thought and codes. The supposedly normal person could be punished in the traditional ways. By equating insanity with a lack of accountability, again, in a dichotomous fashion, other remedies in the form of measures could be introduced for the abnormal.

The *Erklären-Verstehen* Controversy: Explanation versus Understanding

The second way in which the Wittgensteinian 'limits' proposition 5.6 is important is in the close connection between the determinism debate and the *Erklären-Verstehen* controversy as it is called in the German philosophical tradition. It is the epistemological and methodological dispute on whether

---

[12] A. F. A. Hamon, *Vrije wil, misdaad en toerekenbaarheid* (Amsterdam: Buys, 1907), p. 11 (my paraphrase in translation).

the methods of the sciences understood as academic disciplines should focus on the explanation of human behaviour in terms of the rationalistic and empiricist model of the natural sciences, or on the understanding of the meaning of human behaviour in the hermeneutic manner of the humanities. The debate has had far-reaching implications for law and literature.

To the German philosopher Wilhelm Dilthey (1833–1911), the concept of explanation was restricted to the field of the natural sciences, because explanation as a form of action could only pertain to facts. Hence, it was distinguished from the concept of meaning, or hermeneutic understanding, belonging to the field of the humanities. To Dilthey, interpretation was primarily the understanding of a text; however, the object of study of the humanities also included human actions and situations for which the meaning is sought, as is the case in historiography. Thus, Dilthey focused on *Erlebnis*, the inner, lived experience of phenomena, as a starting point for a methodology of the humanities, because human actions and situations cannot be understood by means of the laws of nature or of the explanatory methodology and classifications of the natural sciences. Put differently, meaning is an entity in its own right. Ironically, given the development of hermeneutics, legal positivists picked up the intentionalist hermeneutic theory of Dilthey's intellectual predecessor, Friedrich Schleiermacher (1768–1834), for the very reason that precisely because of the premise of the classical school of legal thought regarding the individual's free will an individual's utterances should be taken literally and at face value as the expression of his intentions. Law's thrust for *Normgerechtigkeit* – the notion that justice follows from the application of the legal norm as German legal theory would have it – and the mistake of legal positivism to adhere to a paradigm derived from the natural sciences can therefore be explained against the background of the '*Erklären-Verstehen*' controversy.

The positivist idea that legal decision making must necessarily opt for guidance based on the system of rules is not an isolated event, but forms part of a wider methodological dispute that can be roughly divided into two camps. Firstly, on one side of the spectrum is the further sophistication of positivism in the twentieth century. The original logical-positivist aims to base scientific knowledge on the unquestioned double basis of logic and observation turned out to be untenable when Karl Popper argued that perception cannot be thought of as independent of theory, and can therefore never be an objective criterion for the assessment of competing theories. Popper's critical form of a more sophisticated rationalist methodology as the basis for objective science that could be applied to all sciences, both natural and social, was initially welcomed. In the case of the social sciences, with law considered as one of them, this approach was translated to imply a programme of empirical science based on the concept of instrumental rationality. Because of the then dominant ideal of value-free science, the selecting of objectives was left to politics so that the competence of the scientist would be limited to giving advice about the applicable means.[13] In law, it occasioned the rise of the legal professional as social engineer, a species already defined with derision by Sir Walter Scott in the novel *Guy Mannering* as a 'mechanic, a mere working mason' in contradistinction to the legal 'architect' who is knowledgeable about the humanities.[14]

Secondly, on the other side of the spectrum, the tradition of the humanities took as their centre hermeneutics, critical theory, and numerous other theories on knowledge. Here the domain of human action is determined by the interrelation of values and culture, of facts and values, and of objectives and means, all inextricably intertwined. When applied to professional life, this view can help prevent lawyers from becoming hired guns only. Another model of rationality applies, in that critical debate takes the place of objective acquisition of knowledge. In this view, rationality is discursive; it recognises diversity as legitimate. The consequence for the heuristic principle of (legal) interpretation is that we should acknowledge the need for interdisciplinary thought. Diverse as the fields in the humanities may be, they share the notion of the refutation of the ideal of objective knowledge based on empirical data as defended by positivism. The domain of human action, determined as it is by values and culture, is ill-suited to the supposedly objective acquisition of knowledge. When the methods used in textual interpretation were expanded to include understanding human actions in general, the central question of the methodological dispute within the social sciences also became whether these methods should focus on explaining human behaviour in terms of the natural science model or in terms of understanding human behaviour in the manner of the humanities. The rediscovery in the late twentieth century of the Weberian hermeneutical methodology for the social sciences is a case in point. What is more, the turn to interpretation in the 1960s and 1970s in the social sciences and law (by then no longer by definition a social science) helped counter the dominant paradigm of positivism.

---

[13] See H. Albert, *Traktat über kritische Vernunft* (Tübingen: Mohr Siebeck, 1975), and *Traktat über rationale Praxis* (Tübingen: Mohr Siebeck, 1978). The pretence of neutrality of law was championed, for example, by the legal process school in the US in the 1950s.

[14] W. Scott, *Guy Mannering* (London and New York: Dent and Dutton, [1815] 1954) p. 259. But see D. Howarth, *Law as Engineering: Thinking about what Lawyers Do* (Cheltenham and Northampton, MA: Edward Elgar, 2013).

Contextualisation and Interdisciplinarity

Contextualisation

The above debate confronts us with the consequences of the scholarly position we take when it comes to interdisciplinary work. After all, as Michel de Montaigne already noted, law as a discipline by its very nature occasions strife and discord, and he refers to Quintilian's thesis, *'difficultatem facit doctrina'*, that it is learning – when thought of as doctrine – and academic scholarship that cause the problem.[15] Furthermore, each discipline is a disciplinary and disciplining practice that inevitably domesticates its practitioners if we think of the original Latin meaning of *disciplina*: education, teaching and ordering device. Hence the continued relevance of the debate, given the use of the dichotomous use of the conjunction in interdisciplinary fields. We should ask ourselves whether we are at all to continue the supposedly mutual incomprehension that results from the putative dichotomy of the scientists versus the scholars in the humanities. The 'Two Cultures' dichotomy that is the heritage of C. P. Snow is the successor of the *'Erklären-Verstehen'* controversy, and it often resurfaces in contemporary interdisciplinary thought. Snow's (in)famous distinction, or so his critics claim, between the scientists and non-scientists, with those working in the humanities grouped under the latter heading, led to a dismissal of the humanities because of their perceived inability to contribute to the solution of real problems: namely, societal, political and global ones. Whether we are inclined to embrace F. R. Leavis's third realm for the existence of literature, or Jerome Kagan's recent distinction between not two but three cultures,[16] what matters to me here is that we need to realise that our choice depends to a large degree on our theory about theory.

The formation of accepted knowledge in any field is indissolubly connected to the articulation of the tension between text and context, logic and experience, premise and result. It can be seen in the development of law from the exclusive domain of the jurist who analyses and systematises what is to be called knowledge in the field to a concept of law as no longer fully autonomous but infused with the findings of other disciplines, such as the empirical sciences (more specifically sociology, economy and psychol-

---

[15] M. de Montaigne, 'Of experience', Book III, Essay 13, in M. de Montaigne (trans. and ed. M. A. Screech), *The Complete Essays* (Harmondsworth: Penguin, [1588] 1991), pp. 1207–69, p. 1210.

[16] C. P. Snow, *The Two Cultures* (Cambridge: Cambridge University Press, [1959] 1993); F. R. Leavis, *Two Cultures? The Significance of C. P. Snow* (London: Chatto and Windus, 1962); J. Kagan, *The Three Cultures, Natural Sciences, Social Sciences and the Humanities in the 21st Century: Revisiting C. P. Snow* (Cambridge: Cambridge University Press, 2009).

ogy). The emergence of new fields on the interface between law and other disciplines also occasioned the movement from multi-disciplinary 'Law plus an auxiliary discipline' to interdisciplinary 'Law ands'. Intimately connected to this development – and still in full swing – is the methodological dispute on the status of jurisprudence itself. Can there still be a dogmatic theory of law: that is to say, a text-oriented science directed to the analysis and systematisation of authoritative texts as jurists have done since the rediscovery of the *Corpus Iuris Civilis*? Or does law move in the direction of the empirical social sciences? The answer to the question determines our methodology: text analysis or empirical surveys? The logic of the syllogism or the acceptance on the basis of experience of what works in practice or what benefits those involved? It is, in turn, immediately connected to the particular view of language that we espouse.

To put interdisciplinary research in an even wider context, it should be noted that in the course of the twentieth century another source for the arising countermovement to the uniform model in the sciences evolved: namely, the development of the philosophy of science in the direction of the history of science. As Thomas Kuhn noted, scientific knowledge began to be viewed less and less as the result of internal dynamics towards the growth of knowledge, and more and more often as the contingent result of scientific practice.[17] This contextualisation of knowledge and science is in itself part of a larger movement that is considered by Stephen Toulmin to be a post-modern return from the theoretical ratio to the practical ratio. Toulmin specifies this development as a return from writing to speaking (from logic to rhetoric), from the general to the specific (from principles to individual cases), and from the universal to the local and the temporary (forms of life and traditions).[18] This new philosophy transcends modernism as it were, in returning to the Aristotelian tradition of the intellectual and moral virtues. The category of the intellectual virtues contains the distinction between what Aristotle called *épistèmè* and *phronèsis*, by which he meant theoretical knowledge, aimed at 'knowing that', and practical knowledge, aimed at 'knowing how' and acting according to the circumstances.[19] *Phronèsis*, a topic of Part II of this book, is necessary to satisfy fully the demands of legal interpretation, on the premise that in a situation of judging one always has to deal with the particulars of a

---

[17] T. S. Kuhn, *The Structure of Scientific Revolutions* (Chicago: University of Chicago Press, 1962).

[18] S. Toulmin, *Cosmopolis, The Hidden Agenda of Modernity* (New York: The Free Press, 1990), pp. 186–90.

[19] Aristotle (trans. H. Rackham and ed. J. Henderson), *Nicomachean Ethics* (Cambridge, MA and London: Harvard University Press, [1926] 2003), II.ii.3–5,1104a4–10.

case, and in a specific situation at that: namely, τα τον ανθροπων πραγματα, in the realm of human affairs. It would perhaps be more accurate here to speak in terms of recontextualisation, when we recall the emphasis on context in the determination of meaning that is characteristic of Renaissance humanism, as noted in Chapter 2.

The problem of translation in interdisciplinary ventures between law and the natural sciences thus returns with a vengeance in the distinction between theoretical knowledge and practical wisdom. The natural sciences epitomise modern science with an emphasis on theoretical knowledge, and the keywords here are universality, objectivity, certainty, and rationality. Disciplines emphasising practical wisdom focus their attention on the particularity of a specific situation – in this sense *phronèsis* is local knowledge – on intersubjectivity as the basis for debate, argumentation, and deliberation on a plurality of viewpoints.

Interdisciplinarity: ands and buts

BUTS

Against the background of the history of ideas sketched in Chapter 2, it is important to note that in the US at the very moment that C. C. Langdell developed his case method for legal education and connected to it a legal theory, comparable to *Begriffsjurisprudenz*, [20] claiming that once a legal concept had been formed by the inductive process of reading case after case, it could deductively be applied to new cases, Oliver Wendell Holmes Jun. had already voiced a strong critique of such a concept of law as an autonomous discipline. [21] Oddly, Holmes spoke of law as a branch of anthropology, rather than the other way around, and pointed to the necessity of law being aided by the new sciences of sociology, economics, and statistics. Following Holmes, sociological jurisprudence and its successor, legal realism, in the first decades of the twentieth century, made a strong claim for the auxiliary function offered to law by other disciplines. [22] The irony is that the very process of the formation of autonomous disciplines that led to the rise of monodisci-

---

[20] To Langdell, it, 'was indispensable to establish at least two things: first that law is a science; secondly that all the available materials of that science are contained in printed books', C. C. Langdell, 'Introduction' to *A Selection of Cases on the Law of Contracts*, in A. E. Sutherland, *The Law at Harvard* (Cambridge, MA: Harvard University Press, 1967), p. 175.

[21] O. W. Holmes Jun., 'Review Langdell Casebook', 14 *American Law Review*, 1880, pp. 233–5.

[22] See Louis Brandeis' 'Brief for the defendant in error' in *Muller v. Oregon*, 208 U.S. 412 (1908), in which he seeks the support of medical science as well as of industrial and labour statistics for his interpretation of contract law.

plinarity did not come to a head until the late nineteenth century, and was followed almost immediately, at least for law, by this demand for auxiliary disciplines, and, in the wake of these trans- or multi-disciplinary ventures, by interdisciplinary fields as diverse as *Law and Economics* and *Law and Literature*.[23]

So there is a paradox in interdisciplinarity when we consider retrospectively the fact that the long process itself of epistemological differentiation as disciplines became academic now necessitates our contemporary use of the conjunction 'and'. This is even more so if we look at the continued dominance of Enlightenment methodological individualism since Hobbes in strands of contemporary *Law and Economics*. Also connected to the natural sciences paradigm of scientific positivism of philosophers such as Auguste Comte, John Stuart Mill, and Herbert Spencer, methodological individualism is another logical conclusion of the quest for certainty, with its central idea of the individual's deliberate agreement to subject himself to the sovereign in exchange for peace. It returns with a vengeance in an economic environment that favours the positivistic hermeneutics that meaning is obvious – again, that facts are entities in the world easily transmissible by words, the encoded perceptions of these very same facts. *Law and Literature* opposes such a language view because it disregards the influence of our conceptual framework on our valuation of the world. The political relevance of the debate is obvious, given our contemporary global financial, economic and humanitarian crises. A humanistic reconsideration of the primacy of instrumental reason in modernity therefore remains acute, lest such instrumental reason enframed in a project of domination threaten our capacity to remake the conditions of our existence.

As Charles Taylor claimed, we risk the growth of 'a disengaged model of the human subject' at the expense of moral deliberation: that is, disengaged from our bodies, emotions, and life forms.[24] Chapters 12 and 13 take up the topic of law, technology, and personhood. On the meta-level of interdisciplinarity, the consequence of the rationalist economic view, put bluntly, is that

---

[23] Trans-disciplinary or multi-disciplinary work, in my view, refers to an exchange of findings between disciplines only, and/or the importation of a technique or methodology from one field to another, for the purpose of solving a specific problem if the solution cannot be found in the original field itself. Thus, it is a form of finding the right point at which opportunities for cooperation are perceived, after reaching the result of which disciplines go their own way. In other words, after the collaborative job is done, everybody retreats to the safety of his own domain, safe once more from further intrusions on disciplinary autonomy.

[24] C. Taylor, *The Ethics of Authenticity* (Cambridge, MA: Harvard University Press, 1991), pp. 101–2.

the discipline whose language is victorious determines the form of cooperation. This leads to what White calls disciplinary imperialism, prioritising the
one language at the expense of the other.[25] The discipline connected by means
of the 'and' is then at best a tool or auxiliary, not a constitutive component.
As one who spends most of her time in judicial practice, I encounter daily
the problems of differences in conceptual cultures; one problem involves
culpability in criminal law, and it is voiced wonderfully by James Boyd White
when he writes,

> Consider, for example, the attempt of the law to rely upon the 'findings' of
> psychiatrists as to the 'sanity' of criminal defendants. While it is not true
> that psychiatrists have nothing useful to say to the law – not at all – it is
> true that their 'findings' are not very usable by the law, for the reason that
> the two systems of discourse, and the two communities, operate on such
> radically opposed premises. Psychiatry thinks in terms of treatment and
> diagnosis and health; the law thinks in terms of guilt, blame, and punish-
> ment. There is a radical incompatibility between the discourse, between the
> conceptions of the human subject and the speaker's relation to him or her,
> that makes any transfer of 'findings' problematic, to say the least.[26]

For the purposes of my argument here, I want to draw attention to one of the
risks that contemporary law and legal theory have to face.[27] If law's current
development depends at least in part on external sources – that is to say, in
contradistinction to its (self)-proclaimed autonomy – it risks the exchange
of the historic bargain between law and politics for a view on law as the
instrument with which to achieve the results that politics desires. Law then
becomes the battlefield of conflicting interests and incompatible values, as
can be seen, for example, in the role of law in what is today euphemistically
known as 'the war(s) on terror', very loosely defined, as exemplified wonderfully in Ferdinand von Schirach's play *Terror*.[28]
    On the meta-level of our discussions of the very idea of interdisciplinar-
ity (methodologically as well as epistemologically), interdisciplinarity can be
thought of as the consequence of an earlier diasporic movement. In other

---

25 J. B. White, 'Establishing relations between law and other forms of thought and language',
    1 *Erasmus Law Review*, no. 3, 2008, available at <https://www.erasmuslawreview.nl> [last
    accessed 1 November 2017].
26 J. B. White, *Justice as Translation* (Chicago: University of Chicago Press, 1990), pp. 13–14.
27 See H. J. Berman, *Law and Revolution: the Formation of the Western Legal Tradition*
    (Cambridge, MA, and London: Harvard University Press, 1983), pp. 33–45; P. Stein and
    J. Shand, *Legal Values in Western Society* (Edinburgh: Edinburgh University Press, 1974).
28 F. von Schirach (trans. D. Tushingham), *Terror* (London: Faber and Faber, [2016] 2017).

words, when we apply the metaphor of diaspora to think about the differentiation of disciplines or *Ausdifferenzierung* that resulted in the formation of
autonomous disciplines with clearly demarcated boundaries, and, also as far
as the development of a positivistic approach to law is concerned, in the idea
that the autarky of the discipline is a precondition for the objectivity of its
results, what implications and/or suggestions would this have with regard to
'Law and' studies?

Obviously, the movement from the disciplinary unity of the heyday
of humanism to the differentiation of knowledge in academic pigeonholes
brought about the development of separate disciplinary methodologies.
More precisely, when law and literature each went their separate ways as
academic disciplines, a natural enmity developed between them, as the
German jurist Gustav Radbruch claimed.[29] Long-shared concepts such as
justice, punishment, and guilt or culpability began to diverge, along with
professional languages generally. This is not just a matter of terminology
or semantics – it is also about 'the limits of my language'. What is more,
within what were originally called the *artes liberales* throughout Europe,
another shift occurred. While the terminology is often used interchange-
ably, the mental images differ. The *Geisteswissenschaften* as they developed
in the German tradition do not totally overlap with what the English
call the moral sciences or humanities; both also differ, however slightly
perhaps, from the *sciences humaines* in France and the American liberal arts.
Furthermore, the concept of literature as a distinct field has come a long
way since the eighteenth century when it still included philosophical and
theological works as well as non-fictional texts from the natural sciences
and politics, under the heading of *letters*, as sources of knowledge and
intellectual pursuits, with Adam Smith's series of *Lectures on Rhetoric and
Belles Lettres* (1762–3) as a case in point.[30] The terms *letters* and science both
denoted knowledge, with the adjective 'literary' connoting the intellectual
in a broad sense.

In other words, disciplinary differentiation can itself be looked upon
as the root of the problem of contemporary terminological and conceptual
(in)translatability between disciplines. It leads to the question that has kept
many interdisciplinary legal scholars busy these past decades: namely, what
is internal and what is external to law, or to any other discipline for that

---

[29] G. Radbruch (eds E. Wolf and H. P. Schneider), *Rechtsphilosophie* (Stuttgart: K. F. Köhler
Verlag, [1914, rev. 1932] 1973), p. 201, 'einer natürlichen Feindschaft'.

[30] See also C. Biet, *La Jeu de la Valeur et de la Droit: droit et littérature sous l'Ancien Régime*
(Honoré: Paris, 2001); T. Pech, *Conter le Crime: droit et littérature sous la Contre-Réforme*
(Paris: Champion Slatkine, 2001).

matter.[31] The question forces us to think not only about disciplinary boundaries, intuitively presumed or authoritatively drawn, but, more importantly, also about the whatness or *quidditas* of law itself, not least because with this development soon came the tendency to place law and literature in opposition as being hard versus soft.

From a law point of view, this comes as no surprise. Law itself from the very start of its development has thrived on classification and systematisation. And, as Stephen Jay Gould claimed, the only reason that we ever developed a model of opposition between the natural sciences and the humanities is our general 'deeply entrenched habit of ordering our categories as oppositional pairs'.[32] There may be nothing wrong with the opposition of law to literature, or its companion, the opposition of economic man (including the authoritarian man of law as science) to literary woman as a heuristic device for purposes of argumentation. We should, however, consider whether or not to continue an antagonistic and gendered reasoning in terms of the deficiency of the one discipline compared to the superiority of the other, as scholars as varied as Kenji Yoshino,[33] Jane Baron,[34] Julie Stone Peters,[35] Greta Olson,[36] Christine Künzel[37] and Desmond Manderson[38] have argued in their critiques of *Law and Literature*. There is good reason to do so, because the very idea of binary opposition and its resulting dichotomous thought that occasioned the starting point for *Law and Literature* from the 1970s onwards – that is to say, its desire to develop its pedagogical aim to do law differently, and to shift from an emphasis on doctrinal issues to a broad, humanistic education that integrates rather than separates disciplines – has by now resulted in a kind of

---

[31] See H. Dagan and R. Kreitner, 'The interdisciplinary party', 1 *Critical Analysis of Law*, no. 1, 2014, pp. 23–31.

[32] S. J. Gould, *The Hedgehog, the Fox, and the Magister's Pox, Mending the Gap between Science and the Humanities* (New York: Harmony Books, 2003), pp. 81–2.

[33] K. Yoshino, 'The city and the poet', 114 *Yale Law Journal*, 2005, pp. 1835–96.

[34] J. B. Baron, 'The rhetoric of Law and Literature: a skeptical view', 26 *Cardozo Law Review*, 2005, pp. 2273–81.

[35] J. Stone Peters, 'Law, literature, and the vanishing real: on the future of an interdisciplinary illusion', 120 *PMLA*, no. 2, 2005, pp. 442–53.

[36] G. Olson, 'Law is not turgid and literature not soft and fleshy: gendering and heteronormativity in law and literature scholarship', 36 *The Australian Feminist Law Journal*, 2012, pp. 65–86.

[37] C. Künzel, '"Aus einem Bette aufgestanden", Anmerkungen zum "Verhältnis" zwischen Recht und Literatur', in G. Hofmann (ed.), *Figures of Law, studies in the interference of Law and Literature* (Tübingen and Basel: A. Francke Verlag, 2007), pp. 115–32. The title refers to Grimm's view on the bond between law and literature as noted in Chapter 2.

[38] D. Manderson, 'Modernism and the critique of law and literature', 35 *The Australian Feminist Law Journal*, 2011, pp. 105–23.

skepticism that this book aims to counter with regard to the relevance of *Law and Literature* for either legal theory or legal practice.

Critics are obviously right in drawing jurists' attention to the question as to what comprises literature. Jurists often without hesitation get into the contentious area of literature as an unproblematic repository of the humane, or they overemphasise the ethical aspects, disregarding literature's wider system of cultural significance. The anxiety this causes touches the sore spot in our scholarship, and highlights an important interdisciplinary issue: the methodological reserve on both sides of the divide, or of the bridge, depending on one's perspective. Therefore, as I hope to have shown so far, we should realise that the supposedly mutual incomprehension that results from the putative dichotomy of the scientists versus the scholars in the humanities is itself the result of the differentiation of disciplines that the advocates of a humanistic study of law ask us to reconsider. If we keep in mind that what today is heralded as contextualisation and interdisciplinarity has a long tradition, we can then find a way out of dichotomous thought that reduces what comes after the 'and' to auxiliary knowledge at the most. Yet we cannot gain new insights if we fail to consider the very construction of law's boundaries itself. Hence, the question will be whether any road of regret at having lost the old connections can lead to salvation, and I will answer this question in the affirmative. Because interdisciplinarity depends on the success of cross-cultural translation, we should ask how successful the 'and' is, given that no exchange or translation of concepts in crossing disciplinary cultures can take place while isolated from the cultural, scholarly-professional, societal and systemic background of its genesis. In short, since we cannot escape hermeneutic circularity, we need to be aware of it.

ANDS

To make a virtue of necessity, based on the view that a single methodology is precisely what *Law and Literature* as one of law's liminal discourses[39] has opposed from its very start by advocating a diversity of approaches, any methodological or theoretical support should, I suggest, be sought at the foundational level of law and literature, and that is in language, not least given the history of ideas of law and legal theory. Erasmus had already pointed to the need for careful and repeated reading as the foundation of understanding so that we could build and rely on 'the storehouse of our reading'.[40] As a

---

[39] Cf. D. Carpi and J. Gaakeer (eds), *Liminal Discourses, Subliminal Tensions in Law and Literature* (Berlin: De Gruyter, 2013).

[40] Desiderius Erasmus (trans. and annot. B. McGregor, ed. C. R. Thompson), *On the Method of Study, de ratione studii ac legendi interpretandique auctores*, in *Collected Works of Erasmus*,

metaphor, it fits perfectly with Sebald's language concept that this book takes as its epigraph. More recently, Thanos Zartaloudis proposed that language itself is the true conjunction of law and literature, because

> it is language that forms this milieu or between (an 'and') that is more originary than both law and philosophy, prose, and poetry and . . . it is language as an experience (an *idein*, an idea) which law and philosophy fervently oust in order to form themselves, but without ever being able to escape confronting its emergence or event if they are to seriously reflect upon their own formation.[41]

Language, then, is the only medium with which we can transmit people's non-linguistic experience – and that includes the legal and literary imagination – into a manageable form for further debate, and for aesthetic as well as critical appreciation in both law and literature.

Therefore, although law and literature have different goals, they are cognate human practices. If we keep in mind that any legal perception is the result of the interpretive movement from fact to legal norm and back, and that both text and human action are constantly subject to our interpretation, the (re)connection of *Law and Literature* to legal practice finds its starting point on the plane of hermeneutics, the topic of Part II of this book. A focus on language is therefore eminently suited to help prevent any new placing of boundary stones, any new form of disciplinary appropriation, if only to prevent the application of the Roman law principle of *uti possidetis*, the demarcation of a new area by means of an addition to an existing field's old spatial boundaries, of having its negative effect on such emerging topics as *Law and Culture*, and *Law and the Humanities*. One thing, however, is certain; the 'and' definitely has a future if we regard law and literature as wider linguistic systems of cultural significance having ethical implications for both theory and practice. But if we do so, we should take the poet Horace's admonition to heart: namely, to understand that 'there is measure in things, for there are boundaries outside of which the just ceases to exist'.[42]

Literary and Educational Writings 2: de copia/de ratione studii (Toronto, Buffalo and London: University of Toronto Press, 1978), p. 671.

[41] T. Zartaloudis, 'Ars Inventio, poetic laws: law and literature – the and', 29 *Cardozo Law Review*, 2008, pp. 2431–59, p. 2432.

[42] Horace, *Satires*, I.1.106, 'Est modus in rebus, sunt certi denique fines, quos ultra citraque nequit consistere rectum' (author's translation).

The Wars of the Disciplines as a Language Problem

Chapters 4 and 5 take Wittgenstein's 'limits' proposition 5.6 both literally and as a conceptual wrench[43] in order to analyse two cases: that of Robert Musil's fictional character, the sex murderer Moosbrugger, and that of the Dutch poet Gerrit Achterberg, who was diagnosed insane and institutionalised on the basis of a literal reading of his poetry. Thus, Chapters 4 and 5 take up modernity's problem of language as a representation of reality, and its concomitant attention to the clash of the empirical behavioural sciences and law on the issue of free will as expressed in the scientific debate on the criminal liability of those who lack the capacity either to appreciate the wrongfulness of their conduct, or to conform to what the law requires. There is a good reason for doing so, because rationalism's emphasis on facts is dominant in its view – in Musil's fictional account and Achterberg's actual psychiatric treatment – that their uses of language are proof of Moosbrugger's and Achterberg's insanity. This is in stark contrast to Moosbrugger's and Achterberg's deeply felt resentment of this view and of its diagnostic consequences in their lives. There is a fracture of the self in Moosbrugger and Achterberg, in that they are unable to locate themselves in terms of the language imposed on them. This points to a mirror image of the modernist fracture between the languages of art and science, of which Musil's narrative and Achterberg's poetry are exemplary. As with Flaubert's Bouvard and Pécuchet, the interpretation of Musil and Achterberg is both inscribed in the text and offers an opportunity for the reader to claim meaning for it. Both Musil and Achterberg are concerned with what it means for a human being to be locked up within the boundaries of his subjective consciousness. With them, therefore, the debate on the methodological division between the subject and the object of inquiry in the sciences comes full circle. They also teach us that subjective (ap)perception is ultimately our only tool to empathise with another, be it a fictional character or a human being: that is, to imagine oneself in the position of the other, the topic of empathy as discussed in Chapters 8 and 11. Thus, from a phenomenological point of view, Musil and Achterberg confront us with the inevitability of subjectivity in a double sense, both with respect to their being objects of inquiry and to the hermeneutic approach of the humanities itself.

[43] R. Weisberg, 'The law-literature enterprise', 1 *Yale Journal of Law & the Humanities*, 1988, pp. 1–67.

4

Understanding Fact and Fiction in Robert Musil's *The Man without Qualities*

Kakania as a State of Mind

Robert Musil's story of the murderer Moosbrugger, whose mental competence to stand trial is at the heart of the novel *The Man without Qualities*, exemplifies Wittgenstein's 'limits' proposition 5.6 in more than one sense. Borders between fact and fiction blur as Musil shows us poignantly to what extent Moosbrugger's use of language is misunderstood by his fictional lawyers and psychiatrists, and for what reasons. This chapter suggests that the key to Moosbrugger's plights is the clash of views on language espoused by those involved in his case.

Musil's biographer, Karl Corino, points out that Musil's life cannot be portrayed without attention to the strong link between the themes in *The Man without Qualities* and its author.[1] That is not to say that the novel can be understood only along the lines of a romantic, psychological hermeneutics as promoted by Friedrich Schleiermacher. It means that some insight at least is required into the man who thought of himself as a being without qualities, because in his portrayal, or perhaps we should say definition, of Ulrich, the novel's protagonist, Musil inscribes his own experience and view on humanity:

> The inhabitant of a country has at least nine characters: a professional, a national, a civic, a class, a geographic, a sexual, a conscious, an unconscious, and possibly even a private character to boot. He unites them in himself, but they dissolve him, so that he is really nothing more than a small basin hollowed out by the many streamlets that trickle into it and drain out of

[1] For biographical information about Musil, I draw on K. Corino, *Robert Musil, eine Biographie* (Reinbek: Rowohlt Verlag, 2003) and A. Thiher, *Fiction Refracts Science: Modernist Writers from Proust to Borges* (Columbia: University of Missouri Press, 2005), Chapter 2, 'Robert Musil and the dilemma of modernist epistemology', pp. 59–99. The edition used for citations from the novel is R. Musil (trans. S. Wilkins and B. Pike), *The Man without Qualities* (London: Picador, [1930–3] 1997). Hereinafter (MWQ + page number).

it again, to join other rills in filling some other basin. Which is why every inhabitant of the earth also has a tenth character that is nothing else than the passive fantasy of spaces yet unfilled. This permits a person all but one thing: to take seriously what his at least nine other characters do and what happens to them; in other words, it prevents precisely what should be his true fulfillment. (MWQ 30)

Robert Musil was born on 6 November 1880 in Klagenfurt, the son of the engineer Alfred Musil and his wife, Hermine Bergauer. The family later moved to Brünn (now Brno, Czech Republic), where Alfred was appointed professor at the Hochschule. Musil's family relations, especially with his mother, were strained, and so in 1892 he left for Eisenstadt to attend an institution for military training in the cadet corps. His career as a cadet, however, was short. In 1897 he was allowed to study at the technical military academy in Vienna. After being honourably discharged from the military, he enrolled in a course in mechanical engineering at the University of Brünn in 1898. In 1902, he left Austria for Germany to continue his engineering studies, and in 1903 he began to study psychology and philosophy at the Friedrich-Wilhelms University (now Humboldt University). His dissertation in 1908 was on the subject of what Musil claimed was Ernst Mach's mistaken epistemological view on causality. To Musil, Mach had wrongly dismissed the traditional, Aristotelian concept of matter and had tried to replace it with a mere functional concept. In short, he defended 'a realist epistemology against Mach's positivism'[2] because Mach's definition of sense data lacked precision to such an extent that his positivism resembled metaphysics. Musil's ongoing struggle with Mach's views is reflected in *The Man without Qualities*. When the First World War broke out, Musil rejoined the army and renewed his experience with the military bureaucracy when he was stationed in South Tyrol.

Written between 1924 and 1942, *The Man without Qualities* was still unfinished at the time of Musil's death. However, on 26 August 1930, shortly before turning fifty, Musil completed the manuscript that at that time comprised some 8,000 pages of typescript. He was suffering from insomnia and palpitations of the heart, brought about by the stress of worrying that the publishers, Rowohlt, would turn him down, as had many other publishers before. Because Musil had no money to pay an assistant, he put considerable effort into whatever corrections he deemed necessary. In 1930, Book One, Parts One and Two, a total of 123 chapters, came out, and was followed by the thirty-eight chapters of Book Two in 1933. Although Rowohlt pressed him for publication of the remaining twenty chapters in 1938, Musil

---

[2] Thiher, *Fiction Refracts Science*, p. 60.

continued re-writing them until his death in 1942 – in exile in Switzerland after the Nazis occupied Austria – obsessed with his attempt to offer a unified theory of knowledge (with respect to *Eigenschaften*, properties) for both the arts and the sciences. Musil the engineer, with his keen interest in the empirical sciences, shows us that forensic psychiatry is unable to explain mental illnesses once it restricts itself to the language of logic and causality. At the same time, however, Musil remains indebted to the postulates of the natural sciences, from the positivist opening lines of the novel to the continued effort to picture Ulrich, who not incidentally is also a mathematician, in great detail. In short, there is a field of tension between the man Musil and his portrayal of the crisis of modernity.

The narrative of *The Man without Qualities* starts in 1913, in the Austro-Hungarian Empire on the brink of the First World War. In it, Musil gives an acute diagnosis of a society that is in a deep cultural and political crisis while at the same time undergoing a radical process of modernisation. Musil's fictional world resembles *Kakania*, the ironical name for the bureaucratic, formalist society of the Austro-Hungarian Dual Monarchy: *kaiserlich und königlich*, shortened to k. und k. and pronounced 'caca'.[3] The account of the determinism debate shows a striking resemblance to the discourse held by those involved in the process of legislation at the end of the nineteenth century throughout Europe, with dichotomies in the texts of law as a result. The notion of literature as a mirror of society therefore proves its worth. The legal institution is depicted as not only being burdened by formalistic particularism but also as being in a state of gradual transition under the impression of modern social and behavioural sciences as well as general cultural developments. The novel forms a huge literary experiment that equals that of James Joyce in radicality and importance. Musil not only wanted to write a good novel, he also intended to make the novel a touchstone for a new vision of the human being.

Musil's War of the Words

In *The Man without Qualities*, the clash between law and psychiatry is prominent. Questions about the autonomy of law as a discipline in relation to the implementation of the findings from auxiliary disciplines in the form of the behavioural sciences are rendered acute in the case of Moosbrugger. The case strikingly illustrates the incompatibilities, on the linguistic level and elsewhere, of the discourse, methodology and values of criminal law with those

---

[3] For Kakania, see A. Janik and S. Toulmin, *Wittgenstein's Vienna* (New York: Simon and Schuster, 1973); C. Schorske, *Fin-de-siècle Vienna: Politics and Culture* (New York: Knopf, 1980).

of psychiatry. The scientific debate on criminal liability of those who lack the capacity either to appreciate the wrongfulness of their conduct or to conform to what the law requires brings us back to the question noted in Chapter 3 regarding the (in)translatability of discourses in interdisciplinary movements in law and other domains.

The emphasis on facts leads to the view – in Musil's fictional account as well as in contemporary science – that there is a direct connection between the way in which Moosbrugger, or any other mentally ill defendant for that matter, speaks and the degree of his insanity. This dominant aspect of scientific positivism vehemently disregards the diagnostic consequences it has in people's lives. Moosbrugger fails to locate his subjective self in the terms of the language that his doctors and his judges impose on him. He is not allowed to constitute himself by means of a language in which he feels comfortable. Alienation is its obvious result.

Although the closed world of a novel is incommensurable with lived experience, and the world of the literary work resists referentiality, the novel itself allows for a comparison of the fictional and the actual because of its motto as far as human understanding and understanding the human are concerned: 'When do you understand another human being? When you feel with him. *Feel with him*' (MWQ 775). This captures the essence of Musil's central thesis in a concept of empathy as the required element of under-standing and the constitution of meaning. None of the fictional authorities involved, however, be they legal or medical, understand Moosbrugger. The question of whether or not Moosbrugger is able to understand the tenor of the criminal proceedings instituted against him is therefore as central to the narrative as it remains unanswered.

Paradoxically, then, it is precisely the concept of personhood that is belied at all levels of the narrative, from Ulrich to Moosbrugger, and with practically all the other characters in different forms in between. Time and again in the novel, the crisis of modernity arises in Musil's depiction of the bourgeois mentality of old Europe that he offers us in a fictional guise of the many domains of 1913 Vienna. The case of Moosbrugger, in which fact and fiction collapse into each other, evokes the modernist desperation regarding the fact that the natural sciences, despite their all-encompassing claims of objectivity, dissociated themselves from culture in the first half of the twentieth century, and that they did so precisely because of the language view espoused.

The Crisis of Modernity Revisited

In the behavioural sciences, the hermeneutic principle of *clara non sunt inter-pretanda*, that whatever is clear needs no interpretation, led to the question of whether the language of psychiatry could be regarded as a descriptive language indicative of the mental state of a defendant, or as a performative speech act, for example when viewed against the background of relevant classificatory manuals such as today's *Diagnostic and Statistical Manual of Mental Disorders* (DSM). The choice made has immediate consequences for law's treatment of the insane.

Cesare Lombroso, the founder of criminal anthropology, applied a positivist methodology so that crime became the product of measurable causes. Criminal anthropology was thought to be superior to law because law did not use scientific methods. Thus, if only law would join the ranks of the social sciences, it too could boast a single scientific methodology. This idea(l) is beautifully and ironically exemplified in the opening lines of *The Man without Qualities;* they are at once truly positivist, totally within the natural sciences paradigm and indicative of the language problem that Musil addresses in the rest of his novel. Musil starts with a long and painstakingly detailed description of the weather (temperature and humidity included):

> a barometric low hung over the Atlantic. It moved eastward toward a high-pressure area over Russia without as yet showing any inclination to bypass this high in a northerly direction. The isotherms and isotheres were functioning as they should . . . In a word that characterizes the facts fairly accurately, even if it is a bit old-fashioned: It was a fine day in August. (MWQ 3)

The opening chapter continues by paying homage to the traditional concepts of the unity of time, place and action in its description of a car accident that also introduces the subject of science and technology, one of the main threads of the narrative. Paradoxically, Musil's fascination with detail and his obsession with exactitude is coupled with an attempt to shed light on the area of the human that is beyond the *recta ratio*: the other condition of man when he is suffering from delusions, hallucinations – in short, from a mental illness. This attempt is in itself meant to exemplify the problems one encounters when trying to do just that: namely, trying to understand the other condition in all its appearances, given the failure of language itself to catch the irrational in the words of the rational. For how can one speak of that which one cannot reach in a rational manner? One must be silent, wrote Wittgenstein in the final proposition of the *Tractatus*.

The problem that Musil confronts and from which he distances himself is that of the function of language as a vehicle to convey thoughts. The novel therefore is self-referential in its search for another philosophy of language: that is, of language as constitutive of the self and the world. This in turn is also emblematic of a view on the literary work as a proposal for a world that the reader can enter. As early as 1906, in the novella 'The Confusions of Young Törless', Musil showed his affinity with scientific positivism, and it is essential to note the development of his thought as laid down in his fiction. Despite this development, however, Musil remains indebted to the postulate of exactitude of the natural sciences. This can be seen in his ongoing painstaking care to describe in detail and as precisely as possible both Ulrich and Moosbrugger, and in Ulrich's own compulsion to describe Moosbrugger in detail – an attempt that Moosbrugger of course escapes.[4]

'Insanity is an all-or-nothing proposition'

'Onward to Moosbrugger' (MWQ 908) then. He is the means by which Musil treats the subject of free will. Inspired by the facts of actual murder cases, Musil draws the character of the carpenter Christian Moosbrugger as that of a physically powerful man who is also a bit of a simpleton with Lombrosian-style atavistic bodily characteristics.[5] Moosbrugger has 'a face blessed by God with every sign of goodness', but he is also a sex murderer who has killed a woman 'in a horrifying manner'; he 'was one of those borderline cases in law and forensic medicine known even to the layman as a case of diminished responsibility' (MWQ 67). Unfortunately, however, the law does not accept nature's gradual transitions, or rather, *natura non fecit saltus*, nature does not progress by leaps and bounds. Law's compass is the premise of the *tertium non datur*. That is why in the dichotomous logic of law, as it says much later in the novel, 'insanity is an all-or-nothing proposition' (MWQ 583). In this view that dominates the fictional debate on legal insanity and free will,

> a person is either capable or not capable of breaking the law; between two contraries there is no third or middle state. It is his ability to choose that makes a person liable to punishment. His liability to punishment makes him legally a person, and as a person in the legal sense he shares in the suprapersonal benefaction of the law. (MWQ 261)

---

[4] See H. Arntzen, 'Sprache und sprechen in Musils "Mann ohne Eigenschaften"', *Duitse Kroniek*, 1976, pp. 69–83, p. 71.

[5] Here too we perceive Musil's emphasis on facts. See Corino, *Robert Musil*, p. 881ff., for the actual cases underlying the novel: for example, the 1910 murder case of the carpenter Christian Voigt; the 1924 case of Fritz Haarmann; the 1929 case of Peter Kürten. See also E. Ostermann, 'Das Wildgewordene Subjekt. Christian Moosbrugger und die Imagination des Wilden in Musils *Mann Ohne Eigenschaften*', *Neophilologus*, 2005, pp. 605–23, p. 606, for the 1900 case of Florian Grossrubatscher as an influence on the Moosbrugger story. In Musil's short story 'The Perfecting of a Love', a psychopath called G. is the embryonic form of Moosbrugger.

In a nutshell, and ironically perhaps, here are the tenets of the classical school of criminal law with free will as a solid foundation. Moosbrugger belongs to the group of patients 'whom the angel of medicine treats as sick people when they come to him in his private practice, but whom he shyly leaves to the angel of law when he encounters them in his forensic practice' (MWQ 262). In other words, forensic psychiatrists shy away from decisions that jurists necessarily make, in that they are reluctant to classify as insane the people they cannot cure. *The Man without Qualities* gives the angel of medicine a sound interdisciplinary warning: namely, not to listen to jurists too long, in case he 'forgets his own mission' (MWQ 263). The same applies, I would say, the other way around. This warning should alert us to the dangers and effects of classification generally. As noted in Chapter 3, what is one to think of the idea that the more you change the classification of the mentally insane, the more patients or criminals you generate? With every new edition of the DSM – still currently in use in forensic practice – the unfortunate complication for jurists and forensic psychiatrists alike is that more mental states unrecognised in earlier editions of the DSM will be deemed unsound. An increase in the number of mental diseases is the result.[6]

Moosbrugger definitely fills the bill, since so far he has lacked the beneficial treatment the new school of criminal law theory wants to bestow on defendants.

> In the course of his life, . . . he had as often been confined in mental institutions as he had been let go, and had been variously diagnosed as a paralytic, paranoiac, epileptic, and manic-depressive psychotic, until at his recent trial two particularly conscientious forensic psychiatrists had restored his sanity to him. (MWQ 262)

Here is a foray into the disciplinary debate on the forced interdisciplinary bond between law and the forensic behavioural sciences, given law's predisposition to seek retribution and deterrence by means of inflicting punishment, which is in sharp contrast to psychiatry's main goal of treating the patient and restoring his mental health. When ends and means differ so much in the setting of disciplinary co-operation, this cannot but lead to tension between the disciplines involved.

While everybody agrees that Moosbrugger is insane, nothing can be done because Moosbrugger cannot be pigeonholed along the lines of the

---

[6] See also T. Szasz, '"Diagnosing" behavior: cui bono?', XXV *Legal Studies Forum*, 2001, pp. 505–17; S. R. Schmeiser, 'The ungovernable citizen: psychopathy, sexuality, and the rise of medico-legal reasoning', 20 *Yale Journal of Law & the Humanities*, no. 2, 2008, pp. 163–240.

conditions of insanity recognised by law. The danger of classification and the legal doctrine of *tertium non datur* painfully resurface. The argument runs like this: 'if one is partly insane, one is also, juridically, partly sane, and if one is partly sane one is at least partly responsible for one's actions, and if one is partly responsible one is wholly responsible' (MWQ 262). So Moosbrugger could and should have used his ability to do the right thing, and left the crime uncommitted, but since he did not, the law demands that a willfully performed crime be punished. Besides, in most insane persons some form of discrimination of right and wrong can be found; this means of course that Moosbrugger should have made the effort to resist his impulses in the first place.

The debate on determinism unfolds as Ulrich's father voices concern about the circumstance that 'in lay circles, but also, sad to say, in scientific circles . . . an extremely dangerous movement has been afoot for a long time to bring about certain presumed reforms and ameliorations in the proposed revision of the penal code' (MWQ 342). Danger lurks then in the effort made to extend the concept of mental disorder so that the scope of the concept of diminished responsibility is widened to include, for example, the feeble-minded. It is almost as if we hear Justice Oliver Wendell Holmes Jun. speak the infamous line for which the case of *Buck v. Bell,* 274 U.S. 200 (1927) is remembered: 'three generations of imbeciles is enough'. To Ulrich's father, the concept of diminished responsibility depends as much on one's definition of full responsibility as on one's total lack of it.

As a legal scholar involved in the legislative process, Ulrich's father proposes Paragraph 318 of the future Penal Code to read as follows: 'No criminal act has been committed if the perpetrator was in a state of unconsciousness or pathological disturbance of his mind at the time he was engaged in the act under consideration, so that . . .' (MWQ 343). His erstwhile friend, Professor Schwung, who, given his name in German, has obviously swung from one point of view on the matter to another – as Ulrich's father does not hesitate to emphasise – starts his proposal for Paragraph 318 identically. However, after the 'so that', Schwung's text reads, 'he could not exercise his free will'; Ulrich's father, however, would have it read, 'so that he did not have the capacity to perceive the wrongfulness of his act' (MWQ 343). Here he inserts what would nowadays be called an excuse defence, such as in a case of insanity, when a person is not held responsible for his criminal conduct if at the time of the conduct, and, as a result of his mental disorder or disease, he lacks the substantial quality either to appreciate the wrongfulness of his conduct or to bring his conduct into conformity with what the law requires. Ulrich's father thinks in terms of intellect and reasoning power, which leads him to claim that as far as the will of a person is concerned,

> volition is simply not a matter of chance but an act of self-determination
> arising from within the person, and so the will is determined by thought,
> and when the thought process is disturbed, the will is no longer the will,
> as the man's action is prompted only by his natural cravings. (MWQ 343)

While Ulrich's father is aware of the more recent perspective on volition,
he observes that this is a newfangled view known only since 1797, while his
own dates from the fourth century BC. The intertextual reference to the year
1797 is obviously to the year of publication of Immanuel Kant's *Metaphysics
of Morals*, which deals extensively – although not convincingly from a legal
pespective – with the concept of free will. Aristotle is of course the originator
of philosophical thought on free will from the fourth century BC.

   At this point in the novel, we already witness the conceptual derailment
of the discussion. In its wake, the philosophical distinction between freedom
of will and freedom to act that is so important in law fades away. For jurists,
the question is: What does it mean that a decision is free, and what are
the conditions, both necessary and sufficient, that enable such a decision?
Significantly, Musil's fictional jurists do not seem to bother about this at all.
This is as odd as it is understandable if we consider the topic of the relation
between subject and object that is so relevant to the discussion in and of
Musil's novel. Philosophically speaking, the ontological dualism of mind and
matter is a necessary presupposition if one wants to assert the working of free
will and the freedom of human agency, in contrast to an all-encompassing
determinism.

   Worse, however, is yet to come in the discussion between Ulrich's father
and Schwung. Ulrich's father draws up an epistemological compromise,
rewriting his proposal so that it reads,

> No criminal act shall have been committed if the offender was at the time of
> his act in a state of unconsciousness or a morbid disturbance of his mental
> activity, so that he did not have the capacity to perceive the wrongfulness of
> his act and could not exercise his free will. (MWQ 343–4)

This will not do for Professor Schwung, who demands the epistemologically impossible: namely, that the 'and' be changed into 'or'. Ulrich's father
adamantly refuses, of course, because Schwung's only aim is to show that
Ulrich's father has not fully grasped the fine distinction between the use of
these conjunctions, and to expose him as a dilettante and superficial thinker
should he accept the 'or'. No wonder Ulrich's father flees into the legal
tertium non datur of his first position and withdraws his compromise. He
does so because his first proposal was based on 'the capacity to recognise
a wrongful act as such', and for good reasons, 'for while empirical logic

recognises the existence of persons who are partly insane and partly sane, the logic of the law must never admit such a mixture of juridical states' (MWQ 344). The debate continues as Ulrich's father points out to Schwung that if one were to follow Schwung's proposal, it would be necessary to determine the influences a defendant had undergone as far as each of his acts of volition is concerned. This is a deliberate sneer at the new school of criminological thought, of course.

Yet Ulrich's father is upset again when Schwung, on top of it all, unimpeded by a desire for conceptual clarity, mingles the opposing concepts, claiming that human beings are more aware of their volitions than of causal relations, and that as a consequence 'it only requires a special effort of the will to resist the causally determined criminal causes' (MWQ 345). It comes as no surprise that Ulrich's father is pushed to the end of his intellectual tether. As a result, he decides to swing as well, and convert to the new social school of thought, and with the same line of reasoning to boot, for he then claims that the more harmful a criminal defendant's behaviour, the greater the decrease in his legal responsibility, his culpability. From this follows in his new logic that the criminally insane, although the least receptive to improvement, must be given the harshest punishment in order to accomplish the best deterrent effect possible on those similarly inclined. This is a brilliant example of how our languages indeed impose limits on our worlds.

Hence, Musil's fictional account of Moosbrugger's trial and tribulations is as painfully accurate in showing the consequences of scientific positivism as it is in rendering adequately the tension that arose at the moment jurists thought that they had managed to arrive at the appropriate compromise as far as the concept of free will and attendant views on the classification of mental and intellectual faculties in this spectrum were concerned, and on the subsequent creation of measures such as the entrustment order. In short, Musil holds a painful mirror up to us.[7]

Disciplinary Action

In the character of Moosbrugger, we witness how the nineteenth-century, Kantian-based priority given to the linguistic representation of thought has by then – in the fictional 1913 Vienna of the novel as elsewhere in Europe on the brink of the First World War – run into serious trouble. If language is to be the means of representation, how can it do its job at all if it is limited in that it does not have names for every situation in the world?

---

[7] For a treatment of criminal liability against the background of the codified criminal law of Musil's era, see B. Pieroth, *Recht und Literatur, von Friedrich Schiller bis Martin Walser* (Munich: C. H. Beck, 2015), pp. 247–71.

For defenders of logical positivism, the language of the natural sciences is a godsend and a safe haven. For the likes of Moosbrugger, however, who suffers from the other condition, the language of rationality does not suffice. Musil shows us that the behavioural sciences, once they confine themselves to the language of causality and logic, can neither achieve nor provide insight into the unconscious. Here it is also important to note that Musil entitled Part III of his novel 'Into the Millenium (The Criminals)', and pinpointed Ulrich and Agathe – whose crimes consist of annihilating bourgeois morality – as the criminals who also suffer the other condition, although in a more symbolically sophisticated, or rather a more socially and legally acceptable form than Moosbrugger's. Thus, Musil's description of Moosbrugger shows how the dominant language paradigm is opposed by the idea of linguistic contingency, with words not being the necessary and sufficient instruments to express thoughts and sense perceptions that the positivists thought they were, but 'at best *metaphors* for what the senses perceive'.[8] To reiterate the point made in Chapter 3 about the *Erklären-Verstehen* controversy, the novel shows the epistemological repercussions for the relation between the natural sciences and the humanities. As John Coetzee succinctly puts it, 'To enter "the other condition" one must abandon the model of science (*Wissenschaft*), whose instrument is logic, and take up the model of poetry (*Dichtung*), whose instrument is analogy.'[9] That is to say, the unconscious cannot be grasped and understood by means of thinking in terms of legal causality.

To Musil, the question of understanding the human being is also the question of understanding what it means to be a writer, since the writer's task differs from that of the scientist. As an empiricist, the scientist looks back to past events in order to make sense of them, whereas the writer with his creative imagination brings forth an idea of, or a proposal for, a future.[10] This also explains the tension in the writer-engineer Musil himself, and the long genesis of the text that is *The Man without Qualities*: literary production can serve as the vehicle to find a way out of the dilemmas that science forces us to confront. If Musil is right in claiming that to understand a person one must feel with him, this capacity presupposes the ability, or at least the attempt, to live with oneself in an empathic manner. The very length of Musil's narrative shows how difficult that is. I suggest that it is justified to say that *The Man*

---

[8] Janik and Toulmin, *Wittgenstein's Vienna*, p. 122 (italics in the original).

[9] J. M. Coetzee, 'On the edge of revelation', on Robert Musil's *Five Women*, 33 *The New York Review of Books*, no. 20, 18 December 1986, p. 33.

[10] See H. Reiss, 'Musil and the writer's task in the age of science and technology', in L. Huber and J. J. White (eds), *Musil in Focus* (London: Institute of Germanic Studies, 1982), pp. 41–53, p. 43.

without Qualities also points to the question of whether it is at all possible to be a good writer at any juncture.[11] Can one capture the spirit of the times at all, and can one write beyond thinking in terms of facts only? Can one find a poetic language to do so? Musil tries to do just that, and he is successful, if only in the way in which the metaphoric aspects of his narrative fulfill a cognitive function by showing us things in an unexpected manner, by having us experience that metaphoric language is not a model that misleads as diehard positivists think it does, but as a model that should alert us to new perspectives, of which we had not previously been aware. As Chapter 7 elaborates, metaphor's performative aspect is what matters. Musil's work is important for the idea and ideal of perspectivism in *Law and Literature*. Any linguistic utterance presupposes a choice, whether implicit or not, to see things from a specific angle. In this sense, language usage is a continuous process of inclusion and exclusion, with the excluded always lingering in the background as a future possibility. In law, both the perception and the valuation of phenomena as relevant facts and their subsequent interpretation are comparable to searchlights – they necessarily show things in a specific light. Hence, in law and elsewhere, the need to be receptive to other possibilities, and to listen to the other side.

Musil makes the problematic aspects of such an enterprise poignantly clear in his description of Moosbrugger's inability to perceive the boundary between himself and other people. The girl who accosted Moosbrugger, and whom he murders, is as invasive as the spirits whom he hears talking, but 'this was no insanity, and Moosbrugger could not bear being called insane' (MWQ 69). She is the 'there it was again, winding its arms around his neck' (MWQ 74), from which Moosbrugger liberates himself with what turns out to be his own knife. Moosbrugger's ability to enter the other as he enters the other condition is misunderstood by those who judge him. Language is the root of all evil for Moosbrugger, who tries to make a good impression on his judges with his idiosyncratic use of forensic language,

> He had eagerly picked up such phrases in the mental wards and prisons, with scraps of French and Latin stuck in the most unsuitable places as he talked, ever since he had discovered that it was the possession of these languages that gave those in power the right to decide his fate with their 'findings'. (MWQ 71)

In addition to attention, this linguistic display eventually results in him being given the death penalty. Moosbrugger, however, is actually proud of

[11] See also P. Payne, 'Musil erforscht den Geist eines anderen Menschen – zum Porträt Moosbruggers im Mann ohne Eigenschaften', *Literatur und Kritik*, 1976, pp. 389–404.

this, because he 'simply wanted his deeds understood as the mishaps of an important philosophy of life' (MWQ 72). He thinks of his deed in terms of a political crime as he fights for his view on the legal issue. What this comes down to is that

> Moosbrugger never missed a chance to demonstrate in open court his own superiority over the psychiatrists, unmasking them as puffed-up dupes and charlatans who knew nothing at all, and whom he could trick into placing him in a mental institution instead of sending him to prison, where he belonged. (MWQ 72)

Moosbrugger's struggle for the recognition of his language is the struggle for the recognition of his *Weltanschauung*. The judge sums up the evidence, calls him quite a character, mentions his vagrancy and recidivism, and thus constructs his guilt, 'while to Moosbrugger it was a series of completely separate incidents having nothing to do with one another, each of which had a different cause that lay outside Moosbrugger somewhere in the world as a whole' (MWQ 75). Noteworthy is that Ulrich learns as well what it means to be a Moosbrugger in a concrete sense at the moment when he is arrested and experiences a form of depersonalisation. Moosbrugger alienates himself from the world of jurists and forensic psychiatrists as he discovers the swindle perpetrated by means of the language of jargon, cliché and power. But, as he explains, 'Since it is I who forced the indictment, I declare myself satisfied with the conduct of the case' (MWQ 76). Moosbrugger's judges construct the unity of Moosbrugger's deeds and his self. To Moosbrugger, such inter-connection cannot exist, and, what is more, he is a universe unto himself. Both worldviews are at loggerheads, and once more the principle of *tertium non datur* does its beneficial work. Moosbrugger is convicted and sentenced to death, and this is Musil's metaphor for the crisis of modernity, 'When the presiding judge read out the psychiatrists' findings that the accused was responsible for his actions, Moosbrugger rose to his feet and announced to the court: "I am satisfied with this opinion and have achieved my purpose"' (MWQ 76). He takes the verdict to be the confirmation of his view of him-self, fractured as that is in and by the legal procedure. This statement is not at all the internal contradiction for Moosbrugger that it would be to the jurists in the novel, because once his worldview is under attack, bad things happen.

While Moosbrugger recognises that others decide his fate on the basis of their language of concepts, which to him is 'this net woven of incom-prehension' (MWQ 75), he nevertheless fails to grasp how this can at all be connected to the interrelation of mind and world that is the foundation of his life and actions. To him, the only solution is one comparable to that of Flaubert's Pécuchet before the police court: namely, 'that the educated ought to have their tongues cut out' (MWQ 254). That is the radical way of taking away the language of those who outtalk him.

But what exactly is injustice in Moosbrugger's view? It is closely connected to his language theory, and it challenges the positivist picture theory. Moosbrugger encounters the difficulties that language as a system of signs poses to its users, '"A squirrel in these parts is called a tree kitten", it occurred to him . . . "In Hesse, on the other hand, it's called a tree fox"' (MWQ 258–9). He astounds his psychiatrists by nominating a picture of a squirrel as 'a fox, . . . a hare or maybe a cat or something' (MWQ 259), because to him everything hangs together. Ironically, by whatever name he is called, Moosbrugger, locked up in prison, still remains the same. To him, the connection between the signifier (in Saussurian terms, the form that the word as a sign takes) and the signified (the concept that the sign represents) is arbitrary.[12] Language is utterly private speech: 'It had happened that he said to a girl, "your sweet rose lips"' when suddenly 'the words gave way at their seams' (MWQ 259). The girl became that rose on a long stem – that is, the word becomes the thing it represents. Moosbrugger could not resist the temptation to cut off the rose, and when he came to his senses after having done so, it was the girl he had killed. In Moosbrugger's other condition, the connection between words and objects in the world is magical. Language is the representation of what the words as hieroglyphic signs denote. This also pertains to his view on law and justice, which coincides with his sense of personal integrity. '"My right", he thought, . . . "It's when you haven't done anything wrong, or something like that, isn't it?" . . . "Right is justice"', and thus, 'he had been cheated of his justice!' (MWQ 255).

Moosbrugger slides back into what we would call pre-logical thinking that is as literal as it is metaphorical in the unmediated way in which it emanates from the human affect. In a literal, though not in the logical-positivist sense, the word coincides with the object. That is why he ends up ensnared in the nets of the law of those who judge him with foreign words without understanding who and how he is. It is also why he escapes the dichotomous thought of the jurists and the psychiatrists; he simply does not fit into their categories. He sees relations where they do not, because their language of concepts disconnects sign and object.

To Moosbrugger, law and the administration of justice are language problems, and they are intimately connected to questions of power. As a result, the question of who has power over the language of law is crucial. The

[12] See F. de Saussure (trans. W. Baskin and eds P. Meisel and H. Saussy), *Course in General Linguistics* (New York: Columbia University Press, [1916] 2011).

answer is simple. Jurists have power over the language of law, while forensic psychiatrists have power over the language of behavioural sciences. That is why language in Moosbrugger's case is both the means to grasp reality and the instrument of his downfall. Truth is indeed not univocal, and modernity's quest for certainty is an illusion. Yet law in Moosbrugger's case demands precision in order to be fair in a positivist vein, in a double sense of positive law and positivism as a scientific worldview. When this does not result in certainty, the only way out is to diagnose Moosbrugger with anything other than a 'hitherto observed syndrome' (MWQ 267), or, as the DSM would call it, Not Otherwise Specified. The Moosbrugger case presents the need for precision in order to exact justice, and at the same time it is an example and an acceptance of ambiguity. Moosbrugger takes poetic licence to voice his innermost experience. His language articulates the essences of things, facts, and emotions by means of metaphor in order to shape reality. If the creation of meaning is language's original intention, metaphor can also help expand the language of concepts and include new situations that are different from ones to which the concept was originally designed to give meaning. In short, metaphor provides an excess of meaning.[13]

The *Erklären-Verstehen* Controversy Inescapable?

To me, Moosbrugger's case demonstrates that our continued attention to the old controversies in the natural sciences and the humanities about methods of research, aims of inquiry, and standards of judgement is important for both interdisciplinary legal research and legal practice. Ulrich's outcry summarises succinctly the professional and societal effect of the ongoing development of science since the start of the scientific revolution: 'Scientific man is an entirely inescapable thing these days; we can't not want to know! And at no time has the difference between the expert's experience and that of the layman been as great as it is now' (MWQ 213). *The Man without Qualities* counsels epistemological modesty, especially when we consider that the abyss between science and the rest of the world has widened even more since Musil showed us how woefully susceptible we all are to the idea that our conceptual corner of the world is the only one that can be perceived veridically. The very form of his extensive narrative taken together with its genesis is a case in point as well. The writer Musil kept writing and writing and rewriting the pages, a selection of which we now know in printed form as *The Man without Qualities*, but which could have been much longer had Musil decided to publish everything

---

[13] In modern parlance, the idea of *Gestalt* psychology, with its claim of unmediated experience of visual and auditory impulses, or occurrences, comes to mind, as suggested by Corino, *Robert Musil*, p. 225ff.

that he had written. Hence, another of the lessons we can learn from *The Man without Qualities* is that closure is an illusion. Nevertheless, there comes a time when choices have to be made. *The Man without Qualities* as we know it is one result, while others are the decisions made in actual cases in law and in the behavioural sciences.

A final lesson to be drawn from the novel is that literature and law are value-laden constructs that cannot be understood in terms of a neutral orientation of the kind that positivistic legal thought endorses. To me, this is all the more reason to replace the *tertium non datur* of scientific discourse with a *tertium datur*: namely, that of interdisciplinary co-operation, with an open eye for – and a strong emphasis on – the discursive, methodological, and epistemological pitfalls and peculiarities of the disciplines involved. We must not forget the devastating consequences of an unmediated application of the one discipline in the field of the other.

5

Poetry that Does not Fade: Gerrit Achterberg's Experience with Law and Forensic Psychiatry

Acid Language

On 15 December 1937, the Dutch poet Gerrit Achterberg (1905–62) fired two shots at his landlady Roel van Es and her daughter.[1] Van Es died of her wounds. The girl survived, so traumatised that as an adult she was unable to give voice to her experience. The circumstances of this manslaughter were kept out of publications about Achterberg's life for a very long time. It was revealed only in 2002 that, on the fatal evening, the landlady's daughter came to bring Achterberg his evening snack a bit earlier than usual. But here the stories diverge. One has it that the girl caught him in the act of masturbation, while another is that Achterberg, stripped to the waist, suddenly tried to grab her. The girl started screaming, her mother rushed to the rescue, and Achterberg panicked and fired the gun he kept in his room.

For years, he suffered the consequences of his deed. On 2 June 1938, the Utrecht regional court ordered Achterberg's entrustment to the care of a forensic psychiatric institution on the basis of what was then Section 37 of the Dutch Criminal Code, because he was judged to be a sexually deviant psychopath. According to Dutch law, unlike a punishment such as imprisonment, a measure in criminal law – of which an entrustment order is an example – can be imposed on an offender regardless of his diminished

---

[1] For biographical information about Achterberg, I draw on W. Hazeu, *Gerrit Achterberg* (Amsterdam: Arbeiderspers, 1988); a special Achterberg issue in 9 *Maandblad Geestelijke Volksgezondheid*, 2003, pp.763–853; G. van Colmjon, 'Letter en Geest', *Trouw*, 16 November 2002, pp. 37–8; F. Abrahams, 'Achterberg', *NRC Handelsblad*, 21 November 2002, <https://www.nrc.nl/nieuws/2002/11/21/achterberg-7615090-a880063> [last accessed 4 December 2017]; H. M. van den Brink, 'De gratie voor Gerrit A.', *Vrij Nederland*, 30 November 2002, p. 59. I am also grateful to Ralf Grüttemeier, professor of Dutch literature at Oldenburg University (Germany), for conversations about the Achterberg case.

responsibility, because the aim of a measure is to promote the safety and security of other people. Thus, if the defendant who suffers from a mental illness or defect is deemed responsible, be it only to a slight degree, an entrustment order may be imposed, with or without another penalty, as happened in the Achterberg case. The defendant then has to undergo treatment in the clinical setting of a forensic psychiatric institution, and the case is reviewed every two years. The decision of whether or not to prolong the measure is taken by a panel of three judges – in Achterberg's days, the Ministry of Justice took the decision – on the basis of new psychiatric reports.

The Dutch debate on the nature and proposed form of the entrustment order raged from 1870 to 1928 before it was brought into effect. The 1886 Dutch Criminal Code followed the classical school of thought, emphasising culpability and retribution on the basis of intent and volition. Since the classical school linked free will to powers of reason and judgement, the determinism debate quite rightly included the question of whether disturbances of the intellectual powers or a mental disease could and should be extenuating factors when it came to the choice between imprisonment and psychiatric treatment. On the basis of this view, forensic psychiatrists in the Netherlands, who were involved as experts in the legislative process concerning the entrustment order, heavily criticised the legal usage of the term mental faculties on the grounds that the legislator should not enter into the scientific debate on the (Cartesian) dichotomy of mind and matter, or, put more simply, on the influence of the mind on the body and its human – all too human – actions. Like the fictional debate between Professor Schwung and Ulrich's father in Chapter 4, the discussion focused on the subtle differences between the mental and the rational in relation to free will. Insofar as free will has become the criterion for legal personhood in its connection to concepts of guilt and culpability, the discussion shows that the position one takes is consequential for one's views on forms of retribution, especially incarceration of 'the body'.

After having been diagnosed initially as mentally deranged, Achterberg underwent harsh treatments as an inmate of various institutions. Later on, a lighter regime was applied when a revision of the applicable laws opened up this possibility. Achterberg could live a more or less normal life, even though it was under the constant supervision of the warden, in whose house he was required to live. It was not until 27 May 1955 that this ban – because that was how he experienced it – was lifted. Amazingly perhaps, or understandably if we consider the fact that he did everything he could to prevent people from knowing about his plight, Achterberg became one of the most renowned twentieth-century Dutch poets. The impact of the treatment he endured was immense. During those seventeen years, Achterberg wrote several poems that give voice to his frustration and anger at being misunderstood on so many levels. The volume of poetry entitled *Blauwzuur* in Dutch, *Acid* in English,[2] was a response to the way Achterberg had been treated by jurists and behavioural scientists. Published posthumously – as Achterberg was afraid that publication would have a negative effect on his release – the poems offer a unique perspective on both law and society, and raise the question with regard to the dehumanising effects of scientific rationality in matters concerning treatment of the criminally insane. In what follows, I do not want to diminish the enormity of Achterberg's crime and its impact on the surviving victim. Most probably Achterberg did suffer from psychopathologies. When asked once whether he felt remorse for his deed, he is said to have answered that he had written beautiful verse about it, had he not?[3] What I want to address are the nineteenth-century concept of law as science, clearly depicted in Achterberg's critical portrayal of the law; forensic medicine, with its attendant concepts of personhood; and the effects of a referential language view.

Madness and Modernity in Achterberg: Another War of the Words

Achterberg's poems about his experience of being hospitalised also exemplify Wittgenstein's 'limits' proposition 5.6. The tension between Achterberg's double identity as a poet and as a criminally insane and sexually deviant person is deeply felt in *Acid*. Here too, as in Musil's *The Man without Qualities*, borders between fact and fiction blur, especially when we realise that Achterberg was diagnosed as insane on the basis of a most unusual criterion: namely, his poetry written prior to the manslaugher. With Achterberg as well, the key to his plight is the clash of views on the language espoused by those involved in his case, and, as with Musil, the question then is whether Achterberg's poetry is commensurable with his lived experience. The epistemological aspect of the *Erklären-Verstehen* controversy resurfaces once more.

The psychiatrist Henri van der Hoeven, who examined Achterberg, used his patient's poems in order to diagnose the form and degree of insanity. Thus, the link between the constellation of Achterberg's personal and/or mental problems and the content of his work became a constant factor in every new attempt at diagnosing him.[4] A causal relation between illness and poem, or

---

[2] The edition of *Blauwzuur* used is The Hague: Bert Bakker, 1969. Unless otherwise noted, the translations of the *Acid* poems are by Pleuke Boyce, who graciously consented to provide a first draft of an English translation in order to clarify those poems unavailable in English translation. She also translated 'Murderballad'.

[3] Namely the volume *Sixteen*, a reference to the girl's age. See also S. Wiersma (trans. and ed.), *A Tourist Does Golgotha and other Poems by Gerrit Achterberg* (Grand Rapids: Being Publications, 1972), p. 55, 'Let me originate in you, creature of sixteen years'.

[4] For another example of a defendant's poetic oeuvre connected to questions of evidence, see

what Achterberg himself called, 'the word which coincides with you', was established along with – on this basis – the diagnosis of psychopathology.[5] How did Van der Hoeven come to this conclusion? His attention was drawn to a line in an early poem entitled 'Murderballad', which read, 'O you who I had massacred', and which as far as Van der Hoeven was concerned should already have been understood in 1931 as a sign of impending madness, unfortunately ignored. Had Achterberg sought psychiatric help then, or so Van der Hoeven claimed, the crime could have been prevented.

This diagnosis became the foundation for a long line of interpretations in which the manslaughter was *ex post facto* related to the early, and constant, theme in Achterberg's work: the search for the lost loved one. No wonder Achterberg later changed the title of the poem to 'Dreamballad'. In addition, the contested line, 'O you who I had massacred', was changed into, 'O you, whom I had waited for', and the line that read, 'my hands dripping with blood' became 'Then you stood up and you undid the knot my hands were in'.[6]

By the time of this astonishing methodology and diagnosis, Achterberg had already been committed more than once for psychiatric problems: namely, in 1927 because of a mental breakdown caused by anxieties concerning his future as a poet, and in 1932 because of a bout of aggression following problems in his relationship with his then fiancée. When Achterberg was released, her father had asked for medical intervention because he feared for his daughter's life. His fears proved to be correct. After his release, Achterberg took a taxi to the girl's house, and asked her to join him on a trip to a nearby wood, where he planned to kill her and commit suicide. Luckily for her, the taxi driver had misgivings about the whole situation, and called the police. Achterberg was found to carry a loaded gun. Again he was committed, this time until October 1933. The central theme of a yearning for death by suicide as well as for the love of the lost one is evident in the poem 'Pavilion'. The loved one is presented as a saviour,

> Will she, while I fall towards the pavement
> be forced to put her faith in me at last?
> In that case I will land in someone's arms.

J. Surdukowski, 'Is poetry a war crime? Reckoning for Radovan Karadzic the poet-warrior', 26 *Michigan Journal of International Law*, 2000, pp. 673–99, on the Karadzic case before the International Criminal Tribunal for the Former Yugoslavia in The Hague.

[5] M. O'Loughlin (ed. and trans.), *Hidden Weddings, Selected Poems Gerrit Achterberg* (Dublin: Raven Arts Press, 1987), p. 18, 'Word'.

[6] P. Boyce (ed. and trans.), *But This Land Has No End, Selected Poems of Gerrit Achterberg* (Lantzville, BC: Oolichan Books, 1989), p. 23.

Hers or an angel's, for they are the same.
Is there love greater than a change of heart
at the last minute, cheating death?

and fellow inmates are described in truly Lombrosian fashion as 'utter idiots, milling about like animals'.

During the six months of his pre-trial detention, Achterberg continued writing poetry. His feeling of impotence with regard to those who interpreted him and his works on the basis of the explanatory model of the natural sciences, and whose superior forces he associated with death, was clearly evident when he wrote that in this house of detention he was weighed and found wanting. On 27 June 1938, Achterberg was committed to the psychiatric asylum Veldzicht. One day later he wrote to a friend to express his disgust at having been judged on the basis of his poetry. His poems, he claimed, were not signs of illness or decadence as some jurists had claimed. He was anxious lest his confinement together with real madmen have negative effects on his poetic capability. He had good reason for this reserve. In 1941, even though other psychiatrists such as Van der Horst and Tammenons Bakker admitted that they were not trained in literary analysis, their lack of expert knowledge did not discourage them from using the same method as Van der Hoeven. They even dragged in later collections of Achterberg's poetry that had been written after the criminal offence.

To Achterberg, the task of the poet is to translate the unspeakable, the inexpressible, into the expressible.[7] The poet dreams reality – his poetry is a hypothesis of life, not a picture of things visible to the eye. To have his poems called *Wortsalat* and autistic verbalisations by his psychiatrist Fortanier in the 1940s was a traumatic experience for the poet, as was the fact that he was forced to read his poetry to students attending Fortanier's medical lectures.[8] It was not helpful that fellow writers disqualified his work as degenerate; nor that his biographer later pointed to his fascination for Dostoevski's protagonist Raskolnikov in *Crime and Punishment,* and to his view that superior people can do whatever they like, murder included.[9]

More recently, these earlier diagnoses were dismissed by the psychiatrist Vink, who nevertheless uses the same methodology when he argues that

---

[7] F. Treffers and D. Bos, 'De loopbaan van Gerrit Achterberg in de psychiatrie', 9 *Maandblad Geestelijke volksgezondheid*, 2003, pp. 804–36, 819–21. The authors draw on previously unpublished expert-witness reports from 1939–41, and reassess the diagnosis.

[8] A. J. Govers, 'Gerrit Achterberg en de psychiatrie', *Bzzlletin*, no. 79, October 1980, pp. 29–38, p. 35.

[9] F. Treffers, 'Ik breng met u geen woorden meer te weeg', 9 *Maandblad Geestelijke volksgezondheid*, 2003, p. 839.

Achterberg suffered from a severe personality disorder with narcissistic and psychopathic aspects. To him as well, 'Murderballad' is conclusive, because the line, 'O you who I had massacred' is prospective of the manslaughter, and the comparison later on in the poem of the eyes of the beloved with 'those mirrored halls' is proof of the poet's narcissism.[10] It would seem, then, that given the importance of this *topos* in western literature, this implies that many poets, Shakespeare probably included, suffered from this mental disorder. One thing is clear though – interpretation of the inexpressible yields astonishing results in the hands of scientific literalists. No wonder Achterberg asked himself, 'In what sewer have I ended up?'[11]

The *Acid* poems, I suggest, are a warning to those whom Achterberg – in a poem originally entitled 'Language' but later – significantly – renamed 'Consultation' – addressed as 'doctors and professors of language and the soul' who are 'people like beasts [who] control me now'. Note the ironic reversal of the Lombrosian view on criminals as dangerous animals. They are the people who 'meet at conferences where they softly speak in broken, obscure languages, while I scream at them, urged by my soul'; they are the people 'who are deaf, who only hold their white bands sacred', and that is clearly a reference to the judge's bands and gown as a metaphor for institutional language as the instrument with which to diagnose and pass sentence. Jurists and psychiatrists alike are given a sound poetic thrashing,

> In their vain monologues
> words are not measured
> for their essence or their import,
> their origin or their direction,
> they are but rented words
> for now.

The experts who use incomprehensible jargon – 'rented words' – are taken to task for their lack of empathy. Their language prevents them from understanding either the poems or the poet. Taken together, this is unmistakably a sneer at the linguistic doings of professionals.

Achterberg wrote poetry as a survival strategy and a form of release during his years in mental institutions under the shadow of the entrustment order, which in the poem 'Sunday' he referred to as 'the plan in which I have no say'. At the same time, he was concerned that any new poem would be

---

[10] J. Vink, 'Spiegelingen, Gerrit Achterberg psychiatrisch bezien', 9 *Maandblad Geestelijke volksgezondheid*, 2003, pp. 767–82, p. 714.
[11] O'Loughlin, *Hidden Weddings*, 'Sewer', p. 64.

taken as yet further proof of mental illness, and that his critical poems might get him into more trouble. 'Regulations' is an expression of that sentiment:

> Lost property. A life condemned to death.
> I can only smile with lowered eyes
> and mutter the required words,
> my head bent down . . .
>
> And with this song I once more go too far,
> expose myself to the execution of
> his judgement.

Nevertheless, writing poetry was also a form of rehabilitation for Achterberg in order to show the world that he was not really mad and deserved a return into society. He heavily criticised the Ministry of Justice in his comparison of the psychiatric hospital to a sewer, where people are 'laid together in hideous suppuration'.[12] In 'Acid', being hospitalised is 'an acid for the soul'. In 'Terror', Achterberg lamented the circumstances in the institutions, a terror exercised by his psychiatrists Van der Hoeven, Palies and Hartsuiker, whom he hoped would apply an ethics of conscientious professional duty, but who failed him, as did the judges in Moosbrugger's case.

Achterberg's fears were justified if we take into consideration that in those days the inmates of forensic psychiatric wards were locked up in iron cages at night, a fate Achterberg escaped only because his day-to-day behaviour was deemed normal. And then there is also the circumstance that castration was one of the standard forms of treatment for psychopaths with sexual deviances such as those attributed to Achterberg. Luckily, he never had to undergo castration, but from the psychiatric reports it has become clear that his psychiatrist seriously considered the option more than once, because he wanted to find out whether it would affect Achterberg's linguistic usage, and, if so, in which way. Of all things, this is as remarkable an example of the direct link supposed by the dominant scientific paradigm and epistemology between the body and its intentions as it is an example of the interrelation of *Eros* and *Thanatos*. Perhaps this is why Achterberg wrote,

> they thought, if we kill him
> We will strip him of his song[13]

---

[12] O'Loughlin, *Hidden Weddings*, 'Sewer', p. 64. Originally, the second line of the poem equated the entrustment order with the sewer, see the historical-critical Achterberg edition by P. G. de Bruijn, *Gerrit Achterberg: Gedichten* (The Hague: Constantijn Huygens Institute, 2000), p. 214.

[13] O'Loughlin, *Hidden Weddings*, 'Epitaph', p. 67.

The figure of the psychiatrist is portrayed most clearly in the 'Director' of the institution, who 'can keep me locked away in here as long as he deems fit'. Achterberg remains fully aware of the impact of his poetry when he writes,

> one wrongly chosen word
> is sure to be in the report that evening
> and will be kept until the end of times.

He rages at the depersonalisation that he feels deeply as the result of the treatment by

> this man who has this one deficiency:
> that he will not give up curing me
> until I'm someone else.

The last line was originally, 'until I hurl myself upon him', but this too was later softened for obvious reasons.[14] Becoming someone else is losing one's personhood, legally as well as poetically, and becoming reified. The only reason the Director wants Achterberg to change is that, 'that way it'll better fit into the blind system of files, that's on his desk', with the blind file reminiscent of positivism's claim of objectivity, empirical repetition of experimentation, and neutrality, and suggestive of the depersonalisation and reduction of a human to just this one dimension – madness. To reiterate the point made in Chapter 2, I have no axe to grind with legal positivism as a theory of law; I only want to warn against a one-sided belief in its supposedly logical consequences as far as volition and authorial intention are concerned, because these are negative fictions when applied to actual legal cases.

The counterpart of 'Consultation' is a poem about legal officials, entitled 'Civil servant'. It turns against those responsible for keeping Achterberg institutionalised year after year, after each new examination. They diagnose the poet from a distance, and are described with venom, because in their paperwork, the ink that details what the officials think they know about the poet dries, and 'thus he will be deemed a danger as long as registers and files make all the big decisions'. In 'Minister', the tension between *Erklären* and *Verstehen* is rendered poetically as,

> You count.
> I name.
> And with one name I reach you in your millions.
> I make the law and move by leaps and bounds.
> The law makes you . . .

[14] De Bruijn, *Gerrit Achterberg: Gedichten*, p. 39.

Between us is a gulf, that can't be bridged.
(From your perspective).

The often monomaniac vehemence that his choice of words demonstrates is misunderstood by those who judge and treat him. The very root of evil is indeed language. Like Musil's Moosbrugger, Achterberg's usage of words is unmistakably pre-modern, and is one that Vico defined as original poetic speech in *La Scienza Nuova*. To Vico, metaphor is essential to linguistic usage in general and to poetry specifically. Indeed, poetry stands out as one of the oldest ways in which human beings express themselves – namely, by means of symbolic and associative language rather than by way of the abstract, theoretical concepts favoured by rationalism. And, as Percy Bysshe Shelley later claimed in 'A Defence of Poetry', poetry acts in a divine manner, above and beyond consciousness.[15] That is why judging a poet's consciousness and mental faculties on the basis of his work is fundamentally wrong. Yet, to both Vico and Achterberg, words in the sense of what we now call concepts are metaphors as well, but in a special way. Primitive man 'found' metaphorical language and used it literally to describe the essence of things as he perceived them. Only after this phase did metaphorical language become a proposal for the linguistic reshaping of reality that, in its modern usage, expands the imagined space of language – and in Achterberg's case, the poem; it also includes another situation not originally taken into consideration, and provides an excess of meaning. In other words, the creation of meaning is language's original game as the word shifts from being a mere sign to creating an image.[16] Poetic thought structure thus differs totally from the rationalist language game with its emphasis on reason and the logic of the syllogism. Achterberg takes poetic licence to seek the words to best voice his individual experience. Phenomenologically speaking, his words have performative power, in that articulating the word gives expression and structure to the underlying subjective feeling. Therefore, the unproblematic acceptance in language of what was originally literally unmediated, combined with the modernist picture theory, leads Achterberg's interpreters – jurists and psychiatrists alike – to a grave misunderstanding of their object of study and of judgement.

Achterberg's metaphorical thinking leads him to gaining insight into other people's sense of things and their actions. Hence his vehemence with regard to what jurists and psychiatrists do to him. 'The word that coincides

---

[15] P. B. Shelley, 'A Defence of Poetry', published posthumously in 1840, available at <https://www.saylor.org/site/wp-content/uploads/2011/01/A-Defense-of-Poetry.pdf> [last accessed 4 December 2017].

[16] See J. P. Sartre, *Qu'est-ce que la littérature?* (Paris: Gallimard, 1948), pp. 19–20.

with you' is not the referential picture of reality that the professionals have in mind, but is a poetic evocation. Preoccupation with language is what matters to Achterberg. It is precisely this preoccupation that shapes his poetic genius, that is, rather than the other way around, that any event in his personal life could result in the use of a specific theme for his poetry, such as the death of the landlady and/or the beloved. Thus, the central theme, of which his poems are the illustrative examples, is always in tension with the ambiguity of the word as the constant interplay between literal and metaphorical language, an ambiguity not recognised by the legal and psychiatric experts since Van der Hoeven's first and fateful diagnosis.[17]

Belief in the magical power of the word makes Achterberg almost a metaphysical poet, given his stylistic use of conceit, his tendency to invent neologisms, and, paradoxically perhaps, his interest in science. A fine example is 'Prayer to the typewriter':

> Machine that holds the song
> That should fall from my fingers:
> Forgive them one and all
> The damage done to you.[18]

However, given the dissociation of sensibility often suffered with the specialisation of knowledge and the differentiation of disciplines since the seventeenth century, being misunderstood leaves him no refuge other than his 'Own Sea' that is 'never a wave short'.[19] All of the above, I suggest, illustrates how tragically mistaken was the poet, of whom it is safe to say that there is no later Dutch poet who is not at least tangentially descended from him.

The Human and the Legal Experience

A web of textuality ties the poet Achterberg to the politics of mental institutions. That is why the *Acid* poems cannot be brought to attention enough in order to make professionals aware of the interpretive pitfalls of their linguistic disciplines. What institutional languages have in common is that they impose their conceptual framework to such an extent that other languages are easily excluded, often without our realising it. Here also is the link with *Law and Literature*, since one of the answers to the question of what jurists can learn from literature is that reading literary works and trying to make sense of them will redirect the jurist's attention to the fact that interpretation both in

---

[17] P. K. King, *Dawn Poetry in the Netherlands* (Amsterdam: Athenaeum, Polak and Van Gennep, 1971), p. 123.
[18] Boyce, *But This Land* (from *Osmosis*, 1941), p. 33.
[19] O'Loughlin, *Hidden Weddings*, p. 65.

law and in literature is a process that demands our active participation and helps promote awareness of our own role in the creation of meaning. Since interpretation is always an act, the outcome of any process of interpretation is never given beforehand. We work out meaning; we do not find it ready-made. Thus, in dealing with language as a form of human behaviour, both law and literature involve consideration of common theoretical issues when the central task of both enterprises is seen as a coming to terms with what another person says and claims for meaning.

Furthermore, the way in which a literary work is a response to law, for example in its description of a conflict between the individual and the system of law, offers the reader a possibility of imagining the world proposed in the literary work. As a reproach to 'doctors and professors of language and the soul', the *Acid* poems also alert us to the way in which literature either affirms the norms and values of the powerful in a particular period or lays bare the ideological structure of society in terms of the assumptions – especially those that are not always explicitly defined or articulated – that permeate any society, and with it the law and literature of any given period. As noted in Chapter 4, epistemologically that is, for the purpose of the creation of theory, both law and literature function as value-laden constructs in any culture. In this sense, Achterberg's asylum poems are yet another literary-legal illustration of the *Erklären-Verstehen* controversy. They can be read as our cultural memory, both in the sense of a legal-historical memory of the period of Achterberg's entrustment and as an expression of an otherwise inexpressible, let alone scientifically explainable, human experience. This justifies, I suggest, a literary-legal diagnosis from a distance.

With this analysis of Achterberg's language problem, or rather that of his judges and psychiatrists, I suggest that – for purposes of interdisciplinary work in law – it is important to keep addressing the old controversies in the natural sciences and the humanities about methods of research, aims of inquiry, and standards of judgement. When James Boyd White writes that in language, 'for each of us there is always an element or dimension of meaning . . . that is irremediably personal',[20] and is one that the language of concepts is unable to recognise and incorporate, Achterberg's story demonstrates the devastating consequences of any misunderstandings in translations between disciplines.

Achterberg is concerned with what it means for a human being to be locked up within the boundaries of his subjective consciousness. Here the debate on the methodological division between subject and object of inquiry

---

[20] J. B. White, *Justice as Translation* (Chicago: University of Chicago Press, 1990), p. 35.

again comes full circle. This should draw our attention to precisely the literary mode of thought that can both illuminate and negotiate the very tension of meaning and context, individually as well as culturally. Inevitably, we also have our habits of the mind, by which we tend to perceive the world according to well-established patterns and expectations. We should therefore ask ourselves as well whether the disciplinary battles are perhaps not themselves fictional, in that our dichotomising is a Baconian 'idol of the theatre', an attracted bias imposed on man by philosophers, rather than an innate 'idol of the tribe', inherent in the very structure of the human mind, a topic that is explored further in Chapter 7.

Like Musil's Moosbrugger, Achterberg experiences alienation. His self is fractured because he is unable to locate himself in terms of the language imposed on him. His poetry and personal experience provide insight into law's underlying assumptions as well as into the legal system's underlying justifications. Another poet, Wallace Stevens, wrote, 'In an age of disbelief it is for the poet to supply the satisfactions of belief'.[21] If anything, Achterberg demonstrates how difficult it is to situate the legal perspective in human experience. Nevertheless, I think it is fair to say that Achterberg remains 'the poet of the verse that did not fade'.[22] His poetry reminds us of the professional assignment to ensure the ethical integrity of not only our individual disciplines when these deal with the individuals left to our care but also of our disciplinary co-operations themselves.

---

[21] W. Stevens, 'Two or three ideas', in W. Stevens, *Opus Posthumous* (New York: Knopf, 1989), p. 259.

[22] G. Achterberg (trans. J. S. Holmes), 'Epitaph' [1941], *Hommage aan Gerrit Achterberg*, 125 *De Gids*, no. 1, 1962, p. 166 (note that Achterberg used the title 'Epitaph' for two poems).

Part II

Iuris Prudentia or Insightful Knowledge of Law

6

Practical Knowledge:
Facts, Norms and *Phronèsis*

Facts and Norms, Theory and Practice

This chapter starts from a double premise. The first is that law as an academic discipline belongs firmly to the humanities precisely because of its historical development since the rediscovery of the Justinian Code, as outlined in Chapter 2. Moreover, law is and has always been characterised as a strong language-oriented, philological-hermeneutical perspective, notwithstanding contemporary developments occasioned by the influx of technologies on the plane of digital and visual media entering the courtroom. It is the view, propounded among others by Hans-Georg Gadamer in *Truth and Method*, that hermeneutics is not merely a methodology for interpretation but is also a philosophical view encompassing a broad mode of inquiry into both text and action or human agency. Judges always try to 'figure out' the variety of meanings of the narratives before them, and to deal with these in terms of their legal consequences, whether or not intended. As a consequence, the second premise is that jurists necessarily combine the practical and the theoretical. I use the term theory deliberately a bit loosely here in order to refer to legal scholarship in the sense of the academic study of and research into law generally, with no doctrinal strings attached, at least not a priori. But why this double premise? Because the art of doing law in its different professional guises always requires attention to the reciprocal relation between fact and norm, as well as to the ways in which the system of substantive and procedural rules and norms is deployed to achieve justice.

Facts and norms

A characteristic feature of legal methodology in the sense of the perception of the case or legal topic at hand is the constant movement from facts to legal norms, and back. Or, as the Latin maxims go, *Da mihi facta, dabo tibi ius*, give me the facts and I will give you the law, and *Ex facta ius oritur*, the law arises from the facts. The facts too, objective as they are often mistakenly called, need a hermeneut. They do not need a *iudex deductor* who subsumes the facts under the rule as if the meanings of both are undisputed and given beforehand, immediately ready for use. The idea of the *iudex deductor* is obviously closely connected to the positivist separation thesis of fact and norm noted in Chapter 2, guided as that is by the view that judging is the unmediated application of objective legal norms to the facts. This idea is false. The movement is always dialectic, a going hither and thither of fact and norm, so to speak, as coined by the German jurist Karl Engisch in the phrase the *Hin-und Herwandern des Blickes*.[1] In performing this movement, jurists should constantly bear in mind the influence of their own interpretive frameworks on both fact and norm, because as humans we cannot escape our hermeneutic situation of being culturally determined, professionally as well as personally.

What is more, the systematisation of knowledge in the field of law as well is subject to a comparable movement back and forth; hence the double aspect of facticity and normativity is inherent in the ordering process of law itself. As a consequence, theoretical knowledge and legal interpretation are intertwined. In other words, when confronted with a new case, the legal professional begins with a diagnosis of what are considered the relevant facts – that is, established facts and/or facts admissible as evidence or with a certain probative value – then proceeds to a first, tentative classification of the materials, deliberating about the next step of formulating a response and fine-tuning his or her classificatory analysis. In all this, one's specific position as a legal professional is of decisive importance, of course, in that a judge will combine this process with her prior experience of hard and easy cases, and a defence lawyer will seek as many anchors as possible for the construction of his legal argument and its accompanying narrative.[2]

Theory and practice

As far as the relation between theory and practice is concerned, it follows from this that for the outcome of the specific case, legal practice always reflects on the consequences of any theoretical, doctrinal assumption. This reflection includes attention to the possible theoretical justification of the position taken when viewed against the background of the wider significance of the combined legal and cultural framework: for example, in high-profile cases

---

[1] K. Engisch, *Logische Studien zur Gesetzanwendung* (Heidelberg: Winter, [1943] 1963), p. 15. See also K. F. Larenz, *Methodenlehre der Rechtswissenschaft* (Berlin: Springer, [1960] 1991), p. 204.

[2] A. Abbott, *The System of Professions: An Essay on the Division of Expert Labor* (Chicago and London: University of Chicago Press, 1988), p. 40, on the tripartite division of diagnosis, reference (or deliberation), and treatment (or response).

that attract societal and/or media attention. In turn, theoretical knowledge in the sense of academic legal scholarship is augmented by the actual *quid-iuris* questions that legal practice raises: for instance, what is the law? These often go far beyond what academic doctrinal discourse can even begin to fathom. The relationship is reciprocal. Where practice turns to theory for justification, theory thrives on practical input. Legal scholars can do research on a scale impossible at the level of the actual case confronting the practitioner. In doing so, they can offer alternative views and innovative arguments that practitioners in turn can use in future cases. Theory, time and again, is thus able to reproduce the overall picture of a field of law. It can synthesise and bring coherence to what seemed initially to be incompatibilities at the case level, thereby giving direction to the application of legal principles. In doing so, theory offers a proposal for the legitimacy of law as well as opens up a site for critique, for the language of the law is by its very nature open-textured. The continuous rise and subsequent development of new subfields of law is a case in point here. Another is the move away since the nineteenth century from the concept of guilt as essential to the assessment of liability towards the concept of risk. Those working in law are therefore necessarily both theorists and practitioners. Their professional gaze shifts between norm and fact, between law as a system of norms and rules and the administration of justice in concrete cases.

In short, the jurist's methodology is never purely deductive or inductive. It is always the combined effort of the perception and assessment of the facts against the background of what legal norm – including the academic propositions made for it – means, and the awareness that the whole process is governed by the dynamics of the interpretive frame that is itself subject to constant developments and challenges of a varied nature (for example, technological or societal). This ontological uncertainty – at any time something new may crop up that challenges existing meanings – also opens up areas of critique and innovation.

When the results of legal scholarship are used to justify practice, they can also help clarify its foundations and connect these to the broader cultural framework of which law is a part. The transference of theoretical knowledge is itself an immersion in a language game; it is a habituation, both conscious and unconscious, in the discourse of law, the visible discourse as much as the invisible.[3] This is important from an interdisciplinary perspective.

---

[3] See J. B. White, *Heracles' Bow* (Madison: University of Wisconsin Press, 1985), p. 63, for the distinction between legal vocabulary and law's 'cultural syntax' or 'invisible discourse': 'Behind the words, that is, are expectations about the ways in which they will be used, expectations that do not find explicit expression anywhere, but are part of the legal culture that the surface language simply assumes.'

Transference of systematised knowledge is a form of reproduction; it is the creation and recreation of a shared background that enables jurists to understand one another. Application and imitation, or *mimesis* as re-presentation, a topic elaborated upon in Chapter 8 in relation to narrative intelligence, are intertwined here. Insights and theoretically supported solutions find their way into practice, which in turn provides feedback to legal scholarship. Reciprocity is the key to the constant renewal of debate and to the growth of new insights. This process also facilitates the introduction of the discourse, methodology, and values of law to newcomers in the field. Thus, theoretical knowledge of law of the kind that scholarship provides is essential, not because those in legal practice can apply it without giving it constant consideration in each case, especially in what are considered easy cases, but because it provides the background knowledge on which to build in acquiring professional knowledge. All this taken together means that theory and practice are the warp and woof of law's fabric and social order or the *ordo ordinans*, the Latin *ordo* being a term derived from the activity of weaving.

The interrelation sketched here also affects legal theory, in that, ideally at least, as George Pavlakos and Sean Coyle argued, it should be understood as engaged in rather than detached from questions underlying doctrinal debates that concern moral and political aspects of law. The aim of legal theory would then be to understand legal ideas as a reflection of values and an explanation of how they came about. This concept of law as a discipline is what Pavlakos and Coyle call jurisprudence. Their view is most congenial to me. Jurisprudence denies 'the possibility of generality in theoretical accounts of the nature of law',[4] because such generality entails a detached form of observation by theory viewed as the legal science of the social institution that is law, and that aims merely to provide an objective account of it. In this perspective, theory and practice exist as disconnected entities. The legal theorist's sole task is then to analyse practice from a safe distance. As Francis Mootz says, in reference to Gadamer on the point of human experience being fundamentally interpretive, 'within legal practice we can understand a binding norm only within a practical context: understanding and application are a unified pact'.[5] Consequently, legal professionals in their actions demonstrate their specific knowledge by way of a 'reflection-in-action'[6] that consists of a

---

[4] G. Pavlakos and S. Coyle, 'Introduction', in S. Coyle and G. Pavlakos (eds), *Jurisprudence or Legal Science? A Debate about the Nature of Legal Theory* (Oxford and Portland, OR: Hart, 2005), pp. 1–13, p. 12.

[5] F. J. Mootz III, 'Foreword to the Symposium on philosophical hermeneutics and critical legal theory', 76 *Chicago-Kent Law Review*, no. 2, 2000, pp. 719–30, p. 721.

[6] D. A. Schön, *The Reflective Practitioner* (New York: Basic Books, 1983), p. 130.

creative interaction with a problem situation. Obviously they then benefit from reflection on what works and what does not. This becomes especially acute when they have to confront the situation in which more than just one response to the problem is possible and/or feasible.

It is here that the topic of practical wisdom or *phronèsis* comes in: namely, the ability to 'see', to determine what might be the best solution under the given circumstances, and to act on it. For the judge, this also means arriving at the decision that does justice to law's demand for coherence. In law, the view intimately connected to *phronèsis* is that professional knowledge is transferred by means of reproduction in the sense of the constant recreation or renewal of a shared background that makes understanding possible, and that all this is done is discursive situations. Before I turn to the Aristotelian source of *phronèsis*, however, a brief excursion into the historical context is appropriate.

Remembrance of Things Past

Because of the inherent combination of facticity and normativity in legal theory and practice, the humanistic study of law should work from that basis, precisely in view of the ongoing process of differentiation of knowledge in law itself (as noted in Chapters 2 and 3), and elsewhere, if we think of new technologies that influence law, discussed in Chapters 12 and 13. And since contemporary literary and language studies themselves are no longer solely rooted in philology, linguistics or literary criticism *per se* but have evolved into broader cultural studies, there is good reason to reflect on interdisciplinary issues pertaining to the bond of theory and practice of the cooperating disciplines, be they of a comparative or a conceptual nature.

Already in the eighteenth century the point was duly noted by Giambattista Vico. This aspect of the humanist tradition in law, however, was unjustly forgotten. Vico propagated a critical attitude in order to preclude the loss of creativity and free thought that the individual should entertain before arriving at judgements. Vico's call for a return to an all-round education, the *enkuklios paideia* as espoused by the ancient Greeks, focuses on the reflective and imaginative qualities of students, and opposes abstract intellectualism because that will stifle the growth of common sense in young people who still have powerful imaginations or *fantasia*.[7] The original act of *fantasia* is the discovery that things have a meaning. It is an act of consciousness that is an essential in the humanities. The Vichean idea of knowledge as the

---

[7] E. Grassi, *Vico and Humanism: Essays on Vico, Heidegger, and Rhetoric* (New York: Peter Lang, 1990), p. ix and pp. 1–17.

result of our human capacity for imaginative understanding also pertains to our having empathic knowledge of other human beings. As such, it is a precursor of the ethical questions that in *Law and Literature* find prominent expression in the works of James Boyd White, Richard Weisberg and Martha Nussbaum. It also has an ethical component, in that it aims at forming the student's ethos for public life, the importance of which has also been argued forcefully by Martha Nussbaum and others in *Law and Literature*.[8] This ethical component of *fantasia* has an uncanny contemporary ring to it. In 2009, for example, Dutch captains of industry complained that young employees with a master's degree fell short when it came to ethical behaviour, and strongly suggested that the universities do something about that. It would seem then that there is indeed nothing new under the sun.

In his oration *De Nostri Temporis Studiorum Ratione*, translated as *On the Study Methods of Our Time*, Vico rejects a one-sided approach that favours the natural sciences above the humanities in education.[9] For the ideas animating this chapter it is also important to note that Vico, in the *Scienza Nuova*, defends the idea of practical knowledge, and postulates the primacy of *ingenium* – literally 'in-sight' – to rational thought.[10] *Ingenium* is the human capacity – and that includes our dispositions and talents – to see what must necessarily be done in a given situation, the excellence of which is also the measure of virtue.[11] This chapter's topic of *phronèsis* is intimately connected to *ingenium*.[12] Furthermore, Vico follows Aristotle when he claims that the deeds of men must be gauged 'by the pliant Lesbic rule, which does not conform bodies to itself, but adjusts itself to their contours', and suggests that prudence and common sense as crucial

[8] For example, M. C. Nussbaum, *Cultivating Humanity: a Classical Defense of Reform in Liberal Education* (Cambridge, MA and London: Harvard University Press, 1997); M. C. Nussbaum, *Not for Profit: Why Democracy Needs the Humanities* (Princeton: Princeton University Press, 2010).

[9] Giambattisto Vico's *De Nostri Temporis Studiorum Ratione, On the Study Methods of Our Time*, is the seventh of a series of inaugural orations, delivered at the start of the academic year in Naples in 1708 as part of what was required of Vico as a Professor of Latin Eloquence, whose duties among others involved helping students achieve the necessary qualifications for the practice of law. The edition used here is G. Vico (trans. E. Gianturco), *On the Study Methods of Our Time* (Ithaca and London: Cornell University Press, 1990). Cf. Vico's remark that 'the greatest drawback of our educational methods is that we pay an excessive amount of attention to the natural sciences and not enough to ethics', p. 33.

[10] T. Goddard Bergin and M. H. Fisch (trans. and eds), *The New Science of Giambattista Vico* (Ithaca and London: Cornell University Press, [3rd edition 1744] 1986).

[11] See also E. Grassi, *Rhetoric as Philosophy: The Humanist Tradition* (University Park and London: The Pennsylvania State University Press, 1980).

[12] Vico, *Study Methods*, p. 34.

to human action work better than abstract science. In other words, the wise man knows when 'to follow a roundabout way whenever he cannot travel in a straight line.'[13] This ties in with the equitable view in and of law, a topic in Chapter 8.

Diachronically, Vico's argument is in accordance with the twentieth-century call in Europe for a renewed contextualisation of knowledge with a focus on the practical rather than the theoretical ratio, as noted in Chapter 3. A remembrance of things past is therefore eminently suitable for the study methods of our time. We are obviously in an inescapable hermeneutic position, because we undertake this recollection from the perspective of hindsight, and hermeneutically speaking we are unable to emigrate from our own historical moment.[14] But that does not mean that we cannot try to do what Aristotle advised: namely, to start 'by wondering that things are as they are',[15] precisely because Vico speaks to contemporary interdisciplinary concerns.

In *On the Study Methods of Our Time*, Vico not only promotes the value of the *litterae humaniores* but he is also highly critical of the Cartesian analytical methodology that insists on its own monistic character, and thereby collapses theoretical clarity and certainty with regard to human knowledge.[16] The jurist who has practical wisdom, in that he combines his knowledge of the geometry of the system of legal rules, *l'esprit de géometrie*, with the ingenuity of *l'esprit de finesse*, as the French philosopher Blaise Pascal called it, therefore personifies Vichean man.[17] In opposition to Descartes, and using a truly interdisciplinary argument, Vico proposes that students should be taught the totality of sciences and arts. As far as the interconnection of disciplines is concerned, with coherence and integrity in the sense of the integration of knowledge and disciplines as the keywords, 'the whole is really the flower of wisdom', Vico's thesis finds a contemporary form in James Boyd

---

[13] Vico, *Study Methods*, p. 35.

[14] F. Kermode, *The Genesis of Secrecy* (Cambridge, MA: Harvard University Press, 1979), p. viii, 'we cannot emigrate from our historical moment'.

[15] Aristotle (trans. W. D. Ross), *Metaphysics* (Oxford: Oxford University Press, 1958) 16, 983a14-15.

[16] The remark that 'Modern philosophical "critique" is the common instrument of all our sciences and arts', and that it claims to supply us 'with a fundamental verity of which we can be certain even when assailed by doubt', is a direct reference to Descartes's *cogito*; see Vico, *Study Methods*, pp. 6 and 9. Descartes obviously held the *litterae humaniores*, and language studies more specifically, in contempt.

[17] See also the translator's note to *Study Methods*, p. xxviii, 'The anti-thesis Vico-Descartes is . . . the contrast between the mentality of the jurist and that of the mathematician, between the spirit of erudition, and that fostered by the "exact" sciences.'

White's view on intellectual integration as making 'a third, a new whole, with a meaning of its own'.[18]

Now that Vico also suggests 'And let them develop skill in debating on either side of any proposed argument',[19] this combined appeal to topical knowledge and practical wisdom presages the premise of *Law and Literature* that imaginative literature ideally produces the value of engagement in reflection. It reflects the idea that literature in the sense of the total of individual literary works is a storehouse of topics and claims of meaning, so that we need this (Erasmian) storehouse of our reading because it provides an ethical-professional *ars topica*.[20] Vico's insistence on 'cultural knowledge as a whole', the appropriate mindset for which is 'the heroic mind',[21] is a return to his claim of unifying the cognitive and creative capacities of the human mind, and, when applied to law, to the necessary connection of reflective thought to contextual understanding and the imagination. Vico promulgates the idea that all our judgements, the aesthetic included, demand such harmony. His exploration of the issue of the choice of authors comes with the claim that reading the best will make you a good reader and writer, one that Benjamin Cardozo drew renewed attention to in the twentieth century. In all, Vico's is a consistent belief that meaningful thought in the humanities joins both the rational and the imaginative figuration of reality with a relational involvement in human beings. In this he is a precursor of important twentieth-century philosophers such as Paul Ricoeur and Emmanuel Levinas, both of whom developed a relational concept of law. This is also why *Law and Literature* could draw a lesson from Vico's consistent emphasis on the integrality of man.

The example of Vico also alerts us to the need for an open view of the relationship between theory and practice in law, because it can help us to move beyond traditionally dominant forms of research in literary-legal studies, in order to rekindle the original desire of interdisciplinary humanist scholarship to have a practical impact. This is to say that methodologi-

---

[18] Vico, *Study Methods*, p. 19; J. B. White, *Justice as Translation* (Chicago: University of Chicago Press, 1990) p. 4. See also J. G. Herder, *Abhandlung über die Sprache*, as cited in R. E. Norton, *Herder's Aesthetics and the European Enlightenment* (Ithaca and London: Cornell University Press, 1991), p. 114, 'I have proven that . . . not the most basic judgment of human reflection is possible without a distinguishing mark: the difference between two things can only be recognized through a third.'

[19] Vico, *Study Methods*, p. 19.

[20] Originating in Aristotle's *The Art of Rhetoric*, the topical approach to law returns in the twentieth-century in T. Viehweg, *Topik und Jurisprudenz* (Munich: Beck, 1954).

[21] G. Vico, *On the Heroic Mind*, oration delivered on 20 October 1732 on the occasion of the opening of the academic year, in G. Tagliacozzo et al. (eds), *Vico and Contemporary Thought* (London: MacMillan Press, 1980), p. 244.

cal premises as well as methodological shifts should be made explicit in interdisciplinary co-operations, especially given the development within the humanities themselves to think more in terms of what Anthony Kronman refers to as the modern research ideal and the culture of political correctness that together have driven questions about the human condition out of the academy.[22] In addition, I would also like to draw attention here to the relationship between practical wisdom and the literary concept of poetic justice. Other than Jon Kertzer, who claims that all justice is poetic justice, although not in the typically legal sense of justice as reward or punishment, but in the sense of its reliance on the moral imagination, I suggest that the legal and the poetic concepts of justice do go together. If poetic justice is about setting things right – in comedy for instance, by uniting the lovers in the final act – then, to me at least, law like justice in both senses of the term aims to design 'temporality to compensate for the pastness of the past'.[23] Compensation for past wrongs, whether in the form of penal retribution, financial compensation or punitive damages, to name but a few examples, all depend on insight into what is right under the circumstances of the past when the facts under consideration occurred, and of the present when the decision has to be made. The importance of the humanities for law is therefore found in their contributions to enhance practical wisdom, remembering the Aristotelian claim that our judgements – whether they are the result of our literary imagination as in the case of judging the Greek tragedies and other literary works, or of our decisions made in the course of legal practice – are directly connected to our humanity because judgement and ethos are intimately connected.[24] Law emphasises this need for attention to the particularity of a specific situation, and its focus is on intersubjectivity and the plurality of viewpoints as a starting point in any legal debate. Legal reasoning, therefore, concerns probabilities, not a priori logical certainties.

[22] A. T. Kronman, *Education's End: Why Our Colleges and Universities Have Given Up on the Meaning of Life* (New Haven and London: Yale University Press, 2007).

[23] J. Kertzer, 'Time's desire: literature and the temporality of justice', 5 *Law, Culture and the Humanities*, 2009, pp. 266–87, p. 267. See also J. Kertzer, *Poetic Justice and Legal Fictions* (Cambridge: Cambridge University Press, 2010).

[24] See K. Eden, *Poetic and Legal Fiction in the Aristotelian Tradition* (Princeton: Princeton University Press, 1986), pp. 4–5, for the notion that the original Aristotelian tradition of law and literature was based on certain common characteristics, such as linguistic-literary methods of proof: that is, that spectators in the theatre and juries at a trial witness with their own eyes what happens, and if the performance is skillful enough, it will provide insight into the 'what' and the 'why'. Eden also analyses the Aristotelian link between the judgement that results from cathartic insight in tragedies and in the (literary) imagination and the human soul (p. 63ff.).

Phronèsis: from Aristotle to Ricoeur

The reason that the distinction between theoretical and practical knowledge matters

The demands of practice and with them the need to do whatever is necessary under the circumstances, Aristotle's προσ τον καίρον (pros ton kairon),[25] in turn, ideally at least, result in the growth of the legal practitioner's *phronèsis* as the application of good judgement to human conduct. This includes the ability to propose changes for the legal system. Knowledge in practical matters such as law is never general, but is always context-dependent and provisional. *Phronèsis* can therefore not be taught in the traditional sense. Practitioners can only acquire it through experience, by gaining insight into the ways in which fields of law develop, and by augmenting their ability to apply such insight to new situations. Furthermore, *phronèsis* is not simply a matter of combining knowledge with technique – it is also specifically a matter of character and morality, a combination of epistemology and ethics. This speaks as well for a continued bond with and input from the humanities.

One might rebut, and say that legal doctrine has focused traditionally on the judge as a model so that with the rise of interdisciplinary studies legal scholarship should grasp the ample opportunities offered in order to dissociate itself from such 'old school' thought. On this basis, one might accuse me of reactionary thinking, and say that I am a celebrant rather than a critic of traditional scholarship. My point, however, is that interdisciplinary studies will die from their own successes if they stick to their self-contained academic discourse and forget that their original lesson to law was aimed at contributing to legal practice. It is precisely here – on the subject of *phronèsis* and otherwise – that the humanities can contribute.

If they do contribute, a caveat is in order, since all discourses impose linguistic and conceptual restrictions on its participants. As humanists, jurists and literary scholars share the written text as their object of inquiry. In literary theory, the single text is the primary object of scholarly research, while the text of literary theory itself is secondary. In law, however, given the interaction of norms and facts, there is always a minimum of two texts that form the primary object of research: the legal rule, or any other substantive text of law, and the narrative construction of the facts. The object of legal theory also includes the text of procedural law, as well as in any given case

---

[25] Aristotle (trans. H. Rackman, ed. J. Henderson), *Nicomachean Ethics* (Cambridge, MA and London: Harvard University Press, [1926] 2003), II.ii.3-5,1104a4-10 (p. 76). In Greek mythology, Kairos is the grandson of the god Chronos. He gives his name to the philosophical term *kairos* in ancient philosophy, referring to the right moment to act.

the text of, for example, the subpoena or the legal brief. Taken together, they guide interpretation.

Furthermore, the text of law is always authoritative to an extent to which the literary text, or the text of literary theory for that matter, cannot aspire. Put differently, the text of law in which human behaviour is captured is one that the jurist helps construct, whereas to the literary scholar, human behaviour as laid down in textual form has been constructed by others. So while the vocabulary used in both disciplinary contexts consists of concepts referring to human behaviour, this does not imply the same hermeneutic freedom nor does it imply the same restrictions. Neither does the literary text aspire to the kind of claims to truth that the legal decision maker builds on in his texts, which are intended to be authoritative. In its freedom of expression, and in a different way, law is more restricted than literature. While both work within a tradition of conventions, law's forms always have as one of their goals the continuity of the discourse and the institution, a restriction that literature does not necessarily have to take into consideration.

When legal theory takes as its goal the application of its interpretive efforts, it does so in order to generate solutions that may be of effective service to legal practice, so that cases may be solved and, as a consequence, law can fulfill its obligation to serve social and societal needs. In literary theory, even though today it has moved beyond philological and literary-linguistic spheres to cultural studies, no comparable, immediate impact on people's lives is the case. As a hermeneutic discipline, law comprises both doctrinal law and hermeneutic methodology. This speaks for an ongoing investigation into the conceptual presuppositions as well as the interpretative strategies in both law and literature, and into the possible ways in which the two can share assumptions, and can penetrate and inform each other.[26]

Carla Spivack pinpoints the heart of the matter when she notes that the methodological questions that arise in the practice of law and literature – namely, that 'lawyers read for the plot', while literary analyses do not necessarily 'take the text at its word about what it says'[27] – also pertain to the methodology of *Law and Literature* research itself, and, more generally, to the very idea of analysing cultural texts, especially those of past cultures. While I think Spivack's definition of legal interpretation is too narrow, her argument that jurists differ from scholars in the humanities when it comes

---

[26] Although sometimes in literature too the distinction is made between literature with aesthetic purposes and literature aimed at influencing society. See Sartre's distinction between 'littérature pure' and 'littérature engagée' in *Qu'est-ce que la littérature?* (Paris: Gallimard, 1948).

[27] C. Spivack, 'Ways of reading', 22 *Law & Literature*, no. 3, 2010, pp. 491–507, p. 495.

to ascertaining to what extent, 'we should take the text at its word for what it is saying' is very much to the point. Legal practitioners are indeed 'trained to take the text at its word because they read it – the case – as a roadmap for actions and consequences'.[28] Such roadmaps are not sought, at least not necessarily, by those working at the academic crossroads. So here is another argument for renewed attention to the ways in which theory and practice are connected in law.

Nevertheless, I would voice a twofold concern. The first is about the tendency of not a few literary scholars of post-modernity to be averse to literary and therefore to linguistic ambiguity when it comes to literary-legal studies. The second is about the tendency by literary and legal scholars alike to maintain an oppositional, dichotomous framework of the 'law is hard and clear' kind versus 'attention to literary narrative can help soften law', as noted in Chapter 3. To me, linguistic ambiguity and its consequences are what legal practitioners deal with in one way or another on a daily basis. It is their core business. If accepted, this premise may offer a way to deal with noted cultural suspicions. If, as I think we should for reasons of law as well as of justice, we cherish poetic faith as an open state of mind and, for judges especially, as a synonym for the prerequisite of impartiality, one that Coleridge called 'that willing suspension of disbelief',[29] the very idea of ambiguity can help form a basis from which to conceive a literary-legal hermeneutics. It would be one that resists thinking in terms of law as the realm of the mono-vocal authoritative voice of the language of legal concepts that are just 'out there', and that cherishes poly-voicedness as well as resistance to the closure while realising at the same time that, as Roman law had it, *lites finiri oportet*, disputes must, at some point in time, be settled.

There is good reason for this as well, given contemporary juridical-political issues. Ino Augsberg, for example, points to the German legal debate where the idea currently in vogue is that 'To be adequately prepared for the challenges of modern society, jurisprudence will have to transform itself from a hermeneutic science of texts into a pragmatic science of actions', with the related claim that 'what we need . . . is a transition from the currently dominant "application-oriented science of interpretation to a law-making-oriented science of actions and decisions"'.[30] To Augsberg, this claim disregards the

---

[28] Spivack, p. 500.

[29] S. T. Coleridge (eds J. Engell and W. Jackson Bate), *Biographia Literaria*, in *The Collected Works of Samuel Taylor Coleridge*, vol. 1 (Princeton: Princeton University Press, 1983), p. 6, 'that willing suspension of disbelief for the moment which constitutes poetic faith'.

[30] I. Augsberg, 'Reading law: on law as a textual phenomenon', 22 *Law & Literature*, no. 3, 2010, pp. 369–93, p. 369.

very concept of a text in law. In his description, the German debate shows an example of a jurisprudence that suffers from an instrumental view on law. This is potentially hazardous in view of the delicate balance in European politics between the rule of law traditionally conceived in democratic societies and the current rise of political parties voicing sentiments aimed at a politics of exclusion. Here as well, a plea for a conception of jurisprudence nourished by a broad range of the humanities as an antidote to more restricted views on text is in order, not least since history has shown that a rule-bound model is often ineffective in situations of international conflict. Transposed to the concrete level of adjudication, this suggests that while theoretical, doctrinal knowledge is obviously a necessary condition for judging, it is not a sufficient one.

This is also why the Aristotelian distinction between *épistèmè* and *phronèsis* is the important linchpin to connect a discussion of the bond of theory and practice in law to the meta-level of the nature of law and legal theory as fields of knowledge. *Épistèmè* pertains to that which is necessarily true because of its universal validity under relevant conditions, such as the law of gravity. *Phronèsis*, in contrast, pertains to what is probable. *Épistèmè* finds its expression in general laws, objective statements, and universally valid principles. It can be put into words, and as such it can, if not always easily, be communicated to others. *Phronèsis* is perceptual knowledge, and it is dispositional in nature. As the capacity to see what the situation demands and to act upon it, it is also a virtue. Furthermore, it is tacit knowledge that can only be learned by doing, because it defies expression by way of logical propositions, and it defies methodological reduction. This has a formidable consequence for reasoning. In the field of theoretical knowledge, argumentation is analytical, aimed at offering linear proof for a specific thesis. In contrast, practical wisdom is characterised by dialectical reasoning aimed at advancing arguments for and against the premise under consideration. It pays homage to the art of persuasion by means of convincing arguments.

In the distinction between theoretical knowledge and practical wisdom, we can also find the root of the problems of translation in interdisciplinary ventures between law and the natural sciences, as noted in Chapter 3. For *phronèsis,* reasoning concerning probabilities is the thing that matters, and it is why we need to reflect on our own theories on theory, so to speak. To reiterate, the formation of accepted knowledge in any field is connected to the articulation of the tension between text and context, logic and experience, premise and result. With this in mind, I now turn to Aristotle's view on *phronèsis* as well as to that of Paul Ricoeur, given the importance that Ricoeur's works have for judicial practice, owing to his insistence on the input of the humanities when it comes to developing judicial *phronetic* intelligence.

Aristotle on phronèsis: *insight into particularities and (dis)similarities necessary to examine human actions*

In the Aristotelian spectrum of the intellectual and moral virtues, *phronèsis* is placed in the category of intellectual virtues. As noted, it is distinguished from *épistèmè*, aimed as that is at 'knowing that'. It is also distinguished from the knowledge of how to make things, the technical skill of the craftsman, which is called art or *technè*, and can relatively easily be taught and learned. Aristotle begins his analysis with a definition of the prudent man, the *phronimos*:

> We may arrive at a definition of Prudence by considering who are the persons we call prudent. Now it is held to be the mark of a prudent man to be able to deliberate well about what is good and advantageous for himself, not in some one department, for instance what is good for his health or strength, but what is advantageous as a means to the good life in general . . . so that the prudent man in general will be the man who is good at deliberating in general. But no one deliberates about things that cannot vary, nor about things not within his power to do. Hence inasmuch as scientific knowledge involves demonstration, whereas things whose fundamental principles are variable are not capable of demonstration, because everything about them is variable, and inasmuch as one cannot deliberate about things that are of necessity, it follows that Prudence is not the same as Science. Nor can it be the same as Art. It is not Science, because matters of conduct admit of variation; and not Art, because doing and making are generically different, since making aims at an end distinct from the act of making, whereas in doing the end cannot be other than the act itself: doing well is in itself the end. It remains therefore that it is a truth-attaining rational quality, concerned with action in relation to things that are good and bad for human beings.[31]

The above demonstrates why *phronèsis* is not just the virtue of knowing the ultimate goals of human beings but also of knowing how to secure them. In other words, the virtue includes the application of good judgement to human conduct, and that is a 'knowing how' rather than a 'knowing that'.[32] As such, it necessarily pertains to the probable in the sense of provisional truths, because whatever theoretical knowledge it incorporates in its reason-

---

[31] Aristotle, *Nicomachean Ethics*, VI.iv.1, 1140a24-29, p.337 and VI. v. 3-4, 1140a32-1140b7 (p. 337). See also A.-H. Chroust (trans.), *Aristotle: Protrepticus; a reconstruction* (Notre Dame, IN: University of Notre Dame Press, 1964), par. 39 and 43. The topic of *phronèsis* is also treated in the *Organon*, the *Eudemian Ethics*, and the *Rhetoric*.

[32] See also G. Ryle, 'Knowing how and knowing that', 46 *Proceedings of the Aristotelian Society*, 1945, pp. 1–16.

ing is always occasioned by the practical aim of action. As the capacity to see what the situation demands and to act upon it, *phronèsis* 'deals with the ultimate particular thing, which cannot be apprehended by Scientific Knowledge, but only by perception.'[33] Its methodology therefore is not deductive. Its main characteristic is deliberation or *bouleusis*, primarily with oneself but always with others as well when transposed to the realm of juridical deliberation.[34] Subsequently, *phronèsis* as a way of reasoning does not aim at arriving at universal truths, but thrives on dialectical reasoning.[35] Its focus is on advancing arguments for and against a specific premise, and weighing or balancing them.

Although categorised as an intellectual virtue, as a virtue in the sense of a dispositional quality that one acquires, for example through instruction or one's education generally, *phronèsis* is nevertheless at the same time a matter of *ethos* or character. It is not a mere combination of knowledge (for example, the knowledge of widely accepted moral rules) and deliberative technique, but rather the ability to apply insight – gained in specific situations, and context-dependent as such insight necessarily is – to new questions as these crop up. Ethics and epistemology thus go hand in hand in *phronèsis* as a *praxis* of concrete action in specific situations, and therefore the critical quality of 'Understanding' answers the imperative quality inherent in and posed by *phronèsis*. To Aristotle, this means that 'its end is a statement of what we ought to do or not to do.'[36] While not identical, understanding and *phronèsis* are about the same objects,[37] as Aristotle points out, because understanding is also about those things that are subjects of questioning and deliberation rather than about the strictly defined, universal givens of scientific knowledge.

---

[33] Aristotle, *Nicomachean Ethics*, VI.viii.9, 1152a27 (p.351).

[34] Aristotle also connects *phronèsis* as Prudence in the general sense, 'Prudence as regards the state . . . Legislative Science' and Prudence as specifically important for the faculty of judging equitably, see Aristotle, *Nicomachean Ethics*, VI.viii.2, 1141b23 (p.347).

[35] For an Aristotelian view on the ideal of the lawyer-statesman who epitomises *phronèsis* in relation to its professional, educational and political consequences, see A. T. Kronman, *The Lost Lawyer: Failing Ideals of the Legal Profession* (Cambridge, MA: Harvard University Press, 1993).

[36] Aristotle, *Nicomachean Ethics*, VI.x.2, 1143a9-10 (p.359).

[37] Aristotle, *Nicomachean Ethics*, VI.x.2, 1143a8 (p.359), 'it [understanding] is concerned with the same objects as Prudence'. Cicero (trans. H. Rackham), *De Finibus Bonorum et Malorum* (Cambridge, MA: Harvard University Press and London: Heinemann, [1914] 1967), Book II, xiii, 40, p. 127, endorses Aristotle's view when he says that 'man, as Aristotle says, was born for two things, thought and action'.

Paul Ricoeur's phronimos

It is precisely this view on *phronèsis* that permeates Paul Ricoeur's perspective on justice and law. It is also constitutive as far as his views on morality and ethics are concerned, as well as his view on equity – the subject of Chapter 8 – as 'the *sense* of justice, when the latter traverses the hardships and conflicts resulting from the application of the *rule* of justice'.[38] This is important to note because of the differences in perspective on the subject throughout Ricoeur's works, and therefore of the philosophical gradations to be discerned and distinguished. In *Oneself as Another*, *phronèsis* is discussed in the ethical realm of deliberation on the good life, so that the emphasis lies on moral judgements in specific and uncertain situations in relation to the ethical aim and goal to be pursued. In *The Just*, the focus is on the relation between the idea of justice conceived as a moral rule and of justice mediated by the institution, which is 'incarnated in the person of the judge, who, as a third party between the two parties, takes on the figure of a second-order third party', so that the concept of justice as 'just distribution'[39] becomes pivotal. As an aside, I might mention that this can be seen clearly in Ricoeur's engagement in *The Just* with John Rawls's *Theory of Justice* and its description of society at the level of the distribution of market- and non-market goods; however, this topic is outside the scope of the present book.

What matters to me here, to start with, is that Ricoeur consistently connects his discussion of the deliberative aspect of *phronèsis* with the idea of the hermeneutic movement, circular as it were, of the 'back-and-forth motion', as he significantly puts it in *Oneself as Another*[40] between the idea that we have about, for example, the good life or justice, and the decision to be made. This ties in neatly with the legal methodology of connecting the facts and the relevant norm, as well as with the above-mentioned tripartite structure of professional practice as diagnosis-classification-response. Ricoeur's view on rule application in the situation of a criminal trial is also apparent when he writes that 'The application consists both in adapting the rule to the case, by way of qualifying the act as a crime, and in connecting the case to the rule, through a narrative description taken to be truthful'.[41]

---

[38] P. Ricoeur (trans. K. Blamey), *Oneself as Another* (Chicago and London: University of Chicago Press, [1990] 1992), p. 262 (italics in the original).

[39] P. Ricoeur (trans. D. Pellauer), *The Just* (Chicago and London: University of Chicago Press, [1995] 2000), pp. iv and xiii.

[40] Ricoeur, *Oneself as Another*, p. 179.

[41] P. Ricoeur (trans. D. Pellauer), *Reflections on the Just* (Chicago and London: University of Chicago Press, [2001] 2007), pp. 55–6.

Ricoeur refers approvingly to the hermeneutic movement of norm and fact when he writes,

> the close tie established by Aristotle between *phronèsis* and *phronimos*, a tie that becomes meaningful only if the man of wise judgement determines at the same time the rule and the case, by grasping the situation in its singularity.[42]

In this view, *phronèsis* is further perceived as an essential component of actual judging. A judge may well be the best there can be as far as her theoretical knowledge of the black letter law of relevant statutes, principles, and precedents is concerned, but if she lacks *phronèsis*, the outcome in the individual case may prove to be unsatisfactory or downright unworkable for the parties involved, and/or others concerned.[43] In Ricoeur's terms, the wise judge is a *phronimos*, a sensitive person who combines attention to the circumstances and insight into the demands of a specific case with the theoretical knowledge that law suggests she should apply. She orients her deliberation at choosing the best of the available legal means in order to translate these into the appropriate action. She possesses 'the aptitude for discerning the right rule, the *orthos logos*, in difficult situations requiring action'.[44]

An example from my Dutch practice serves to illustrate how demanding these requirements are. In 1998, the Dutch Supreme Court ruled that the involuntarily reception of a French kiss fell under Article 242 of the Criminal Code on the subject of statutory rape, on the basis that this act qualified as the unlawful penetration of another person's body.[45] This proved to be problematic, however, not only in terms of conclusive evidence when connecting the fact to the norm but also especially in terms of the judicial sanctioning of such behaviour, which, as most jurists agreed, differs in gravity from a violent and forceful vaginal or anal penetration of another person's body. How, for example, to punish an eighteen-year-old young man who gave a sixteen-year-old girl a French kiss at a school party, a kiss that, only with hindsight perhaps, she would rather have not received? What is going to be the impact of a conviction for rape on his life and career? This is absolutely not to diminish the impact on the victim with regard to what happened; it is simply

---

[42] Ricoeur, *Oneself as Another*, p. 175.

[43] See also Cicero (trans. W. Miller), *De Officiis* (London: Heinemann, 1968), Book I, x, p. 31ff., for the view that the actions of the good man are guided by fundamental principles of justice, such as the classical Roman precept 'that no harm be done to anyone', as much as by contextual aspects that depend on time and place.

[44] Ricoeur, *Reflections*, p. 54.

[45] Hoge Raad (Dutch Supreme Court) 21 April 1998, ECLI:NL:HR:1998:ZD1026.

to give a cautious example of interpretation and qualification. And from yet another perspective, how are judges to explain and justify to the general audience that an act may well be called rape and yet not deserve incarceration? In 2013, the Supreme Court therefore reconsidered its 1998 decision and ruled that the demand for legal certainty did not stand in the way of disqualifying the French kiss as rape.[46] This change of mind, however, caused great confusion and uncertainty in the legal profession because the Supreme Court still defined the French kiss as 'the penetration of the body with sexual intent', with the result that the qualification of such specific human behaviour was still uncertain. Again the Supreme Court had to reconsider. Finally, it ruled that the French kiss does not provide grounds for the qualification of rape.[47]

Furthermore, *phronèsis* as an actual form of reflective human judgement is also a form of self-reflection and therefore self-knowledge, since good reasons for a person's specific decision unfold, and subsequently legitimise why in a particular situation this rather than that is what is required under these circumstances. In the sphere of the juridical, self-reflection is therefore always a constitutive element required of the judicial *habitus*. This is already beautifully exemplified in the iconography of the virtue of Prudentia herself. When Giotto painted her in 1306 in a fresco in the Scrovegni chapel in Padua, he depicted her holding a mirror up to herself to indicate that the wise person knows it is essential to look deeply into herself and to know herself.

What makes Ricoeur's perspective especially attractive from a point of view of humanistic legal studies is not only that it is embedded in the literary tradition, canonical as we now perhaps critically perceive it, starting with the Greek dramatists Sophocles and Euripides, but also that Ricoeur consistently argues that the particularity of the exemplary 'profiles of virtue' we find there invites rereading and rewriting in the sense of adapting what they teach us for our contemporary situation.[48] A fine example is Ricoeur's analysis of Sophocles' *Antigone*,[49] in which *phronèsis* is the lens through which to view tragic conflict on the plane of the political when it comes to just distribution. If we combine this with what Ricoeur calls analogy at the level of forming

---

[46] Hoge Raad 12 March 2013, ECLI:NL:HR:2013:BZ2653. European decisions that have a European Case Law Identifier (ECLI) can be accessed via the European e-justice portal <e-justice.europa.eu>.

[47] Hoge Raad 26 November 2013, ECLI:NL:HR:2013:1431.

[48] Ricoeur, *Reflections*, p. 54.

[49] Ricoeur, *Oneself as Another*, pp. 240–96. Adaptations of *Antigone* are J. Anouilh, *Antigone* (1944); B. Brecht, *Antigone* (1977); F. Ost, *Antigone Voilée* (2004) and K. Shamsie, *Home Fire*. Adaptations of Aeschylus's *Oresteia* are G. Ernst, *Blutbad* (1990); Y. Farber, *Molora* (2008) and C. Tóibín, *House of Names* (2017).

judgements and making decisions in spheres like the juridical, that 'imprint praxis with a tragic stamp',[50] the need to develop our understanding of the close tie between the particular and *phronèsis* becomes acute. The next chapter therefore examines how augmenting our insight into metaphor contributes to this understanding.

That Depends

To conclude the current chapter, one more aspect of the reciprocity of theory and practice deserves to be highlighted. It is the epistemological question hovering in the background on the subject of categorisation and conceptualisation of knowledge in law – that is to say, the status of knowledge as compared or opposed to beliefs, opinions or accumulated ideas. Most importantly, given the way in which facts have a place in law, the question is whether facts can be thought of as objects or simply as the way things just are.[51] And, one step further, the next question concerns how we can recognise epistemological issues dominant in the one discipline and integrate them with those of the other discipline without the fundamental philosophical despair with regard to whether or not we can at all know propositions about the world around us, cognitively burdened as we are by our disciplinary conceptual frameworks, and prone as we are to the cognitive dissonances resulting from them. These questions are as important as they are difficult. But that does not mean that we do not have to try and question our cultural, disciplinary and professional assumptions.

One lens with which to view these assumptions can be found in another definition of theory and its uses as offered in the idea of '*interdisciplinary cultural analysis*' proffered by Jonathan Culler, Mieke Bal and others.[52] Culler's claim is that theory is the name for

> the unbounded corpus of works 'that succeed in challenging and reorient-
> ing thinking in domains other than those to which they ostensibly belong
> because their analyses of language, mind, history, or culture offer novel and
> persuasive accounts of signification, make strange the familiar and perhaps

---

[50] Ricoeur, *Reflections*, p. 57. Cf. C. Michelon, 'Practical wisdom in legal decision-making', in A. Amaya and H. Hock Lai (eds), *Law, Virtue and Justice* (Oxford and Portland, OR: Hart Publishing, 2013), pp. 29–49.

[51] See M. Wood, *Literature and the Taste of Knowledge* (Cambridge: Cambridge University Press, 2005); B. Vermeule, *Why Do We Care About Literary Characters?* (Baltimore: Johns Hopkins University Press, 2010); G. Currie, *Narratives & Narrators: A Philosophy of Stories* (Oxford: Oxford University Press, 2010).

[52] M. Bal, 'Legal Lust: literary litigations', 15 *Australian Feminist Law Journal*, 2001, pp. 1–22, p. 5 (italics in the original).

persuade readers to conceive of their own thinking and the institutions to which it relates in new ways'.[53]

Here is both an intellectual challenge and a litmus test for the success of interdisciplinary fields. What is it in my field that may interest others from outside, and in what ways does that invite me to rethink my own cognitions and discursive idiosyncrasies? What is more, the conjoined view that 'theory is, to some extent at least, to be defined in terms of practical effects: as what changes people's views, makes them conceive of their objects of study and their activity of studying differently'[54] opens up the possibility of probing issues concerning the bond between theory and practice as sketched above. The issues are both in law and its interdisciplinary partners, precisely because theory so conceived is no longer exclusively *épistèmè* – blocks of knowledge easily conveyed in an unadulterated form – but is part of *phronèsis* as the activity of studying discourses and their interrelations in order to learn a new way of perception. The days of the relatively calm possession of theory in late modernity and early post-modernity are definitely over.

Central to all this remains the question of whether objectivity is at all possible when, as is the case in the humanities, the human is both the object and the subject of our inquiries. Can the ultimate premise of any scholarly research be grounded scientifically, or is interpretation our only key to valuation? The critical question then is whether a view on law grounded on *phronèsis* does not open the door to legal, moral, or cultural relativism of the anything-goes type. A focus on *phronèsis,* on the prudence in the term jurisprudence, however, does not insist on a lack of evaluative standards but merely on the impossibility of abstract, a priori standards claimed to be valid irrespective of time and place. In short, it rejects the standards that are cherished by those who aim to build legal science solely as *épistèmè*, such as a variety of legal positivists. Or, viewed the other way around, as Pavlakos puts it, '*Prudentia* understands legal practice as a genuinely practical activity in which the members of a legal community synthesise the law through a combination of fact and value.'[55] Today's contextualist thus always reasons in terms of 'that depends'.[56] Nevertheless, a contextual approach does not invalidate the idea

---

[53] J. Culler, 'What's the point?', in M. Bal and I. E. Boer (eds), *The Point of Theory: Practices of Cultural Analysis* (Amsterdam: Amsterdam University Press, 1994), pp. 13–17, p. 13.

[54] Ibid.

[55] G. Pavlakos, 'Normative knowledge and the nature of law', in S. Coyle and G. Pavlakos (eds), *Jurisprudence or Legal Science?* (Oxford and Portland, OR: Hart Publishing, 2005), pp. 89 and 101.

[56] See M. Blaauw (ed.), 'Introduction: epistemological contextualism', 69 *Grazer Philosophische Studien: Internationale Zeitschrift für analytische Philosophie*, 2005, pp. i–xvi.

of standards; it finds them in 'law in context' itself. Contexts do not spring into existence *ex nihilo*, but are themselves the products of socio-historical circumstances and interpretive frameworks. And this is the reason that the interdisciplinary humanistic study of law should also be a *praxis*, a lived, integrated practice.

I conclude this chapter with a metaphor. Recalling Thomas Aquinas's definition of beauty can help form a threshold test for our conversation on how to unite practice and theory as well as for a further discussion of the role of *phronèsis*, because it is highly appropriate as an evaluative and aspirative criterion. Aquinas wrote, '*Ad pulchritudinem tria requiruntur . . . integritas . . . consonantia . . . claritas*';[57] for something to be called beautiful, three things are necessary: integrity, coherence and clarity. I suggest that, keeping in mind the notion of integrity as wholeness, we have an excellent guideline in order to pursue not only an integral view on our subject in the sense of an all-encompassing, well-rounded one but also one that is intellectually sound and unbiased. Consonance or coherence then adds to integrity the idea and ideal of a harmonious whole, with, minimally, an internal consistency as the result of a dialectical process of the kind favoured in the humanities. If *Law and Literature* is to thrive, we will need to make it organically sound and coherent, and structurally a whole that is integrative and intellectually sincere and conscientious. Only then might it stand a chance of bringing to full fruition – literally and figuratively – the luminous ideas that gave rise to it in the first place. Only then can it be truly interdisciplinary as far as intellectual integration is concerned. While clarity for Descartes meant theoretical and methodological certainty, clarity in the definition used here refers not only to the idea of something being clear, intellectually and perceptually, but also to that of being radiant, when what really matters to us comes into focus, and inspires and guides our actions.

It is therefore important to pay careful heed to the continuity in the history of ideas from Aristotle to Aquinas and from Vico to twentieth-century phenomenological philosophical hermeneutics. Hans-Georg Gadamer approvingly cites Vico's *De Nostri Temporis Studiorum Ratione* as his source for 'the human sciences' mode of knowledge',[58] and shows the importance of Vico's grasp of *phronèsis* for the act of judging. For Gadamer, in order to accomplish the evaluation of facts and norms needed when reaching a decision, the judge must have a sense of whether her evaluation is in keeping with everything else that she has. This is crucial when it comes to viewing the

---

[57] Thomas Aquinas, *Summa Theologica*, vol. 1 (Westminster, MD: Christian Classics, 1948), Part Ia, question 39, response 8, p. 201.
[58] H.-G. Gadamer, *Truth and Method* (London: Stagbooks, 2001), p. 19.

outcome as a coherent whole. To arrive at the correct judgement at the level of an individual case, the general principles of law and the legal rules must of course be applied, not rigidly and with the sole aim of arriving at subsuming the particular under the general, but always in such a way that the judgement in terms of what the law demands in the theoretical sense of law in the books is supplemented by what the circumstances of the case demand from us. In this way as well, each new judgement is a contribution to the further development of what comprises the law, and for this reason the continued need exists for *Bildung* and an engagement in action in legal practice itself.

7

Metaphor and (Dis)belief

The Metaphoric Spark

My next building block for a humanistic model of doing law is insight into metaphor. Seeing similarities and dissimilarities in a particular situation is what *phronèsis* and metaphorical insight hold in common. Ricoeur emphasises that 'la métaphore vive' or 'the rule of metaphor',[1] when viewed as a combined process of cognition and imagination, is essential for judgement. It ties aspects of *phronetic* intelligence to 'the semantic role of imagination (and by implication, feeling) in the establishment of metaphorical sense'.[2] Here, too, Ricoeur turns to Aristotle, who denotes metaphor as, 'the application of a word that belongs to another thing: either from genus to species, species to genus, species to species, or by analogy'.[3] Ricoeur shares Aristotle's interest in the semantic gain of metaphor as a dynamic process: that is, ' "to metaphorize well" is "to see *resemblance*" '.[4] Ricoeur argues for the assessment of the role of the imagination, for 'it is in the *work of resemblance* that a pictorial or iconic moment is implied, as Aristotle suggests when he says that to make good metaphors is to contemplate similarities or . . . to have an insight into likeness'.[5] Etymologically, μετα φερειν (*meta pherein*) means 'to carry beyond'. In the figure of metaphor, this means beyond descriptive language.

Precisely because there is semantic gain in a successful metaphor, we

---

[1] P. Ricoeur (trans. R. Czerny, K. Mclaughlin and J. Costello), *The Rule of Metaphor: Multidisciplinary Studies in the Creation of Meaning in Language* (Routledge: London, [1975] 1986). The English translation of the title seems to favour the normative aspect at the expense of the literal vivacity of metaphor prominent in the French title.

[2] P. Ricoeur, 'The metaphorical process as cognition, imagination, and feeling', *Critical Inquiry*, 1978, pp. 143–59, p. 144.

[3] Aristotle (trans. S. Halliwell), *Poetics* (Cambridge, MA and London: Harvard University Press, 1999), 21, 1457b7-9 (p. 105), and Aristotle (trans. J. H. Freese), *The Art of Rhetoric* (Cambridge, MA, and London: Harvard University Press, 2006), 1405a3ff (p. 355).

[4] Ricoeur, *Rule of Metaphor*, p. 23.

[5] Ricoeur, 'Metaphorical Process', p. 145 (italics in the original).

should develop our ability to understand how resemblance works in the creation of meaning. The premise that insight into the metaphorical is essentially a contemplation of similarities leads not only to the requirement of insight into what is deemed a likeness but also, and more importantly, for what reasons. What matters then is the *lexis* of a text: that is, *how* something is said as compared to *what* is said (the *logos* of a text).

This distinction had already been made in Plato's *Republic*.[6] Vico connected it to the bond linking poetry with law and jurisprudence.[7] In *Law and Literature*, it is re-emphasised in the axis initiated on the basis of Cardozo's claim that legal professionals need to develop a linguistic antenna sensitive to peculiarities beyond the level of the signifier, because the form and content, the 'how' and the 'what' of a text, are interconnected. To Ricoeur, this bond means that there is a strong '*picturing function* of metaphorical meaning'.[8] Think, for example, of Cardozo's opinion in *Hynes v. New York Central Railroad Co.* (231 N.Y. 229, 131 N.E. 898 [1921]), and of Lord Denning's sketch of rural England as the decisive factor in *Miller v. Jackson* ([1977] 1 QB 966), although the jury is still out on the effect of Lord Denning's metaphors. A successful metaphorical performance makes us say, literally and figuratively, and without double-entendre, 'Oh, but now I *see*'. This can be fruitfully connected to *phronèsis*. Firstly, *phronèsis* and metaphor necessitate the ability to see similarities and dissimilarities in a particular situation. Secondly, because *phronèsis* implies the *phronimos*' professionally trained intuition of 'knowing by doing', it immediately perceives what matters in a given situation.[9]

This connection is clearly apparent in the scheme that Ricoeur offers to elaborate on the combination of metaphor and imagination. Its first step is to ask us to understand imagination as the insight that metaphor offers when it asks us to contemplate resemblance. This insight is both cognitive and perceptual when the imagination is viewed as the 'ability to produce new kinds by assimilation and to produce them not above the differences, as in

---

[6] See S. Halliwell, 'Diegesis-mimesis', in P. Hühn et al. (eds), *The Living Handbook of Narratology* (Hamburg: Hamburg University), available at <http://www.lhn.uni-hamburg. de/article/diegesis-mimesis> [last accessed 20 January 2017].

[7] See T. I. Bayer, 'Vico's principle of senus communis and forensic eloquence', 83 *Chicago-Kent Law Review*, 2008, pp. 1131–55, p. 1154, for Vico's view in the *Scienza Nuova* that Roman law and the jurisprudence of the ancients generally was '*una severa Poesia*'. See also H. Arendt, *The Life of the Mind* (New York, Harcourt: 1981), for imagination and metaphor in relation to thought on the view that metaphor connects thinking and poetry.

[8] Ricoeur, 'Metaphorical process', p. 144.

[9] Ricoeur, *Rule of Metaphor*, p. 6 (italics mine), '"To metaphorize well", said Aristotle, "implies an *intuitive* perception of the similarity in dissimilars"'.

the concept, but *in spite of and through* the differences',[10] also as an antidote to the initially anamorphic effect of metaphor. What matters then is the *phronètic* combination of thinking – in judicial *phronèsis* that obviously includes recognising the relevant legal aspects – and then understanding by grasping the particularity of the new situation that metaphor suggests.

The second step is that of incorporating the pictorial dimension of the imagination. Both *phronèsis* and metaphor depend on our capability to see what precisely this specific thing is that connects that which we already know to the new significance of the particular that we have discerned. This is the productive step from the semantics of metaphor to our literally figuring out what the new thing is. It is the moment that the ordinary reference of a word is abolished in favour of the new meaning produced by the metaphor. This requires not only imagination but – in order to preclude jumping to conclusions about the legal meaning of it all, both new and old – also Coleridgean poetic faith, and what John Keats called 'negative capability'.[11] A small disclaimer is perhaps in order here. Despite my avowed avoidance of Romanticism, I nonetheless offer poetic faith and negative capability as a metaphor for what it means to write – and to be – a great work of literary art, because it draws the attention to a quality that is normative for the way in which jurists should treat their materials: impartially, with full attention to the different aspects of a case, and without the inclination to arrive hastily at a final stand. The ability to be in uncertainties resembles an ideal judge's being open to contingency and ambiguity. Methodologically, the suspension of judgement – or ἐποχή, *epoché* in Greek philosophy – is normative for the legal profession. In the sense claimed here, it also points to an articulation of the conjunction in *Law and Literature*.

Ricoeur's third step is the final move to the cognitive import of metaphor. This combination of the cognitive and the imaginative also ties in with the division of knowledge in *épistèmè* and *phronèsis* in that it highlights the critical element of judicial *phronèsis*. The judge's imagination enables her to see what ties the singular situation of the case before her to the existing framework of law. At the same time, it asks her to determine which aspect of the singular situation calls for an adjustment in the application of the normative framework, an 'unforeseen reading' as it were, brought about by 'the

---

[10] Ricoeur, 'Metaphorical process', pp. 147–8 (italics mine).

[11] S. T. Coleridge (eds J. Engell and W. Jackson Bate), *Biographia Literaria*, in *The Collected Works of Samuel Taylor Coleridge*, vol. 1 (Princeton: Princeton University Press, 1983), p. 6; J. Keats, 'Letter of 21 December 1817 to his brothers George and Thomas', in M. H. Abrams et al. (eds), *The Norton Anthology of English Literature*, vol. 2, 1974, p. 705, 'that is when man is capable of being in uncertainties'.

metaphoric spark',[12] however slight this adjustment may be in the case before her. *Phronèsis* thus enables the judge to bridge the gap between the generality of the legal rule and the particular of the situation. Here is a connection to the right discrimination of the equitable in law.

The pictorial or iconic moment cannot do without interpretation of whatever meaning is already in existence and accepted, and of the new meaning suggested in and by the metaphor. This too demands insightful creativity. As Ricoeur points out, metaphor is 'a commerce between thoughts, that is, a transaction between contexts', so that 'metaphor holds together within one simple meaning two different missing parts of different contexts of this meaning'.[13] It is in this way that 'the metaphoric spark' is central in Ricoeur's hermeneutics, the goal of which is to bring about an understanding of what it is that we do when we interpret, and what that means for us as human beings endowed as we are with both reason and feeling.[14] The traditionally favoured view that interpretation is merely the act of decoding the codified rule falls short as an interpretive strategy. Ricoeur's view is thus ontological as well as epistemological. Other than what many jurists long thought – and some still do – 'The real problem . . . is not so much "what is a metaphor?" as "What is a literal statement?"'[15]

When Ricoeur states that metaphor 'implies an intuitive perception of the similarity in dissimilars', he stands firmly in the Aristotelean tradition.[16] Obviously, such imaginative perception needs to be tested. Yet in my view, the very concept of this quality of perception is linked to the imagination as it is conceived in the continental European hermeneutic tradition, in the sense attributed to it by Immanuel Kant in his *Critique of Judgment* (1790): for example, as *Einbildungskraft* or *imaginatio*. And why is this the case? It is because Kantian imagination is linked with the idea of metaphor as the connection or linchpin between two fields of meaning. Through the individual's imagination, the texts she reads are recognised in their similarities, and these similarities are subsequently translated into specific images, mental pictures, and, finally, into a reflective judgement. Thus, it augments the other Kantian idea, also found in the *Critique of Judgment*, of judgement as the application of common sense, *sensus communis*: namely, the result of

---

[12] J. M. Coetzee, *Diary of a Bad Year* (New York: Viking, 2008), p. 23, 'the metaphoric spark is always one jump ahead of the decoding function, where another, unforeseen reading is always possible'.

[13] Ricoeur, *Rule of Metaphor*, p. 80.

[14] Ricoeur, *Rule of Metaphor*, pp. 173–215.

[15] E. H. Gombrich, *Symbolic Images* (Oxford: Phaidon Press, 1972), p. 166.

[16] Ricoeur, *Rule of Metaphor*, p. 23.

a dynamic growth over time in a specific setting in which specific meanings are held in common.

As transported to a legal context, the metaphorical contemplation of (dis) similarities adds something new to the reservoir of accepted meanings, and can help provide insight into the jurisprudential development of the rule of law in common law as well as in civil law jurisdictions. I say this not least because Ricoeur also suggests that 'to understand a story is to understand both the language of "doing something" and the cultural tradition from which proceeds the typology of plots'.[17] What is more, Aristotle's treatment of metaphor in two domains – poetics and rhetoric – as a linchpin so to speak between them connects metaphor to the enthymeme as the figure of speech in rhetoric that persuades by means of what is contingent or usually the case in a specific setting. Both start from what is probable in a given situation. The performative aspect of metaphor and enthymeme can therefore not be understood without insight into the cultural-specific locus of their production and their import with regard to the story they tell. Chapters 9 and 10 address in more detail the topic of narrative and plot in law and literature. What matters to me here is that if we translate Ricoeur's work into a legal typology and setting, this idea of the cultural tradition suggests that the concept of understanding the story or narrative – and metaphor is a mini-narrative – would include its procedural aspects as well as the evidentiary settings in specific jurisdictions.

Metaphor in Action in Law

Understanding the way in which legal categories and concepts are coined and developed by means of such comparisons is but one example of where a perceptive attitude is crucial. Given the reciprocal relation between theory and practice in law, I think it justified to suggest that insight into the ways in which metaphor works is important in the formation of legal concepts, for the development of legal doctrine, and for success in legal practice.[18] Therefore, we should consider carefully the way in which the rule of metaphor works, because the introduction of a new metaphor in a specific field entails the generation of new meanings, along with new interpretive challenges: for example, when the metaphor of 'the ship of state' is introduced in public law, 'the neighbour principle' in tort law, not to mention 'the man on

---

[17] P. Ricoeur (trans. K. McLaughlin and D. Pellauer), *Time and Narrative* (Chicago: University of Chicago Press (vol. 1) 1984, (vol. 2) 1985, (vol. 3) 1988), vol.1, p. 57.

[18] Ricoeur, 'Metaphorical process', p. 149, where he refers to 'the fundamental metaphoricity of thought to the extent that the figure of speech that we call "metaphor" allows us to glance at the general procedure by which we produce concepts'.

the Clapham omnibus', or 'the bad man' as in Oliver Wendell Holmes Jun.'s theory of law.

What is more, it is precisely because the need for intuition in both *phronèsis* and metaphorical insight is one for an informed intuition that the hermeneutic project is so important for law. Ricoeur's proposal is that we accept a structural analogy between the imaginative and the cognitive elements of the process of dealing with metaphor. In other words, new meanings are generated by means of the introduction of a new metaphor in a specific field, or by taking a metaphor from one field to another. And as a side effect, the original meaning may be suppressed, even if that is only for a time, or in a specific context, given that meaning in law is dynamic, never static; after all, Supreme Courts can also change their minds. All this should be done against the background of the local knowledge of a specific legal system and a specific legal practice, for we need to ground our research in concrete circumstances if we are to understand this research as 'an inquiry into the capacity of metaphor to provide untranslatable information and, accordingly, into metaphor's claim to yield some true insight about reality'.[19]

Allow me to give just one example from Dutch criminal law on the development of the concept of theft. Article 310 of the Dutch Criminal Code reads,

> A person who removes any property belonging in whole or in part to another, with the object of unlawfully appropriating it, is guilty of theft and liable to a term of imprisonment of not more than four years or a fine of the fourth category.[20]

Originally, the concept of property was understood to refer only to tangible objects. In 1921, however, the Dutch Supreme Court ruled that electricity, intangible as it is, could also be viewed as property because it has an economic value. In 2012, the Court had to decide the question of whether or not a digital amulet and a mask in the online computer game Runescape were also objects that could be unlawfully appropriated under the provision of Article 310.[21] The facts of the case were simple. A boy who was very wealthy in terms of Runescape paraphernalia had been threatened by another boy into giving him the data from his Runescape account, allowing the coercive boy to transfer the digital amulet and mask to his own account. The Court ruled that the virtual character of the objects under consideration had real value for

[19] Ricoeur, 'Metaphorical process', p. 143.
[20] See L. Rayar et al. (trans.), *The American Series of Foreign Penal Codes: The Dutch Penal Code* (Littleton: Fred Rothman & Co., 1997).
[21] Hoge Raad 31 January 2012, ECLI:NL:HR:2012:BQ9251.

game players, and that these objects were the fruits of a prolonged investment of time in the game. Thus, digital objects were included in the concept of property.[22]

So, metaphor can have a heuristic function for law: 'seeing as' – both a *what* and a *how* – enables us to see before our eyes potentialities as actualities. In view of these metaphorically based mini-narratives concerning the status of digital objects, it becomes obvious that judges must have a pre-understanding of the way in which specific forms of human action usually take place in the world as we know it. It is this contingency that forms the basis of metaphorical, probable argument. Ricoeur calls this a form of pre-understanding that is necessarily based on '*the pre-narrative quality of human experience*'.[23] Insight into the specifics of any given context is everything, for as Ricoeur claims,

> it is always against the background of ordinary language, of conventional meanings, that there is a breakthrough of metaphorical language . . . when we enter in the problematic either of metaphor or narrative, there is already a background. There is, in the case of narrative, an experience of action, of what a human action is, and how it has been already recounted by previous stories, and then we retell in a new way what has been told already in a certain way.[24]

Besides judicial imagination, this also requires attention to the fact that judicial pre-understanding is itself always informed by other cultural as well as professional narratives on what people, judges included, usually do, and on what may be good reasons for specific decisions. Chapter 8 elaborates on Ricoeur's view on *mimēsis* that incorporates such pre-understanding. What this means for a legal narratology is a topic addressed in Chapter 10. The point is also noted in cultural studies. Mieke Bal, for example, argues that it makes sense to think about the idea of theory in terms of metaphor. She wants us to ask in what way a theoretical concept is imbued by metaphor – for example, the concept of rape. I suggest that one has only to think of the value-laden concept of terrorism during these past decades, the ambiguity

---

[22] See J. C. Rideout, 'Penumbral thinking revisited: metaphor in legal argumentation', 7 *Journal of the Association of Legal Writing Directors*, 2010, pp. 155–91, for relevant common law examples. On the visual, see R. Moran, 'Seeing and believing: metaphor, image, and force', 16 *Critical Inquiry*, 1989, pp. 87–112.

[23] P. Ricoeur, 'Life: a story in search of a narrator', in M. C. Doeser and J. N. Kraaij (eds), *Facts and Values* (Dordrecht and Boston: Martinus Nijhoff Publishers, 1987), pp. 121–32, p. 129 (italics in the original).

[24] See C. E. Reagan, 'Interview with Paul Ricoeur', in C. E. Reagan, *Paul Ricoeur: His Life and His Work* (Chicago: University of Chicago Press, 1996), pp. 100–9, p. 106.

of which often leads to heated debates on legal precision or the lack of it in international humanitarian law without probing its narrative, be it implicit or explicit. So metaphor can indeed function as a 'searchlight . . . to specify, analyze, get an eye for differences'.[25]

This speaks for continued attention to metaphor, especially when we assign prominence to the metaphorical element of legal concepts in our literary-legal research, not just when dealing with concepts within a legal system but more so when we have to deal, as is the case today in Europe and elsewhere, with aspects of supranational and international law, and therefore also with comparative aspects of law and legal theory. Global developments in, for example, new technologies of the digital age only increase this need. Furthermore, think of the cultural differences that exist between the various member states of the European Union, and that find their way into national legal concepts that subsequently have to be 'translated' – the Latin root, the verb *trans ferre,* like metaphor, means 'to carry beyond' – if they need to function and be dealt with at the European level: that is to say, cultural differences informing the cognitive load of such concepts as 'right' when concepts are rendered into the official languages of the EU, or when they become the subject of legal debate in the European Court of Justice in Luxembourg or the European Court of Human Rights in Strasbourg. Semantic ambiguity often crops up in the official texts of the European Convention on Human Rights: for instance, in the immensely important Article 6, the right to fair trial, in the only two authentic languages, English and French. In English, it reads, 'everyone is entitled to a fair and public hearing', but the French text has, '*toute personne a droit*'. So, we have 'entitled' in English and the French idea that 'everyone has a right'. Not only are these concepts dissimilar as far as the place in their legal systems are concerned, they are also culturally dissimilar in that the idea of a legal right in French thought is deeply connected to the history of the demise of the *Ancien Régime* and the French Revolution, as compared to the United Kingdom's long tradition of an unwritten constitution.

All this is even more pertinent for those member states whose languages have not gained official status but that must nevertheless feel included in the European project. At the time of this writing, the European Union has 28 member states, although the *Brexit* procedure is in full swing. They all have specific national legal systems and concomitant frames of thought. For this reason, whenever a member state submits a proposal for new supranational

---

[25] M. Bal, 'Scared to death', in M. Bal and I. E. Boer (eds), *The Point of Theory: Practices of Cultural Analysis* (Amsterdam: Amsterdam University Press, 1994), pp. 32–47, p. 40.

legislation, it does so inescapably from its own context. And what if member states work together to propose new legislation? How can they translate and reconcile their own specific modes of thought? An illustrative example is the way in which Canada's two official languages that theoretically enjoy the same status as a language of the law get on in practice. In *Justice as Translation*, James Boyd White refers to a 1971 study by the Canadian Royal Commission on Bilingualism and Biculturalism that showed the many problems the legislator had to confront.[26] Should new legislation be drafted in one of the official languages and then translated into the other? Or should it be framed in both languages at the same time? The practice at the time was to draft new legislation in English and then have it translated into French. The trouble was not only that the translators in the civil service lacked any specific legal expertise but also that cultural differences proved to be insurmountable. As a result, the French official text was often incomprehensible to French-Canadian lawyers. In the words of the report,

> The way an Englishman likes to develop an idea bears scarcely any resemblance to the way a Frenchman would do it. The mentality, turn of mind, and method are different. One may thoroughly grasp the idea of law as expressed in one language, and yet be unable to translate it properly into the other. Unless the two languages have a common genius and the intellectual processes of both peoples are identical, any attempt at translation is vain if it is not preceded by a complete dissimilation of the legal idea to be transplanted.[27]

Comparable issues can be found in the interpretive debates on the scope of the concept of 'family life' under Articles 8 and 12 of the European Convention on Human Rights. Family life includes a variety of human relations, inside and outside the traditionally conceived marriage bond. Conservative definitions of marriage and family as found in the Irish Constitution, for example, or Italy's failure to recognise same-sex unions therefore provoked legal disputes, and showed that having political agreement to be a Union is not enough.[28] Think also of those wanting to join such a Union. In Ismael Kadare's novel *Spring Flowers, Spring Frost*, we read how at the end of the twentieth century

---

[26] J. B. White, *Justice as Translation* (Chicago: University of Chicago Press, 1990), pp. 241–4; C.-A. Sheppard, *The Law of Languages in Canada: Studies of the Royal Commission on Bilingualism and Biculturalism*, no. 11 (Ottawa: Information Canada, Queens Printer, 1971).

[27] Sheppard, *The Law of Languages*, p. 114.

[28] For example, *Johnston and others v. Ireland*, European Court of Human Rights 18 December 1986, [1986] ECHR 17, 9697/82; *Keegan v. Ireland*, 18 EHRR 342 [1994].

traditional Albanian customary law known as the Kanun became a subject of interest to the Helsinki Committee and the International Criminal Court in The Hague. This interest was because of the Kanun's provisions on blood feuds, a subject that was neither officially acknowledged in the Albanian legal system nor incorporated into its penal code, on account of there being a memorandum from the Council of Europe denouncing blood feud. In short, we suffer an inexhaustibility of contextual differences. This is all the more reason never to stop investigating them, and to continue our research into the literary works of a legal era to help inform our views on legal concepts. To jurists, therefore, attention to (dis)similarities and metaphor always matters.

Given the history of ideas of interdisciplinarity, a historical approach is indispensable, not least because, as a result of this process of differentiation of disciplines, concepts long held in common began their separate disciplinary tracts. This approach could be nourished by input from comparative literary studies: for example, on the subject of how the literary representation of legal concepts in the genre of the *Bildungsroman* or the realist novel of the nineteenth century generally has taken place, and what such development means for the culture of law. In this respect, I suggest that in view of the concept of family life noted above, a detailed study of family relations in the novel would be called for to help provide a background for current societal issues. If this project were undertaken in a broader international setting, we would also gain much more insight into the differences between the common law and the civil law approaches to such concepts.[29] Since proposals for standards with respect to significant research and its valorisation are the order of the day in academia – and precisely because it differs from armchair theorising remote from social realities – it could also stand a fair chance of being accepted as having the kind of 'impact' that humanities research supposedly needs more of.

Now, one might argue that a judge has no need of metaphorical insight because her analytical and logical competences not only prevail but suffice, and, furthermore, that incorporating metaphor easily leads easily to category mistakes and/or forbidden usage of analogy, precluded as that is in criminal law. In defence of resemblance as the guiding feature, Ricoeur refutes the accusation of logical weakness by pointing to the structure of the similar itself, because 'in the metaphorical statement "the similar" is perceived *despite* difference, *in spite of* contradiction'.[30] As a result, resemblance brings near what was initially perceived as being distant and different. In terms of a lan-

---

[29] See M. Williams, 'Socio-legal studies and the humanities – law, interdisciplinarity and integrity', 5 *International Journal of Law in Context*, no. 3, 2009, pp. 243–61.

[30] Ricoeur, *Rule of Metaphor*, p. 196.

guage strategy, metaphor breaks down established logical structures in order to build new ones, because that is what is required to be able to see things anew. This is not a deviation but is basically the same operation by means of which any classification of concepts into categories takes place.[31]

Metaphor's impact on our way of looking at the world therefore deserves our careful consideration, not least since, firstly, all language runs the risk of becoming cliché. As Ralph Emerson famously coined in 'The Poet', 'Language is fossil poetry', thus reiterating Vico's view on the origins of language in metaphorical usage. The novelty of a word and its initial meaning wear off through our continued usage of it, up to the point we no longer actively consider how the word came into being in the first place. Once they have lost their original semantic power, the concepts that we use daily run the risk of becoming reified, while they may have gained much in social functionality.[32] Turned the other way around, an uninformed use of conceptual language only helps in replicating epistemological and methodological preoccupations. Secondly, empirical research shows that often we are unaware of metaphor's impact. Recent findings suggest strongly that metaphor also covertly influences the way that people reason and decide about societal issues. Metaphors frame decisions, but people do not consciously recognise that this occurs.[33] In other words, there is a relation between linguistic framing and conceptualisation, and this influences our reasoning. I am not thinking here in terms of blatantly negative metaphors such as populist suggestions to halt 'tsunamis of asylum seekers', but of the more subtle 'this-is-how-we-always-do-things' mode that all too often pervades our lives. Metaphor pertains directly to psychological defects to which we all run the risk of falling prey.

If we agree that judicial practice presupposes for the actual moment of persuasive argument the willingness to suspend disbelief, the judge should be able to comprehend contraries: that is to say, balance discordant arguments, narratives and human qualities. To accomplish this requires imagination, and that is itself, ideally at least, the harmonised result of one's own contraries

---

[31] See C. S. Bjerre, 'Mental capacity as metaphor', 18 *International Journal for the Semiotics of Law*, 2005, pp. 101–40.

[32] A. C. Zijderveld, *On Clichés: The Supersedure of Meaning by Function in Modernity* (London: Routledge, 1979), p. 20.

[33] See P. H. Thibodeau and L. Boroditsky, 'Metaphors we think with: the role of metaphor in reasoning', available at <http://www.plosone.org/article/info:doi/10.1371/journal.pone.0016782> [last accessed 1 March 2015]. Of related interest is that IARPA (Intelligence Advanced Research Projects Activity, a US government agency) has a Metaphor Program aimed at finding out what foreign cultures' metaphors may tell about foreign peoples' beliefs (see D. Soar, 'Short cuts', *London Review of Books*, 30 June 2011, p. 22).

and complexities.[34] Suspending judicial disbelief then is an acceptance, if only for that moment, of the world portrayed by others in legal proceedings, before coming to a harmony of diverging points of view as a starting point for further argument, a *concordia discordantium*, a harmony between different, or dissenting opinions, both in a literal and a figurative sense, as it was originally called in the scholastic tradition before this degenerated into casuistry.[35] It is difficult enough on its own to be able to fully recognise opposites in all their aspects. After the heuristic phase of deliberate uncertainty, however, comes the explicit demand for a judicial answer to the problem. In the discursive practice of law with its system of remedies – appeal, cassation, annulment or review – the answer may be provisional. Yet the judgement stands out in that it is accepted at least momentarily as a correct rendition of applicable law, and of the truth in the sense of the correct interpretation of the facts. That is the classical Roman law notion of *res iudicata pro veritate habetur*.

For judges, therefore, combined attention to all the workings of meta-phor, both positive and negative, is essential. Judges should also always ask themselves whether, or rather, to what extent, their private worldviews influence their legal thought, and question how prejudice – also in its Gadamerian meaning of prior judgements, private and professional – may hamper the requirement of impartiality. None of us can escape Henry James's metaphor of 'the house of fiction' with its million windows, at each of which a person is watching. I use the image here to draw attention once again to the importance of perspective and context. The Jamesian watchers at all these windows 'are watching the same show, but one seeing more where the other sees less, one seeing black where the other sees white, one seeing big where the other sees small, one seeing coarse where the other sees fine'.[36] And I suggest that for some the window does not open at all, and when this happens to judges, the consequences may be terrible for everyone concerned. The impact of choices made in law on people's lives makes the topic of metaphor even more urgent for judges, because when judges speak, people's lives are literally changed.[37]

---

[34] Coleridge, *Biographia Literaria*, pp. 16–17: 'This power . . . reveals itself in the balance or reconciliation of opposite or discordant qualities: Of sameness, with difference; of the general, with the concrete; the idea, with the image'.

[35] The source of *concordia discordantium* is Cicero's idea of the harmony of the spheres in *De Republica* (51 BC); see also Gratian, *Decretum*, in E. L. Richter and E. Friedberg (eds), *Corpus Iuris Canonici* (Leipzig: Tauchnitz, [1140] 1879–81).

[36] H. James, 'Preface' to *The Portrait of a Lady* (Harmondsworth: Penguin, [1881] 1976), p. ix.

[37] See R. Cover, 'Violence and the word', 95 *Yale Law Journal*, 1986, pp. 1601–29.

Understanding Dissonance

If it is indeed the case that the metaphors we live by make us who we are and tell us something about the consequences of our epistemological premises and chosen methodologies,[38] the next question would be 'What if the dissonance inherent in comprehending contraries makes us fall into the trap of cognitive dissonance?' The psychological phenomenon that goes by the name of cognitive dissonance is the feeling of uncomfortable tension that is caused by holding two conflicting options, including our own thoughts about them, in our mind at the same time, yet it is the obverse of the positive Coleridgean version of comprehending contraries. It can arise as well from engaging in behaviour that is in conflict with an individual's beliefs. As a psychological term, it denotes more specifically the feeling that occurs in the individual when she perceives an incompatibility between her cognitions – namely, between elements of knowledge and beliefs. Such dissonance will then motivate her to reduce the dissonance by actively avoiding 'information which would likely increase the dissonance'.[39]

I suggest that the question is acute, in that the most often sought solution to cognitive dissonance, once it is perceived and literally felt as a problem, consists of the combination of two other ways to explain and reason away opposites: confirmation bias and belief perseverance. These are mutually reinforcing, and together as well as apart are thought of as ways of avoiding the unpleasant in the event of our experiencing cognitive dissonance. Therefore, a confirmation bias is the inclination to seek and to interpret evidence in such a manner that it confirms an existing conviction, expectation or hypothesis. That is to say, we have an idea or an intuition with respect to the world around us, and this becomes our guideline when we try to gather and then judge information, or, in legal surroundings, evidence. New information confirming one's preconceptions is accepted. Information and interpretations contradicting one's prior beliefs are actively avoided. This is where belief perseverance enters the fray. It is the tendency to keep on believing what one has decided that one believes a priori even in the face of disconfirming evidence.[40] A confirmation bias as a form of selection bias often takes the form

---

[38] G. Lakoff and M. Johnson, *Metaphors We Live By* (Chicago: University of Chicago Press, 1980). See also G. Lakoff, 'The contemporary theory of metaphor', in A. Ortony (ed.), *Metaphor and Thought* (Cambridge: Cambridge University Press, 1993), pp. 202–51, p. 244, for metaphor as a way to understand concepts.

[39] L. Festinger, *A Theory of Cognitive Dissonance* (Stanford, CA: Stanford University Press, 1957), p. 3.

[40] See R. S. Nickerson, 'Confirmation bias: a ubiquitous phenomenon in many guises', 2 *Review of General Psychology*, 1998, pp. 175–220.

of an active search by a decision maker for evidence that confirms her initial hypothesis, to which she then subsequently assigns more weight, while at the same time she tends to ignore evidence that disconfirms the hypothesis. What happens is that even slightly potentially confirmatory evidence is taken at face value, while potentially disconfirming evidence is scrutinised extremely critically.[41] In short, there is no, or not enough, constant revaluation of the evidence relevant to the belief that a person holds. Consequently, there is a failure to resist what James Boyd White calls the empire of force.[42] As White notes, law

> depends entirely upon the way in which law is done, upon the quality and direction of the lawyer's or judge's mind at work: does it seek to understand the empire of force at work in the world and in the self and learn how not to respect it?[43]

If we have then acted on the confirmation bias and belief perseverance, and our action cannot be undone, it is only after-the-fact dissonance that compels us to change our beliefs. This is not least so because of our human tendency to think that when mistakes are made, they are made by others.[44] A literary example of the phenomena is Shakespeare's *Othello*, in which the question of whether Desdemona is faithful is resolved at the cost of her life. Othello wants 'ocular proof' of his wife's infidelity (III, iii, 365) in truly empirical fashion, but he clings to his a priori view that Michael Cassio is Desdemona's lover. He immediately assumes a guilty act, and does not look any further for evidence, let alone for anything that might disconfirm his view.[45] His desire to prove his assumption of Desdemona's infidelity is both an example of a confirmation bias and a form of belief perseverance. Literary variations of

---

[41] See L. Ross and C. A. Anderson, 'Shortcomings in the attribution process: on the origins and maintenance of erroneous social assessments', in D. Kahneman et al. (eds), *Judgment under Uncertainty: Heuristics and Biases* (Cambridge: Cambridge University Press, 1982), pp. 129–52; T. Gilovich, *How We Know What Isn't So: The Fallibility of Human Reason in Everyday Life* (New York: Free Press, 1993).

[42] J. B. White, *Living Speech: Resisting the Empire of Force* (Princeton and Oxford: Princeton University Press, 2006), p. 5.

[43] J. Gaakeer, 'Interview with James Boyd White', 105 *Michigan Law Review*, 2007, pp. 1403–19, p. 1405.

[44] Cf. C. Tavris and E. Anderson, *Mistakes Were Made (But Not by Me): Why We Justify Foolish Beliefs, Bad Decisions, and Hurtful Actions* (Harcourt: Orlando, 2007).

[45] See also L. Hutson, '"Lively Evidence": legal inquiry and the *evidentia* of Shakespeare drama', in B. Cormack et al. (eds), *Shakespeare and the Law: A Conversation among Disciplines and Professions* (Chicago and London: University of Chicago Press, 2013), pp. 72–97.

the Othello theme abound, from Leo Tolstoy's *The Kreutzer Sonata* to Nicci French's *The Memory Game*.

Why is all of this important for the legal professional? For the very simple reason that we ourselves are not exempt from the psychological processes that we are called upon to judge. Sometimes we also misjudge what we see, or we miss part of the information before us. Biological and cognitive factors may cause illusions and delusions, and our expectations can lead to our experiencing stimuli that are not really 'out there'. A practical application may prove useful to illustrate my point. What if the police, on the basis of their perceived dissonance and their inability to hold opposites in their minds long enough, knowingly and willingly select evidence in such a way that rigorous critical scrutiny and logical thought processes are applied only to evidence supporting their preconceived views, but not to evidence challenging their preconceptions? What if the public prosecutor goes along with that, without even recognising the misdeeds of the confirmation bias-oriented empire of force? Festinger was right when he posited that dissonance persists once it comes into being, because it is so difficult to change either one's behaviour or one's cognitions, not least because the dominant culture defines what is consonant and what is not.[46] There are often very prosaic reasons that beliefs persevere despite evidence to the contrary. It is most embarrassing to have to withdraw a belief that you have earlier declared publicly – for example, in the early phase of investigation of a case that attracts considerable media attention. There is always hope that evidence supporting what you now declare will crop up very soon, is there not? And surely you know what you are doing, because you have been in this business for so long that you recognise 'it' when you see it[47] – even though evidence is produced under the pressure of a huge workload – so you do not have to forego your stubbornness in clinging to a preconceived idea, do you? Furthermore, the police are used to selecting evidence that fits the scenario of the offence, and anything inconsistent with the scenario easily runs the risk of being explained away as incorrect, or of being simply ignored without a moment's thought. There are, so to speak, vested interests to be protected, and therefore the failure to search impartially for information looms large all along the way. And this can hardly be prevented, because of the partial role of the police, the public prosecutor, and the defence lawyer, especially if he thinks of himself as a hired gun. How is one to suspend belief as well as disbelief?

The question is especially acute for civil law legal systems that favour an inquisitorial rather than an adversarial approach. If the case comes to trial at

---

[46] Festinger, *Cognitive Dissonance*, pp. 6 and 14.

[47] See US Supreme Court Justice Potter Stewart in *Jacobellis v. Ohio* (378 U.S., 184, 1964), for the 'I know it when I see it' attitude.

the end of the chain of gathering evidence under the influence of the psycho-logical processes described here, the only thing a judge can and will do is go through the process of verification of evidence. That is why it is extremely dif-ficult for the judge not to fall into the prejudice trap. The confirmation bias in combination with a form of belief perseverance therefore entails a huge risk for judges. When they have read the file, it is the information in that file that will direct their attitude during a trial, during an oral hearing. The discomfort incidental to difficult choices is all too easily reasoned away if a judge can point to evidence that favours a direct and obvious solution, as Robert Cover had already pointed out in his seminal book *Justice Accused*.[48] Cover offered the dissonance hypothesis with regard to judicial responses in cases of the doctrinal divergence that has to be confronted by the judge who is struck by the impossibility of seeing herself as an impersonal rule-enforcer and the moral human being that she is. I suggest that his thesis is also applicable to the forms of dissonance discussed here. The greater the commitment to one cognition, the less likely the cognitive framework will change.[49]

So, suppose there are grave doubts as to the veracity of a defendant's con-fession, but he pleads guilty to a heinous crime: what do you do as a judge? You are damned if you do and damned if you do not convict him. How can you let a criminal who confesses go free? How could you have convicted him, when later on it proves that even though he confessed to the deed, he did not commit it? There is a grave risk of becoming an O'Brien, the cynical character in Orwell's *Nineteen Eighty-Four*, who has elevated 'doublethink' – that is, 'the ability to *believe* that black is white, and more, to *know* that black is white, and to forget that one has ever believed the contrary'[50] – to an art of negatively comprehending contraries in a most devious way, so that the oppression of, and with, language gradually becomes increasingly subtle. Here is the empire of force, as the novel's protagonist Winston Smith finds out in the infamous Room 101, where he is tortured psychologically in a way that the not-so-fictional *Torture Memos* improved upon.[51]

In the Netherlands, an example of miscarriage of justice exemplifies the point. In 2000, a ten-year-old girl was raped and killed in a park. A man

---

[48] R. Cover, *Justice Accused: Antislavery and the Judicial Process* (New Haven and London: Yale University Press, 1975), ch. 13.

[49] Cover, *Justice Accused*, p. 227.

[50] G. Orwell, *Nineteen Eighty-Four* (London: Book Club Associates, [1949] 1967), p. 218. Think also of Alfred Hitchcock's film *Witness for the Prosecution* (1957) and Pat Barker's novel *Border Crossing* (2001).

[51] See D. Cole, *The Torture Memos: Rationalizing the Unthinkable* (Oxford: Oneworld Publications, 2009).

confessed, but later withdrew his confession. He was sentenced to a long term in prison and to forensic psychiatric treatment. The decision was upheld in appeal and cassation. In 2004, the case was reopened when another man confessed. It then turned out that certain information concerning relevant DNA materials, known at the time of the first defendant's trial, was more or less 'withheld' from the judges, even though expert witnesses had pointed out to the police and the public prosecutor that the DNA evidence was problematic to say the least. Thus, the judges were simply never informed that there was a problem.[52] A special research committee was appointed afterwards to investigate this case, and a 200-page evaluation of the facts was the result, with recommendations on how to do things differently in future cases.

All of this suggests that we should pay more detailed attention to the empires of forces at work in ourselves and in others, especially since judges read for the plot. They select the facts, and structure reality with an eye to a final answer in the form of a decision, a topic taken up in detail in Chapters 9 and 10. Here it suffices to say that the psychological predispositions discussed are obvious dangers to judicial emplotment. It would seem then that 'the palace of the mind', where Francis Bacon would have us reside, may prove to be deceptive, 'for man always believes more readily that which he prefers'.[53] Bacon's interest in mistaken ideas and methods, or what he calls Idols, 'the deepest fallacies of the human mind', was a visionary intuition if we consider that cognitive psychology and neurological research have by now confirmed that we are indeed prone to falling prey to the combined shortcomings of the *idola specus*, the errors peculiar to the individual, and the *idola tribus*, the tendency, once an opinion has been formed, to adhere to it in the face of contrary evidence with the help of continual rationalisations.[54] Our mind cannot but go wrong, because the human brain and sensory system have undergone an evolutionary development to such an extent that human beings in any new situation can do nothing other than very quickly evaluate, subconsciously for that matter, states of affairs, other people's behaviour, ideas, and emotions. When we then act on that initial impression, which consequently tends to last in our memory, we do so with a literal unwillingness to change our minds.[55]

[52] Hoge Raad 25 januari 2005, ECLI:NL:HR:2005:AS1872.
[53] F. Bacon (ed. J. Devey), *The Physical and Metaphysical Works of Lord Bacon, including The Advancement of Learning and Novum Organum* (London: George Bell and Sons, [1605; 1620] 1901), here *Advancement*, p. 115 and *Organum*, p. 393.
[54] Bacon, *Advancement*, p. 209.
[55] For example, D. Westen et al., 'The neural basis of motivated reasoning: an fMRI study of emotional constraints on political judgment during the U.S. presidential election of 2004', 18 *Journal of Cognitive Neuroscience*, 2006, pp. 1947–58.

Seeing Things as We Are?

Metaphor, therefore, is not an embellishment but a mode to learn why things happen, both in text and in human action, and in us as their readers. The metaphors we live by indeed make us who we are, and the work of metaphor does not take place outside law. On the contrary, it is inherent in it. This is even more so now that the days in which the legalistic and positivist idea of law as restricted to a set of codified rules are long behind us, and law in civil law countries since the early twentieth century includes principles, the interpretation and application of which by their very nature demands a deliberation about and a balancing of the interests involved. The Aristotelian attention to resemblance therefore also forms an argument in favour of a discursive view of metaphor, given the way in which metaphor elaborates both terms of the comparison in their reciprocal relation. As noted, this pertains to the way in which conceptualisation and classification in law takes place, in the sense that like scientific language it aims to eliminate as much as possible any ambiguities. But the language of legal concepts cannot do without the legal fiction, especially when viewed as the counterfactual mode of the as-if.[56] It comes then as no surprise that Ricoeur describes his project as one concerned with 'the rhetorical process by which discourse unleashes the power that certain fictions have to re-describe reality'.[57]

That is why the recognition of a diversity of rationalities is essential. It is also why the recognition that telling stories is a way of knowing is essential.[58] The etymological and epistemological connection between *narrare*, telling stories, and *gnarus*, knowing, should also make legal professionals return to *narratio* in the classical sense used by Quintilian, of *evidentia in narratione*, where *narratio* refers to the exposition of facts as demonstrated by documentation, or, rather, the ability to depict one's case persuasively. This is because here too is an important lesson to be learned if we are to create an awareness of the pitfalls of cognitive dissonance and their consequences for our treat-

---

[56] See H. Vaihinger (trans. C. K. Ogden), *The Philosophy of As-if* (London: Routledge and Kegan Paul, 1924); P. J. J. Olivier, *Legal Fictions in Practice and Legal Science* (Rotterdam: Rotterdam University Press, 1975). For the legal fiction, see L. L. Fuller, *Legal Fictions* (Stanford, CA: Stanford University Press, 1967); M. Del Mar and W. Twining (eds), *Legal Fictions in Theory and Practice* (Cham, Switzerland: Springer International Publishing, 2015); S. Stern, 'Legal and literary fictions', in E Anker and B. Meyler (eds), *New Directions in Law and Literature* (Oxford: Oxford University Press, 2017), pp. 313–26.

[57] Ricoeur, *Rule of Metaphor*, p. 7.

[58] See M. C. Nussbaum, *Love's Knowledge* (Oxford: Oxford University Press, 1990), and *Poetic Justice* (Boston: Beacon Press, 1995); J. Bruner, *Making Stories* (Cambridge, MA, Harvard University Press, 2002).

ment of evidence and narratives in forensic environments. The disordering literary reality may serve as a mirror to expose our innate prejudices, keeping us from being trapped in our legal myopia, or, even worse, dystopia, as I also intend to illustrate with more literary examples in Chapters 12 and 13. Now that we are prone to see the world in a way that fits the stories we tell about it and 'as we are', this ontology of our existence by means of stories recapitulates epistemology.[59] From a methodological point of view, narrative knowledge by means of literature can therefore help us to integrate experience and interpretation, as well as the sorely needed critical, professional reflection in order to instill in us a legal conscience of integrity. If Aristotle was right when he claimed that narrative tells us not only what happened but also what is probable,[60] we will do well to become *theoroi* again – from the Greek θεωρειν (theorein), to watch carefully, *theoroi* were the people sent to the Games to watch the tragedies, and who, upon returning to their villages, told others the lessons of what they had seen – rather than to remain theorists. And we will do so by reading literary works in order to learn, by way of the skilful representation of events, why things happen.

Ours should be a positive outlook on the simultaneousness inherent in metaphor as referred to by Paul Ricoeur when speaking of narrative coherence: that is, the creation of a whole in which both the story being told and the means expressing the story, discordant concord or concordant discord, should be the subject of our investigation.[61] In the sense that metaphor can make us say, 'I thought I knew, but now I see that it can also be otherwise', it ties in with *phronèsis* as 'a truth-attaining rational quality', noted in Chapter 6. Metaphorical truth and the pictorial moment are eminently suited to illustrate the importance of, on the one hand, the interconnection in good judging of *phronèsis* and metaphor, and, on the other, narrative and the equitable. When judges select what they consider the relevant facts of the case, and grasp them together with the relevant circumstances, they are authors trying to figure out what happened, and then performing the act of configuring a new narrative. As Ricoeur wrote, '*to figure* is always *to see as*'.[62]

---

[59] D. Mitchell, *number9dream* (London: Sceptre, 2001), p. 115, 'We don't see things as they are, we see things as we are'. Condillac had already made the point in *Essai sur l'origine des connaissances humaines* (Amsterdam: Pierre Mortier, 1746), p. 1, 'Soit que nous nous élevions, pour parler métaphoriquement, jusques dans les cieux; soit que nous descendions dans les abymes; nous ne fortons point de nous-mêmes'.

[60] See Aristotle, *Poetics*, 1451b5-b12, p. 59.

[61] P. Ricoeur (trans. D. Pellauer), *Reflections on the Just* (Chicago and London: University of Chicago Press, 2007), p. 79.

[62] Ricoeur, *Rule of Metaphor*, p. 61 (italics in the original).

Narrative intelligence is therefore of crucial importance to a judge's professional iconic moments. All of this also suggests that jurists generally will do well to learn how specific forms of narrative transfer their stories: namely, how they address their readers and are formative in constituting their readers' responses to the events that they relate. Thus, human agency and human responsibility, both with respect to the production and to the reception of narratives, are topics shared by law and literature.

8

Narrative Intelligence:
Empathy, Mimesis and the Equitable

The Literary Jurist

The sometimes discomfiting effects of metaphor help loosen the habits of the heart and mind, and urge jurists to cultivate their story sensibility or, more broadly, their narrative intelligence to prevent them from falling into the professional abyss of the psychological errors to which all humans are prone.[1] The same obviously goes for satire, irony, hyperbole and tropes in general when found in a legal setting. Cognitive psychology also shows convincingly that professionals rely on a variety of skills rather than simply applying the relevant rule. Thus, sophisticated knowledge of how narrative works both in the world and in us is crucial, and for the simple reason that misreadings and misunderstandings – reinforced by our natural tendency to cling to our initial beliefs when combined with professional overconfidence about how things are habitually done – easily lead to miscarriages of justice. The epistemological question to be kept specifically in judicial minds should always be whether there is indeed a chain of circumstance 'out there', or whether someone carefully fits together the evidence with other established facts. And whether that someone is you.

We can complement this cautioning approach with a more constructive one. 'Seeing as', especially when connected to the requirement of using the imagination, suggests yet another reason for the development of the jurist's narrative intelligence. *Law and Literature*'s strand that premises the idea that literary works appeal to the emotion as well as to the intellect, and thus engender the reader's empathy, elaborates on this. Martha Nussbaum argues that literature 'speaks *about us*, about our lives and choices and emotion, about our social existence and the totality of our connections', so that 'our interest in literature becomes . . . cognitive: an interest in finding out (by seeing and feeling the otherwise perceiving) what possibilities (and tragic

[1] R. N. Bellah, *Habits of the Heart* (Berkeley: University of California Press, 1985).

impossibilities) life offers to us, what hopes and fears for ourselves it under-writes or subverts'.[2] Nussbaum builds on earlier work in which she combines ethical philosophy along Aristotelian lines with the suggestion to study the narrative and emotional structures of novels. It is intimately connected to her construction of the truly moral judge whose phronetic virtue lies in correctly applying the equity of the flexible ruler.[3]

The crux of the argument about the literary-legal construction of a good judge is that real judges should read fiction, because the lessons it teaches can be applied directly to decision making.[4] Its premise is that literary works with legal themes, however remote perhaps from the traditional jurispru-dential themes, can offer insight into the struggles and tensions that are created by law by the very way in which it regulates society and the lives of individuals. Literature is also an indispensable medium to learn about law itself when literary authors portray professional lives of jurists and hold them up as a 'mirror for magistrates'. The experience of viewing the world of the text and its inhabitants empathically can be transformed into a norm for judging human relations in general. Thus, reading literature can make us aware of the complexity of the human condition, and can help promote an empathic capability 'to imagine the concrete ways in which people different from oneself grapple with disadvantage'.[5] At the heart of this approach is the emphasis on the particularity of human experience rather than an abstraction formulated on the basis of presuppositions that are hard to test. Nussbaum refers to this 'ability to see one thing as another, to see one thing in another' as 'metaphorical imagination' or 'fancy'.[6] It requires from the reader as a judicious spectator the ability to imagine what it is like to be in the other person's shoes.[7]

Robin West claims that reading literature helps us understand aspects of our own character, and she also offers literature as an aid to mitigate law's rougher political edges. Furthermore, social intercourse forces us to recognise the needs of others. Reading literature is formative in a double way; it helps us develop our empathic capacity, because that is not only a product of but

---

[2] M. C. Nussbaum, *Love's Knowledge* (Oxford: Oxford University Press, 1990), p. 171 (italics in the original).

[3] M. C. Nussbaum, *The Fragility of Goodness* (Cambridge: Cambridge University Press, 1986).

[4] P. J. Heald (ed.), *Literature and Legal Problem Solving* (Durham, NC: Carolina Academic Press, 1998), pp. 3–13.

[5] M. C. Nussbaum, *Poetic Justice* (Boston: Beacon Press, 1995), p. xvi.

[6] Nussbaum, *Poetic Justice*, p. 36.

[7] Nussbaum, *Poetic Justice*, p. 73.

also a precondition for reading well. The issue is deeply political for West, as shown in her debate with Richard Posner on Franz Kafka's story 'The Hunger Artist'. It goes to the core of predominant aspects of our legal and economic culture, such as individual autonomy and freedom of contract.[8]

The practical aspect of judicial empathic imagination is promoted eloquently by US Supreme Court Justice Stephen Breyer when he writes that,

> Law requires both a head and a heart. You need a good head to read all those words and figure out how they apply. But when you are representing human beings or deciding things that affect them, you need to understand, as best you can, the workings of human life,

and that especially in hard cases,

> where perfectly good judges come to different conclusions on the meaning of the same words . . . it is very important to imaginatively understand how other people live and how your decisions might affect them, so you can take that into account when you write.[9]

Related to this is the premise that judges should seek nourishment in literary works to preclude an insular view of life. It is connected to who judges are, to how they view their societal role and legal persona in daily practice, and thus to practical *phronèsis* as a judicial disposition.[10] This calls for continued attention to the relation between law and society, and between law and morality in their connections to theories of adjudication in their historical contexts.[11]

In short, the main premise is that the combined study of law and literature joins cognitive insights with empathic understanding of the plight of those affected by law. Because law and literature are both producers and products of culture, and thus they reflect as much as they critique, ideally at least, the prevailing societal convictions and conventions, the investigation of the literary creation of human experience helps us understand the ways in which narratives (re)construct reality. Furthermore, such an investigation

---

[8] R. A. Posner, 'The ethical significance of free choice', 99 *Harvard Law Review*, 1986, pp. 1431–48; R. West, 'Submission, choice and ethics', 99 *Harvard Law Review*, 1986, pp. 1449–56.

[9] E. Gerber, 'Stephen Breyer on intellectual influences', available at <https://fivebooks.com/best-books/stephen-breyer-on-intellectual-influences/> [last accessed 12 January 2018].

[10] *Hearings before the Committee on the Judiciary*, 103rd Congress, 2nd session 232-233, 1994, statement of Stephen G. Breyer, Supreme Court Nominee: 'I've found literature very helpful as a way out of the tower.'

[11] See W. J. Brennan, Jun., 'Reason, passion, and "the Progress of the Law"', 10 *Cardozo Law Review*, 1988, pp. 3–23, p. 9, no. 20, referring to Thomas Jefferson's *Dialogue between my Head and my Heart*.

forces us, as the authors and readers of legal narratives, to acknowledge that law's instrument is an institutional language that also imposes its conceptual framework on its users, so that it behooves us to develop literary-linguistic sensibilities. This includes attention to a broad range of aspects of alterity, not least because law is socially organised as power. Thus, fostering the imagination as the capability of entering imaginatively into the lives of others also helps foster a capacity for empathy upon which we can act.

Against this background, I suggest that the term *narrative jurisprudence* focusing on 'story' in law, in contradistinction to *literary jurisprudence* focusing on what literature may teach us, may be useful for heuristic or methodological purposes in legal theory, but that these two strands are not distinct when it comes to their application in legal practice.[12] *Law and Literature* need not strive to read pervasive legal subtexts into literary works, or vice versa. We would then run the risk of ending up in an intellectual ghetto. To reiterate the point made in Chapter 3, introducing new dichotomies is counterproductive. What matters is that in each casuistic account of the facts the theoretical knowledge of legal doctrine is necessarily confronted with the narrative, situational knowledge that literature can help provide. This is also to say that when I talk about narrative intelligence, I do not suggest that in law we have to choose between either traditional legal reasoning, with a focus on logic and rationality, or narrativity, and then fight to defend our position. Nor do we have to force a duality of law as a system of rules versus the subjective experience of the unmediated, brute facts in our lives. That would mean introducing the pretence that narrative is a superior form when it comes to offering a picture of reality as we think we know it. As I was taught in an early stage of my literary-legal studies, that would have as its consequence that the very idea of narrativity in a hermeneutic approach to law would vie with the positivist (empirical-social) sciences. That is exactly what a humanist approach rejects.

Narrative Intelligence II

Ricoeur's insistence on judicial narrative intelligence leads him to take up the Aristotelian thesis that knowledge of a thing requires insight into its mimetic representation. Only at the moment that the experience of an event or a human action is actually laid down in a text can the result be questioned for its aesthetic or cognitive contents. At the macro level, *locus classicus* for this narrative paradigm is Robert Cover's '*Nomos* and Narrative'. Cover's central

---

[12] For this distinction, see G. Minda, *Postmodern Legal Movements: Law and Jurisprudence at Century's End* (New York and London: New York University Press, 1995), p. 155.

theme is the position of the judge in the conflict between law and other normative worlds. To him, the normative world of law consists not only of a system of rules but also of a narrative that serves as its backdrop:

> We inhabit a *nomos*—a normative universe. We constantly create and maintain a world of right and wrong, of lawful and unlawful, of valid and void . . . No set of legal institutions or prescriptions exists apart from the narratives that locate it and give it meaning. For every constitution there is an epic, for every decalogue a scripture. Once understood in the context of the narratives that give it meaning, law becomes not merely a system of rules to be observed, but a world in which we live.[13]

Examples abound. The narrative of how a specific society came into being, such as the French after the demise of the *Ancien Régime* or the American after the Declaration of Independence, or, at the level of the narrative of a specific group within a larger society, that of ultra-orthodox Dutch Protestants hesitant about the gender equality that the Dutch constitution proclaims. Without knowledge of these narratives, legal interpretation in conflict situations cannot be successful. Thus, we can also not forgo the constitutive narratives of the *nomos* that law itself is.

On the micro level of narrative, *locus classicus* is Aristotle's *Poetics*. Aristotle points to the productive aspect of mimesis as representation when he says, 'I use "plot" to denote the construction of events', so that 'the plot is the mimesis of the action'.[14] This presumes an author who as a mimetic artist 'must produce (at any one time) a mimesis of one of three things: reality past or present; things as they are said or seem to be; or things as they ought to be'.[15] This act of emplotment is called *muthos*; it is a way of organising the events together with the plot of a story itself (plot as 'the story told').[16] On the concept of story, Aristotle confers the simple but essential elements of a beginning, a middle, and an end.[17] At the same time, he warns us not to mistake the fact that an individual performs many acts when deliberately conferring unity on them. This is a lesson not to be taken lightly by jurists. We should take heed not to presume that the term *praxeis* in the sense of separate actions automatically coincides with *praxis* in the sense of a unified whole. What

---

[13] R. Cover, '*Nomos* and Narrative', 97 *Harvard Law Review*, 1983, pp. 4–68, pp. 4–5.

[14] Aristotle (trans. S. Halliwell), *Poetics* (Cambridge, MA, and London: Harvard University Press, 1999), 6, 1449b 35-36,1450a 2-3 (p. 49).

[15] Aristotle, *Poetics*, 25, 1460b 8-11 (p. 125).

[16] See S. Halliwell, *Aristotle's Poetics* (London: Duckworth, 1986), p. 141, '*muthos* is defined (as is tragedy itself) as the mimesis or enactment of the (or a) *praxis*'.

[17] Aristotle, *Poetics*, 7, 1450b (p. 55).

Aristotle points out, and Ricoeur has elaborated upon, is the importance of our being sensitive to the question of who it is that brings unity in the form of a plot to what are previously loose elements representing single events. Thus, Ricoeur's hermeneutics 'is led by the question, *who*: who speaks? Who acts? Who tells a story? And who is the subject of moral imputation?' That is why Ricoeur's concept of narrative identity is closely connected to the philosophy of action, 'since narrative is "imitation of action" (*mimesis*)'.[18]

What are the consequences then if we do not properly understand the way in which *muthos* is constructed? This is unquestionably relevant for law. It is important to note two things, the one ontological and the other methodological.[19] Not only is a human being always *homo narrans*, but, as Aristotle notes,

> It is an instinct of human beings, from childhood, to engage in mimesis (indeed this distinguishes them from other animals: man is the most mimetic of all, and it is through mimesis that he develops his earliest understandings).[20]

Furthermore, the applicability of the components and principles of tragedy noted in the *Poetics* is much wider, because the requirement of structural unity and the criteria of necessity and probability have a far greater range than tragedy.[21] This is even more so if we agree that what and how we see is influenced by the mental frames through which we perceive the world, the formation of which is informed by our local cultural imaginations and scripts that are themselves the narratives we live by. In other words, the idea that what we call reality is always already – at least to a certain extent, depending on the field of knowledge – an interpretation made by man as an interpretive, narrative being. That too informs my plea for the future of *Law and Literature* to keep the hermeneutic totality in mind, and to probe the figures of the humanistic project that are valuable for the context sketched here.

Ricoeur makes a point clear when he writes,

> when a judge tries to understand a suspect by unraveling the knot of complications in which the suspect is caught, one can say that, before the story is being told, the individual seems entangled in the stories that happen

[18] C. Reagan, 'Interview with Paul Ricoeur', in C. E. Reagan, *Paul Ricoeur: His Life and His Work* (Chicago: University of Chicago Press, 1996), pp. 75–6.

[19] Aristotle, *Poetics*, 6, 1449b 25 (p. 47).

[20] Aristotle, *Poetics*, 4, 1448b 4-8 (p. 37). See also A. MacIntyre, *After Virtue: A Study in Moral Theory* (Notre Dame: University of Notre Dame Press, 1981), p. 201; J. B. White, *Heracles' Bow* (Madison: University of Wisconsin Press, 1985), p. 169.

[21] Halliwell, *Aristotle's Poetics*, p. 12.

to him. This 'entanglement' thus appears as the pre-history of the story told in which the beginning is still chosen by the narrator.[22]

This draws our professional judicial attention both to emplotment and to the way in which events and actions are described in law. It also incites us to consider the background of the individual if that individual is a party before us. When the judge herself as the reader is subsequently the mimetic producer, her own background, including her legal knowledge, is itself in need of critical attention. This point has already been well noted in narratological research with respect to the reader generally: that is, as one who takes decisions as she judges a literary narrative. Chapter 10 elaborates on it. The circumstance that 'mimesis comes naturally to us'[23] can obviously work as much to our advantage as to our disadvantage. This is even more so because the concept of 'likeness' is what rouses fellow feeling (*philantropia* in the sense of both sympathy and justice).[24] One thing, however, is clear; *phronèsis*, metaphoric imagination and empathic understanding are three of a kind.

Firstly, Ricoeur draws the attention to the beginning that the narrator-defendant chooses for his story, in relation to the competing stories as found in, for example, a victim's statement to the police or witness statements and/or written testimony. Is the story coherent? Is the sequence of events and the way in which it is told at all probable? Questions about the story's plausibility and the narrator's credibility require the active reader's insight into narrative on the level of what Ricoeur elsewhere calls 'the act of the plot, as eliciting a pattern from a succession'.[25] Why? Because in order to answer these questions, the judge must be able to understand what it means to grasp firmly and to combine what were initially considered separate events into a story with a plot, 'the intelligible whole that governs the succession of events in any story'.[26] Therefore, the success of the judicial configurational act at this level depends on the ability to decide whether an event is just a singular one or a crucial element in the development of the narrator-defendant's plot. It is here that the contribution of the humanities comes to the fore. Precisely because she has to be able to read for the plot, the judge can learn from the wealth of literary examples of plotting, including but not limited to legal plots in trial situations. In this sense, *le lecteur-juge*, as Christian Biet explains, combines being a reader and a

---

22 P. Ricoeur, 'Life: a story in search of a narrator', in M. C. Doeser and J. N. Kraaij (eds), *Facts and Values* (Dordrecht and Boston: Martinus Nijhoff Publishers, 1987), p. 129.

23 Aristotle, *Poetics*, 4, 1448b 19-20 (p. 39).

24 Aristotle, *Poetics*, 13, 1453a 1 (p. 69).

25 P. Ricoeur, 'Narrative time', *Critical Inquiry*, 1980, pp. 167–90, p. 178.

26 Ricoeur, 'Narrative time', p. 171.

spectator of exemplary plotting, and in both settings she needs to test the veracity of the evidence.[27]

Secondly, judges are themselves narrators in the active, authorial act of comprehending the facts and circumstances of the case, and deciding in any presented succession of events what is and what is not relevant for the legal plot. This plotting in the form of a selection is always done with the aim of arriving at a decision, or, as Ricoeur put it succinctly, 'To tell and to follow a story is already to reflect upon events in order to encompass them in successive wholes.'[28] Thus, the judicial configurational act has as its ultimate goal the (re)structuring of reality; like drama, it is aimed at a *dénouement*, a solution of the problem.[29] This is always done with the normative framework of law in mind. Here too, as with metaphor, being able to perceive difference and resemblance is important for the narrative construction of facts. What James Boyd White had already emphasised as an essential ability for any jurist becomes poignantly clear: the ability to bridge the originally fundamental difference – both in herself and when recognised as competing tugs in other people's texts – between the narrative and the analytical, or the literary and the conceptual. White calls this the difference between 'the mind that tells a story, and the mind that gives reason', because 'one finds its meaning in representations of events as they occur in time, in imagined experience; the other, in systematic or theoretical explanations, in the exposition of conceptual order or structure'.[30]

The professional demand for thorough judicial reflection before action is especially important, now that the judicial construction of the plot is not only the arrangement of events in a dramatic sequence but also the determination of what and who is to be included, and what and who will be left out. And that itself is already a judgement. Or, viewed the other way, the outcome of the judicial configurational act gives insight not only into the judgement itself but also into the judge's *ethos*. If judicial configuration is to be more than an automatism, it needs to be informed, and that, I suggest, settles the case for the humanities as providers of insight into how narratives work in the world. Because judges are the producers of sentences in at least two meanings – that is, they decide about the lives of others, and in writing down their decisions

[27] C. Biet, 'L'empire du droit, les jeux de la littérature', *Europe, revue littéraire mensuelle*, 2002, pp. 7–22, p. 20.

[28] Ricoeur, 'Narrative time', p. 178.

[29] W. W. Holdheim, *Der Justizirrtum als literarische Problematik* (Berlin: De Gruyter, 1969), p. 7.

[30] J. B. White, *The Legal Imagination: Studies in the Nature of Legal Thought and Expression* (Boston: Little, Brown and Company, 1973), p. 859.

they have to state the grounds the decision is based on so that others can form an opinion about its correctness – Ricoeur's thesis that 'to narrate is already to explain'[31] points to the success demanded of a judicial decision as far as bringing together heterogeneous and contradictory facts and circumstances in one coherent whole that, as a story, must have an acceptable conclusion. This also links the ability to narrate well to *phronèsis* as a virtue. Here as well, literature can contribute to judicial training and to legal education generally, because when people contemplate resemblance, 'they understand and infer what each element means, for instance "this person is so and so"'.[32]

Mimesis and the Re-presentation of Human Action

The input of philosophical hermeneutics and narratology aimed at providing insight into how the human mind deals with the very idea of narrative as story[33] is therefore of the utmost importance in order to instill into judges an awareness of what it is that they do and of what that means. Ricoeur's elaboration of Aristotle's view that knowledge requires insight into mimetic representation provides an important source of inspiration for law and legal practice. His proposal to view *mimēsis* as consisting of three consecutive steps ties in with his point of a necessary reflection on events before encompassing them in a narrative sequence, as well as with his analysis of the discursive view on metaphor that has *muthos* and *mimēsis* as its constitutive elements.[34] That is to say, firstly, that narrative fiction as a composition shows us – in the sense distinguished by Aristotle – that *muthos* or emplotment is both fable in the sense of an imaginary and imagined story and plot in the sense of a well-constructed story. This obviously requires attention to what it is that is imagined and constructed. It also means that the act of emplotment is an integrative process. Moreover, secondly, Ricoeur goes beyond Aristotle, who restricts *mimēsis* to drama and epic, in that he focuses on narrative as emplotment in a general sense. To Ricoeur, narrative fiction as emplotment or figuration of events also has the power to re-describe them. In this view, therefore, metaphorical re-description and *mimēsis* as an imitation or representation of an action, if not 100% interchangeable, are at least closely related. As Ricoeur explains, 'The mimetic function of narrative poses a problem exactly parallel to the problem of metaphorical

---

[31] P. Ricoeur (trans. K. McLaughlin and D. Pellauer), *Time and Narrative* (Chicago: University of Chicago Press), vol. 1, p. 178.

[32] Aristotle, *Poetics*, 4, 1448b5 (p. 39).

[33] M. Fludernik and G. Olson, 'Introduction', in G. Olson (ed.), *Current Trends in Narratology* (Berlin: De Gruyter, 2011), pp. 1–33.

[34] Diacritics as used in the original.

reference. It is, in fact, one particular application of the latter to the sphere of human action.'[35]

Ricoeur distinguishes three stages of *mimēsis*. The first is prefiguration, or *mimēsis₁*. This term denotes the temporality of the world of action. As jurists call it, the brute facts that need to and will at some point in time be named, understood, and valued as such-and-such on the basis of our pre-understandings of the narratives of human actions. That in turn is the pre-understanding we have of the order of a specific type of human action: for example, in criminal law it is what we know about how a robbery is usually planned and how it takes place as an event. That is why, as noted in Chapter 7, we need to take good notice of '*the pre-narrative quality of human experience*', not least because this hermeneutic trajectory is inescapably a vicious circle, as Ricoeur admits, because if human life is thought of in terms of stories, as '*an activity and a desire in search of a narrative*', then any human experience is itself 'already mediated by all kinds of stories we have heard'.[36] Chapter 10 elaborates on this topic. These stories help form our pre-understandings, also in the sense already distinguished by Gadamer with the term *Vorverständnisse*: that is, not our pre-judices in the negative sense of biases but in the sense of our present understandings of the world prior to any new judgement of it. In law, the idea of pre-understanding is also, partly at least, constituted by law's institutional characteristics and the general principles that are the foundation of the institution, as much as by the cultural aspect of the invisible discourse of law (noted in Chapter 6). Thus, we need to force ourselves to remain critical regarding its possible effects on our view on, for example, narrative probability, lest we accept unconditionally this basis for pre-understanding.

In short, these 'stories we have heard' also influence and colour our views and expectations of what the as-if of *mimēsis* as representation may be in terms of acceptability.[37] The circularity involved here should alert us to our task of acknowledging our own all too human tendency to stick to a story once we have located it or told it ourselves, as noted in Chapter 7. Thus, Ricoeur quite rightly points out that 'to understand a story is to understand both the language of "doing something" and the cultural tradition from which proceeds the typology of plots.'[38] Any profession has its specific plots

---

[35] Ricoeur, *Time and Narrative*, vol. 1, p. xi.

[36] Ricoeur, 'Life', p. 129.

[37] See also T. Helenius, '"As if" and the surplus of being in Ricoeur's Poetics', 3 *Ricoeur Studies*, no. 2, 2012, pp. 149–70, p. 152, for the view that Ricoeur's 'as-if' is both a saying and a seeing as, the iconic moment of metaphor.

[38] Ricoeur, *Time and Narrative*, vol. 1, p. 57.

with regard to how things are done and how things work out, with the legal 'whodunit' story as a case in point. Furthermore, in the actual legal setting, that includes procedural aspects as well as evidentiary settings, and these differ depending on jurisdiction.

The second stage of *mimēsis* is configuration, or *mimēsis₂*. This term denotes the world of the narrative emplotment of events: namely, the world of *poiēsis* as making something or as composition.[39] *Poiēsis* as a term is based solidly in the classical tradition of Plato and Aristotle of the *poeta faber*, who by means of his skills as a craftsman becomes the creator of something new, and gains authority because of his specialised knowledge.[40] As Ricoeur points out, 'Artisans who work with words produce not things but quasi-things; they invent the as-if.'[41] Since what is constructed in fiction is *mimēsis* as *poiēsis* – that is, not just imitation but construction in and as the act of composition – to Ricoeur, metaphor too shows the deviation from the ordinary in the sense of what is expected. And there is also a direct connection to the topic of *phronèsis*. Precisely because the activity of jurists is *poièsis*, they should cherish the imaginative challenge that unfolds in emplotment, and ask what they bring to it as professionals. Interpretation and deliberation cannot thrive without *phronèsis*, because, unlike knowledge in the Aristotelian sense of *épistèmè*, legal knowledge is not a pre-existing truth. It is always a form of applied understanding, bringing together rules that are not self-applying, and contexts that obviously differ from case to case.

The prerequisites of *mimēsis₂* are 'the composition of the plot . . . grounded in a pre-understanding [i.e *mimēsis₁*] of the world of action, its meaningful structures, its symbolic resources, and its temporal character'.[42] This means that

> an event must be more than just a singular occurrence. It gets its definition from its contribution to the development of a plot. A story, too, must be more than just an enumeration of events in a serial order; it must organize

---

[39] Ricoeur, *Time and Narrative*, vol. 1, p. xi.

[40] *Poiēsis* is handcraft as the creation and artistic bringing into appearance, a 'making'. See Plato's 'Symposium', in Plato (trans. R. E. Allen), *The Dialogues of Plato*, vol. II (New Haven and London: Yale University Press, 1991), p. 149; H.-G. Gadamer (trans. N. Walker, ed. R. Bernasconi), *The Relevance of the Beautiful and Other Essays* (Cambridge: Cambridge University Press, 1986), p. 117, on *poiesis* and *poietes* as poetic creation and the poet; J. Schönert, 'Author', in P. Hühn et al. (eds), *Handbook of Narratology* (Berlin: De Gruyter, 2009), pp. 1–13.

[41] Ricoeur, *Time and Narrative*, vol. 1, p. 45.

[42] Ricoeur, *Time and Narrative*, vol. 1, p. 54.

them into an intelligible whole, of a sort that we can always ask what is the 'thought' of this story. In short, emplotment is the operation that draws a configuration out of a simple succession.[43]

To Ricoeur, the importance of Aristotle lies in his already equating the plot with the configuring of opposite views, which is why Ricoeur refers to this simultaneousness as 'concordant discordance'.[44] What we call narrative coherence combines the concordance of the ongoing plot and the discordance of the *peripateia* (changes in fortune, reversals, upheavals, unexpected events and so forth). As a result, 'with *mimēsis₂*, opens the kingdom of the *as if*. I might have said the kingdom of fiction.'[45] Here is yet another tie with metaphor as discussed in Chapter 7. Metaphor also illustrates the deviation from the ordinary in the service of the *lexis* of a text, or how something is said, as the demonstration of what happened. This confirms the Keatsian idea of negative capability. The judicial virtue of impartiality demands that judges give full attention to all the different aspects of a case, the manifold possibilities for meaning, always asking 'But what if this had been the case rather than that?', and in the meantime suppressing the inclination to come too quickly to a final decision.

Translated to the narrative aspect of a legal conflict, this also means that the chaos and tension of the initial phase of 'what happened' are, ideally at least, translated into a manageable form in the various legal documents, culminating in the trial phase that finds its (re)solution, or catharsis, in the new order imposed on reality by the judicial decision. In this sense that the legal situation resembles drama, we find here an opening to connect Ricoeur's thought to contemporary discussions on visuality and mediality in law, for there too attention to metaphor and narrative construction is of great importance. Narrative intelligence ties in with the topic of professional ethos in yet another way, in the sense that any story of a professional's actions – and the written version of the judicial decision in which her line of thought unfolds is a prime example here – provides its author with a narrative identity. And this, ideally at least, leads to self-knowledge, or to knowledge of the activities of which the judge as the knowing subject is the author, when it seriously engages with the criticism it engenders in others. If the judge's deliberation is oriented towards choosing the correct legal ends and means, and to translating these into the appropriate legal action, this implies judicial integrity that transcends the obvious demands of clarity and coherence of the judicial

---

[43] Ricoeur, *Time and Narrative*, vol. 1, pp. 54 and 65.
[44] Ricoeur, *Time and Narrative*, vol. 1, p. 66.
[45] Ricoeur, *Time and Narrative*, vol. 1, p. 64.

decision. It includes the ethical aspect in the sense of the judicial disposition to keep probing her inner motives and to reflect on the tensions that arise when one has to get a firm grasp on two conflicting views on the facts of the case or the point of law, or both. To Ricoeur, narrative intelligence is 'much closer to practical wisdom and to moral judgment than it is to science and, more generally, to the theoretical use of reason'.[46] In short, in narrative intelligence we witness the triumph of *phronèsis* over *épistèmè*, for story belongs to 'phronetic intelligence'.[47]

Thus, we can learn about the important features of *mimēsis praxeos* as the imitation of an action (Aristotle's definition of story) by reading (literary as well as other forms of) stories, and in turn we can apply what we learn as best as we can in our own *mimēsis praxeos* in legal practice. In the sense that by means of literature we can gain insight into examples of the particularities of the human condition that may otherwise be inconceivable or beyond our reach, literary examples of the process of mimesis are therefore crucial. Not least because,

> An essential characteristic of a literary work . . . is that it transcends its own psycho-sociological conditions of production and thereby opens itself to an unlimited series of readings, themselves situated in different socio-cultural conditions. In short, the text must be able . . . to 'decontextualise' itself in such a way that it can be 're-contextualised' in a new situation – as accomplished, precisely, by the act of reading.[48]

Mimēsis₁ and *mimēsis₂* can also form the basis for a comparison of other theories of (re)presentation. These include, for example, the principle of minimal departure endorsed by Marie-Laure Ryan, stating 'that we construe the central world of a textual universe in the same way we reconstrue the alternate possible worlds of nonfactual statements: as conforming as far as possible to our representations of AW [Actual World]'.[49] Or Kendall Walton's Reality Principle, with its premise that we make fictional worlds in conformity with the real ones that we know, as well as its modified version, the Mutual Belief Principle, that

---

[46] Ricoeur, 'Life', p. 123.

[47] Ricoeur, 'Life', p. 124.

[48] P. Ricoeur (trans. and ed. J. B. Thompson), *Hermeneutics and the Human Sciences* (Cambridge: Cambridge University Press, 1981), p. 139. For the heuristic force of fiction and the idea of intersubjectivity, see P. Ricoeur (trans. K. Blamey and J. B. Thompson), *From Text to Action: Essays in Hermeneutics, II* (Evanston, IL: Northwestern University Press, 1991).

[49] M.-L. Ryan, *Possible Worlds, Artificial Intelligence, and Narrative Theory* (Bloomington: University of Indiana Press, 1991), p. 51.

focuses on reception and perception in a specific environment.[50] Developed for a theory of literary fiction, these principles are meaningful for legal fiction as well. The kingdom of the as-if suggests that the function of mimesis is to let an already existing reality emerge in a new way by adding something to it in the form of its (re)presentation of action: that is, precisely this rather than another, equally plausible representation. The importance of mimesis in its connection to the nature of fiction in the sense of referentiality inside and outside literature can therefore not be underlined enough.

An example given by Terry Eagleton poignantly illustrates this. The test that foreigners wanting to become British citizens are required to take contains the question 'Where does Santa Claus live?'[51] Now obviously only one answer is possible to those literally or positivistically inclined: namely, that Santa does not exist. But that, equally obviously, does not get a person the desired British citizenship. More broadly viewed, the example alerts us to the circumstance that the value of literature for law is often diminished on the basis of literature's lack of a referential character. That is to say, while the comparison as far as the fictional aspect is concerned may not be a revolutionary notion in the humanities, in law it has not yet become received wisdom. What the question also shows is that 'Human beings do not go to work on a raw, inert environment but on one always-already "textualised", traced over with meaning'.[52] Or rather, we understand the fictional aspect of Santa Claus – as much as that of unicorns, mermaids, or artificial legal persons such as corporations, for that matter – but nevertheless accept its truth value as a fact within the context of the narrative.

Finally, there is the third stage called refiguration, or $mim\bar{e}sis_3$. It refers to the moment when the reader appropriates the text into his own world. Thus, this term refers to the moment at which the worlds of $mim\bar{e}sis_1$ and $mim\bar{e}sis_2$ interact and influence one another. Translated to law, the sole aim of emplotting in judicial practice is to arrive at a decision. The judicial configurational act is the (re)structuring of reality by means of a decision followed by a written judgement, after which the world of the parties involved is changed, as is

---

[50] K. L. Walton, *Mimesis as Make-Believe* (Cambridge, MA: Harvard University Press, 1990), p. 4, 'What all representations have in common is a role in *make-believe*'. Walton investigates the question regarding the ontological standing of fictional characters. Like Ricoeur, Walton emphasises imaginative understanding: namely, only by imagining ourselves in certain situations do we learn to understand and accept other people. To Walton, this is the *Verstehen* in philosophical hermeneutics, the mode of understanding human action as noted in Chapter 3.

[51] T. Eagleton, *The Event of Literature* (New Haven: Yale University Press, 2012), p. 201.

[52] Eagleton, *The Event*, p. 171.

the world of law by what the decision adds to doctrine, if only by confirming it. In hard cases more specifically, such (re)structuring of reality may take the form of an unexpected jurisprudential paradigm shift. Therefore, when *mimēsis₁* and *mimēsis₂* interact, we are in the stage of application, and, as a result, our earlier pre-understanding is also changed by this act of configuration. That is why narration is explanation. In bringing together heterogeneous facts and circumstances woven into competing narratives of opposing parties, the judge draws on the written and unwritten sources of law that are themselves part of the stage of *mimēsis₁* as much as they are the result of an earlier application: namely, an earlier *mimēsis₃* when viewed in the dynamic process of law's development.

The connection of narrating well to *phronèsis* as good judgement is imperative if the judicial decision that is the conclusion of the judge's narrative as an explanatory plot of what happened is to be acceptable and accepted. As Ricoeur notes, 'What is at stake . . . is the concrete process by which the textual configuration mediates between the prefiguration of the practical field and its refiguration through the reception of the work.'[53] In other words, *mimēsis₃* is the stage of application in legal hermeneutics. It is the moment when our pre-understanding is informed and changed by *our* act of configuration when figuration executes its power of redescription and becomes effective. What matters, therefore, is awareness of the reader's capability as far as reception is concerned, informed as that is by the context in which application takes place, an idea comparable to the reader response theories of Hans Robert Jauss and Wolfgang Iser. The moment is crucial when the reader involved is the judge in her act of deciding, because she tries both to reduce the tension of antagonistic positions of the parties involved in a case, and, as the one deciding, to construct or configure what she deems relevant facts and circumstances, her own activity as well being a mimetic, both creative and integrative.[54] Hence, it can also be read as a warning to judges to pay full attention, by way of phronetic exercise, to all the different aspects of a case, and to the manifold possibilities for meaning, by always asking 'But what if this had been the case rather than that?', and in the meantime suppressing the inclination to arrive too quickly at a final decision, not least because *mimēsis₃* is concerned with 'a refined grasp of the real world'.[55]

---

[53] Ricoeur, *Time and Narrative*, vol. 1, p. 53.
[54] See also N. Meuter, 'Narration in various disciplines', in P. Hühn et al. (eds), *Handbook of Narratology* (Berlin: De Gruyter, 2009), pp. 242–62.
[55] See K. Kukkonen, 'Plot', in P. Hühn et al. (eds), *The Living Handbook of Narratology* (Hamburg: Hamburg University), available at <http://www.lhn.uni-hamburg.de/article/plot> [last accessed 12 December 2016].

The Right Discrimination of the Equitable

Attention to narrative can also be translated into a meaningful vantage point from which to resist the reification that is the result of a one-sided, positivist attention to the language of legal concepts. Rules and norms are not self-applying. They are applied by man, who in turn is responsible for any reductive tendency, for, as Ricoeur put it, 'One massive fact characteristic of the use of our languages [is]: *it is always possible to say the same thing in a different way*.'[56] A judge's ethos in the sense of professional attitude cannot be separated from the persuasiveness of her judgement. If a lack of reflection on this bond may rightly be deemed an ethical defect, this is another reason that we need the input from the humanities in the process of going from the abstract, general norm to its particular application in a concrete situation, for the justice of the outcome depends on it. What Ricoeur shows us is that it is precisely because the statutory norm is general that we need a perspectival reaction to which literature and philosophical hermeneutics may help give form. This is also why the right discrimination of the equitable is another building block in a humanistic model of doing law.

In the *Nicomachean Ethics*, Aristotle argues that equity not only parallels written law but, where necessary, also prevails over it as a corrective, so that any error arising from the fact that any law is a general statement can be rectified by

> deciding as the lawgiver would himself decide if he were present on the
> occasion, and would have enacted if he had been cognizant of the case in
> question . . . This is the essential nature of the equitable: it is a rectification
> of law where law is defective because of its generality.[57]

He then ties *phronèsis* to judgement as the right discrimination of the equitable. Equitable man is above all others a man of empathic judgement, who shows consideration to others – also in the sense of forgiveness – 'that consideration which judges rightly what is equitable, judging *rightly* meaning what is *truly* equitable'.[58] Thus, Aristotle ties both understanding of a case and correct judgement to *phronèsis*. The term justice, therefore, denotes the virtue as well as the idea of just distribution and a just corrective. As such, it is directly connected to the activity of *doing* law. Equity can help close the gap between legal justice in the sense of the right application of the rule, and of justice as

---

[56] P. Ricoeur (trans. D. Pellauer), *Reflections on the Just* (Chicago: University of Chicago Press, 2007), p. 116 (italics in the original).

[57] Aristotle (trans. H. Rackham and ed. J. Henderson), *Nicomachean Ethics* (Cambridge, MA, and London: Harvard University Press, [1926] 2003) V.x.7-8, 1137b30-33 (p. 317).

[58] Aristotle, *Nicomachean Ethics*, VI.xi.1, 1143a24 (p. 361) (italics in the original).

a virtue. It can help offer a just solution where legal justice in the sense of the exclusive application of positive law fails. The lawgiver deals with legal justice when he determines the rule, but he does so necessarily in general terms. The judge is the one who interprets the lawgiver's texts, and, to her, the technical acuity of the kind the lawgiver ideally possesses is not enough. She needs the metaphorical 'leaden rule used by Lesbian builders: just as that rule is not rigid but can be bent to the shape of the stone, so a special ordinance is made to fit the circumstances of the case'.[59]

The doing of equity therefore depends on the particular circumstances of each case, as it combines the virtue of legal justice and the moral virtue that is the product of ethos. Aristotle, in examining the nature of human actions, says that

> matters of conduct and expediency have nothing fixed or invariable about them ... the agents themselves have to consider what is suited to the circumstances of each occasion (πρoσ τον καίρον), just as is the case with the art of medicine or of navigation.[60]

Applied to our subject, the reciprocity of facts in their various contexts and the normative precepts of law are obviously what make law and justice. On the basis that Ricoeur is right and it is indeed possible to say the same thing in a different way, our very act of configuring law and justice has to solve the paradox of rule-following: namely, that language requires a user who knows how to use it in concrete situations, because the words of the rules are not self-applying. This means that legal concepts also derive their meaning from the contexts in which they are developed and applied, including the fundamentally unpredictable nature of our social environments.

As a result, the interpretation of language – not incidentally, to Aristotle, language and speech are the only means through which the *zoon politikon* (the political animal) can discuss (in)justice[61] – becomes a precondition for the development of law. From the perspective that interpretation is always linked to argumentation, debate is necessarily a special form of practical reasoning within, to reiterate, institutional and procedural boundaries, and these are subject to our deliberative reasoning as well. The right to speak within this framework implies a membership in the social and legal system, and is therefore of enormous political and moral significance:

---

[59] Aristotle, *Nicomachean Ethics*, V.x.7-8, 1137b30-33 (p. 317).

[60] Aristotle, *Nicomachean Ethics*, II.ii.3-5,1104a4-10 (p. 77). See also J. Gaakeer, 'Scraping the judge's conscience', *Pólemos*, no. 2, 2008, pp. 193–214.

[61] Aristotle (trans. B. Jowett [1895]), *The Politics*, I.ii,1253a, available at <http://classics.mit.edu/Aristotle/politics.html> [last accessed 13 January 2015].

Stating the law in the singular circumstances of the trial, hence within the framework of the judicial form of institutions of justice, constitutes a paradigmatic example of what is meant here by the idea of justice as fairness or equity.[62]

Since to Aristotle justice comprises both the just as a regulative idea and ideal, and the legal as the domain of positive law, Ricoeur points to the social aspect, because 'Argumentation is the site where the bonds between self, neighbor, and others are established'.[63] Combined with the development of *phronèsis* by means of literary works as a matrix for ethics and law, and the exercise of this virtue as inseparable from the personal qualities of the capable *phronimos* in action, the conjunction between the self – legal and otherwise – and the rule shows that self-reflection is constitutive of the judicial *habitus*, and that includes her narrative habitus as the sum total of the stories she has read and that affect her.[64] Since, as Ricoeur claims, 'Interpretation of the facts of what happened [is] in the final analysis of a narrative order',[65] this is even more crucial in hard cases.[66] Equity's knowledge is narrative in its attention to the particular aspects of the case, which are necessarily connected to the stories of the parties involved, not least because judging requires hearing the other side in full.[67]

Ricoeur's line of thought can be combined with the important topic recently addressed by Miranda Fricker. Taken together, these authors offer yet another argument for a humanistic perspective on law. Perceptual as the tie of *phronèsis* and judgement is, it is important for our dealing with

---

[62] Ricoeur, *Reflections*, p. 63.

[63] Ricoeur, *Reflections*, p. 7.

[64] See also A. W. Frank, *Letting Stories Breathe: A Socio-Narratology* (Chicago: University of Chicago Press, 2010), pp. 52 and 54.

[65] Ricoeur, *Reflections*, p. 69.

[66] For example, *Riggs v. Palmer*, 115 N.Y. 506, 22 N. E. 188 (1889). The literary equitable attitude of 'the spirit' of the law is exemplified in Edward Hake's poem 'Of him that steales through Neede' (E. Hake (ed. D. E. C. Yale), *Epieikeia, a Dialogue on Equity in Three Parts* (New Haven: Yale University Press, [1597] 1953), pp. 64–5). The judge personifying the letter of the law is found in an exchange between a judge and a desperately poor woman facing a demand for damages because her son had hit a ball through a neighbour's windowpane while playing: 'She asked . . . "But then, by law, I can of course pay for the pane of glass by installments?" And the judge, dry as dust: "That you could only do if your little boy had broken the window-pane by installments"' (F. Bordewijk (trans. E. M. Prince), *Character: A Novel of Father and Son* (New York: New Amsterdam Books, [1938] 1990), p. 244).

[67] See G. Samuel, 'Equity and legal reasoning', 11 *Pólemos*, no. 1, 2017, pp. 41–53; G. Watt, *Equity Stirring: The Story of Justice Beyond Law* (Oxford and Portland, OR: Hart Publishing, 2009), for a common law view on equity.

(in)justice in the discursive situation in court, because, as Fricker puts it, it depends on 'the virtuous hearer's perceptual capacity . . . understood in terms of a sensitivity to epistemologically salient features of the situation and the speaker's performance.'[68] She offers an illuminating discussion of two types of epistemic injustice from which discourses can suffer. The first is hermeneutical injustice, which occurs when a gap in collective interpretive resources puts someone at an unfair disadvantage when it comes to making sense of their own social experiences. So, we should mind the gap. The second is testimonial injustice, which occurs when prejudice causes a hearer to give a deflated level of credibility to a speaker's word – either an excess of credibility or a deficit. Fricker illustrates the problems resulting from such injustice by means of Harper Lee's *To Kill a Mockingbird* and Patricia Highsmith's *The Talented Mr Ripley*. The ideal situation is when 'the hearer exercises a reflexive critical sensitivity to any reduced intelligibility incurred by the speaker owing to a gap in collective hermeneutical resources'.[69] And that sensitivity is an ethical as well as an intellectual virtue. But because as humans we are fallible, it is almost impossible to escape testimonial injustice. To the extent that we lack reflection on the effects of specific societal conditions and biases – for example, with respect to gender, race, or class – the risk of hermeneutical injustice increases. Therefore, we should at the very least strive to attain a reflective optimum. To do so as jurists, we need to understand the elements of our professional self-fashioning, even though such self-discovery and self-knowledge can be painful when we are confronted with our own prejudices. For example, when in the courtroom we ignore 'hermeneutically marginalized persons' because they simply have not been assigned a place in our collective understanding given the dominance of identity prejudices, so that they suffer a 'situated hermeneutical inequality: the concrete situation is such that the subject is rendered unable to make communicatively intelligible something which it is particularly in his or her interest to be able to render intelligible'.[70] This ties in with the subjects of belief perseverance and confirmation bias discussed in Chapter 7, and deserves our continued attention.

To me, Pat Barker's character Billy Prior in the novel *Regeneration* exemplifies such hermeneutic injustice.[71] The main theme of *Regeneration* is the ethical dilemma that the psychiatrist Rivers is forced to face when he has to treat Siegfried Sassoon, whose publication in 1917 of *A Soldier's*

---

[68] M. Fricker, *Epistemic Injustice: Power and the Ethics of Knowing* (Oxford: Oxford University Press, 2007), p. 72.

[69] Fricker, *Epistemic Injustice*, p. 7.

[70] Fricker, *Epistemic Injustice*, p. 162.

[71] P. Barker, *Regeneration* (Harmondsworth: Penguin, 1992). Hereinafter (R + page number).

Declaration, an indictment of the First World War as a war of aggression with unnecessary sacrifice of soldiers' lives, had forced Sassoon to choose between a court martial or treatment for neurasthenia. Barker's fictional portrayal of the doctor-patient relationship is interesting here because of its parallel narrative of the treatment of Billy Prior. Prior, who suffers from mutism, is an intelligent lower-class boy who has become an officer. Empirical research shows that the rate of war neurosis was four times higher among officers than among the regular soldiers, so it should not come as a surprise that words fail Prior, whose poor background makes him a loner among the upper-class officers to boot. No wonder then that at the end of the first treatment Prior writes 'NO MORE WORDS' (R 43) as a response to his psychiatrist Rivers' method. No wonder, either, that Prior reproaches Rivers for his methodology, 'All the questions from *you*, all the answers from *me*. Why can't it be both ways?'(R 50). Yet it is precisely Prior's antagonism and his constant probing that gives Rivers the awkward feeling that his method is not beyond criticism. Rivers' tendency to play the dependable father figure does not work for everybody, 'I just think you might consider the possibility that *this* patient might want you to be *you*' (R 64). Thus, Prior also forces Rivers to think about the question of why he is there, at Craiglockhart, and what he is doing professionally. And Rivers, inadvertently perhaps, does just that when he explains the background of Prior's mutism to him, 'Mutism seems to spring from a conflict between *wanting* to say something, and knowing that if you *do* say it the consequences will be disastrous. So you resolve it by making it physically impossible for you to speak' (R 96). As far as the fictional Rivers is concerned, this physical symptom is rare in officers, who suffer instead from neurasthenic stammering. Or is he perhaps having a dig at the lower-class boy Prior? To the fact that officers experience this symptom, Rivers ascribes their prolonged education and more complex mental life. Prior is aghast. He confronts Rivers with the fact of his own stammer, 'It's even more interesting that you do', and Rivers is taken aback, 'That's d-different' (R 97). It is painfully clear that Rivers is face to face with his own elitist prejudice that his stammer is lifelong and even genetic. Now we also understand why he had taken a liking to Sassoon from the very start, because he had 'a distinguished stammer, perhaps, but a life-long stammer . . . not the recent, self-conscious stammer of the neurasthenic' (R 10).

When Prior tells Rivers that he feels that it is Rivers who needs to have the upper hand in their encounter, Rivers answers, 'This may come as a shock, Mr Prior, but I had been rather assuming we were on the same side' (R 80). That is exactly what Prior does not assume, because he is sorely aware of the difference in the treatment he receives compared to Sassoon. *Regeneration* celebrates the moral perspective as well, in that it shows, both in the narrative and at a meta-level, how literature can help link experience, interpretation and critical reflection with mutism also as a metaphor for a pervasive inability or unwillingness to engage in dialogue. I say so not least because the novel's picture of the different doctor-patient relationships also shows a striking resemblance to that of the possible lawyer-client relationships, in terms of institutional constraints to be faced, the danger of reduction of the patient's or client's emotion when translated into the language of medicine or law, the acceptance of the doctor's diagnosis or the judge's verdict, and the power structure that is always present in the relationship. This is also to say that our exposure to narrative can help us realise that what we call the facts and reality is to a large extent the product of our own way of thinking, and all too often proves to be illusory. In this respect, the story as genre may be looked upon as a gateway to a truth hidden behind the veil of facts with which we often exclusively concern ourselves. If anything, the literary approach can fight the disease of legal dysnarrativa, a disease that leads to an impairment in the ability to tell or to understand stories, and to read other minds.[72]

Kiran Desai's *The Inheritance of Loss* provides another insightful example of both lack of voice and of discrimination. The novel's protagonist is a retired judge, Jemubhai Popatlal Patel, who lives high in the northeastern Himalayas with his beloved dog Mutt, his orphaned granddaughter Sai, and his cook. The son of poor parents – his father, ironically as far as voice is concerned, makes a living by procuring false witnesses to appear in court – Jemubhai left his home in Piphit in 1939 to go to Cambridge with the money provided for by his arranged marriage to a fourteen-year-old bride of rich descent, but without his marriage consummated because the uneducated girl is frightened out of her wits and barely speaks. In England, he is being discriminated against, and 'for entire days nobody spoke to him at all, his throat jammed with words unuttered',[73] so that he himself begins to mumble rather than to speak in order not to be noticed. At the time of the exams, most non-native speakers 'had crisp-ironed their speech, but Jemubhai had barely opened his mouth for years and his English still had the rhythm and the form of Gujerati' (I 112). But he passes. At twenty-five, he returns home, and 'Except for exchanges with landladies and "How do you do?" in shops, he hadn't spoken to a woman in years' (I 165). The theme of his alienation, from himself, from his home country, and from his wife, is constantly connected to voice. As a student, he 'learned to take refuge in the third person . . . to keep

[72] J. Bruner, *Making Stories* (Cambridge, MA: Harvard University Press, 2002), p. 86.
[73] K. Desai, *The Inheritance of Loss* (Harmondsworth: Penguin Books, [2006] 2007), p. 39. Hereinafter (I + page number).

even himself away from himself' (I 11). He does not use 'I' but 'one' when referring to himself and constructing his own narrative identity. He works 'at being English with the passion of hatred and for what he would become, he would be despised by absolutely everyone, English and Indians, both' (I 119).

The Realm of Human Affairs

The ideas informing this chapter come full circle. The particularity of an equitable interpretation and decision, nourished by a rich array of contexts – that is, texts woven and joined together, with, given the primacy of language in law, the narrative context in and of literature animating and constituting the way in which the human mind makes sense of experience – epitomises the link between human beings and their products of law and literature as typically human, social artefacts. In this sense, equity's knowledge is also narrative in its attention to the particular aspects of the case that are necessarily connected to the stories of those involved. And turned the other way around, the argument justifies the idea that *Law and Literature*, as well as law and equity, can be understood as the hendiadys that they are: a single idea conveyed through a pairing of two nouns linked by the conjunction 'and'.[74] When speaking of good judging, Aristotle emphasises the combined importance of action (*praxis*) and speech and narrative (*lexis*) for our living together in society (the *bios politikos*). He does so – on Raphael's famous fresco *The School of Athens* in the Stanza delle Signatura in the Vatican, with, significantly the *Nicomachean Ethics* in his hand – by explicitly pointing to the realm of human affairs, τα τον ανθροπων πραγματα, where there is always the possibility that things are otherwise than we thought. This suggests that if we read well, equity and the other building blocks of a humanist, literary-legal jurisprudence discussed so far are what they have always been: namely, essential parts of just law.

[74] C. Reich, 'Toward the humanistic study of law', 74 *Yale Law Journal*, 1965, pp. 1402–8, p. 1408.

9

Towards a Legal Narratology I:
Probability, Fidelity and Plot

Points of Departure

This chapter continues the search for the specific building blocks for a humanistic approach to law that favours the idea of language as our cultural software. The suggestion that judges need narrative intelligence leads me to consider the possible elements of a narratology applicable in and for law. To be able to make the distinction, important for practice, between narrative in the sense of the story that is told and narrative as the way in which a story is transferred in a specific manner and has a specific impact on its audience, jurists need guidance as far as the production and the reception of narratives is concerned.[1] That is why this chapter is prompted by Benjamin Cardozo's succinct reminder of the intertwinement of theory and practice in law: 'the perplexity of judges becomes the scholar's opportunity.'[2] At the moment that it becomes apparent that judges crave more guidance than usual, academic scholars are offered a topic for further research. So here is an opportunity for interdisciplinary co-operation on the plane of narratology that can illuminate for practice its foundation in a broader cultural framework of which law is a part; hence the title of Part III of this book, which offers three examples of developments that may cause judicial perplexity.

Jerome Bruner has already argued that because 'narrative constructions can only achieve "verisimilitude"' they are 'a version of reality whose acceptability is governed by convention and "narrative necessity" rather than by empirical verification and logical requiredness'.[3] Jurists, therefore, should learn to differentiate between the construction of a narrative as text and narrative as operative in terms of how we construct the world as we know it. These aspects of narrative have recently been elaborated upon in connection

---

[1] G. Currie, *Narratives and Narrators: A Philosophy of Stories* (Oxford: Oxford University Press, 2010).

[2] B. N. Cardozo, *The Growth of the Law* (New Haven: Yale University Press, 1924), pp. 5–6.

[3] J. Bruner, 'The narrative construction of reality', 18 *Critical Inquiry*, 1991, pp. 1–21, p. 4.

with the notions of credibility and persuasiveness when these are judged against the background of factual evidence – or the lack of it – in legal cases, a topic closely related to the bond between facticity and normativity, as discussed in Chapter 6. Here too the human psychological make-up returns with a vengeance. What happens if our mind's natural proclivity to structure reality by means of narratives falls into the pitfall of their becoming set stories, and therefore, as will be addressed in Chapter 10, results in our applying them as set rules? We first need to do the groundwork as far as the 'how' and the 'what' of narratology is concerned. To do so, I will say more about my points of departure, and these include a few caveats.

It was argued in the previous chapters that philosophical hermeneutics is crucial for the development of a humanistic methodology for the process of judging. To confer legitimacy on my project, I have a second, related train of thought. I received my first training in literary theory, narratology included, in the late 1970s, at a time when Wellek and Warren's seminal *Theory of Literature* (1948) was still *de rigueur*. Todorov built on the Aristotelian definition of a story's elements as a beginning, a middle, and an end, and introduced the term narratology.[4] Greimas and Courtès delineated the concept of narrativity in the sense of story as the organising principle of any discourse.[5] Not incidentally, Greimas was one of the first scholars to apply semiotic insights to legal discourse, claiming that law as code is omnipresent.[6] All of these theorists paid homage to Propp's *Morphology of the Tale*.[7] However, it was only when I became a judge that I began to understand much of what had until then remained purely theoretical, also in terms of my own research in *Law and Literature*. Theory became practice when I had to make sense of and assess the narratives of authors and/or characters who literally stood before me as defendants in actual cases. When I looked for further guidance, I found that a terminological wreckage had occurred since the early days of narratology, and of the kind that the *glossatori* of the Justinian Code – not to mention the positivistic Benthamites, given their view on fiction – would have envied.

Some examples suffice to explain my perplexity. Wilhelm Schernus offers a short definition stating that 'narratology is a theory of narrative', complemented by the more sophisticated definition 'narratology is the humanistic

---

[4] T. Todorov, *Grammaire du Décaméron* (Paris and The Hague: Mouton, 1969).

[5] A.-J. Greimas and J. Courtès, *Sémiotique, Dictionnaire raisonné de la théorie du langage* (Paris: Hachette, 1979).

[6] A.-J. Greimas and E. Landowski, 'Analyse sémiotique d'un discours juridique', *Sémiotique et Sciences Sociales* (Paris: Seuil, 1976), pp. 79–128.

[7] V. Propp, *Morphology of the Folktale* (Research Center: Indiana University, [1928] 1958).

discipline dedicated to the study of the logic, principles, and practices of narrative representation.'[8] Derek Kiernan-Johnson distinguishes three concepts: story, narrative, and storytelling. Story and storytelling are limited to events and people, while narrative is the broader term that can also be used in legal reasoning; narrativity, then, is the overarching concept.[9] Christy DeSanctis defines storytelling as narrative reasoning. To her, there are currently three interrelated trends in the field: (1) narrative/story in contrast to hard logic; (2) the practice of storytelling as distinguished from narrative theory; and (3) the combination of these two trends: that is, the equation of narrative and storytelling, with an emphasis on how narratives are received by the audience (with, ideally, an empathic reaction).[10] In turn, Jerome Bruner and Anthony Amsterdam differentiate between 'endogenous theories of narrative', which are based on the view of the human as *homo narrans*, as noted in Chapter 8, and 'a second sort of theory' that argues 'that narratives and genres of narratives serve to *model* characteristic plights of culture-sharing human groups', this being the form with which legal narrative tends to conform.[11]

From the perspective of legal theory, these definitions suggest the need for conceptual clarity when it comes to *the* or to *a* project of developing a legal narratology, or, more modestly, developing narratological insights that are geared to application in legal research and legal practice. As Greta Olson aptly notes, 'The term "narrative" is often used in an undifferentiated fashion in work on the narrative properties of law to include a number of phenomena.'[12] As a result, what narratology is supposed to be or to do remains undecided, as does, as a consequence, its interdisciplinary goal, impact, and status.[13] Clarity

---

[8] W. Schernus, 'Narratology in the mirror of codifying texts', in G. Olson (ed.), *Current Trends in Narratology* (Berlin: De Gruyter, 2011), pp. 277–96, p. 281. Schernus takes the second definition from J.-C. Meister, 'Narratology', in P. Hühn et al. (eds), *Handbook of Narratology* (Berlin: De Gruyter, 2009), pp. 329–50. See G. Andersson, 'Is there a narrative method of text analysis and interpretation?', in G. Rossholm and C. Johansson (eds), *Disputable Core Concepts of Narrative Theory* (Berlin: Peter Lang, 2012), pp. 279–305, for an overview of approaches to narratology.

[9] D. H. Kiernan-Johnson, 'A shift to narrativity', 9 *Legal Communication and Rhetoric: JALWD*, 2012, pp. 81–98, pp. 81–2.

[10] C. H. DeSanctis, 'Narrative reasoning and analogy: the untold story', 9 *Legal Communication and Rhetoric: JALWD*, 2012, pp. 149–71, p. 151.

[11] A. G. Amsterdam and J. S. Bruner, *Minding the Law* (Cambridge, MA: Harvard University Press, 2000), pp. 115 and 117.

[12] G. Olson, 'Futures of law and literature: a preliminary overview from a culturalist perspective', in C. Hiebaum et al. (eds), *Recht und Literatur in Zwischenraum/Law and Literature in-between* (Bielefeld: Transcript, 2015), pp. 37–69, p. 43.

[13] Schernus, 'Narratology', p. 290, 'The disciplinary status of narratology appears unclear or at least somewhat uncertain'.

in terms of the legal is essential, given existing differences between legal systems and the specifics of their procedures, also as distinguished according to subfields of, for example, criminal law, trade law, or administrative law.

From the perspective of narratology, much can therefore be gained by exemplifying what is meant by the term 'narrative' in a specific legal context. However, when Stefan Iversen discusses narratives in rhetorical discourse, which in my view is a profoundly legal subject, he does not mention law as a topic for further investigation.[14] What is more, when law is mentioned in narratological studies, it is usually oriented to common law settings. Obviously, narratological findings that are applicable in common law settings cannot immediately be translated to civil law surroundings. Therefore, we need to keep in mind that we are dealing with contested definitions (including different terms for the same object) as far as their scope is concerned. It is important to bear this in mind when, as jurists, we look to narratology to find food for thought for practice. In other words, here too, for reasons of conceptual clarity, one must choose.

Related to narratology's definitional problem is the claim found in the field of *Applied Legal Storytelling* as a recent separate branch on the narrative tree: namely, that it goes beyond traditional *Law and Literature* concepts to explore the role of narrative in law practice, judging, and teaching.[15] On the one hand, *Applied Legal Storytelling* is obviously quite right in emphasising the practical aspect, for the lack of it is precisely what made many legal practitioners unresponsive to *Law and Literature*. On the other hand, however, its claim is bold. As the adjective 'applied' already indicates, its focus seems primarily instrumental, geared as it is to tactics of persuasion in legal argument. What is more, the common law versus civil law dichotomy looms large here as well – or rather, insofar as a common law orientation is predominant in *Applied Legal Storytelling*. Therefore, given procedural differences, there may be a risk of misunderstanding, an implication that Chapter 10 addresses. Inasmuch as *Applied Legal Storytelling* emphasises the importance of the facts, it too has much to win by turning to the foundations of narrative theory in philosophical hermeneutics. Here, then, is another reason for continued attention to what philosophical hermeneutics can bring to our understanding of narrative and narratology. Charles Reagan in his Ricoeur study had already

---

[14] S. Iversen, 'Narratives in rhetorical discourse', in P. Hühn et al. (eds), *The Living Handbook of Narratology* (Hamburg: Hamburg University), available at <http://www.lhn.uni-hamburg.de/article/narratives-rhetorical-discourse> [last accessed 10 December 2016].

[15] Call for papers for the 4th Biennial Applied Legal Storytelling Conference held at the City Law School of City University London, July 2013, available at <http://www.city.ac.uk/events/2013/july/applied-legal-storytelling-conference> [last accessed 4 July 2013].

argued that 'Narrative already contains, even in its most descriptive mode, evaluations, estimations, and value judgments'.[16] Consequently, the task of hermeneutics – and to me this includes legal hermeneutics broadly conceived, for the claim pertains to the descriptive mode of ascertaining the facts and circumstances at the case level as well – is to keep in mind the methodological decisions that we take, and to resist hasty closure. In doing so, we need to bear in mind, as Ricoeur had already acknowledged, that the difference is of degree, not of kind, even though 'in the tribunal there is a moment when the procedures of appeal are exhausted. But it is because the decision of the judge is implemented by the force of public power'.[17]

A caveat as far as the meta-level of interdisciplinary co-operation is concerned would be what Pierre Schlag calls the dedifferentiation problem. Ironically or not, Schlag claims that we suffer from it now that our theories of the 'Law and' kind have become sophisticated to the point of being useless because they take foundational similarities to their logical extreme. As a consequence, 'the dedifferentiation problem is that there is nothing to be said about the relations between the two entities because we were never entitled to separate them out in the first place'.[18] As I read Schlag, he warns interdisciplinarians to resist overemphasising foundational similarities of co-operating disciplines to the detriment of the necessary inclusion of other aspects such as institutional power relations and social relevance. After all, courts do not exist in a social vacuum. This suggests that we should not only reflect on the uses and abuses of narrative theory and/or narratology but also rethink the idea of literary narratology functioning as, as Werner Wolf puts it, 'the mother country of many colonies, domains outside literature where narrativity also plays a role'.[19] In short, disciplinary colonisation comes with risks. Some are of the traditional kind, whether the one discipline is the auxiliary of the other, or whether the two disciplines remain relatively autonomous, as noted in Chapter 3. Another risk is addressed by Wolf: namely that, on the one hand, 'the question arises of whether abandoning literature as the original home domain of narratology does not bespeak literature's loss of status as a

---

[16] C. E. Reagan, *Paul Ricoeur: His Life and His Work* (Chicago: University of Chicago Press, 1996), p. 83.

[17] P. Ricoeur (trans. and ed. J. B. Thompson), *Hermeneutics and the Human Sciences* (Cambridge: Cambridge University Press, 1981), p. 215.

[18] P. Schlag, 'The dedifferentiation problem', 42 *Continental Philosophy Review*, 2009, pp. 35–62, p. 37.

[19] W. Wolf, 'Narratology and media(lity): the transmedial expansion of a literary discipline and possible consequences', in G. Olson (ed.), *Current Trends in Narratology* (Berlin: De Gruyter, 2011), pp. 145–80, p. 156.

whole', and, on the other hand, the export of literary narratology into other fields may cause miscommunication when narratologists who are not experts in the colonised field must deal with experts who are not narratologists.[20] To reiterate the important question posed in Chapter 6: What is it in my field that can be usefully connected to another object from a discipline outside mine, and in what ways does that invite me to rethink my own cognitions and discursive idiosyncracies? The starting point should not be the deductive idea of narratology as the master discipline from which, syllogistically, our view of legal narrative is derived and by which it is informed. If our point of departure is that many discourses are organised narratively, we can make similarities productive if our research is informed by the bond of theory and practice so that the comparable movement to and fro between discourses can be made.[21]

Let us return to Aristotle. When he perceives a direct link between *phronèsis* and 'understanding' because the latter shares with *phronèsis* the same goal of 'what we ought to do or not to do', and is concerned with the same objects,[22] this is especially relevant in the context of narratology in view of the *Erklären-Verstehen* controversy on the meta-level of epistemology and interdisciplinarity, as noted in Chapter 3. This is also to say that the new trends in mediality and visuality in law, to me at least, do not herald the demise of textuality, and neither do they diminish the importance of hermeneutics for law. The same goes for the technological influx in law when jurists have to give meaning to what others consider relevant for the case at hand. My view is informed here by Bruno Latour's claim that despite the process of postmodernisation, the humanistic elements such as 'the hermeneut', 'the inner self' and 'the thee and thou of dialogue' remain indispensable as the objects of reflection and research, and that this is even more so because they have been abandoned or even orphaned by those studying scientific-technological developments.[23] That is to say, the contemporary favouring of the empirical, aka the hard sciences, has led to a positivistic methodology with which to tackle its objects of research. That is why we need to realise that as far as the relationship between the empirical and the human sciences is concerned, 'So long as humanism is constructed through contrast with the

---

[20] Ibid. p. 157.

[21] For a comparable but not identical argument, see W. Rhee, 'Law and practice', 9 *Legal Communication & Rhetoric: JALWD*, 2012, pp. 273–313.

[22] Aristotle (trans. H. Rackham and ed. J. Henderson), *Nicomachean Ethics* (Cambridge, MA, and London: Harvard University Press, [1926] 2003), VI.x.2, 1143a8-10 (p. 359).

[23] B. Latour, *We Have Never Been Modern* (Hempel Hempstead: Harvester Wheatsheaf, 1993), p. 135.

object that has been abandoned to epistemology, neither the human nor the nonhuman can be understood', and that this is why for the empirical sciences too it is important to ask, 'Where are Mouniers of machines, the Lévinases of animals, the Ricoeurs of facts?'[24] The very idea that the objective facts are in need of a hermeneut in the natural sciences as much as in the humanities is as obvious as the fact that it has been too long forgotten in the quest for epistemological certainty – that is, along the lines of the logic of Cartesian reason that characterises modernity. After all, law always deals with the realm of human affairs, and doing law is the work of humans. That is why narratology can contribute to legal theory and practice when it comes to understand better what is at work when we figure out the story of the facts in its various forms and at different levels. In this respect I remain confident that nothing has changed since the legal humanism of the Renaissance: *Si bene facta notes, consultus, iura sequentur. Factum praecedens ordine ius sequitur*: that is, when you, jurist, determine the facts adequately, what follows will be the law. The facts come first, the legal assessment comes next.[25]

Probability and Fidelity

In the *Poetics*, Aristotle claims that plots are subject to the laws of probability.[26] So it is no coincidence that the link between action and character is the core of his view on tragedy, with a flaw in the protagonist's character, *hamartia*, as the trigger to dramatic agency. Here is already a foundation of facts in narrative. And here is another reason that Ricoeur consistently refers to the particularity of literary profiles of virtue to show how these are historically and culturally informed.

Given the resemblance of tragedy or drama generally to the trial situation as the site in which fates are decided, Peter Brooks' remark that 'narrative is in large measure the *impensé* of the law'[27] alerts us to the fact that the idea of narrative is all too often taken for granted. That situation is to be deplored, since adjudication is always about deciding competing stories, for as Brooks contends, '"Conviction" – in the legal sense – results from the conviction created in those who judge the story'.[28] As a consequence, the judge should, on the one

---

[24] Latour, *We Have Never Been Modern*, p. 136.

[25] Cited in G. Radbruch, *Kleines Rechts-Brevier* (Göttingen: Vandenhoeck & Ruprecht, 1954), p. 58 (my translation). The source is J. Gobler, *In legem respiciendam explanatio* (Basel, 1543).

[26] See also, S. Halliwell, *Aristotle's Poetics* (London: Duckworth, 1986), p. 12.

[27] P. Brooks, 'Narrative in and of the law', in J. Phelan and P. J. Rabinowitz (eds), *A Companion to Narrative Theory* (Oxford: Blackwell, 2005, pp. 415–26), p. 415.

[28] Brooks, 'Narrative', p. 416.

hand, be trained to become aware of how human actions and events that were, initially at least, viewed separately are woven together in a story with a claim for specific legal meaning, and, on the other hand, to become aware of the influence of her own view of human behaviour and narrative fit on her judicial decisions about the veracity of a story in court, and of her own cultural beliefs that always hover in the background. As I read Brooks' argument, two points are of special importance: firstly, the argument of construction – namely, that what matters is 'how the "narratees" or listeners – juries, judges – hear and construct the story';[29] and secondly, that in law '(N)arrative understanding is retrospective'.[30] To me, this would mean two things. One is that such understanding is to a large degree dependent on the narrative elements provided by others, with the result that when a crucial element – crucial, that is, for the judge – is found missing, usually nothing can be done to bridge the gap. This is especially important to keep in mind in view of the fact that higher courts in many jurisdictions reconsider the facts only in as far as they have been ascertained by the lower courts. What is more, it also means that ascertaining the facts in the sense of the selection of what may be looked upon as relevant legal facts by the judge is always done literally *ex post facto*. That too provides a good reason for more research on how a number of facts 'out there' come to be regarded as a string of causally connected events with consequences as far as imputation and accountability are concerned. To reiterate, my insistence on the bond between theory and practice leads me to reject the idea of legal science purely positivistically conceived, because that traditionally presupposes the disconnected existence of legal theory and doing law, with the result that the legal theorist's task would be to analyse practice from a scientifically neutral, objective perspective. This, I am convinced, is both unrealistic and undesirable.

The narrative paradigm noted in Chapter 8 also comprises the notion that we are all born into a world of narratives that constitute a large part our own lives. It implies an image of humans as authors who interpret and subsequently help form the narratives that they encounter. These can either be stories told in people's private (family and working) lives, or they can be texts as well as emplotted social institutions, law and legal practice among them. At the level of a methodology for jurisprudence, the narrative paradigm was viewed initially as being especially fruitful for a discussion of the moral dimension of law, based on the view that literary narratives offer alternative ways of learning about values in law.[31] The subsequent rise of narrative juris-

---

[29] Brooks, 'Narrative', p. 424.
[30] Brooks, 'Narrative', p. 425.
[31] For example, T. Phelps, 'Narratives of disobedience', 40 *Journal of Legal Education*, 1990, pp. 133–43.

prudence cannot be seen in isolation from the turn to interpretation in the social sciences.[32] In the sense that it is posited against the idea(l) of scientific neutrality and objectivity in law, it is indebted to Walter Fisher, who in the early 1980s developed and coined the term narrative paradigm in literary theory. This provides a good starting point for interdisciplinary discussions because Fisher's narrative paradigm can be employed in the interpretation and assessment of a text in which there are claims to knowledge, truth, or reality. This aim is intimately connected to the quest, in law and elsewhere, to determine 'whether or not one should adhere to the stories one is encouraged to endorse or to accept as the basis for decisions and actions'.[33] Fisher pays tribute to Aristotle's concept of *phronèsis*, and acknowledges indebtedness to Ricoeur's discussion of metaphor.[34] His work ties in with continental-European philosophical hermeneutics in as far as it examines what occurs at the very moment that something is said or written. Therefore, it highlights the question of the relationship between human action and communicative experience, the nature of the rationality of this experience, and the contents of its values.[35] Nevertheless, it is undeservedly underrated in contemporary research.[36]

To Fisher, 'people are as much valuing as reasoning animals'.[37] His project demonstrates this by drawing on Aristotle's view on metaphor and the cognitive aspects of rhetoric. The representation of reality in literary works bears a relationship to our world at the very moment that we claim to recognise and to understand the literary reality, because in doing so we make use, consciously or unconsciously, of the concept of mimesis as representation. The narrative paradigm aims at achieving a synthesis of argumentative reasoning and its literary-aesthetic counterpart.[38] It does so

---

[32] See C. Geertz, *The Interpretation of Cultures* (New York: Basic Books, 1973), and *Local Knowledge* (New York: Basic Books, 1983).

[33] W. R. Fisher, 'The narrative paradigm: an elaboration', 52 *Communications Monographs*, 1985, pp. 347–67, p. 348.

[34] Fisher, 'Narrative paradigm', p. 355.

[35] See also S. IJsseling, *Rhetoric and Philosophy in Conflict* (The Hague: Nijhoff, 1976).

[36] But see A. E. Ralph, 'Not the same old story: using narrative theory to understand and overcome the plausibility pleading standard', 26 *Yale Journal of Law & the Humanities*, no. 1, 2014, pp. 1–57.

[37] W. R. Fisher and R. A. Filloy, 'Argument in drama and literature: an exploration', in J. R. Cox and C. A. Willard (eds), *Advances in Argumentation Theory and Research* (Carbondale, IL: Southern Illinois University Press, 1982), pp. 343–62, p. 343.

[38] W. R. Fisher, 'Narration as a human communication paradigm: the case of the public moral argument', 51 *Communications Monographs*, 1984, pp. 1–22, p. 2, the narrative paradigm being 'a dialectical synthesis of two traditional strands in the history of rhetoric: the argumentative, persuasive theme, and the literary, aesthetic theme'.

in contrast to the rational-world paradigm of the natural sciences, in that it thrives on 'symbolic actions – words and/or deeds – that have sequence for those who live, create, or interpret them'.[39] As a paradigmatic mode of human decision making, it is founded on phronetic reasoning that is both medium- and context-dependent. It embraces a concept of stories as the symbolic interpretations of aspects of the world shaped by history, culture, and character in the sense of an individual's qualities. Therefore, narrative rationality,

> is determined by the nature of persons as narrative beings – their inherent awareness of *narrative probability*, what constitutes a coherent story, and their constant habit of testing *narrative fidelity*, whether the stories they experience ring true with the stories they know to be true in their lives (narrative probability and narrative fidelity, it will be noted, are analogous to the concepts of *dramatic* probability and verisimilitude).[40]

For a coherent story to be probable, it must be a sequence of thought and action that is free of contradictions and makes sense. Its fidelity depends on 'the soundness of its reasoning and the value of its values'.[41] Fisher's philosophical point is an epistemological one, as can be seen from the phrase 'they know in their lives'. What is more, narrative rationality so conceived posits the concept of narrative as an independent meta- or master discourse that can be put to use outside its original rhetorical surroundings rather than as a disciplinary grounded concept with colonising tendencies.[42] The point about narrative rationality as 'an account, an understanding, of any instance of human choice and action'[43] alerts us to the question of mimetic re-presentation of human actions, as posed by Heidegger and Gadamer, and to whom Fisher is also indebted. The importance of the topic of mimesis in its connection to the nature of fiction in the sense of referentiality inside and outside literature cannot be underlined enough for law, especially when we consider Terry Eagleton's example, noted in Chapter 8, of the question about where Santa Claus lives.

What matters to me here specifically is that Fisher claims that narrative rationality is connected to *phronèsis* because it 'recognizes a contingent world, the particularities of practical existence and the possibility of wisdom – a virtue that involves an interest in matters that transcend immediate

---

[39] Fisher, 'Narration as communication', p. 2.
[40] Fisher, 'Narration as communication', p. 8 (italics mine).
[41] Fisher, 'Narrative paradigm', p. 349.
[42] See also Wolf, 'Narratology and media(lity)', p. 156.
[43] Fisher, 'Narration as communication', p. 9.

circumstances'.[44] Therefore, his thesis about the determination, by means of the narrative paradigm, of whether or not to adhere to the stories one is encouraged to accept as the basis for decision making and action, combined with a foundation in good reason, is deeply rooted in the Aristotelian tradition of emphasising *phronèsis* as a quality indispensable to good judgement. In the sense that *phronèsis* pertains to the probable – that is, to provisional truths – we find the connection to Fisher's narrative probability and fidelity, not least because these are products of experience.[45] What is more, Fisher offers the narrative paradigm as the meeting ground *par excellence* for scholars in the humanities. Therefore, it is also eminently appropriate to legitimise a discussion on the future of *Law and Literature*, both from the culturalist perspective promoted by Greta Olson among others,[46] and from my own legal perspective, because it is the judge's everyday challenge to determine 'whether or not one should adhere to the stories one is encouraged to endorse or to accept as the basis for decisions and actions'.[47] Fisher's concepts of narrative probability and fidelity, to me at least, go beyond the demands of mere internal coherence of a story, in that together they also point to narrative persuasiveness, and can thereby be connected to narrative affect as much as to the task of the judge to connect the case to the rule by means of a truthful description of the facts. Furthermore, Fisher already draws attention to the fact that stories may mislead deliberately when he writes that we should always try to determine 'whether or not a story is a mask for ulterior motives'.[48] This not only presages Peter Brooks, whose views are discussed below, but it is of equal importance for literary-legal studies in general, when it comes to detecting linguistic perversions in relation to totalitarian tendencies of the kind noted in Chapter 1.

Something that has already been richly documented in narratological research with respect to the reader generally – for example, as the person who takes decisions as she judges a literary narrative – is that her own background is itself in need of critical attention. This insight should be applied to the judge. It is she who, after the act of reading and of attaching meaning to what she has read, subsequently constitutes a new state of affairs as 'reality', with at least a minimal presumption of the re-presentation of how things were at the moment that she writes her decision. Thus, as Fisher notes, we require both knowledge of the agents in order to find which is *reliable* or *trustworthy*

---

[44] Fisher, 'Narrative paradigm', pp. 350 and 354.
[45] Fisher, 'Narration as communication', p. 15.
[46] See Olson, 'Futures'.
[47] Fisher, 'Narrative paradigm', p. 348.
[48] Fisher, 'Narrative paradigm', p. 364.

and knowledge of the objects in order to discover what has the quality of *veracity*.[49] This observation can be transposed seamlessly to the requirements at work in a legal narratology.

Mimesis Revisited

Before I address the question of how the narrative paradigm may be employed in texts with truth claims, such as the texts of law in court surroundings from the perspective of criminal law in practice,[50] I want to highlight certain other examples of narratological scholarship that I am convinced will help to guide the envisaged project of creating a narratology of European civil law jurisdictions.

In literary theory, Ansgar Nünning and Michael Basseler take up the challenge provided by Ricoeur's model of mimesis. And they do so against the background of the two main problems they perceive in the humanities: firstly, that of the life sciences as humanities' opponents that take over all of the topics traditionally connected to the humanities; and secondly, that the notion of literature as knowledge is itself not uncontested in literary circles, on the grounds that it fails the 'threshold test' definition of 'justified true belief' for lack of attaining the minimal criterion of truth.[51] This already makes the authors' analysis worthy of attention, because the concept of 'truth' in legal environments is not the 100% certainty and universality of the laws of the natural sciences; instead, it is one of probabilities, of interactional and inter-relational expectancies, and of attribution and the 'beyond reasonable doubt' threshold of criminal law. Furthermore, it provides jurists with insight into current issues in literary theory that are important to note in view of the idea of narrative as a form of knowing.

Nünning and Basseler offer a modest proposal to demonstrate that literature does indeed 'know' something. Their thesis is twofold. Firstly, they argue that 'literature has something important to contribute to our concepts of human life and knowledge of how to live with one another', while

---

[49] Fisher, 'Narration as Communication', p. 18.

[50] My choice is inspired not only by my own judicial practice but also by the view that the narratives in the field of criminal law are most suitable for a narratological approach. See also M. Sette Lopes, 'Clarice Lispector and forgiveness: incidences and coincidences', in M. Paola Mittica (ed.), *Dossier Law and Literature, Discussion on Purposes and Method* (2010), pp. 43-63, p. 46, available at <http://www.lawandliterature.org/> [last accessed 2 January 2015]: as a law student, the Brazilian writer Clarice Lispector told her professor that she opted for criminal law, and he replied 'You became interested in the literary part of law'.

[51] A. Nünning and M. Basseler, 'Literary studies as a form of "Life Science": The Knowledge of Literature', in G. Olson and A. Nünning (eds), *New Theories, Models and Methods in Literary and Cultural Studies* (Trier: WVT, 2013), pp. 189–212.

acknowledging the possibly unfavourable critique that such a view may undermine the very autonomy of the field of literature as well as be refuted immediately by the empirical predominance of the natural sciences, given how hard they supposedly are on the plane of facts. Secondly, the authors focus on the question of 'to what extent can literature be regarded as a force or an agent that reflects on, produces, and disseminates "life knowledge" and how can literary studies be regarded and (re-)conceptualized as a "form of life science"'?[52] The authors look for the way in which literary works draw on pre-figured knowledge of the textual repertoire – for example, the stage of *mimēsis₁* – based on the view that there is a reciprocal relationship between *mimēsis₁* and *mimēsis₃*. They do so because 'on the one hand, literary life knowledge is directly linked to and shaped by extra-literary forms of life and ways of living', while 'on the other hand, life itself is shaped by literary representations'.[53]

This is an argument on the plane of narrative knowledge connected to the thesis that reading literary works can contribute to the development of jurists' empathic qualities, with which I wholeheartedly agree. At the same time, I maintain that broadening the scope of the application of Ricoeur's model is necessary if we are to take up the interdisciplinary task of thinking through the implications of developing a legal narratology. In law as much as in literature, the construction of narratives is based on the idea that there are acceptable or at least feasible renditions of what happened, even if only in the moment in which they are transmitted in court and elsewhere. Consequently, the phase of configuration of *mimēsis₂* – that Nünning and Basseler conceive of as the presentation of alternative forms of knowledge and life in the literary work, and as a test case in the form of an alternative fictional world that reflects as much as challenges the actual world – has already always had a legal counterpart. Refiguration or *mimēsis₃* opens up new horizons of expectancy in law as to what will, for example, be covered by the concept of theft. Refiguration changes the interpretation of a chain of precedents when arguments rejected earlier are suddenly deemed feasible. In common law and civil law alike, a phase of determinative judgement follows the reflective effort to seek the relevant legal norm to apply to precisely the case at hand. This phase of judgement ends the process of the parties' dialectical argument. Reflective judgement as such, however, is not limited to the end of a trial. In the sense that a decision becomes an authoritative precedent, the act of judging

---

[52] Nünning and Basseler, 'Literary studies', p. 191. See also Reagan, *Paul Ricoeur*, pp. 100–9, for Ricoeur's elaboration on Dilthey's idea of *Verstehen*: *Verstehen* is not restricted to the humanities, and therefore the supposed gap between the 'two cultures' needs reconsideration.

[53] Nünning and Basseler, 'Literary studies', p. 197.

in a specific case does not exhaust the meaning of the act itself.[54] What is more, Ricoeur emphasises that only in law is there a last word, in the sense that proceedings at some point are finalised by the judicial decision, after which public power takes over in order to implement the decision, whereas, 'Neither in literary criticism, nor in the social sciences, is [there] such a last word. Or if there is any, we call that violence.'[55]

To conclude, any text of law can potentially be de-contextualised and re-contextualised. That is why Ricoeur's threefold distinction of *mimēsis* provides a good working model for a legal narratology, because 'What is at stake . . . is the concrete process by which the textual configuration mediates between the prefiguration of the practical field and its refiguration through the reception of the work.'[56] If the practical field is taken to be the existing legal background, and reception is taken to refer to both the reception by the legal professionals and the larger field of societal reception including, in the end, societal acceptance, Ricoeur is also right to emphasise that while the short-term goal of judging is to end the uncertainty for the parties involved, the ultimate finality of the act of judgement is social peace rather than ongoing strife.[57] This point, noted already by Thomas Hobbes, although for different reasons, is all the more relevant in our contemporary societies when catastrophic events such as acts of terrorism occur, which result in political pressure on the judiciary and/or the legislator that all too often disregards or deliberately puts aside long-cherished principles of law and values of democratic societies under the rule of law.

Law and Narrative: Reading for the Plot

My preliminary investigation of narrative from a legal practitioner's perspective continues with the question posed by Peter Brooks as to whether law needs a narratology.[58] This is to ask whether or not it is important to develop a *legal* narratology that has a status as a legal methodology rather than to make do with specific elements derived from literary narratology *per se*. Further, if a legal narratology is to be developed, what form should it take? I pose these questions not least because the practice both of law and of legal theory are

---

[54] P. Ricoeur (trans. D. Pellauer), *The Just* (Chicago and London: University of Chicago Press, 2000), pp. 129–30.

[55] Reagan, *Paul Ricoeur*, p. 77.

[56] P. Ricoeur (trans. K. McLaughlin and D. Pellauer), *Time and Narrative* (Chicago: University of Chicago Press, 1984), vol. 1, p. 53.

[57] Ricoeur, *The Just*, p. 128.

[58] P. Brooks, 'Narrative transactions – does the law need a narratology?', 18 *Yale Journal of Law & Humanities*, no. 1, 2006, pp. 1–38.

for obvious reasons very much attached to the concept of the rule of law rather than the rule of men. The very idea of the role of narrative in judging when viewed from a traditional doctrinal and/or a legal-positivist perspective would seem to open the door to subjective elements that supposedly threaten logocentric reasoning and rationality, judicial impartiality, objectivity and equality before the law. And this too is in itself a specific viewpoint as far as the whatness of law is concerned. My voice is that of a legal practitioner in the field of criminal law in a civil law jurisdiction, who has immediate experience of narrative's failures and successes at various levels. Another aim of the present book is that this praxis-oriented perspective may help to inspire narratologists to turn to law.

Studying the field of narrative from the perspective of a judge has often made me feel like monsieur Jourdan in Molière's play *Le Bourgeois Gentilhomme*; I have experienced that I had been reading for the plot all my judicial life. Nonetheless, I am often perplexed, and look for more guidance. At the same time, however, I repeat that the narrative turn in law needs more congruity and articulation as far as its focus is concerned, even though the pioneering works of the 1970s have now been supplemented by sophisticated views on how legal discourse is organised narratively at different levels. What Peter Goodrich as early as 1987 called 'the glaringly obvious fact'[59] that legal theory and practice depend on tools of rhetorical and linguistic analysis has still not yet been fully internalised, not even in the various interdisciplinary subfields of *Law and Literature*. More importantly, to voice perhaps yet another caveat, narrative is not the panacea for all our legal woes. As Ruthann Robson and James Elkins have noted, citing narrative can close down inquiry as well as open it up, since narratives – like legal rules – do not come with inbuilt explanations: 'Instead, . . . narratives are particularized explorations of particular people (or non-human forms of existence) in particular situations, and at their best they illuminate the ambiguities, the contradictions, and the un-theorizability of life.'[60] This is an important point, given that, due to law's historical connections to narrative, many intuitive notions of narrative are part of it. Think, for example, of the etymological significance of the old terms to denote the function of advocate in Middle English – namely, narrator and *counter*, derived from the French *conter*, to tell a story and plead in a court of law.[61] One might then argue that since jurists have been telling

---

[59] P. Goodrich, *Legal Discourse: Studies in Linguistics, Rhetoric, and Legal Analysis* (New York: St Martin's Press, 1987), p. 1.

[60] R. Robson and J. R. Elkins, 'A conversation', 29 *Legal Studies Forum*, 2005, pp. 145–72, p. 159.

[61] See A.-H. Chroust, *The Rise of the Legal Profession in America* (Norman: University of

stories since time immemorial, why bother at all with the intricacies of narrative? Or, viewed from a different angle, consider the late Cornelia Vismann's point about the German judge's traditional responsibility to convert the disputed *Ding* – that is to say, disputed matter – into some 'thing' that could be spoken about, a development that she claims gained momentum with the spread of Roman law in Europe in the twelfth century and the subsequent theoretical development of an emphasis on punishment rather than damages in criminal law.[62] In other words, the matter under dispute evolves into a matter of fact to be adjudicated by means of judicial narration. This historical fact also provides another good reason to focus on the judicial function as being important for research geared to developing a legal narratology. Why? Because initially the turn to narrative in the field of *Law and Literature* literally remained academic. In other words, the first revaluation of narrative within jurisprudence developed a theoretical antidote to the technicalities perceived in formalism and positivism, but it did not find its way into the courtroom.

In narratology, a comparable development can be seen in the fact that the early narratologists focused on narratological model-building. Thus, perhaps it comes as no surprise at all that, until recently, narratologists did not immediately treat things legal as topics for consideration. David Herman offers a list of topics, derived from Wellek and Warren, that, I suggest, might already have included law as a target field in the 1970s. For example, Wellek and Warren posit that narrative fiction is only one subtype of narratively organised discourse. From the legal perspective, this insight can immediately be connected to the problem of temporality in evidentiary settings. Further,

> the notion that the 'truth' of narrative fiction arises from the way its components hang together to form a *Kosmos* sufficient unto itself, whereas the truth of a historical account depends on the extent to which it matches, in some sense, the way the world is,[63]

could obviously have been translated long ago into questions of veracity and verisimilitude in legal settings.

Oklahoma Press, 1965); R. Pound, *The Lawyer from Antiquity to Modern Times* (St Paul: West Publishing Co., 1953), p. 78.

[62] C. Vismann, 'Die unhintergehbare theatrale Dimension des Gerichts', in C. Vismann, *Medien der Rechtsprechung* (Frankfurt am Main: S. Fischer Verlag, 2011, pp. 19–37). Think also of the Islandic term *Althing* and the German term *Thingstätten* for the place where people gathered to render or to receive justice.

[63] D. Herman, 'Histories of narrative theory (i): a genealogy of early developments', in J. Phelan and P. J. Rabinowitz (eds), *A Companion to Narrative Theory* (Oxford: Blackwell Publishing, 2005, pp. 19–35), p. 21.

Another reason to focus on the work of the judge also relates to the topic of temporality; the judge was not present when the brute facts that she has to decide about took place. For that reason, the actions that occasion the lawsuit can only be re-enacted before the judge by means of a variety of narratives that may differ as far as their story-time and their discourse-time is concerned.[64] To reiterate, this demands on the part of the judge an understanding of the temporal order of an action that is itself informed by other cultural and professional narratives, including the pre-understanding that we have of the order of an action, which is based on 'the pre-narrative quality of human experience'. This understanding of narrative re-enactment obviously entails a departure from the correspondence theory of language as an objective vehicle for communicating information, the *adequatio rei et intellectus* noted in Chapter 2, including for law the mimetic theory that facts are entities in the world, and can be transmitted by means of words as the encoded thoughts that are our perceptions of these very same facts. Facts are always to a certain extent perspectival products.[65] It is precisely because of the need for this awareness of the influence of our conceptual frameworks on our valuations that work needs to be done on the concept of narrative in legal surroundings.

Consequences for Law and the Humanities: Two Examples

Peter Brooks

I mention all of these considerations in order to reiterate my point that jurists – when they use language to translate brute facts into the reality of a legal narrative – should be imaginative with regard to both the law and the people whose fates they determine. If the way in which the facts of a case are narrated, and, more specifically, the order in which they are narrated determines the outcome of a case, jurists then need to develop and to value narrative knowledge, for no small reason because the events that were overlooked and/ or, for some reason, did not ultimately become the relevant facts may be of

---

[64] Story-time defined as the narrated time within the story, 'the sequence of events and the length of time that passes in the story', and discourse-time as 'the length of time that is taken up by the telling (or reading) of the story'; available at <http://www2.ang listik.uni-freiburg.de/intranet/englishbasics/Time02.htm> [last accessed 26 March 2016].

[65] See M. Riffaterre, *Fictional Truth* (Baltimore: Johns Hopkins University Press, 1990), pp. xiii–xiv, for the view that 'the narrative need not be judged true because it corresponds to an external image of the world, but because it is consistent with the linguistic usages current in a given social context, at a given moment in time'.

equal importance.[66] This has also been Peter Brooks' consistent argument. He defends the epistemological view on narrative when he claims that narrative is 'the way we make sense of meanings that unfold in and through time'.[67] He is, however, also critical of this process as it unfolds in legal practice, for while law always concerns competing stories, these stories may mislead, and they may do so deliberately. Further, Brooks repeats Robert Cover's view on law as violence when he warns us not to forget that law 'sends people to prison, even to execution, because of the well-formedness and force of the winning story'.[68] His lament is that law seems to disregard the importance of narrative knowledge and intelligence. These considerations lead to a quest guided by the question, 'Could one say that law needs a narratology? What would be its elements?'[69]

Brooks' methodological emphasis resembles that of Ricoeur, in that he emphasises the importance of plot as a way to structure time and experience.[70] His definition of 'narrative glue' as 'the way incidents and events are made to combine in a meaningful story', as well as his argument that 'the substance of this narrative glue depends in large part on the judges' view of standard human behavior, on what words and gestures are to provoke fear, for instance',[71] ties in with what Ricoeur claims about the mediation of human experience through prior narratives. From this perspective, the *doxa* that Brooks finds in Roland Barthes's definition – though I would suggest that Aristotle discovered it long before Barthes – as 'that set of unexamined cultural beliefs that structure our understanding of everyday happenings'[72] has to be incorporated into this narrative glue. In other words, because context and perspective matter, they deserve careful investigation, not least because 'perspectival narratives'[73] in law depend, I suggest, on the specific procedural surroundings in which they take place: for example, within an adversarial or inquisitorial setting, but also based on a set of expectations constituted by judicial professional culture.

On the basis of these theoretical considerations, Brooks analyses Justice

---

[66] I. D. F. Callinan, 'Stories in advocacy and in decisions, the narrative compels the result', 12 *Texas Weslyan Law Review*, 2005, pp. 319–30, p. 323, 'It is . . . not only the way the actual facts are narrated that determines the case, but also the order in which they are narrated and the facts that are omitted'.

[67] P. Brooks, 'The law as narrative and rhetoric', in P. Brooks and P. Gewirtz (eds), *Law's Stories: Narrative and Rhetoric in the Law* (New Haven and London: Yale University Press, 1996), pp. 14–22, p. 14.

[68] Brooks, 'Narrative', p. 416.

[69] Brooks, 'Narrative transactions', p. 24.

[70] Brooks, 'Narrative transactions', p. 24.

[71] Brooks, 'Narrative', p. 417.

[72] Brooks, 'Narrative', p. 418.

[73] Brooks, 'Narrative transactions', p. 10.

Benjamin Cardozo's opinion in *Palsgraf v. Long Island Railroad Company*, and, with respect to Helen Palsgraf's injuries, criticises Cardozo's statement of facts for only telling 'the story of the event under adjudication. He recasts the story events so that they make a legal point, rendering it a narrative recognisable in terms of legal principle.[74] Accordingly, Brooks blames Cardozo for stacking the deck by beginning with the doctrine of foreseeable harm in tort cases and then, in a Procrustean exercise, telling the story to fit the doctrine, thereby introducing narrative coherence *ex post facto*.[75] The point made here about the construction of a story is a salient one when it comes to developing a general theory of legal and/or judicial narratology. However, Ayelet Ben-Yishai quite rightly suggests that

> What Brooks finds problematic – 'only appears to tell the story' – I regard as instructive. Narrative analysis is indeed as important an analytical tool for legal studies as Brooks claims it is. However, I argue that its importance lies not in revealing how legal stories should be written but rather in revealing the judicial, historical, political, and social stakes in their having been written the way they were.[76]

This important observation pertains to the direction that interdisciplinary narratological research should take. More specifically, I want to suggest that for narratological research, a diachronic analysis of law's story within specific national jurisdictions needs to be developed as well, and then used for comparative purposes. To my knowledge, this line of research has so far not been taken up. Furthermore, Ben-Yishai's point illuminates the need for attention to the bond of theory and practice that this book advocates.

Monika Fludernik

Brooks' suggestions, however, have, already been taken up in narratological studies in a different way. Monika Fludernik points out that the narrative

---

[74] Brooks 'Narrative', p. 419, and Brooks 'Narrative transactions', p. 14. Noteworthy is Justice Rehnquist's opinion in *DeShaney v. Winnebago County Department of Social Services[DSS]*, 489 U.S. 189 (1989), on the question of whether or not the DSS, who knew that 4-year-old Joshua DeShaney was beaten repeatedly by his father, were responsible for his ultimate brain damage because of failure to intervene. The opening statement 'The facts of this case are undeniably tragic' suggests compassion, but it is followed by a cold enumeration of reasons that DSS were not responsible, which tells us that Justice Rehnquist's narrative was mainly driven by doctrine.

[75] P. Brooks, 'Retrospective prophecies: legal narrative constructions', in E. S. Anker and B. Meyler (eds), *New Directions in Law and Literature* (Oxford: Oxford University Press, 2017), pp. 92–108.

[76] A. Ben-Yishai, *Common Precedents: The Presentness of the Past in Victorian Law and Fiction* (Oxford: Oxford University Press, 2013), p. 22.

turn in literary theory forces narratologists to accept that other disciplines will appropriate their conceptual framework. One such contemporary extension of the term narrative is that 'narratology is now held responsible for explaining . . . narrative representations in . . . legal contexts.' [77] Fludernik engages with Brooks' analysis of *Palsgraf* in terms similar to those of Ben-Yishai.[78] With Brooks, she observes, 'Narrative presumes a logic of events that may not happen in real life . . . we may base our judgments on fictions that have no purchase on what really was the case.'[79] Fludernik's analysis underlines a salient point for the development of a legal narratology: namely, professional acculturation may render jurists oblivious to their choices with respect to the facts, but it also alerts us to the other problem noted: what indeed is meant by 'real life' or 'what really was the case'? Views of the facts and the case may differ, depending not only on one's disciplinary background but also because differences in substantive and procedural law, as well as in accompanying theories of evidence, are constitutive.

Fludernik's discussion of law as code renders this point poignantly clear. As she rightly claims, code is 'a much more difficult area of the law, where narrativity has traditionally been regarded as non-existent'.[80] For example, in her analysis of the New York Penal Law Section 10, which defines offences, violations, felonies and crimes, she writes, 'Note that the definition of the transgression is related not to a particular act but to the punishment imposed.'[81] To a jurist, this is not at all notable, because the addressee of a statutory provision in a criminal code is not the individual citizen but the judge, at least in civil law jurisdictions. Nevertheless, this is likely not different in common law jurisdictions in which sentencing is the judge's prerogative after the jury decides on whether or not a defendant is guilty. Fludernik concludes that 'transgression of the law is not defined as an issue of morality but as an issue of bureaucracy and of the imposition of rules that

[77] M. Fludernik, 'Histories of narrative theory (II): from structuralism to the present', in J. Phelan and P. J. Rabinowitz (eds), *A Companion to Narrative Theory* (Oxford: Blackwell, 2005), pp. 38–58, p. 50.

[78] M. Fludernik, 'A narratology of law? Narratives in legal discourse', 1 *Critical Analysis of Law*, no. 1, 2014, pp. 87–109, available at <http://cal.library.utoronto.ca/> [last accessed 2 January 2017], p. 88, 'One of the key features of such narratives is not (only) cultural preconceptions about ranges of causality, but the various narrators' deliberate (or perhaps sometimes unintentional) selection of circumstances, that is to say their neglect or repression of other important evidence'.

[79] Fludernik, 'Narratology of law', p. 89.

[80] Fludernik, 'Narratology of law', p. 92.

[81] Fludernik, 'Narratology of law', p. 102, referencing the N.Y. Penal Law § 10.00ff. (2009).

need to be obeyed'.[82] From the point of view of legal theory, this remark about transgression not being defined as a moral issue seems to refer to a view, inspired by a conception of natural law, of the interrelation between law and morality. Paradoxically, however, in its reference to bureaucracy, the comment seems to imply a view of judging as an automatic application of a given set of rules, the outcome of which is known beforehand, because the judge is merely *iudex deductor*. What is more, it does not take into consideration the difference in law and legal theory between norms and rules. The norm is 'Thou shalt not steal'. The codified rule tells us, 'But if you do, this is what will happen to you, if and when your act is discovered and there is enough evidence to convict you'.

While I fully agree with Fludernik that 'Crime is necessarily agentive and therefore can be conceived of as a narrative',[83] I still remain a bit puzzled by her contention that 'more contemporary law codes deliberately suppress the narratives that abound in the courtroom and outside it and try to transform the defendant even before conviction into the anonymous representative of a category'.[84] The statutory rule is necessarily always general, because the legislator cannot think of all the possible situations to which it might apply. Therefore, the legal rule finds its meaning only in its application in the individual case. Furthermore, the fact that the addressee of the rule is the judge who must determine its application does not mean that the narratives in court are 'denarrativized . . . once the sentencing project takes over'.[85] Instead, a general division of tasks occurs in the legal process. To be clear, however, this is not to quibble or to take an esteemed colleague from the humanities to task, but to offer a cautious reminder that attention needs to be paid to the *quidditas* issue, the whatness of law or any other discipline, as noted in Chapter 3. Interdisciplinary co-operation is urgently needed to undertake this task, or we will run the risk of forgoing the chance to implement highly relevant observations in the project of outlining a judicial/legal narratology. In other words, European jurisdictions deserve the kind of careful and considered narratological analysis that Fludernik has performed on US American statutes.

Conclusion

On the basis of the conceptual framework sketched above, we can engage fruitfully in interdisciplinary research in law and narratology concerning

[82] Fludernik, 'Narratology of law', p. 102.
[83] Fludernik, 'Narratology of law', p. 108.
[84] Fludernik, 'Narratology of law', p. 109.
[85] Fludernik, 'Narratology of law', p. 109.

topics like narrative rationality, emplotment, and narrative glue in their interconnection with regard to legal practice. This is especially the case if we also connect these topics to the requirement that judges possess narrative intelligence and deliberative judicial *phronèsis*, the situational knowledge that Ricoeur advocated for jurists. Why? Because they inform the hermeneutic movement from the facts to the rule and from the legal concept to the judicial decision, always back and forth, and they guide the way in which the judge develops her own perspectival narrative that, in turn, allows her to constitute the decision making process. Put differently, the act of judicial emplotment and application when taken literally as *ad plicare* – the folding of the fact and the legal rule into a reciprocal union in order for a new meaning to unfold – requires a narratology. The first reason for this is because this process is guided by one's interpretive framework, while the second is because of the similarity between narrative and legal interpretation. They do not constitute the application of the abstract rule to the story of the case, but involve a judgement about probability, verisimilitude and truth on the basis of the whole of one's knowledge of the world, 'connecting the case to the rule, through a narrative description taken to be truthful',[86] as noted in Chapter 6. The third reason for a narratology is because in the whole process, judges play the role of someone who brings about a reversal of fortune, a *peripeteia* for others, and they may fall short of the necessary quality of recognition, the Aristotelian *anagnorisis* of what is indeed the truth in a specific case.[87] This is especially so since – to reiterate – judicial understanding is retrospective. Nothing, for example, can be done if parties to a case are negligent when it comes to incorporating relevant elements into their narratives in situations where rules of procedure require the judge to be passive rather than active in her search for the truth. But if narratological research on law is to have an actual impact, some pitfalls need to be avoided, as the next chapter will argue.

---

[86] P. Ricoeur (trans. D. Pellauer), *Reflections on the Just* (Chicago: University of Chicago Press, 2007), pp. 55–6.

[87] Aristotle (trans. S. Halliwell), *Poetics* (Cambridge, MA, and London: Harvard University Press, 1999), 11, 1452a, 29 (p. 65).

10

Towards a Legal Narratology II: Implications and Pathologies

Implications: The Influence of the Master Narrative

Common law v. civil law dichotomies?

From a jurist's perspective, the first pitfall of legal narratological research is the false dichotomy frequently made between common law and civil law reasoning. It is certainly the case that common law reasoning has an affinity for the concept of narrativity, because it is normatively based on precedent. Nevertheless, it is often ignored that civil law reasoning also includes precedent as a source of law; precedent, however, is given less weight when it comes to bowing to its authority in the sense of the *stare decisis* characterising common law reasoning. Here we find a comparable rather than a dissimilar situation. I emphasise this point for interdisciplinary reasons, since in academic discussions with scholars from other disciplines of the humanities, I often encounter the misconception that civil law reasoning is merely syllogistic rule application that is deductive in nature, because it supposedly moves from abstract codified legal norms to a decision about a specific case. In other words, in contradistinction to common law reasoning, civil law reasoning supposedly espouses the idea of law as a mere set of codified propositions, a domain of written rules.[1]

As I hope to have shown in this book so far, from a *hermeneutical* point of view, the above is hardly the case, because while the written rule may be the starting point of reasoning, it is not the sole determinant of the outcome. Nor is it the case that the judge has a partly prosecutorial function. The position of the judge between the prosecuting government official and the defendant

---

[1] See G. Olson, 'De-Americanizing law-and-literature narratives: opening up the story', 22 *Law & Literature*, 2010, pp. 338–64, p. 352, 'legal reasoning proceeds through a process of deduction from abstract norms of codified law to the particular case at hand'; H. Porsdam, *From Civil to Human Rights, Dialogues on Law and Humanities in the United States and Europe* (Northampton, MA: Edward Elgar, 2009), p. 174, 'Civil law starts with certain abstract rules, that is, which judges must then apply in concrete cases'.

in criminal cases, or as the arbiter of the dispute between two civilian parties, is that of the impartial third party, who indeed connects the relevant statutes and principles of law to the case at hand, and who functions as a check, either against the abuse of government power in the asymmetrical relationship between the state and the citizen, or against a comparable abuse of power between civilian parties. But she does so, ideally at least, not by means of a deductive methodology but, as noted in Chapter 6, by way of a combined effort of grasping together the relevant facts and the legal norms. What is more, she is able to make law. In the event that the law is not clear and decisive on a specific question, the decision of the judge generates the new rule. Obviously, this new rule so generated can later be adjusted when the legislator decides to codify, or when later judicial decisions change direction. On the ethical plane of judging, the judge's work is an 'open work'[2] in that any human act – if in law it is to be called a fact – waits for our conscientious interpretation.

At the same time, a second pitfall may entail the risk of overlooking procedural differences between common law and civil law systems, as often happens when scholars use the word law loosely. For example, in discussing storytelling at the appellate level in civil cases in US courts, a contradistinction needs to be made to most civil law systems as well as to UK courts of appeal, in which a second level of consideration of both questions of law and fact occurs, which includes hearing defendants and witnesses and sentencing. The same risk can be found on the level of substantive law when differences involving the mental pictures that jurists have of civil law and common law when dealing with legal concepts may cause them to act like ships passing in the night. To give one example, in nineteenth-century English common law, when the writ system evolved into a system in which 'a cause of action' became the start of a lawsuit – 'a cause of action' being a factual situation that one person stated in order to obtain a remedy against another person – old classifications such as trespass evolved into torts. Torts are actions *ex delicto*, whereas the writ of *assumpsit* (damages) was brought under the heading of contract, an action *ex contractu*.[3] In contrast, a civil law jurist thinks more in terms of rights. In the Dutch system, civil damages to be paid in the event of an '*onrechtmatige daad*', a figure that is often – all too loosely, which is

---

[2] See P. Ricoeur (trans. K. Blamey and J. B. Thompson), *From Text to Action: Essays in Hermeneutics, II* (Evanston, IL: Northwestern University Press, 1991), p. 155ff.

[3] For these examples, I draw on G. Samuel, *A Short Introduction to the Common Law* (Cheltenham: Edward Elgar, 2013), pp. 55–6. See also B. Grossfeld and E. J. Eberle, 'Patterns of order in comparative law: discovering and decoding invisible powers', 38 *Texas International Law Journal*, 2003, pp. 291–316.

precisely the point – translated as torts, are not thought of as arising out of contract. Therefore, Stephen Paskey is correct when he suggests that the dichotomy between rule-based reasoning and narrative reasoning is a false one, because the legal rule can also be read as a story, and, more specifically, as a stock story.[4] Of course, stock stories differ, depending on the specific rule and the legal system. That is why we have to take into account the specifics of the many legal cultures and respective languages in civil law European countries when developing a legal narratology. Jack Balkin has already urged us to reflect on the premise that 'cultural software always creates the possibility of critical engagement with itself'.[5] He does so from the perspective, firstly, of culture as the set of collectively created tools of understanding and cultural know-how, and therefore as a form of 'cultural software', with, secondly, linguistic ability as both constitutive of the human and formative when it comes to articulating human understanding, language being 'the most prominent form of collective cultural software'.[6] And that is precisely the point when engaging in interdisciplinary research aimed at developing narratological insights geared towards legal surroundings.

Inquisitorial v. accusatorial approaches?

A third pitfall of legal narratological research is that in the criminal law context, most civil law countries have an inquisitorial approach that favours a process of verifying evidence, with written evidence gathered before the case comes to trial. At this stage, the falsification principle is honoured more in the breach than in the observance, even though the aim is to arrive at the substantive truth. This is markedly different from an accusatorial approach, because evidentiary standards and processes differ. Yet, unlike professionally appointed judges who have to legitimise their decisions by stating legal grounds as well as the grounds that contributed to their judicial conviction, the common law jury represents a black box; it provides no reasons for its decision. Furthermore, in a system in which the search for the truth is laid more prominently in the hands of the involved parties and lay people – in other words, in a system that includes cross-examination and a jury – the

---

[4] S. Paskey, 'The law is made of stories: erasing the false dichotomy between stories and legal rules', 11 *Legal Communication & Rhetoric: JALWD*, 2014, pp. 51–82. See also on story skeletons, e.g. the betrayal story in divorce stories, F. Jannidis, 'Character', in P. Hühn et al. (eds), *The Living Handbook of Narratology* (Hamburg: Hamburg University), available at <http://www.lhn.uni-hamburg.de/article/character> [last accessed 16 February 2016].

[5] J. M. Balkin, 'Ideology as cultural software', 16 *Cardozo Law Review*, 1995, pp. 1221–33, p. 1233.

[6] Ibid. p. 1228.

judge's role is more passive. Plea bargaining also strengthens the idea of a partial truth. On this basis, we may safely assume that the rhetorical and discursive strategies that contribute to narratives in court may differ, depending on the respective legal system in which they occur. I specifically use the word 'strategies' here. When it comes to determining what the legally relevant facts are, opposing narratives – there is *always* another side to the story, for it cannot be otherwise – may for obvious reasons focus more on explaining away contradictory evidence, and this may lead to ignoring other facts that are equally or even more relevant. In situations in which forensic evidence such as blood samples, DNA tests, and so forth are lacking, this pattern proves even more problematic: for example, when the basis for judging is narrow to begin with.

The 'whatness' of narratological notions

Furthermore, Greta Olson has taken up the *quidditas* issue, and noted that jurists' notions on narrative 'are insufficiently critical and lacking in theoretical acuity'.[7] Honesty compels me to consider that this applies to my own argument. She has urged us not to use the term 'narrative' for all kinds of phenomena that need to be properly differentiated if the narratological project for law is to be successful. To add to the already rich array of distinctions addressed in Chapter 9, and to show how definitions themselves can augment the jurist's perplexity, I repeat some provided by Olson, precisely because she has also recognised them as contested within narratological studies. 'Narration', then, refers to the act of relating, and 'story' in a legal setting denotes the facts and/or the sequence of events, and that, I suggest, would be viewed as the same act by most jurists; 'discourse' would refer to the form of the telling, while 'narrativization' refers to 'the procedure in which a text is processed in someone's mind in response to its narrativity, or story-like qualities'.[8]

What are facts anyway?

I agree with Olson that we need to focus more on the specific forms that the narrative structures take in the texts and procedures of the law. And not least because in narratological studies so far Anglo-American common law settings are offered as the default. More importantly, the way in which jurists look upon the facts also depends on jurisdiction, and that would include insight

---

[7] G. Olson, 'Futures of law and literature: a preliminary overview from a culturalist perspective', in C. Hiebaum et al. (eds), *Recht und Literatur in Zwischenraum/Law and Literature In-Between* (Bielefeld, Transcript, 2015), pp. 37–69, p. 40.

[8] Ibid.

into the history of ideas informing their views on the differences between the *quaestio iuris* and the *quaestio factis*. Two examples illustrate the point. For the contemporary criminal law setting, Floris Bex offers an Aristotelian definition: 'The *facts of the case* often denote the events or states of affairs that are assumed, at least for the moment, to have happened or existed.'[9] In court, facts are indeed assumed to have happened 'at least for the moment' as the requirement of judicial suspension of disbelief, as discussed in Chapter 7, suggests. Barbara Shapiro has shown that historiography became imbued by the concept of fact as developed in the English legal tradition, and subsequently spread to the natural sciences. The distinction between matters of fact and matters of law, a *factum* being an action or event in which individuals participate, as opposed to a *datum*, a given in and by nature, came to the fore in the way common law dealt with the issue of the evaluation of the truth or falsity of evidence by the jury, leaving the facts to the jury and legal doctrine to the judge. Eventually, reciprocity became the key word. 'Fact oriented surveys, reports, and descriptions were so familiar that fictional "matters of fact" imitated real narratives.'[10] The struggle between rhetorical persuasiveness and legal truth as fought out in today's courts, be it in adversarial or inquisitorial criminal law, makes all the more urgent the importance of an inquiry into this part of the history of ideas of law and literature.[11] This is especially so because within the development of the natural sciences, empiricism and rationalism culminated in a theory of scientific positivism, and thereby became instrumental in propounding, firstly, that law's value lies in its objectivity, and secondly, that law as a body of rules exists separately from those who are called upon to decide cases in practice. Furthermore, such inquiry when that includes comparative aspects could help illuminate the influence of context on the development of legal concepts. All of this suggests that a unilateral process of cultural adaptation by jurists of narratological insights that evolved in other disciplines should be avoided, and that a multilateral re-contextualisation of important research topics that avoids any

[9] F. Bex, *Arguments, Stories, and Criminal Evidence* (Dordrecht: Springer, 2011), p. 12.

[10] B. Shapiro, 'The concept "fact": legal origins and cultural diffusion', 26 *Albion*, 1994, pp. 227–52, p. 238. See also L. Hutson, *The Invention of Suspicion: Law and Mimesis in Shakespeare and Renaissance Drama* (Oxford: Oxford University Press, 2007); C. Biet, 'Judicial fiction and literary fiction: the example of the factum', 20 *Law & Literature*, no. 3, 2008, pp. 403–22; P. Haldar, 'The articles of law: Renaissance theories of evidence and the poetic life of facts', 10 *Law and Humanities*, no. 2, 2016, pp. 281–99.

[11] See P. Schneck, *Rhetoric and Evidence, Legal Conflict and Literary Representation in U.S. American Culture* (Berlin: De Gruyter, 2011); L. Hutson, 'Proof and probability: law, imagination, and the forms of things unknown', in E. S. Anker and B. Meyler (eds), *New Directions in Law and Literature* (Oxford: Oxford University Press, 2017), pp. 144–59.

'-centrism' is called for. To tie the above arguments together and illuminate the theoretical considerations, I now turn to criminal law in order to elaborate on the interdisciplinary requirement that more work be done on a theoretical plane of legal narratology. This could then serve as a basis for research on legal practice that would also include empirical research.

Pathologies of Narrative in Criminal Law

Choices

To judge is to choose. Paul Scholten, the greatest Dutch legal theorist of the twentieth century, observed,

> The judge does something other than observing in favor of whom the scales turn, he decides. That decision is an act, it is rooted in the conscience of he who performs the act. That which is expected of a judge is a deed . . . It is the task of the judge to deliver judgment. I think that there is more than merely observation and logical argument in every scientific judgment, but in any case, the judicial judgment is more than that — it can never be reduced to those two. It is not a scientific proposition, but a declaration of will: this is how it should be. In the end it is a leap, just like any deed, any moral judgment is.[12]

Applied to our topic, this means to choose between events and human acts considered to be – or not to be – legally relevant facts; between stories that are plausible in a legal context and those that are not; between narratives to which a legal value can be attached or not, and for what reason, because at the end of the day, the judge as reader-narrator tells the world how she interprets and evaluates what others have told her; and lastly, to choose between the consequences of different choices. What weight should be attached to specific facts? What pieces of evidence should be valued as sufficient proof? Is, as the premise of the theory of anchored narratives claims, a 'good story' in criminal law not only compatible with the available evidence but also anchored in our general knowledge of the world?[13] The success of this evalu-

---

[12] P. Scholten, *General Method of Private Law. Mr. C. Asser's Manual for the Practice of Dutch Civil Law* (Amsterdam: Digital Paul Scholten Project, [1931] 2014), vol. 1, Chapter 1, available at <http://www.paulscholten.eu/research/article/english/> [last accessed 1 April 2016]. But see R. Ferguson, 'The judicial opinion as literary genre', 2 *Yale Journal of Law & the Humanities*, 1990, pp. 201–7, p. 207: 'The one thing a judge never admits in the moment of decision is freedom of choice'.

[13] W. A. Wagenaar et al., *Anchored Narratives: The Psychology of Criminal Evidence* (Harvester Wheatsheaf: St Martin's Press, 1993).

ative and interpretive process depends on the quality of the judge's phronetic discernment. If we follow Kant in his *Critique of Judgment*, the first stage of any judgement is the imaginative one, and this includes reflecting upon what is 'not there'. This is to acknowledge what may not have risen to the surface among the available materials and arguments, as much as what has simply been overlooked or missed because of how judges are influenced by cultural, personal and professional backgrounds.

To complicate matters even further, the way in which we use the term 'culture' is also indicative of our overt or covert ideologies. Do we think in traditional terms of Matthew Arnold's *Culture and Anarchy*, or T. S. Eliot's *Notes Towards the Definition of Culture*, or do we invoke Terry Eagleton or Zygmunt Bauman? Or is culture 'ordinary', as claimed by Raymond Williams, who co-founded the field of *Cultural Studies* in the early 1960s?[14] The *quidditas* issue of culture is not easily resolved.[15] Furthermore, the move away from high culture to popular culture in cultural-legal studies – or rather, the turn from Dostoevsky and Shakespeare to *Crime Scene Investigation* and *Boston Legal* – is often accompanied by what I perceive as popular culture's law-bashing or farcical, perverse portrayal of law. And at the same time, para-doxically, the gist of so many products of popular culture is that law is the great redeemer, and that in the end law and justice will prevail. That as well is often in sharp contrast to everyday legal reality. One thing is clear, the legal *nomos* that Robert Cover distinguished, and the narratives that constitute it as well as the effects of its own narratives on others, undoubtedly channel the jurist's narratives in any given case.

The point, I suggest, is important, given the weight of judicial narra-tivisation and research in cognitive narratology.[16] This is even more the case when we broaden the scope of our topic to include the visuality and mediality of law, because focusing on what Kenneth Chestek calls the judicial 'sweet spot' by means of narrative can easily be translated to persuasion by means of images in order to activate judicial narrative empathy.[17] After all, in all

---

[14] R. Williams, 'Culture is ordinary', in R. Williams, *Resources of Hope: Culture, Democracy, Socialism* (London: Verso, [1958] 1989), pp. 3–14.

[15] See a.o. R. Post (ed.), *Law and the Order of Culture* (Berkeley: University of California Press, 1991); A. Sarat and T. R. Kearns (eds), *Law in the Domains of Culture* (Ann Arbor: University of Michigan Press, 1998), pp. 1–20; A. Sarat and J. Simon, 'Beyond legal real-ism?: Cultural analysis, cultural studies, and the situation of legal scholarship', 13 *Yale Journal of Law & the Humanities*, 2001, pp. 3–32; P. Burke, *Cultural Hybridity* (Cambridge: Polity Press, 2010).

[16] See D. Herman, 'Cognitive narratology', in P. Hühn et al. (eds), *Handbook of Narratology* (Berlin: De Gruyter, 2009), pp. 30–43.

[17] K. D. Chestek, 'Judging by the numbers: an empirical study of the power of story', *Journal*

jurisdictions alike, what is done with the facts in order to persuade the judge, and this goes for both the texts of law and other media, is done deliberately, and it may be done for rhetorical purposes only – that is, discarding legal relevance in favour of trying to affect judicial mental shortcuts that are based on judicial emotion. For this reason, we should also consider cautiously the insight occasioned by the metaphoric understanding of the 'Oh, now I *see*' kind, because, as with metaphor, narrative can also work to our detriment when it activates – without our perceiving it – what DeSanctis called the 'deep frames – cognitive principles that are so fundamentally a part of our identity that, once activated, evoke subconscious reactions that can lead us to real decisions'.[18] This is also to say that *phronèsis* in relation to truth necessarily encompasses reflection on this cognitive aspect of fiction as knowledge as well. The next chapter elaborates on this topic.

In a comparable way, Richard Sherwin has addressed the manner in which our making sense of things depends on our organising the various components of cultural knowledge, ranging from interactions with family members to textual sources of all kinds, as well as all sorts of non-textual media. One important type of organising framework is the 'schema', which 'acts like a familiar story that we carry in our head asking for completion', and another is the 'script', a representation of 'knowledge about events that are widely known and shared', consisting of 'an ordered sequence of action', such as how to behave in a restaurant.[19] Sherwin's point is that if our thinking about and behaving in the world – the sum total of our knowledge – depends to a large extent on schemata and scripts, this should incite us not only to consider our frameworks more carefully but also to allow our traditional perceptions of credibility and persuasion in law to include such notions, because they affect the ways in which we judge. And is not Johnny Cochran's powerful suggestion to the jury in the O. J. Simpson trial, 'If it doesn't fit, you must acquit', a form of script and a metaphoric mantra that needs judicial consideration? Viewed differently, one might compare the risk of script to that of syllogistic reasoning; namely, the idea of a script can make us cram the facts into the script in the same way that facts are squeezed into the Procrustean bed of the syllogism's major premise. Furthermore, the risk

---

of the Association of Legal Writing Directors, 2010, pp. 1–35, p. 34, 'that sweet spot where a deep frame is activated . . . without it being so obvious that the reader's natural defenses are triggered'.

[18] C. H. DeSanctis, 'Narrative reasoning and analogy: the untold story', 9 *Legal Communication and Rhetoric: JALWD*, 2012, pp. 149–71, p. 159.

[19] R. K. Sherwin, 'Law frames: historical truth and narrative necessity in a criminal case', 47 *Stanford Law Review*, 1994, pp. 39–83, p. 50.

that, on the one hand, the stock story, the deep frame, and the sweet spot and script, and, on the other hand, confirmation bias and belief perseverance are mutually reinforced should give us cause for concern if we consider that – as Francis Bacon had already taught us – we all most readily believe that which we prefer to be true.

As with narratives, also with images the question of what justifies credibility is crucial. On this issue, Sherwin's contribution, precisely because his perspective is nourished by American law, is important for comparative reasons, because as he himself claims, 'Every culture has its own way of imagining the real'.[20] That obviously includes legal cultures other than those rooted in common law. When it comes to deciding whether or not an image presented in a courtroom may count as evidence, the question is 'What is it that we see?' And that should obviously include our asking whether or not images are fabricated or manipulated. Think of the huge evidentiary problem with photoshopped images in child pornography or in cybercrime generally, with the fabrication of images being one of the big problems in our digital age, which brings us back to the questions of representation and reality. Photographs and images, as much as diagrams and MRI scans – all too often manipulated by inserting colours not found in the original object that was scanned – used in evidentiary settings tell stories that we need to learn how to read, while realising that the familiar stories we carry with us in our heads are dominant guides of our expectancies with respect to their plots and narratives.[21] In this context, the CSI effect should not be underestimated either; popular TV series such as CSI, CSI Miami, CSI New York, Bones and so on and so forth affect the popular perception of forensic science(s) to such an extent that the legal professional needs to reckon with this perception when he has to deal in his daily practice with the findings of forensic technologies.[22] Consequently, the question of how to put our trust in visual images is acute. In the US American context, Francis Mootz, for example, lauds Sherwin's analysis of how visual images have distinctive qualities, but rejects his view that the visual age is a totally different phenomenon. Textuality returns with a vengeance, since 'Visual images hold power only by virtue of their

---

[20] R. K. Sherwin, 'Law, metaphysics, and the new iconoclasm', 11 *Law Text Culture*, 2007, pp. 70–105, p. 70.

[21] Cf. W. Wolf, 'Narratology and media(lity): the transmedial expansion of a literary discipline and possible consequences', in G. Olson (ed.), *Current Trends in Narratology* (Berlin: De Gruyter, 2011), pp. 145–80, pp. 159–60.

[22] See P. Goodrich, 'Screening law', 21 *Law & Literature*, no. 1, 2009, pp. 1–23; R. K. Sherwin, 'A manifesto for visual legal realism', 40 *Loyola of Los Angeles Law Review*, 2007, pp. 539–791.

embeddedness in a linguistically structured and mediated cultural reality', meaning that visual images perform the evocation of narrative structures even though they themselves are not textualised.[23] That is why I suggest that we keep in mind the fundamental hermeneutic question, 'What is it that I do when I say that I attribute meaning to narratives, including visual images, and which are the determining factors in that process?'

Equally important is the question, 'How do we incorporate what we see in our legal system's procedures?' It is here, I think, that many continental European legal systems differ greatly from Anglo-American ones, as do the professional scripts of European jurists. In Dutch criminal procedure, for example, if the defence or the prosecutor presents pictures or shows the results of CCTV recordings of what happened in the streets of a city's entertainment district, in order for the judge to be able to use these as evidence, the minutes of the trial session must mention the judge's observation of the tape. This, of course, is the first area of contention, since the very reason for bringing in such evidence involves the parties' disagreement about what happened, which is why they demand the judge's opinion on these materials, and, furthermore, the judge's reading of the pictures is undoubtedly informed by doctrinal assumptions and evidentiary standards.[24] So in the realm of the visual as well, the 'seeing as' of metaphor co-constitutes decisions.[25]

Another notable topic in this context is the effect of media and visuality on juries. It is exemplified in the heated debate that ensued in October 2010 in Belgium after a jury in the *Court d'Assises* convicted a woman of murder, and she was subsequently sentenced to thirty years imprisonment, presumably mainly on the basis of the unpleasant impression she made during the trial, and in a situation where there was no directly incriminating evidence. The defendant denied all of the charges. The facts were seemingly simple. The victim and the defendant had been having a love affair with the same man; they both belonged to the same parachute club; the victim's parachute had not opened when she jumped from a height of 4 kilometres; and the defendant was deemed to be knowledgeable about how to sabotage a parachute and how to enter the parachute club without being detected. The decision was not

---

[23] F. J. Mootz III, 'Law among the sight lovers', 75 *New York Law School Law Review*, 2012, pp. 61–74, p. 71. See also C. Vismann, 'Image and law – a troubled relationship', in C. Vismann (eds M. Krajewski and F. Steinhauer), *Das Recht und Seine Mittel* (Frankfurt: S. Fischer, 2012), pp. 417–27.

[24] See P. Haldar, 'Law and the evidential image', 4 *Law, Culture and the Humanities*, 2008, pp. 139–55.

[25] See P. Brooks, '*Scott v. Harris*: The Supreme Court's Reality Effect', 29 *Law & Literature*, no. 1, 2017, pp. 143–9, on police videos as 'self-interpreting evidence'.

quashed by the Belgian Court of Cassation.[26] While Belgium is now thinking of abolishing the jury system, the Netherlands over the past few years has discussed the possibility of introducing it. If the medium is indeed the message, the question here is what are the combined effects of the medium's form and its narrative content. This is so because the change from word-based information to medialisation has certainly contributed to democratising information, but it does not always answer to calls with regard to its veracity; therefore, the risk of 'garbage in, garbage out', to use another metaphor, is not hypothetical. In short, the critical question that Clive Baldwin aptly suggests – 'Who needs facts, when you've got narrative?' – can be broadly applied.[27]

To reiterate, this book's leading premise – that law is a textual discipline – is not done away with by new trends in mediality and visuality in law, the importance and impact of which I of course acknowledge, if only perhaps because I encounter them in daily practice. As far as mediality is concerned, we must consider whether or not perhaps the maxim 'Give me the facts and I will give you the law' is not under serious pressure from the new trend of trial by media, or the charivari of 'Give me the tweets and I will give you the law' in this day and age in which facts are often ominously called 'alternative' rather than lies as old school parlance would have it, and media vilification of parties to a trial can affect sentencing. Furthermore, we need to consider, far more than is done to date in the legal professions, in which way social media can be – and are – put to use in order to force a defence lawyer to consider declining to act as counsel, a prosecutor to consider a strategy different from the one originally envisaged, or a judge to consider recusal, and all for the wrong reasons from a legal point of view.

And then there are the scripts of popular or informal justice that I use here in the sense of the dispute resolution that the general public seeks, or hopes to get, either in TV courts – that is to say, in contradistinction to state law and its institutions – or by means of media attention for the legal

---

[26] Court of Cassation, Belgium, 3 May 2011, N292_3.5.11, available at <https://justitie.belgium.be/sites/default/files/downloads/AC%202011%2005.pdf>.

[27] C. Baldwin, 'Who needs facts, when you've got narrative? The case of P, C & S vs United Kingdom', 18 *International Journal for the Semiotics of Law*, 2005, pp. 217–41; see also D. Herman, 'Narrative as cognitive instrument', in D. Herman et al. (eds), *Routledge Encyclopedia of Narrative Theory* (Abingdon and New York: Routledge, 2008), pp. 349–50. An intriguing movie in this context that any judge should see is *Presumé Coupable* (2011, English title *Guilty*). It is based on the Outreau affair in France, a case in which many men and women in the town of Outreau were charged with incest and paedophilia from 2000 to 2006, on the basis of testimony of the victims' parents, who had made up the whole story. See also A. Garapon and D. Salas, *Les nouvelles sorcières de Salem, leçons d'Outreau* (Paris: Seuil, 2006).

procedure they are involved in.[28] Essentially homologous to institutional law in its legal representations, the cultural location of popular justice, in contrast, lies in the presumed views of the general public on what the right outcome of a case should be. I will skip the topic of the representation of the judge in reality television, and of the fascinating hybrid creature of postmodernity, the judge-show judge.[29] For my example, I draw on a personal experience. In spring 2012, we tried a case of a ghost-driver who was driving the wrong way on a motorway and who was also under the influence of alcohol, who was charged with culpable homicide after having caused a fatal car accident in which a young man died. The Dutch Supreme Court had already referred the case back to the Court of Appeal on a technical point of law with respect to the deadline for sending in the defendant's blood sample for forensic investigation. The young man's bereft mother hoped for legal and emotional closure, but she was extremely anxious that because of legal technicalities the defendant would get away with a less severe punishment than she hoped for. So she turned to the makers of a then new TV series entitled *Pro Deo*,[30] in which a team of well-known Dutch defence lawyers helped people to seek justice as they perceive it. The *Pro Deo* team then asked permission to record the proceedings in court on the day of the trial. Given the rules and regulations Dutch courts have, this comes down to what is called the 'penguin shot' – the entrance of the members of the judicial panel in full attire with black robes and white bands – the introduction of the case, and the charging speech of the public prosecutor, and, two weeks later, the session in which the judgement is pronounced. So far, so good. But when the episode was televised, the court was not amused when the images of the reading of the judgement to the defendant were followed by shots of the defence lawyer, whom we knew had definitely not been present at that crucial moment. What was more, we found that much of this episode was filled with attempts by the TV host to get into contact with the defendant outside the courtroom. He had gone to

[28] Popular justice as defined in A. Norrie, *Law and the Beautiful Soul* (London: GlassHouse Press, 2005), pp. 33–49.

[29] But see C. D. Bond, '"We, the judges": the legalized subject and narratives of adjudication in reality television', 81 *UMKC Law Review*, 2012, pp. 1–60; D. R. Papke, 'From flat to round: changing portrayals of the judge in American popular culture', 31 *The Journal of the Legal Profession*, 2007, pp. 127–51; P. Robson and J. L. Schulz (eds), *A Transnational Study of Law and Justice on TV* (Oxford and Portland, OR: 2016). For a culturalist view on women judge shows, see G. Olson, 'Intersections of gender and legal culture in two women judge shows: *Judge Judy* and *Richterin Barbara Salesch*', in H. Petersen et al. (eds), *Contemporary Gender Relations and Changes in Legal Cultures* (Copenhagen: DJØF, 2013).

[30] See http://www.rtl.nl/programma/prodeo; Episode 2, broadcast 30 December 2012 in the Netherlands on channel RTL8.

the defendant's home to try and talk about the case. Given the presumption of innocence that we hold dearly, and also from a point of view of privacy before and after sentencing, such an attempt is reprehensible in judges' eyes, for it resembles an *auto-da-fé*. My example also serves as a caveat to those involved in cultural studies, and that would be to mistrust deeply what they see when they see court proceedings of any kind.

A thoughtful consideration of how scripts and so forth work on the case level is also necessitated by the increasing use of Bayesian statistics to guide the decision making processes in the criminal trial. Two remarks suffice. Firstly, in Bayesian statistics, the 'garbage in, garbage out' principle applies equally, so that if the choices made with respect to the *prior odds* are nudged both by biased views and the deliberate usage of scripts, the subsequent *likelihood ratio* and *posterior odds* will fail tragically to lead to a just outcome. Secondly, in the sense that such scientific discourse is also narratively structured, it uses its own rhetoric and metaphor on the plane of the representation of its premises.[31] And, to add another caveat, what if we forget about the importance of statistical significance – or rather, the lack of it – in a situation where a story seems to make good sense? The acknowledgement that scientific explanations as well as humanistic understandings are forms of story-telling, related although distinct, is important when we deal with the problem of the valuation in law of scientific reports and the testimony of expert witnesses. For judges unaccustomed to the specifics of a discipline other than their own, it can be most helpful to gain insight into the way other forms of cognition function, but they need to do so carefully.

This brings us back again to the epistemological debate about the facts and the concept of cognition and knowledge, and reminds us of the distinction, problematic as that is – as legal pratice shows – between the *factum probandum*, the fact that is the subject of proof, and the *factum probans*, the fact from the existence of which that of the *factum probandum* is inferred. In short, is there a chain of circumstance out there or does (some)one carefully fit together the facts and evidence, along with the other established facts and so on and so forth? Truth in law is not written in stone. Psychological proclivities to which we are all prone may easily lead to serious errors of judgement and to the miscarriage of justice when a judge explains away as incorrect anything inconsistent with the story and, in hindsight, confabulates and creates the illusion that there were all kinds of good and conscious reasons to decide as she did. After all, chunks of evidence always diverge, and

---

[31] J. J. Bono, 'Science, discourse, and literature: the role/rule of metaphor in science', in S. S. Peterfreund (ed.), *Literature and Science, Theory and Practice* (Boston: Northeastern University Press, 1990), pp. 59–89.

the environment is always dialectical. Obviously, a judge's past experience of specific people and situations leads her to construct trait patterns with respect to stereotypical behaviours that she applies to future situations. The prejudice trap always looms large.

I still recall – and on a regular basis – the error I almost made many years ago when I was sitting as a single judge, and the case before me was that of a young man charged with vandalism. After the closing time of the bar where he had spent the evening drinking, he had wrecked the mirrors of numerous cars parked in the vicinity. Standard script involving an intoxicated youth using some form of violence? When he entered the courtroom, a middle-aged woman walked in behind him. I immediately thought that she was his mother, coming to convince me that her son was usually such a nice guy, and to ask that the punishment not be too severe. This had often happened in my judicial practice, because the regional court was in a predominantly rural area where, in comparable cases, parents practically always came along. Already I felt a twinge of irritation. But how wrong I would have been to follow the script. At the end of my conversation with the young man, I asked the woman who she was, and she replied that she was a psychologist, and had helped treat the young man for his post-traumatic stress disorder. The condition was the result of his having been a member of the Dutch Battalion – part of the UN peacekeeping force – that served in Bosnia in the former Yugoslavia in the 1990s, and that had been unable to guarantee the safety of many deportees, who then fell victim to the ethnic cleansings by local armed forces. This stress disorder was the cause of the young man's sudden and violent behaviour, although the alcohol may have helped. The case taught me the hard way not to go along with my own scripts and prejudices.

Let us turn to another aspect of judicial choosing. The awareness of the constraints brought about by legal principles and rules of procedure is all too easily forgotten in the focus on legal narrative; for example, consider *Nullum crimen, nulla poena sine lege*, the principle of legality brought forward by Beccaria in *On Crimes and Punishment* (1764), according to which human conduct is punishable only when there is a legal basis, such as in a codified rule designating it as a crime. The wording of the criminal charge – the allegations with respect to the defendant's actions at a certain point in time and in a certain place – guides the search for relevant facts and circumstances, and these points in turn all have to be established. To complicate this, the underlying substantive offence in the accusation may depend on further investigations; for example, when a defendant is caught in the act, his role – as well as the nature and the full magnitude of what happened – may not be immediately clear. In short, what matters in the end is the legal qualification of a criminal act: namely, the qualification of facts such that they fall under the provision of a specific article of the criminal code, and the modality of the deviation from the legal norm as exemplified in the codified rule that is the point of reference. The search for this qualification governs the act of reading. Therefore, once you have named the fact, you have got it. All this is important to note, since criminal law is a highly specific mode of regulating human behaviour in a social context that aims at restoring the social balance disrupted by the criminal act.

To reiterate, at the very moment we use language to name things in the world, selection and restriction take place. We cannot help but see things from a specific angle, from the perspective, the position that we take. This means that language in the sense of speech and of writing and reading narrative is a continuous process of deciding what can and will be said, and what will – literally – not be spoken of. In short, language usage is in itself a selective interpretation. There are always roads not taken. The twentieth-century German philosopher Martin Heidegger compares this process with a searchlight that illuminates specific phenomena in a specific way, while leaving others in the dark. Consequently, our articulation of reality as we perceive it by means of language is the result of a process of selective interpretation on the basis of the perspective that we take. This opens up possibilities at the very same moment that it delimits when that which is not spoken of remains obscure in the background. The choice for a specific use of language precedes dialogue, and is always already a decision concerning meaning. Heidegger emphasises that the process of reciprocity – man forms and is formed by language and reality – does not preclude us from falling into the trap of thinking that language is 'just' the objective tool that 'we' use to describe 'the world'. In other words, it is *hubris* to think that this mediation is neutral.[32] For law and legal interpretation, this should lead to the application of a critical hermeneutics. '*Wem Gott ein Amt gibt, dem gibt er allerdings Verstand*', wrote Hegel – that is, 'if God gives someone an office, he also gives him sense'.[33] Others, whether appointed for life or elected, will do well to develop the *iuris prudential* and practical wisdom of law that the present book promotes.

---

[32] M. Heidegger (trans. G. Fried and R. Polt), *Introduction to Metaphysics* (New Haven: Yale University Press, [1935] 2000). Heidegger is widely regarded as one of the greatest contributors to philosophical hermeneutics. It should also be noted that his career was severely tainted by his association, however brief, with the National Socialists when he was rector of the University of Freiburg in 1933–4. This controversial aspect does not prevent me from referring to Heidegger here and in Part III of this book, but it does call for a critical scrutiny.

[33] G. W. F. Hegel, *Grundlinien der Philosophie des Rechts* (Hamburg: Felix Meiser, 1967), p. 12; G. W. F. Hegel (trans. H. B. Nisbet and ed. A. W. Wood) *Elements of the Philosophy of Right* (Cambridge: Cambridge University Press, 2003), p. 18.

To complicate legal-narratological matters even further from an epistemological point of view, we find in the jurist as reader-narrator a subject who describes not only the world as she finds it but also the world on which she will pronounce judgement. The knowing subject and the known object converge, and that is, not incidentally, another reason that law belongs to the humanities. That the referential world of criminal law as the legal translation of the pre-legal reality[34] is constituted by criminal law itself opens up a field for interdisciplinary research. Such research could include, firstly, the important question, for linguists and jurists alike, of whether or not this pattern seems to imply a return to the descriptive view of language that we thought we had by now left behind. This problem was pointed out as early as the 1980s by the Leyden professor of criminal law A. C. 't Hart, but to my knowledge it has so far not prompted research.[35] And secondly, it could involve a further study into how legal narrative re-presents reality: that is, if we start from the view that the interpretive process constitutes the move from the ambiguous to the unequivocal. Put differently, society demands from the judge answers in situations in which she cannot know everything, not only because complete information is an illusion but more specifically because the files never fully represent what happened. How does that affect her narrative? Furthermore, research on sequentiality within the narrated story in law – for example, narrated time and narrative time – could help elucidate issues that legal practice has to deal with.

Suggestions

What else should we keep in mind when developing the interdisciplinary project of a narratology of law? I would like to offer some suggestions that are by no means exhaustive. First of all, the pre-trial needs to be differentiated from the trial stage of the proceedings. In the pre-trial stage of police interrogations, narratological research should focus on plot and narrative constitution as well as on narrative coherence.[36] The most important reason for doing so consists in the circumstance that it is not immediately obvious to the reader who it is who has structured the action of the recorded action, and how they did so. The leading narrating voice is that of the interrogator, but

---

[34] A. Ben-Yishai, *Common Precedents: The Presentness of the Past in Victorian Law and Fiction* (Oxford: Oxford University Press, 2013), p. 43.

[35] A. C. 't Hart, *Strafrecht en Beleid, essays* (Zwolle and Louvain: W. E. J. Tjeenk Willink and ACCO, 1983).

[36] See also M. H. Weresh, 'Morality, trust, and illusion: ethos as relationship', 9 *Legal Communication & Rhetoric: JALWD*, 2012, pp. 229–72; B. Jackson, *Law, Fact and Narrative Coherence* (Liverpool: Deborah Charles Publications, 1988).

the written record does not always give information on the form, length and circumstances under which the interrogation actually took place. The interrogator is the one who selects what goes into the record. If the record does not show the questions asked – and many interrogations do not follow the open questions suggested by Quintilian (and applied by Thomas Aquinas and most members of the Inquisition after him), *Quis, quid, ubi, quibus auxiliis, cur, quomodo, quando*? Who? What? Where? With what auxiliaries? Why? How? When?[37] – but instead the defendant is asked to confirm the events that the investigation has produced, the judge-qua-reader cannot know whether the story suggests a linearity of events and a chronology where there in fact was none, or whether parts of the defendant's account were left out, accidentally or deliberately filtered away, and, if so, for what reasons. Were these elements justifiably left out because they were not legally relevant or because they were not what the police wanted to hear? What if the record is presented as a first-person narrative, or if it consists only of selected legally relevant passages presented as a unified narrative whole?[38] The judge cannot check the gaps if there is no audio(-visual) recording. What is more, the assumption that – other than in the fictional world – in the real world of law there are no gaps should not lull us into complacency.[39] In the sense that any narrative is a recounting, it can suffer from gaps that judges should indeed mind, for they can be deliberate 'plot holes'.[40] In other words, the record invites the judge to accept the narrative account as real, as having evolved organically, and subject to the laws of probability and necessity, as noted in Chapter 9. But all too often the record is a form of 'hint fiction', a short story that may or may not be – but how is the judge to know? – suggestive of a larger, complex story. This makes the judge's decision based on the *facta probanda* more difficult. This point must be made to highlight procedural differences that are dependent on jurisdiction; for example, it matters a great deal whether the

---

[37] Quintilian, *Institutio oratoria* (Cambridge, MA: Harvard University Press, 1996), L.V ch.10, par. 20ff.

[38] P. Brooks, 'Narrative Transactions – Does the law need a narratology?', 18 *Yale Journal of Law & Humanities*, no. 1, 2006, pp. 1–38, p. 7, for the example of Justice Potter Stewart in *Bumper v. North Carolina*, 391 U.S. 543 (1968) lamenting that 'The transcript of the suppression hearing comes to us . . . in the form of narrative; i.e., the actual questions and answers have been rewritten in the form a continuous first person testimony. The effect is to put into the mouth of the witness some of the words of the attorneys'.

[39] On gaps, see S. Wistrand, 'Time for departure? The principle of minimal departure – A critical examination', in G. Rossholm and Ch. Johansson (eds), *Disputable Core Concepts of Narrative Theory* (Berlin: Peter Lang, 2012), pp. 15-44.

[40] M.-L. Ryan, 'Cheap plot tricks, plot holes, and narrative design', 17 *Narrative*, no. 1, January 2009, pp. 56–75.

written file forms the basis of the trial proceedings or whether all witnesses are questioned by the judge(s) in open court, as is the situation in Germany.

The same consideration applies to the trial stage with regard to witness testimony and the need to be able to recognise perjury and strategies of equivocation. It also applies to victim impact statements, including aspects connected to their scope. With respect to scope, it is crucial to know whether in any given legal system a victim impact statement is literally just that – restricted to a statement, that is – about the impact of the crime on a victim's life, or whether the victim is allowed to say something about evidence and sentencing in open court. If it is a matter of the impact, how is one to deal with emotions that may run high? If the victim is permitted to address the evidence and sentencing, how will that guide or influence the judge's behaviour towards both defendant and victim during the proceedings and afterward in chambers, and affect deliberation on the outcome? After all, criminal law is traditionally all about the asymmetrical relation between the defendant and the state represented by the public prosecutor; therefore, the introduction of the victim's story may be thought of as problematic or at least uneasy, given the presumption of innocence.

Similarly, the same consideration applies to whether or not the defendant testifies in court, which also depends on procedural factors. What is the value of a story of confession, troubling as it may be in the pre-trial stage, as Brooks has noted?[41] Should a confession have an untimely effect on the judge's valuation of the evidence and ultimately on her conviction, which, taken together, form the basis of her ruling? If conviction and proof are dissociated, as in legal systems with a jury not formally required to justify its decision also in the sense of its underlying conviction, the valuation of narrative takes place in a situation markedly different from the one in legal systems such as the Dutch one, where proof and judicial conviction are the two pillars on which the judgement rests, or the French one, in which the judicial *conviction intime* is accepted in the *Court d'Assises* as the sole justification for the judgement. For this reason, a confession 'should make us worry',[42] not least because of the risk of a miscarriage of justice.

In the trial situation, narrative competence is presumed. But what if the defendant remains silent, either because the defence lawyer advised doing so,

---

[41] P. Brooks, *Troubling Confessions: Speaking Guilt in Law and Literature* (Chicago: University of Chicago Press, 2000). See also P. Brooks, *Enigmas of Identity* (Princeton: Princeton University Press, 2011), ch. 5.

[42] E. Scarry, 'Speech acts in criminal cases', in P. Brooks and P. Gewirtz (eds), *Law's Stories: Narrative and Rhetoric in the Law* (New Haven and London: Yale University Press, 1996), pp. 165–74, p. 167.

or because he or she is unable to tell in an adequate manner the story of what happened? How, then, is this voice, or the lack of it, to be recognised in the battle of competing stories? In the trial stage, criminal law's specific truth conditions and procedural constraints, including the rules of evidence, have an own impact on the stories that are told. The presumption of innocence confers an individual's right to a fair trial as laid down in Article 6 of the European Convention for the Protection of Human Rights and Fundamental Freedoms (comparable to the Miranda rule in American law, *Miranda v. Arizona*, 384 U.S. 435, 1966). It rests on the classical principle laid down in the phrase *nemo tenetur prodere se ipsum* (no one is obliged to incriminate himself). And it is indissolubly connected to the rule of law in a democratic society in the protection that it guarantees against unlawful intrusions into people's lives. As a prohibition against putting pressure upon a person suspected of having committed a crime, it refers to the deference in law for the defendant as a party in criminal proceedings when it comes to respecting human dignity in the sense of both the free will and physical and mental integrity.

But what if the narrative strategy employed by the defence lawyer backfires?[43] Obviously, a defendant needs a lawyer to translate his or her view of the facts into legal terms. The story needs to cohere with the semantic demands of the legal qualification of his or her act on the basis of the charge, but also to stay clear of them at the same time. Similarly, if defendants honestly try to tell their stories in their own words, they do not always understand the negative legal consequences. The point is beautifully illustrated by the late Willem J. Witteveen in his analysis of Pirandello's short story 'The Truth'. In it, a farmer called Tararà stands trial for having murdered his wife after she had been discovered in the marital bed with her lover. The lover's spouse had called the police and the lovers had been arrested. Tararà admits that he had known about the love affair for a while but that he had not acted on this knowledge until the wife dishonoured him by causing such a scandal, an aspect of the narrative that, unfortunately, does not save the day for Tararà.[44] All of this is also to point to the aspects that may influence the focalisation within the narrative of the court: that is, the selection and/or restriction as far as the information used is concerned.[44] At the end of the day, the court chooses its characters with which to tell its story as the reflection of how to legitimise its decision.

---

[43] E. Merz and J. Yovel, 'Court room narrative', in D. Herman et al. (eds), *Routledge Encyclopedia of Narrative Theory* (Abingdon and New York: Routledge, 2008), pp. 86–8.

[44] W. J. Witteveen, 'Seeing Rhetoric as Law as Literature', in R. Kevelson (ed.), *Conscience, Consensus, & Crossroads in Law* (New York: Peter Lang, 1995), pp. 387–402.

Viewed differently, another narrative problem area arises with respect to the presumption of innocence. While an appeal to the right to remain silent may not be used as proof, a defendant who fails to offer an explanation for an incriminating witness statement will find that this circumstance can and will be used against him or her,[45] especially when there are expert witness statements, the narrative relevance and the credibility of which are often valued higher. Hence, a failure in litigation skills and narrative strategies may trigger a judicial conviction and *libido puniendi,* the desire to punish; this factor needs to be reckoned with, especially in those cases in which there is no long and clear jurisprudential background.[46]

Narrating Oneself

A literary example that exemplifies the above points is John Coetzee's novel *Disgrace.*[47] Set in post-apartheid South Africa, *Disgrace* is a human rights *Bildungsroman* [48] in a double sense: on the one hand, as the narrative of the protagonist David Lurie's self-destruction and subsequent self-recreation, and, on the other hand, as the narrative of violence and the possibility of redemption and reconciliation that the novel holds before us in its depiction of the plight of Lucy, Lurie's daughter. Central to the novel are parallel narratives regarding violations of human dignity, a literary microcosm of human rights issues. The tone is set at the very start of the narrative when David Lurie, former professor of modern languages in Capetown but recently demoted to adjunct professor of communications, is ironically described as a professional failure who lacks personal dignity. As a result, 'Because he has no respect for the material he teaches, he makes no impression on his students' (Dg 4).

Lurie's weekly visits to Soraya of Discreet Escorts reveal both his egocentric, misogynistic views and his desire to engage in a personal relationship. When he chances upon a student of his, Melanie Isaacs, thirty years his junior, he invites her for supper and asks her to stay and spend the night with him. She refuses. Lurie knows 'that is where he ought to end it. But he does not'

---

[45] See *Krumpholz v. Austria*, European Court of Human Rights 18 March 2010, Application no. 13201/05.

[46] I derive the term *libido puniendi* from M. R. Damaška, 'The competing visions of fairness: the basic choice for international criminal tribunals', 36 *North Carolina Journal of International Law and Commercial Regulation*, no. 2, 2011, pp. 365–87, p. 369.

[47] J. M. Coetzee, *Disgrace* (London: Vintage/Random House, 2000). Hereinafter (Dg + page number).

[48] My reading of *Disgrace* is informed by J. R. Slaughter's magisterial *Human Rights Inc.: The World Novel, Narrative Form, and International Law* (New York: Fordham University Press, 2007).

(Dg 18). He takes her out for lunch and back at his house he makes love to her on the living-room floor, realising she is no more than a child but unable to check his desire. A week later he goes to her flat and, unlike Soraya, 'she is too surprised to resist the intruder' (Dg 24), so 'All she does is avert herself . . . Not rape, not quite that, but undesired nevertheless, undesired to the core' (Dg 25). Lurie realises his mistake. The whole thing explodes in his face when Melanie lodges a complaint against him, and it turns out that he had also drawn up a fraudulent record, because she had skipped classes and he covered that up. Symbol and symptom of domination, Lurie sorely lacks *dignitas*. He does not fulfil the duties proper to his rank as a university teacher, and when having to face the committee examining the complaint, he does not exhibit the proper language of respect, the deference required in the situation. While Lurie pleads guilty to both charges – it is important to note that only the attendance fraud is mentioned explicitly, the sexual harassment is not voiced – he refuses to say he is sorry about what happened, 'Guilty as charged. That is my plea. That is as far as I am prepared to go' (Dg 51). The committee immediately understands what he is after – 'There is a difference between pleading guilty to a charge and admitting you were wrong, and you know that' (Dg 54). Lurie, however, refuses to sign a statement for the very reason that it contains an apology. His guilty plea should suffice. Lurie prioritises the private above the public sphere. He asks what the point is when his apology is not sincere. The answer is simple: 'The criterion is whether you are prepared to acknowledge your fault in a public manner and take steps to remedy it' (Dg 58).

This scene is of great significance, not only for what follows in the narrative as far as Lucy's rape is concerned but also for broader issues of law when it comes to dealing with the truth and reconciliation that the eponymous South-African committee had to confront. I am thinking here of the place of the victim in legal procedure as far as standing and voice are concerned. To tie my argument to the discussion of hermeneutic and testimonial injustice in Chapter 8, there is, of course, the problem that criminal law starts from the premise of individual responsibility, whereas systemic violations of human rights of the kind perpetrated by oppressive, totalitarian regimes are much harder to redress when the perpetrators are either no longer alive or – if we recall the defendants in the Nuremberg and Tokyo tribunals – are pleading that they merely obeyed higher authorities. When the problem of voice is viewed from the perspective of the victim, it is exactly because of the dominant asymmetrical vertical relation between the state and the individual in criminal law, with the defendant as its focal point that finding a language with which to give voice is hard. Or, as Benjamin Berger put it succinctly, 'The point here is that the gravamen of victimhood lies in the senselessness of suffering, not in the fate or blame of the perpetrator. Criminal law can speak to the latter, but has nothing to say about the former', and, as a result, 'the criminal law inescapably exposes the chaos and injustice of experience'.[49] Being allowed to tell one's story and to be heard is a way to be recognised as a human being. Such procedure also confers, if only for the moment in court, dignity on the speaker in that it honours her autonomy as a legal subject. Therefore, in order to demand one's rights, both a forum to do so and an individual voice are required, as much as the guarantee of decent treatment. Although judges obviously always have to strike a balance between personal and institutional contexts, their respectfulness towards the people before them, be they defendants, victims, or other parties to a case, is always required, as can also be seen from various codes of judicial conduct.[50]

After having been asked to resign, Lurie leaves for a visit to his daughter Lucy, who lives on a smallholding in a rural area, and has boarding kennels for dogs. One day, two black men and a boy come to the farm, hit Lurie on the head, and lock him in the lavatory, after which they rape Lucy, shoot all the dogs and leave them to die, and steal what little of material value Lucy owns. Not only does Lucy refuse at first to tell Lurie what happened, mirroring his view on the distinction between the public and the private – and is the story of her being raped not voiced in the newspapers comparable to Melanie's harassment being reduced to an incident – but when she finds out she is pregnant, she decides to keep the baby and stay on the farm. Even though Lucie's existence is initially disintegrated by adverse personal circumstances, her further development is not at risk. She opts instead for agency and presence, and is able to narrate herself. In the end, her individual narration redeems both herself and Lurie.

The Judge's Voice

Still another complication may arise as far as narrative is concerned when at the end of the day the judicial panel has to decide about the value and force of the evidence laid down in competing narratives. The difficulty arises from the narratological question of 'Who speaks?' when applied to the judge's voice. The narrative perspective of the judicial decision is that of an impersonal, omniscient third-person narrator whose authorial voice speaks with authority.

---

[49] B. L. Berger, 'On the Book of Job, justice, and the precariousness of the criminal law', 4 *Law, Culture and the Humanities*, 2008, pp. 98–118, pp. 108 and 109.

[50] See the *Recommendation CM/REC (2010)12 of the Committee of Ministers to Member States on Judges: independence, efficiency and responsibilities*, a European Code adopted on 17 November 2010 by the Committee of Ministers; the *ENCJ* (European Network of Councils for the Judiciary) *Working Group Judicial Ethics Report 2009–2010. Judicial Ethics: Principles, Values and Qualities*, adopted in 2010 by the ENCJ General Assembly.

To paraphrase Charlotte Brontë's protagonist Jane Eyre, 'Reader, I convicted him'. The agency of this voice pretends not to be that of individual persons. Judging, however, is a human activity, and this third-person-narrator mode conceals several first-person narratives. What if a judicial panel finds that it cannot get its set of first-person narratives to cohere with one another? Where common law and supra-national European courts offer the solution of having concurring and dissenting opinions, rendering poly-narration acceptable, there is no such problem for the individual judge. But if a judicial panel has to speak in a single voice, that of 'the Court', and the views of individual panel members differ, writing a decision as a judicial narrative of compromise becomes a very difficult task indeed.

Furthermore, the lower courts' narratives are always also composed in view of their being scrutinised by a higher court in appeal or cassation: namely, with an eye on the legal and factual feasibility of the evidence chosen to legitimise the decision. In this sense, they do well to follow Aristotle's advice that the plot should leave out anything unnecessary, anything that distracts from the main storyline, which in the legal situation could give the higher court reason to reverse or to quash. That, too, may compromise both voice and narrative, as judges translate what were originally perhaps episodic facts into a causally related string of events with legal consequences.[51] This is yet another reason that the form and content of judicial narratives matter, and why judges need to consider carefully their *mimesis praxeos*.

If law is indeed a matter of narrative, and narratives legislate meaning in many different ways,[52] probably no judge can plead not guilty to a charge of disciplinary parochialism. By way of conclusion, I offer a small paideic suggestion in order to encourage even the most sceptical jurist to consider the value of hermeneutics and narratology. My own experience from the summer course 'Language, Literature and the Judiciary', which I co-design and co-teach in collaboration with the Dutch Training and Study Centre for the Judiciary as part of Dutch professional judges' permanent education, is that it works brilliantly to rattle the judicial cage by means of a reading of the French writer Raymond Queneau's *Exercises in Style*.[53] In it, Queneau offers ninety-nine re-tellings of the same tale in different modes and styles. Reading a selection of these aloud, one after the other, and then trying to paraphrase

---

[51] On episodic plots, see Aristotle (trans. S. Halliwell), *Poetics* (Cambridge, MA, and London: Harvard University Press, 1999), 10, 1451b, 33-35 (p. 63).

[52] M. Aristodemou, *Law and Literature: Journeys from Her to Eternity* (Oxford: Oxford University Press, 2000), p. 3.

[53] R. Queneau (trans. B. Wright), *Exercises in Style* (Richmond: Oneworld Classics, [1947] 2009).

or re-write them with an eye to plot, content, and style confronts judges with the possibility that the same things can be said differently, and with their often unconscious personal choices as far as word usage and focalisation is concerned. My argument so far has been that we should not work to privilege one discipline – law or narratology – over the other. In order to honour a plurality of views in terms of narrative, we must try to engage in truly interdisciplinary work lest we run the risk of methodological shallowness and – if you will excuse the garden metaphor – end up on an intellectual compost heap. Such interdisciplinary and theoretical work on law and narratology is best begun by addressing specific jurisdictions; it should then move on to address comparative aspects of common law and civil law legal systems. Building on this basis, viable research combining theory and practice will follow. This is of considerable importance because of the contemporary public and political demand concerning efficiency of the judicial process. My point would be that the demands of quality and credibility and the need for critical judicial thought necessitate such research precisely because it can also contribute to efficiency. It is as yet undecided whether investigative efforts will lead to a full-fledged legal narratology that also addresses the specificity of legal systems, and the various types and procedures of law practiced within them. Nevertheless, hope remains for the fruition of legal narratology if we keep in mind Cardozo's dynamic view on law: 'Law never is, but is always about to be'.[54]

---

[54] B. N. Cardozo, *The Nature of the Judicial Process* (New Haven: Yale University Press, 1921), p. 126.

Part III

The Perplexity of Judges

11

Empathy Revisited:
Who's in Narrative Control?

An Understanding Heart

Almost every morning when I walk from The Hague Central Station to the Court of Appeal, I come across a pile of blankets and rags close to the wall of the Royal Library. I presume that a homeless person is sleeping there, and that it is the same person every day. I do not really know, of course, because I always hurry along to the caseload that awaits me. I do not 'see' this person, either literally nor figuratively. In the city centre of The Hague, I sometimes encounter a street vendor who is trying desperately to sell copies of a newspaper as part of a project for the homeless and the addicted. I never buy one. Who needs that kind of paper, right? One time – as I walked past him as usual – I heard him say, 'Nobody sees me'. This struck me, because his observation was as correct as it was tragic. Nobody saw him for who he was, a fellow human being, down-and-out. I felt a pang of remorse for not having bought a newspaper and given him some attention.

What does seeing someone actually mean? Does it imply the understanding that comes with feeling with someone, as Musil's *The Man without Qualities* claims in Chapter 4? What does it mean for the connection between narrative intelligence and empathy, which Chapter 8 has already highlighted? If we agree that, in order to understand, we must be prepared to take a leap of meaning in that we have to try to break through the wall of our own limited individual existence, that requires, at least for the moment of our encounter with the other, that we accept his or her position and try to grasp the circumstances that this person is in. That is what I hope we do in law when we really try to hear the other side, because, as Martha Nussbaum suggests, 'we are invited to concern ourselves with the fates of others like ourselves . . . to do unto ordinary men and women as to ourselves, viewing the poorest as one who we might be, and seeing in the most ordinary and even squalid circumstances a place where we have made in fancy our dwelling'.[1]

---

[1] M. C. Nussbaum, *Poetic Justice* (Boston: Beacon Press, 1995), p. 35.

Promoting the idea that jurists need to develop their imagination by means of increasing their narrative intelligence in order to gain insight into the *miseria hominis,* or the human mind and heart as much as its aberrations, has long been discouraged in the dominant positivistic tradition of legal methodology. It is also mirrored in literature. In the novel *number9dream,* for example, David Mitchell has the fictional character Akaito Kato say, "'I am a lawyer", "I am not paid to imagine".'[2] And in Jane Gardam's novel *Old Filth,* the schoolmaster tells his pupil Terry Feathers, "'Yes. You'll be a lawyer. Magnificent memory. Sense of logic, no imagination and no brains. My favourite chap".'[3] These views obviously tap into a widely held view on jurists, but that is odd if we consider that Solomon already begs his God to furnish him with 'an understanding heart to judge thy people, that I may discern between good and bad' (1 Kings 3:9 (AV)). Or if we think of the essential quality of a good tragedy, the site of difficult decisions *par excellence,* it is that it arouses *philantropia,* fellow feeling that is both an empathic stance with respect to the fate of the protagonist and a form of justice, based on recognition of likeness. These sources suggest that the topics of empathy and emotion have a rich history that merits our further attention. I say this for the simple reason that what James Boyd White wrote in 1985 obviously is still valid for our legal culture of argument: 'Law and literature are alike in that they both give voice to the voiceless and thus aim at "the extension of our sympathies".'[4] So far, however, both the legal-theoretical and the judicial implementation of this proposition have been geared predominantly towards a common law judicial setting, with a focus on the competing narratives of judicial opinions.[5] Furthermore, the paradigm shift in common law adjudication towards Holmesian favourites such as economics and statistics, or, as Robin West calls it, 'scientific judging', has led to, 'the demise of judicial empathy . . . as a piece of the collateral damage'.[6] This observation can be transposed neatly to contemporary civil law jurisdictions that face the challenges resulting from the influx of Bayesian statistics among others, as noted in Chapter 10.

This chapter therefore revisits the topic of empathy, and elaborates on the question posed in Chapter 10 with regard to the uses of narratological

---

[2] D. Mitchell, *number9dream* (London: Sceptre, 2001), p. 34.

[3] J. Gardam, *Old Filth* (London: Abacus, [2004] 2014), p. 68.

[4] J. B. White, *Heracles' Bow* (Madison: University of Wisconsin Press, 1985), p. 104.

[5] See A. McArdle, 'Using a narrative lens to understand empathy and how it matters in judging', 9 *Legal Communication & Rhetoric: JALWD,* 2012, pp. 173–206.

[6] See R. West, 'The anti-empathic turn', in J. E. Fleming (ed.), *Passions and Emotions: NOMOS LIII* (New York: New York University Press, 2012), pp. 243–88, p. 288.

insights into modes of persuasion. To illustrate my point, I turn to Ian McEwan's novel *The Children Act*. In it, the judge Fiona Maye's 'sweet spot' is activated to such an extent that she loses her phronetic capability. This leads to a terrible result in terms of judicial ethics and human responsibility. Now, emotion may seem a strange bedfellow if we consider that the demands of legality in contemporary jurisdictions order the judge to stay clear of her subjective persuasion, so that the rule of law rather than of men can be guaranteed. In other words, is the emotion of empathy to be accepted as an essential and/or normative component of the art of judging, more specifically in hard cases when the law, if not silent, is not particularly outspoken? That is to say, can the judge then give her discretion, coloured as it may well be by personal emotion, free rein?[7] The threat to the logocentric reasoning that we have cherished since the Enlightenment looms large for those of legal-positivist denomination. The heart and the head may obviously not be of one mind, so to speak.

My perspective is geared specifically towards empathy as a response to the emotions of others, such as anger, jealousy, love, or hate. In other words, on what – from a literary-theoretical point of view – is delineated as the combination of aesthetic empathy, empathy felt for a person whom we know to be fictional – for instance, Nicholas Nickleby, Effi Briest, Lady Macbeth, Anna Karenina, or Hannibal Lecter – and the empathy that we ourselves develop, as a professional habitus or a private character trait. The success of professional empathy can be deduced from the reaction of those affected by such a decision. That is why we should ask ourselves what kind of relation we are building – or not – when we use the language of the law in a specific way in the texts that we write. To James Boyd White, this is an ethical enterprise, in that,

> a writer always gives himself a character in what he writes; it shows in the tone of voice he adopts, in the signals he gives the reader as to how to take that tone of voice, in the attitude he invites his reader to have toward the world or toward people or ideas within it, in the straightforwardness or trickiness with which he addresses his reader – his honesty or falseness – and in the way he treats the materials of his language and culture.[8]

The success of professional empathy, therefore, is intimately connected to the readers' response to the texts of law, and such response, in turn, co-constitutes

---

[7] See T. Hobbes, *Leviathan* (London: J. M. Dent and Sons, Everyman's Library, [1651] 1987), ch. 21, for the use of discretion if the law is silent.

[8] J. B. White, *When Words Lose Their Meaning: Constitutions and Reconstitutions of Language, Character, and Community* (Chicago: University of Chicago Press, 1984), p. 15.

the legitimacy and authority of the judge as author. When the judicial text is logocentric and cold, this can evoke violent emotion. A recent example in the Netherlands is that of a father who was present to hear the decision of a lower court with respect to the defendant, the driver of a car that ran over and killed his two-year-old daughter and both her grandparents, who were cycling on a bicycle track. Out of sheer disappointment and frustration, he threw a chair at the judge who read the decision in open court. The decision itself was correct in terms of traffic law and criminal law, also as far as the sentencing was concerned – the punishment did not involve a jail sentence, since the text of the relevant article of the Road Traffic Act does not incorporate criminal intent – but did not at all, or not explicitly, acknowledge the enormous suffering of the couple who lost both a child and a set of parents.[9] In other words, the judicial decision performed its legal function of decision making and criminal law dispute resolution only in the abstract sense. It failed in its communicative and societal function, because it did not show an empathic stance towards the bereft parents, who had understandably hoped that a severe punishment would be given to the offender in the form of a jail sentence by way of retribution. Nor did it explain why the law did not allow such punishment in light of the court's qualification of the criminal act. As a concomitant result, the general public felt with the parents; it did not accept the decision as fair. Therefore, the performativity of the text of the judicial decision is intimately connected to the narrative identity of the judge taking the decision, whether or not this identity is consciously chosen.[10] And obviously we should also bear in mind other and more mundane circumstances, such as the Dutch practice that the judge pronouncing sentence need not necessarily be the judge who wrote the decision. In the Dutch criminal law system, the verdict has to be delivered exactly fourteen days after the closing of the investigation in court. For this reason, it can happen that the judge who wrote the decision is already in the middle of a new trial, and so another judge pronounces sentence. In other words, if as a judge you are given another judge's text shortly before pronouncing sentence, how are you to anticipate the reactions of those present in the court room if you lack

---

[9] Rechtbank Limburg 21 November 2014, ECLI:NL:RBLIM:2014:10041.

[10] For law as performance and event, see J. S. Peters, 'Legal performance good and bad', 4 *Law, Culture and the Humanities*, no. 2, 2008, pp. 179–200; 'Law as performance: historical interpretation, objects, lexicons, and other methodological problems', in E. S. Anker and B. Meyler (eds), *New Directions in Law and Literature* (Oxford: Oxford University Press, 2017), pp. 193–209. See also the family court decision of High Court Justice Peter Jackson, Re A: Letter to a Young Person, [2017] EWFC 48 (26 July 2017), <http://www.bailii.org/ew/cases/EWFC/HCJ/2017/48.html>

adequate information about the whole context of the case and, for obvious reasons, you cannot make any changes to the wording of the message that you have to bring?

Narrative Empathy in Law and Literature

After two decades on the bench, my experience is that in every case that comes before a judge, emotions are involved in at least two related ways. To start with, the emotions of the parties usually trigger the legal conflict, even though in corporate and commercial disputes this is mostly couched as a rights discourse involving money. In criminal law, if we abstract from emotion written into the legal rule itself – for example, in the excuse of self-defence – the emotions of both victim and perpetrator take centre stage. The judge has to be aware of these emotions and act upon that awareness. This is already a huge task if we consider the findings of victimology with respect to victim impact statements. But, more importantly, the judge has to be aware of the subtext, the stories important to the litigants that are all too often filtered away in the course of the proceedings, geared as they are towards the finding of relevant facts in light of possibly applicable rules and norms. This requires of the judge a legal imagination that includes a concrete reflection both on what is and what is not actually argued, in either oral or written form, and what the emotional aspect really is. Since a judge, too, suffers the slings and arrows of outrageous fortune, such imagination should include professional and personal self-reflection on what she recognises and accepts as valid, and why, and on what remains unacknowledged, given her own blind spot(s). The aspect of lack of acknowledgement is the most difficult, of course, not only because *hubris* may preclude the acceptance of the fact that judges too have blind spots but also because it is extremely difficult to figure out what one's blind spot is. After all, if it were not a blind spot, we would not have to locate and then act on it.

Thus far, I have used the term empathy loosely, as a kind of umbrella concept, as do many authors in the field of *Law and Literature*. Before we proceed, however, we need to consider more carefully some definitional differences relevant to my project. Originally, the translation of the German *Einfühlung* as used in nineteenth-century aesthetics and in the then developing discipline of psychology was 'empathy', and the term was used in contradistinction to sympathy. It fits in with the psychological perspective taken on literary interpretation in the nineteenth century by Friedrich Schleiermacher (1768–1834), as noted in Chapter 3, characterised as that is by the idea of understanding texts and human beings, the *Verstehen*. While compassion as a 'feeling for' dominates sympathy, empathy is a 'feeling with' others that encompasses a certain distantiation in order for it to be used in situations requiring judgement. Suzanne Keen recently defined, 'narrative empathy [as] the sharing of feeling and perspective-taking induced by reading, viewing, hearing, or imagining narratives of another's situation and condition'; while I would hesitate to include the word 'feeling' here, the contrast between narrative empathy and what Keen denotes as 'empathetic aversion', or 'personal distress', that we can experience as a negative response to what and to whom we encounter fictionally or elsewhere, is helpful. In a positive sense, narrative empathy enables the reader-spectator to give meaning to 'the emotions and sensations of a representation'.[11] But once we experience discomfort at what we see or read, followed by a form of dissonance with our own feelings, the result is aversion, literally and figuratively. In other words, where Nussbaum's hope is that the empathy that results from reading literary works will make the reader a good citizen, Keen is critical because there is no empirical evidence that such empathy will engender morally correct action. What is more, I would add, should we not differentiate between our empathic reaction to a novel when we read it during adolescence and our reaction or response when re-reading the same novel at a riper age? And also ask ourselves whether perhaps our being in conditions somewhat similar to those of the fictional character evokes our empathy?

That is why I turn to the distinctions made in cognitive narratology, helpful as they are for my analysis of McEwan's *The Children Act*. The point of departure in narratology is that both aesthetic and practical empathy are intimately connected to emotion. As Patrick Colm Hogan suggests, 'Our emotional response to stories is inseparable from our empathic response to the characters, their situations, actions, capacities, and so forth.'[12] That is relevant for law in the sense that there are multiple forms of empathy that help nourish the legal imagination. Within aesthetic empathy, Hogan differentiates between, firstly, 'allocentric empathy' that enables us to feel with what happens to the other; secondly, 'projective empathy' that asks us to imagine what it would be like if we were in the other's specific situation ourselves; and, finally, 'normative empathy' that encourages us to think about what the average person would do in such and such a situation.[13] The third distinction is familiar to jurists in the sense that they are used to dealing with 'the man on the Clapham omnibus', 'the good neighbour' and other 'reasonable men',

---

[11] S. Keen, 'Narrative empathy', in P. Hühn et al. (eds), *The Living Handbook of Narratology* (Hamburg: Hamburg University), http://www.lhn.uni-hamburg.de/article/narrative-empathy, par. 1 and 2 [last accessed 4 April 2016].

[12] P. C. Hogan, *What Literature Teaches Us About Emotion* (Cambridge: Cambridge University Press, 2011), p. 276.

[13] Ibid. p. 284.

concepts all formed on our notion of what specific circumstances require of us in terms of responsible action. All of these differ from the kind of empathy that, ideally, we develop as a character trait,[14] and from the third form, the practical empathy that as jurists we can show in both our dealing with the people before us, and in the texts that we write.

All forms of empathy are connected to emotions(s). This is also to say that while we can distinguish between our emotional responses to literary works and our empathic response to people and events, we cannot fully separate them.[15] Furthermore, we have to make careful distinctions with respect to emotions as such. Our empathic response can be triggered by another person's first-order emotion, such as his anger or grief. Then our response is itself a second-order emotion. Ideally, all of this has a practical consequence – namely, that we develop 'the capacity to make morally significant decisions in the light of empathy with the emotions of others'.[16] What interests me most from the point of view of the field of narrative jurisprudence is, on the one hand, whether – and, if so, how – judicial first-order emotions like vanity, anger, distress, uncertainty, unwarranted pride (a pleonasm?) can be influenced unconsciously by the other person's story, or, on the other hand, become the deliberate target of another person's linguistic strategy. One cannot be a good judge without imagination and empathy, and I agree wholeheartedly with Gary Watt when he writes, 'Too much respect for law and a lack of humane imagination is a terrible thing in a judge'.[17] But judges are humans, so nothing human is alien to them. When it comes to the phenomenology of perception and judgement, we should be alert to signs of unconscious activation of the judicial brain.[18] We should not only probe below the surface of the texts and utterances of the people before us but we

---

[14] Ibid. p. 276.

[15] Ibid. p. 276, 'Our emotional response to stories is inseparable from our empathic response to the characters, their situations, actions, capacities, and so forth'. See also P. C. Hogan, *Affective Narratology: The Emotional Structure of Stories* (Lincoln, NB, and London: University of Nebraska Press, 2011).

[16] T. Morawetz, 'Empathy and judgment', 8 *Yale Journal of Law & the Humanities*, no. 2, 1996, pp. 517–31, p. 523.

[17] G. Watt, *Equity Stirring: The Story of Justice beyond Law* (Oxford and Portland, OR: Hart Publishing, 2009), p. 20.

[18] See already E. Stein (trans. W. Stein), *On the Problem of Empathy. The Collected Works of Edith Stein*, vol. 3 (Washington, DC: ICS Publications, 1989), a translation of Stein's 1916 doctoral dissertation done under Edmund Husserl, with a strong foundation in the phenomenology of perception. See also on the question of how narrative functions as a mode of mental access, M. Fludernik and G. Olson, 'Introduction', in G. Olson (ed.), *Current Trends in Narratology* (Berlin: De Gruyter, 2011), pp. 1–33.

should also examine our private persona hidden under the robe of our public persona, and search for our judicial Achilles heel.

On the political level, it is interesting to note that the 2016 US presidential candidate Hillary Clinton spoke of the necessity to promote empathy – she used the term as 'imagining being in someone else's shoes' – in order to fight racial discrimination,[19] while later on in the heat of the campaign she used the metaphor of the 'deplorables' to point to her presidential rival's electorate.[20] The 2009 confirmation hearing of US Supreme Court Justice Sonia Sotomayor also showed that judicial empathy is not a truth held to be self-evident. Or, rather, that a nominee for the bench risks vilification if she deviates from the enlightened path of rationality as the predominant factor in adjudication. When her views on the importance of her personal identity as a Latina in its connection to empathy as a criterion for judging were challenged, Sotomayor was quick to join the traditional ranks. While she acknowledged the existence of judicial empathic emotion, she dismissed it as harmful in actual decision making.[21] Nor did then-president Obama's warm plea for the empathy criterion survive the public debate. Such vilification is not new. One has only to think of the empathic interpretive stance employed by US Supreme Court Justice Blackmun, who joined Justice Brennan's dissenting opinion in *DeShaney v. Winnebago County Department of Social Services*, and added a voice of his own when he wrote,

> Today, the Court purports to be the dispassionate oracle of the law, unmoved by 'natural sympathy' . . . But, in this pretense, the Court itself retreats into a sterile formalism which prevents it from recognizing either the facts of the case before it or the legal norms that should apply to those facts . . . I would adopt a 'sympathetic reading', one which comports with the dictates of fundamental justice and recognizes that compassion need not be exiled from the province of judging . . . Poor Joshua . . . It is a sad commentary upon American life, and institutional principles that this

---

[19] Speech at the National Urban League meeting held at Ford Lauderdale, Florida, 31 July 2015, CNN Newsreel 31 July 2015.

[20] Ms Clinton used the word deplorables at the 'LGTB for Hillary Gala' in New York, 9 September 2016.

[21] Confirming that 'the job of a judge is to apply the law. And so it's not the heart that compels conclusions in cases, it's the law', Nomination of Judge Sonia Sotomayor to Associate Justice of the Supreme Court before the Senate Committee on the Judiciary, 111th Congress, 1st Session, 14 July 2009. Cf. T. Maroney, 'Emotional regulation and judicial behavior', 90 *California Law Review*, 2011, pp. 1481–551, p. 1485; Sotomayor first brought forward the identity argument in a speech at Berkeley in 2002, see L. Martín Alcoff, 'Sotomayor's reasoning', 48 *The Southern Journal of Philosophy*, no. 1, 2010, pp. 122-138.

child, Joshua DeShaney, is now assigned to live out the remainder of his life profoundly retarded. [22]

Blackmun was widely taken to task for his first-order emotional exclamation, 'Poor Joshua', and his jurisprudence of sentiment.[23]

In short, the ideal image is that of the judge Fiona May in *The Children Act*, whose colleagues praise her for her sound judicial mind, and who in the case involving permission being sought for the surgical separation of the conjoined twins Mark and Matthew starts her decision with the firm statement, '"This court is a court of law, not of morals, and our task has been to find, and our duty is then to apply, the relevant principles of law to the situation before us – a situation which is unique"'.[24] Yet I wholeheartedly agree with Martha Nussbaum when she claims that we need literature, 'that talks of human lives and choices as if they matter to us all'.[25] It is a claim in the Herderian tradition of developing our humanity, our *Humanität*, by means of the *Bildung* we obtain by reading literary works.[26] To Herder, self-reflection leads to

[22] 489 U.S. 189 (1989). In 1984, Joshua DeShaney was subjected by his father, with whom he lived after his parents had divorced, to a battering so severe that he suffered permanent brain damage. He was profoundly retarded for the rest of his life. The evidence showed that the Winnebago Department of Social Services (DSS) knew what was happening in the DeShaney home. After the final beating, Joshua and his mother brought suit against the county, the DSS, and several of its workers. They complained that Joshua had been deprived of his liberty in the sense of bodily integrity without due process of law, in violation of his rights under the Due Process Clause of the Fourteenth Amendment, because the DSS et al. had failed to intervene to protect Joshua against his father's beatings. The majority opinion of the Court held that failure to protect an individual against private violence does not constitute a violation of the Due Process Clause, because no affirmative obligation is imposed on the State to provide this type of protection. The Court also held that the State's knowledge of Joshua's dangerous situation did not itself establish a special relationship which might give rise to such an affirmative obligation either, since the State did not hold Joshua in its custody during the final beating, which incidentally was not by a State official but by his father.

[23] J. Rosen, 'Sentimental journey: the emotional jurisprudence of Harry Blackmun', *The New Republic*, 2 May 1994, p. 13.

[24] I. McEwan, *The Children Act* (London: Jonathan Cape, 2014), pp. 26–7. Hereinafter (CA + page number).

[25] See M. C. Nussbaum, *Love's Knowledge* (Oxford: Oxford University Press, 1990), pp. 23–4 and 171.

[26] Herder developed the term *Humanität* in his essay '*Humanität* Erziehung', and in 'Briefe zur Beförderung der *Humanität*'. See J. G. Herder (ed. Walter Flemmer), *Schriften, eine Auswahl aus dem Gesamtwerk* (Munich:Wilhelm Goldmann Verlag, 1960), pp. 175–9 and pp. 196–205. *Humanität* has its roots in *humanitas* in the Roman sense of the *eruditio et institutio in bonas artes*, in short *Bildung*, as Costas Douzinas explains. See C. Douzinas, 'A humanities of resistance: fragments for a legal history of humanity', in A. Sarat et al. (eds),

self-knowledge, and together these constitute our capacity for self-determination and empathy. In the sense that Herder advocates having as our life's aim to do everything possible in order to maximise our capabilities, he also foreshadows Nussbaum's 'capabilities approach'.[27] Furthermore, *Humanität* is presented as the basic attitude for human contact in society, one that is connected to the virtue of *phronèsis*, as discussed in Chapter 6. It is therefore intimately connected to Vico's primacy of *ingenium* and to his emphasis on *fantasia*, as noted in Chapter 6.

What, then, does this mean for the judge in actual legal practice? 'Narrative imagination', as Nussbaum also calls it,[28] obviously has to be translated into the language of judging, for literature and law are alike in that they need,

> a language that is expressive of the kind of imagination that's capable of perceiving the individual humanity of the people involved and their circumstances; recognizing that each has a complicated story with factors that make it not the same as anyone else's.[29]

The very idea of narrative imagination is applicable not only in a concrete manner in any act of judgement, so that in common law and civil law jurisdictions alike it makes sense for juries and judges to try and imagine as best as they can the other's situation before delivering justice in the form of a final judgement.[30] It is also essential when reading the paper files, as is mostly the case in civil law jurisdictions. At the same time, we should not forget that words themselves can never describe fully the emotions at work in, for example, the story of what happened as told by a witness of a horrendous crime. That is also why employing one's narrative imagination as a judge can help in fostering one's suspension of disbelief as an aspect of *phronèsis*.[31] With this in

---

Law and the Humanities: An Introduction (Cambridge: Cambridge University Press, 2010), pp. 49–72.

[27] M. C. Nussbaum, *Frontiers of Justice* (Cambridge, MA: Harvard University Press, 2007) and *Creating Capabilities: The Human Development Approach* (Cambridge, MA: Harvard University Press, 2011).

[28] M. C. Nussbaum, *Not for Profit: Why Democracy Needs the Humanities* (Princeton: Princeton, University Press, 2010), p. 95.

[29] M. C. Nussbaum, 'Emotion in the language of judging', 70 *St. John's Law Review*, no.1, 1996, pp. 23–30, p. 24.

[30] Cf. J. B. White, *Living Speech: Resisting the Empire of Force* (Princeton: Princeton University Press, 2006), p. 90: 'imagination is the root of justice'.

[31] See also A. Reichman, 'Law, literature, and empathy: between withholding and reserving judgment', 56 *Journal of Legal Education*, no. 2, 2006, pp. 296–319, p. 297, 'I propose that the benefit of literature as a learning tool is not that it makes readers judge empathetically;

mind, I turn to McEwan's fictional judge Fiona Maye, whose emotional trials and tribulations are excellent examples of the arguments brought forward in this book so far, as well as a warning.

Empathy Unbound or Unbounded Empathy?

The opening scene of the novel portrays the High Court judge Fiona Maye, professionally the paragon of legal rationality – 'Among fellow judges, Fiona Maye was praised, even in her absence, for crisp prose, almost ironic, almost warm, and for the compact terms in which she laid out a dispute' (CA 13) – recovering from the shock of her husband Jack's declaration that, at fifty-nine, he wants to have a love affair with a young woman as a last shot before old age sets in, and also because he longs for the physical intimacy he no longer has with Fiona. Even now, Fiona prioritises her professional duty. She starts to work on the decision in a case, which has to be ready the next day, and it is one that foreshadows well the rest of the novel's plot: the choice between religion and life. It is a divorce case in the Jewish Chareidi community, in which, contrary to religious custom, the wife wants an education both for herself and her children. When writing about the moral dispute between the litigants, Fiona 'listed some relevant ingredients, goals towards which a child might grow . . . and having at the centre of one's life one or a small number of significant relations defined above all by love', and becomes painfully aware of the fact that 'Yes, by this last essential she herself was failing' (CA 15). But the job comes first. 'Her judgment must be ready for printing by tomorrow's deadline, she must work. Her personal life was nothing' (CA 16). The topic of religion versus life returns in Fiona's musings about a high-profile case she had decided some weeks earlier, that of the conjoined twins Mark and Matthew. The hospital needed judicial permission to separate them in order to save Mark, whose chances of leading a normal life were highest, as Matthew was unable to live independently of his sibling. The parents refused because they did not want to interfere with God's purpose. In both cases, Fiona's decision favoured life.

At ten o'clock that very same night, the phone rings. Fiona, who is on duty as a Family Division judge, gets another case, that of a hospital looking for a court order to proceed with the transfusion of a leukaemia patient, seventeen-year-old Adam Henry, against the wishes of his parents, who, as Jehovah's Witnesses, are opposed to a blood transfusion on religious grounds. Even at this time of night, and under these specific personal circumstances

---

rather literature teaches one to withhold judgment so that when judgment is ultimately rendered it is more profound and meaningful'.

– her husband is leaving to visit his lover – Fiona immediately instructs her clerk what to do. Next day, at the Royal Courts of Justice, however, Fiona thinks back on her successful career and how she has postponed for years the decision about having children; she realises 'the game was up, she belonged to the law as some women had once been brides of Christ' (CA 45). For Fiona, the law is her life-absorbing religion. During the hearing later that week, the statement of the haematological expert Carter gives Fiona reason to believe that without a transfusion Adam Henry will soon die a horrible death. Adam Henry, it is established, is extremely intelligent and fully aware of the consequences of his refusal of treatment. His parents dote on him, but their faith and his is so strong that they accept he will die. Fiona announces that she will go to the hospital to hear from Adam Henry himself, or, rather, to determine 'his understanding of his situation, and of what he confronts should I rule against the hospital', and to tell him 'that I am the one who will be making the decision in his best interests' (CA 89). Here Fiona's private persona comes to the surface, since it is the social worker rather than the judge who is supposed to make such visits. Furthermore, 'She would have liked to see this boy for herself, remove herself from a domestic morass, as well as from the courtroom for an hour or two' (CA 35). Is the pleasurable period she herself spent in hospital when she was thirteen the trigger? Or is it her maternal interest in 'young Adam', who is intelligent and writes poetry, this 'young patient', 'a lovely boy' who seems to be 'one confused little puppy' (CA 69, 97, 98)? In hospital, within minutes, Fiona is telling Adam about a court case involving parents prosecuted for satanic abuse of their children, a charge that proved to be totally unfounded. She realises 'she had strayed onto his ground. Satan was a lively character in the Witness construction of the world' (CA 102–3). She also realises that by asking 'Would it please God, to have you blind or stupid and on dialysis for the rest of your life?' (CA 105) she has crossed a line that law cherishes.

The intimacy between them develops when Adam asks Fiona whether he can call her 'My Lady', the honourific court term that he obviously uses more in the chivalric and private sense. They discuss his poetry, he reads to her, and plays the violin for her; it is Benjamin Britten's setting of Yeats's poem 'Down by the Salley Gardens', one of the encores Fiona habitually plays with the barrister Mark Berner when they perform together at the Inns of Court. This prompts her to sing along with him. Back at the court, later that evening, Fiona delivers her decision. She sets out the facts, acknowledges that Adam Henry is well aware of his situation, and then when everything seems to lead into the direction of finding for Adam and against the hospital, Fiona suddenly points out that her decision is 'not ultimately influenced by whether he has or doesn't have a full comprehension of his situation. I am guided instead by the decision of Mr Justice Ward' (CA 123). In short, Fiona reverts to the legal domain by employing the basic principle derived from this precedent that the welfare of the minor is the concept guiding the decision. So Adam Henry 'must be protected from his religion and from himself' (CA 123).

This oscillation between public role and private feeling will ultimately lead to professional transgression. It starts when Fiona gets a letter from Adam. He has had the transfusion and his parents are joyful. Why? Because Adam is alive. They remained true to their faith, so the blame can be put on the judge and the legal system. It becomes clear from what Adam writes that he has developed feelings for Fiona, and that the Yeats poem is immensely influential in that development. Fiona writes a short and cool letter, impersonal to the core, which she then does not send. A second letter from Adam arrives, now at her home address. Fiona asks the social worker to go and see Adam, who is doing fine at school. At home, the relationship with her husband seems less strained.

Later that day, in Newcastle, when Fiona is having dinner at Leadman Hall, her clerk tells her that Adam is there. Fiona goes to see him in the kitchen. He has followed her to thank her for saving his life, for she saved him from his religion. He is eighteen now and has left home. It is immediately obvious that he is smitten with Fiona, and that the Yeats poem has been instrumental in the development of his feelings. Baffled when Adam announces that he wants to come and live with her, Fiona knows no better than to respond that she will ask her clerk to bring Adam to a hotel. However, before he gets into the taxi,

> she took the lapel of his thin jacket between her fingers and drew him towards her. Her intention was to kiss him on the cheek, but as she reached up and he stooped a little and their faces came close, he turned his head and their lips met. She could have drawn back, she could have stepped right away from him. Instead, she lingered, defenseless before the moment. (CA 169)

She senses that it was 'more than a mother might give her grown-up son' (CA 169). And thus ends their brief encounter. Fiona probes her state of mind: Did she act on an impulse? If so, what prompted it? Then she swings back to the legal mode as she considers 'the ludicrous and shameful transgression of professional ethics, that occupied her. The ignominy that could have been hers' (CA 172). Back at her London court, she receives a poem from Adam Henry. It is a ballad reminiscent of 'The Salley Gardens', and it ends with Jesus saying to the protagonist, 'Her kiss was the kiss of Judas, her kiss betrayed my name' (CA 180–1). Even though Fiona realises that his infatuation differs from hers, she dismisses the idea that she is the Judas of the poem, convinced as she is that he will move on, do well at university, and forget about her. Again the expected rational response. In December, however, she breaks down after a concert with Mark Berner. The trigger is their playing of 'The Salley Gardens', combined with a phone call from the social worker saying that Adam is dead. He had refused a transfusion when the leukaemia returned. Fiona has to admit to herself that she was indeed the Judas in Adam's poem. With Adam too, 'The Salley Gardens' led to Fiona forgetting the law, but this has come at a high price. She realises that as a human being she has failed Adam completely. She kissed him on an impulse and left it at that. She failed to read the message in his poem, and now he is dead.

I suggest that the importance of McEwan's novel is that it is literally and figuratively a 'mirror for magistrates'. Its documentary character as far as the choice of legal cases is concerned, based as that choice is on McEwan's view on the parallels between the legal and the writing profession,[32] as well as the development of the main character, Fiona Maye, together offer a basis for judicial self-reflection on professional behaviour and judicial regulation of emotion, in and out of court, as much as on the demand to balance the private and the public persona. This is also to say that when we read for the plot, the 'ethics of the story told' should be complemented by the 'ethics of reception', on how the narrative influences us as readers, as James Phelan suggests when he writes,

> Narrative ethics explores the intersection between the domain of stories and storytelling and that of moral values. Narrative ethics regards moral values as an integral part of stories and storytelling because narratives themselves implicitly or explicitly ask the question, 'How should one think, judge, and act – as author, narrator, character, or audience – for the greater good?'[33]

This question can be transposed seamlessly to legal practice.

---

[32] In an interview in *The Guardian*, 5 September 2014, available at <http://www.theguard-ian.com/books/2014/sep/05/ian-mcewan-law-versus-religious-belief> [last accessed 26 November 2016], McEwan tells how at a dinner he attended, Alan Ward 'got up and took a volume of his own judgements from a shelf', one that upon reading McEwan greatly admired: 'It was the prose that struck me first. Clean, precise, delicious. Serious, of course, compassionate at points, but lurking within its intelligence was something like humour, or wit, derived perhaps from its godly instance, which in turn reminded me of a novel-ist's omniscience.' See also R. Herz, 'Anatomy of a judge', 9 *Law and Humanities*, 2015, pp. 123–35.

[33] J. Phelan, 'Narrative ethics', in P. Hühn et al. (eds), *The Living Handbook of Narratology* (Hamburg: Hamburg University), available at <http://www.lhn.uni-hamburg.de/article/narrative-ethics> [last accessed 2 December 2016].

Narrative Control: Judging and the Cognitive Turn in Narratology

What is it that judges especially can learn from reading *The Children Act* if they read the novel with the necessary care and empathy? It is that they should concern themselves more than is done to date with the normative issue of the role of emotion in judicial decision making.[34] The story of Fiona Maye shows how her completely internalised methodology of distinguishing the relevant facts is predominant. It also shows how her initially second-order, allocentric empathy for the individuals whose lives she decides about long remains one of the normative kind as she looks for precedents to decide the cases, the recognition of relevant precedent being a metaphorical process, as noted in Chapter 7, of dealing with similarities and dissimilarities so that one arrives at the imaginative creation of the average person in that specific situation. It changes into first-order empathy, however, as a result of pressures in her personal life. From a judicious spectator of the kind that Nussbaum delineates in *Poetic Justice*, Fiona Maye changes into a judge who loses her phronetic capacity to act and judge correctly under the circumstances. Would she have acted the way she did if she had had children of her own, and/or if she had not met Adam Henry in the vulnerable emotional state that she was in as a result of the problematic relationship with her husband? What is the emotional trigger of the song 'The Salley Gardens'? Why did Fiona act as she did when, on her way to meet Adam for the first time, she already had hesitations about the rationality of what she was doing?

> This, Fiona decided as her taxi halted in heavy traffic on Waterloo Bridge, was either about a woman on the edge of a crack-up making a sentimental error of professional judgement, or it was about a boy delivered from or into the beliefs of his sect by the intimate intervention of the secular court. She didn't think it could be both. (CA 91)

Therefore, we as readers are asked whether we can feel with her. Can we develop aesthetic empathy for her, and can we develop empathy as a professional and/or a character trait? This is also to ask whether we can feel for fellow-judges like her in real life. In the 2015–17 editions of the summer course 'Language, Literature and the Judiciary' mentioned in Chapter 10, *The Children Act* was the set novel. Responses to Fiona Maye widely differed. While most of my fellow judges responded empathically, recognising the dilemmas Fiona faces and the circumstances in which she finds herself, some found the scene in which Fiona kisses Adam utterly implausible,

---

[34] See also Maroney, 'Emotional regulation', p. 1488.

because 'no real judge would do a thing like that'. I would say that it all depends. For a great deal depends on who we ourselves are, and that would include not only our professional 'subconscious loyalties'[35] and cultural background but also our private values, which for judges are, mildly put, usually solidly middle class. It also depends on prior experiences that add to our emotional colouring, from our youth as much as from our professional life. Our being hermeneutically situated and culturally determined is an inescapable fact of all human life.[36] It is therefore important to be knowledgeable about how narrative works to activate our deep frames of (re)cognition, because what affects us in a fictional narrative may be indicative of what affects us in other texts as well. The judge's past experience of specific situations and the people in them can engender expectations with respect to human behaviour that will, in turn, guide her application of such expectations in future cases. To reiterate, it can lead to psychological errors such as the confirmation bias and belief perseverance when not corrected by self-reflection on what it is that guides her. Obviously, it is hard to change one's mind once one has literally and figuratively made it up.

As the findings of neurosciences suggest, empathy is embodied.[37] As such, it has a basis in '*mirror neurons*, which fire both when a person performs an action or feels an emotion and when that person views someone else having the same experience'.[38] This process, too, is dependent on context and culture. So there is even more reason to be alert to subconscious activation of the judicial mind as far as the phenomenology of perception and judging is concerned, not least because we are all prone to the influences of scripts and expectations on the basis of the texts that we read. What, then, if the judge's fear, anger or distress takes centre stage as the objective of other people's narrative goals? Notably, the topic of how to influence the judge's mind and decision has been with us since Aristotle. Cicero's *De Inventione* also deals with the topic of the plausibility of a narrative that convinces those who judge. Judicial narrative imagination and phronetic intelligence therefore

---

[35] B. N. Cardozo, *The Nature of the Judicial Process* (New Haven: Yale University Press, 1921), p. 178.

[36] See also McArdle, 'Using a narrative lens'.

[37] See G. Bruner Murrow and R. W. Murrow, 'A biosemiotic *body* of law: the neurobiology of justice', 26 *International Journal for the Semiotics of Law*, 2013, pp. 275–314, p. 298, 'embodied empathy, broadly defined, involves the sharing, or automatic neural simulation, of the actual neural affective, neural somatosensory, or neural motor states of others with whom one "empathizes"'.

[38] See A. Jurecic, 'Empathy and the critic', 74 *College English*, no. 1, 2011, pp. 10–27, p. 10 (italics in the original).

need an education in narrative affect heuristics, in order to be able to recognise the narrative techniques that are used in any text to deliberately guide the
judge-reader's perception and cognition, her combined seeing and thinking,
as noted in Chapter 6, including an empathic stance. Greta Olson shared a
fascinating example of visuality and affect: namely, that of the picture of the
dead body of the two-year-old Syrian boy, Alan Kurdi, washed ashore on the
Turkish coast in 2015. The image went viral as an emblem of the refugee
crisis in Europe. Olson's point is that we empathise more with an individual
than with a group, and even more with that individual if we know his or her
name.[39]

The expansion of literary-legal studies into the domain of cognitive
narratology offers guidance in what it is that can trigger judicial emotion
– necessary in view of the requirement of judicial impartiality and equal treatment under the rule of law – and can help the judge in suspending judgement
by teaching her to recognise what anti-suspension elements are deployed
(that is, other than case load and time pressure).[40] The demand of integrity
of both judgement and judge transcends the general demands of clarity and
coherence of the decision, in the sense that the judge's disposition should
also be aimed at probing her inner motives and reflecting on the tensions that
arise from the conflicting views, in herself and others, not least because the
correctness of her decision is to a large degree measured by the losing party's
acceptance. The judge's narrative identity, therefore, is intimately connected
to self-knowledge, in the sense of knowledge of the activities of which the
judge, as the knowing subject, is the author.

Self-knowledge and Self-recognition

To tie the strands together, I turn once more to Paul Ricoeur. To Ricoeur,
self-knowledge is essential for identity as *ipse*, and for the view behind it:
namely, that the self and identity are dialogically constituted. With *ipse*,
Ricoeur denotes the way one perceives oneself in the course of a lifetime's

---

[39] See also G. Olson, 'The turn to passion: has law and literature become law and affect?',
28 *Law & Literature*, no. 3, 2016, pp. 335–53. For a treatment of affect in relation to law
and Kazuo Ishiguro's *The Remains of the Day*, see R. Reichman, 'Law's affective tickets', in
E. S. Anker and B. Meyler (eds), *New Directions in Law and Literature* (Oxford: Oxford
University Press, 2017), pp. 109–22.

[40] See T. Maroney, 'The persistent cultural script of judicial dispassion', 99 *California Law
Review* 2011, pp. 629–81; T. Maroney, 'Law and emotion: a proposed taxonomy of an
emerging field', 30 *Law and Human Behavior*, no. 2, 2006, pp. 119–42; M. C. Belleau et
al., 'Faces of judicial anger: answering the call', 1 *EJLS* no. 2 special issue 'Judging Judges',
2007, pp. 1–41, available at <http://www.ejls.eu/issue/2> [last accessed 2 May 2015]; M. L.
Minow and E. V. Spelman, 'Passion for justice', 10 *Cardozo Law Review*, 1988, pp. 37–76.

development. Therefore, *ipse* refers to one's diachronic identity in the sense of human authenticity and uniqueness. In the sense that *ipseity* is reflexive selfhood,[41] a hermeneutics of selfhood is required, and one that connects *ipse* to *idem*, which is the term denoting the way in which the other perceives me. For example, that and how I am thought of as a legal subject when the situation is legal; or, on the physical level, how the correspondence between who we ourselves say we are and our bodily evidence or biological, genetic codes in the form of DNA, fingerprints – think of Mark Twain's novel *The Tragedy of Pudd'nhead Wilson* for the first literary work in which fingerprints are put to forensic use – physiognomy, voice, gait, as well as stable, acquired habits, or the specific but accidental marks by which individual persons are recognised may be relevant in many situations. As regards accidental marks, think of the scar as the sign by means of which Odysseus is recognised upon his return home,[42] or the distinctive tattoo that a witness at a crime scene later recognises in a line-up. The distinction and combination of *ipse* and *idem* is highly relevant to my project, because Ricoeur elaborates on it on the plane of voice and narrative when he writes that the important thing for the human is learning to 'narrate oneself'.[43] This, I suggest, also opens up a possibility of connecting the legal persona to the contemporary varieties of identity that technology now facilitates, a topic that I turn to in Chapters 12 and 13.

The hermeneutics that Ricoeur proposes in connection with the ability to narrate oneself include the following features: firstly, 'taking into account the capacities to be found in the mode of the "I can"', and this is the mode of the subject; secondly, 'the "object" side of experiences considered from the point of view of the capacities employed', and here the what and the how enter the stage; and thirdly, 'in order to give a reflexive value to the self . . . the dialectic between identity and otherness'.[44] Personal identity is therefore indissolubly tied to the act of narrating, both in the sense of being able to narrate one's experiences and being able to narrate oneself, to talk about oneself in different contexts and from different perspectives.[45] This

---

[41] P. Ricoeur (trans. D. Pellauer), *The Course of Recognition* (Cambridge, MA: Harvard University Press, 2005), p. 89. Ricoeur initially made the distinction between *ipse* and *idem* in (trans. K. Blamey), *Oneself as Another* (Chicago and London: University of Chicago Press, [1990] 1992), in the context of a contribution to moral philosophy on the subject of human relations, and applied it to law and justice in P. Ricoeur (trans. D. Pellauer), *The Just* (Chicago: Chicago University Press, [1995] 2000).

[42] Ricoeur, *Course of Recognition*, p. 102.

[43] Ibid. p. 101.

[44] Ibid. p. 93.

[45] Ibid. p. 99.

ties in with *Law and Literature* approaches that focus on the individual's ability to make him- or herself be heard in a court of law. In the sense that the individual can 'emplot' her- or himself[46] – and here is the connection to Ricoeur's view on emplotment and mimesis in *Time and Narrative* – the problem of understanding that arises from the temporal dimension of the self throughout the individual's life and of his or her actions – and with it, its different *ipseities* in the seven ages of man, as Shakespeare famously coined them – can be solved. To do so, we should take carefully into consideration that 'the personal identity, . . . as enduring over time, can be defined as a narrative identity, at the intersection of the coherence conferred by emplotment and the discordance arising from the peripeteia within the narrated action'.[47]

Narrative identity is obviously crucial in legal settings, as legal conflicts arise precisely when expectations about what should have happened are thwarted by realities. Put differently, the narrative identity-approach is a tool to bridge gaps between the *idem* and *ipse*. While the *idem* stands for the more immutable kind of identity, its connection to the *ipse*'s changing identity thoughout a lifetime takes place by means of narrative, thereby connecting biological sameness to selfhood, and urging us to consider who we are now and who we were in earlier stages of our lives.[48] It is also eminently suited to a discussion of the challenges that law faces when it comes to finding a just way to deal with contemporary issues of gender and transsexuality.

Taken together, the above suggests to me that the mental breakdown of our fictional judge Fiona Maye is the result of the circumstance that at the precise moment that her private and professional *ipse* and *idem* coincide, she falls short when it comes to her narrative identity; namely, by not responding to Adam's letters in an appropriate manner. She fails to understand Adam's perception of her and how that came about. She fails to respond to Adam's alterity. She fails in her ethical and professional responsibility towards another human being, which, as the philosopher Emmanuel Levinas insisted,

> is not a cold juridical requirement. It is all the gravity of the love of one's fellowman . . . An ethical culture, in which the face of the other – that of the absolute other – awakens in the identity of the *I* the inalienable

---

[46] Ibid. p. 100.

[47] Ibid. p. 101.

[48] See also A. Lieblich and R. Josselson, 'Identity and narrative as root metaphor of personhood', in J. Martin and M. H. Bickhard (eds), *The Psychology of Personhood: Philosophical, Historical, Social-Developmental, and Narrative Perspectives* (Cambridge: Cambridge University Press, 2013), pp. 203–22.

responsibility for the other man and the dignity of the chosen . . . It is commanded by the face of the other man, which is not a *datum* of experience and does not come from the world. A breach made by humanness in the barbarism of being, even if no philosophy of history guarantees us against the return of barbarism.[49]

When we do what Aristotle wanted us to – that is, to realise as spectators and readers that we too can end up in comparable unfortunate circumstances, so that, as Nussbaum suggests, we can truly view the other as one whom we might be[50] – this can help us practise law in the sense that Ulpian had already written in his definition of law as the *constans et perpetua voluntas ius suum cuique tribuere*, the constant and eternal desire to render to each his own: namely, as the minimum requirement of justice, we can give the other person what is hers, a voice, and we can hear her.[51]

At the same time, we need to keep in mind that this principal requirement may also be hampered by yet another aspect of professional life: that is, what Arlie Hochschild calls the 'managed heart'.[52] Professionals always possess certain characteristics that set them apart as a group. Judges, then, play a role, and they do so wearing their professional masks: that is to say, the mask that both symbolises their objectivity, fairness and impartiality, and that shields their private lives; the mask of which the bands and gown are the outer signs.[53] To end on a sobering note, I would add that this mask also hides their 'managed heart'. Hochschild builds on the idea proffered by Erving Goffman 'of how we try to control our appearance even as we unconsciously observe rules about how we ought to appear to others'.[54] Her thesis is that most jobs today do not involve only physical or mental labour but also emotional labour that is 'the management of feeling to create a publicly observable facial and bodily display' that requires the twin tasks of handling other people's feelings and one's own.[55] Translated to the judicial task, and from the perspective that judges are and should be seen to be human too, this means that when

---

[49] E. Levinas (trans. M. B. Smith and B. Harshav), *On Thinking-of-the-Other: Entre Nous* (London: The Athlone Press, [1991] 1998), pp. 186–7.

[50] Nussbaum, *Poetic Justice*, p. 35.

[51] Ulpian, *Digests*, D.1,1,1 and 10.

[52] A. R. Hochschild, *The Managed Heart: Commercialization of Human Feeling* (Berkeley: University of California Press, 1983).

[53] See also J. T. Noonan, *Persons and Masks of the Law* (Berkeley: University Of California Press, [1976] 2002).

[54] Hochschild, *The Managed Heart*, p. x.

[55] Hochschild, *The Managed Heart*, pp. 7 and 11.

serving as a judge – of whom impartial sang-froid is the emotional labour that is expected under all circumstances in- and outside the courtroom – one has to learn to deal with the tensions between one's public face and mask and one's private, subjective feelings, both about the case at hand and generally.[56] An infamous example of the combination of private anger and vanity can be found in the reaction of the Cypriotic judges to an advocate who referred to the notes that he saw the judges exchange during his cross-examination as 'ravasakia', love letters. They placed him in custody to await his trial for contempt, because they had been deeply offended as private individuals, and not as professional personae.[57] James Clarke's poem about the judge who reads 'the criteria in the Handbook for Judges for appointment to the bench' and realises that what is asked of judges – that they 'be honest, intelligent, sympathetic, patient, courteous, healthy, industrious' – is 'the embodiment of perfection' therefore offers sound advice: 'the judge looked . . . in the mirror, grateful he had a sense of humor'.[58]

The story of Fiona Maye is a perfect example, illustrating the pitfalls and peculiarities of our private and professional identities as they unfold in human and judicial fallibility.[59] A humanistic perspective on law that includes narrative fiction may therefore help us ask the right questions necessary for probing our awareness of ourselves and of others, and, ideally, lead to a critical reflection on the social roles we play, professionally and privately, and the expectations these roles engender in ourselves and in others.[60] This is especially important for judges, precisely because the judicial professional mask has this double function. That is why judges should keep asking the question, 'Who am I and what is my role in the world, as a judge and a human being?', and come to terms with the answers. I suggest that when it comes to law, empathy and emotion, the legal professional can benefit greatly from what literature and narratology are able to offer by way of education and caution. And since as human beings we are all prone to mistakes – after all, to err is human too – in doing so, it behoves us to keep

---

[56] For empirical research conducted in Australian courts, see S. Roach Anleu and K. Mack, 'Magistrates' everyday work and emotional labour', 32 *Journal of Law and Society*, no. 4, 2005, pp. 590–614.

[57] European Court of Human Rights, Case of *Kyprianou v. Cyprus*, Application no. 73797/01, 15 December 2005.

[58] J. Clarke, 'When he read', *The Juried Heart* (New York: Pleasure Boat, 2015), p. 21.

[59] See also M. L. Minow, 'Identities', 3 *Yale Journal of Law & the Humanities*, no. 1, 1991, pp. 97–130.

[60] For an insightful study on judges' working personalities, see P. Darbyshire, *Sitting in Judgment: The Working Lives of Judges* (Oxford and Portland, OR: Hart Publishing, 2011).

clearly in mind Franz Kafka's remark in a letter to his friend Oskar Pollak:
'Many a book is like a key to unknown chambers within the castle of one's
own self.'[61]

---

[61] Originally, 'Manches Buch wirkt wie ein Schlüssel zu fremden Sälen des eigenes Schlosses',
Letter to Oskar Pollak, dated Sunday 8 November 1903, in M. Brod (ed.), *Briefe, 1902–
1924*, available at <http://homepage.univie.ac.at/werner.haas/1903/br03-002.htm> [last
accessed 10 September 2017].

12

Person and *Poiesis* in Technology and Law: Questioning Builds a Way

Loci in Law and Literature

Chapters 12 and 13 further the project of developing our thoughts on a hermeneutics of selfhood by turning to the bond of law, literature and technology, in order to illuminate the questions arising from Ricoeur's distinction between *ipse* and *idem*. Modern technology brings a variety of challenges to the physical aspects of our *idem*, which may affect not only our legal *idem* in the sense of legal personhood but also our *ipse*. As a consequence, it affects our ability to make sense of technology when it comes to narrating ourselves, as well as being able to acknowledge alterity and to do justice.

Ricoeur explains the dialogical constitution of the self as identity – selfhood and legal personhood – as one mode of thought on justice. The other mode is the philosophical inquiry into the way in which the predicates that qualify human actions in terms of morality are hierarchically constituted in institutional forms, such as, for example, the scope of criminal responsibility, the duty of care, or the good neighbour principle. The just is situated at the intersection of the two modes. To Ricoeur, this means that, 'the self only constitutes its identity through a relational structure that places the dialogical dimension above the monological'.[1] Obviously, there is always a distance between me and the other. In the dialogue of friends, the other is you. On the plane of justice, law as an institution mediates human relations so that the other is anyone, as in Ulpian's definition of law, as noted in Chapter 11. If a being is able to narrate its *ipse* identity adequately, this enhances its options to fully achieve the *idem* identity of legal personhood, and, with it, the rights-and-duties-bearing consequences. After all, what matters for success in law is mutual recognition. What the prosecutor said in the case of a slave girl against whom a criminal charge was brought exemplifies this notion, at

---

[1] P. Ricoeur (trans. D. Pellauer), *The Just* (Chicago: University of Chicago Press, [1995] 2000), p. xiii.

least if we take him literally: 'I cannot prove more plainly that the prisoner is a person . . . than to ask your honors to look at her. There she is.'[2] If, in law, we let ourselves be touched by the claims of our fellow creatures, and if we focus on their dignity and vulnerability, seeing them literally and figuratively face to face,[3] then we act in an ethical manner, because in doing so we accept a shared existence as well as alterity, and we celebrate autonomy as well as mutual dependence. But can we do so in technological surroundings?

The depiction of science and technology has fascinated literary writers for centuries. Mary Shelley's novel *Frankenstein* (1818) is the landmark novel. This fictive depiction of technological progress is already anticipated, however, in Jonathan Swift's *Gulliver's Travels*. In the Academy of Lagado, the narrator encounters a huge engine of knowledge that can write books because in it are pieces of paper with 'all the words of their language in their several moods, tenses, and declensions, but without any order', and when an iron handle is turned 'the whole disposition of the words was entirely changed', so that all the available knowledge in the world could – in principle at least – be connected in 'a complete body of all arts and sciences'.[4] This wonderful fictional precursor of computational and corpus linguistics – it can make computations of all parts of speech in a text – is emblematic of the human fascination with the idea of code in its various forms and its interconnection to control and power. Furthermore, it already suggests that code is made by us.[5] Satiric as Swift's portrayal is, it also offers a sobering thought to all technocrats in the sense that literature has foreseen what technology could accomplish, as early twentieth-century dystopian literary works illuminate.[6]

From a disciplinary point of view, law and technology broadly conceived are obviously separate domains of knowledge. But given their interconnection on the plane of the regulation by law of technological implementations, they can be complimentary as forms of cultural reflection, and literature can

---

[2] *United States v. Amy*, 24 F.Cas. 792 (1859). See also D. Fagundes, 'What we talk about when we talk about persons: the language of a legal fiction', 114 *Harvard Law Review*, 2001, pp. 1745–68, p. 1748.

[3] See E. Levinas (trans. A. Lingis), *Totality and Infinity* (Pittsburgh: Duquesne University Press, [1961] 1969), and P. Ricoeur (trans. K. Blamey), *Oneself as Another* (Chicago and London: University of Chicago Press, [1990] 1992).

[4] J. Swift (eds P. Dixon and J. Chalker), *Gulliver's Travels* (Harmondsworth: Penguin, [1726] 1977), pp. 227 and 229.

[5] L. Lessig, *Code version 2.0* (New York: Basic Books, 2006), p. 6.

[6] For example, H. James, *In the Cage* (London: Martin Secker, [1919] 2005); K. Čapek (trans. P. Selver and N. Playfair), *R.U.R* (Mineola, NY: Dover Pub. Inc., [1920] 2001); R. Tokko (pseud. of L. Dexheimer), *Das Automatenzeitalter* (Berlin: Shayol Verlag, [1930] 2004); Y. Zamyatin, *We* (New York: Dutton, [1921] 1924).

be their linchpin. As Italo Calvino wrote, literature 'creates autonomous figures that may be used as terms of comparison with experience or with other constructions of the mind'.[7] That is also why the metaphors of technology, literary and otherwise, have cognitive relevance for law.[8] Furthermore, the issue of mimesis as representation, acute in literature and law, is relevant for science as well.[9] Translated into terms of the argument animating this book, I suggest that one way to investigate the possible form and meaning of the interrelation of law, the humanities and science could be guided by the question: What if code, in whatever guise, takes over the human?[10]

From the already imagined human look-alike clones in the classic *The Invasion of the Body Snatchers* to the creatures in Margaret Atwood's *MaddAddam* trilogy, and the computer as an object of love, without a human body but with a consciousness, in Spike Jonze's film *Her*, on all fronts the question is also one of personhood as artificiality in relation to personhood and selfhood as personality and authenticity. So if what Montaigne held before us is still valid when he wrote,

> We are all framed of flaps and patches, and of so shapeless and diverse contexture, that every piece, and every moment plays its part. And there is as much difference found between us and ourselves, as there is between ourselves and others,[11]

then we can reiterate the intriguing caption that I read on a portrait of a veiled woman by Ridolfo del Ghirlandaio (*c.*1510) in the Pallazo degli Uffizi in Florence, and ask, *Sua cuique persona*, to each his own person and mask?[12] This chapter focuses on biotechnology. Chapter 13 considers the effects of information technology and digital code(s).

---

[7] I. Calvino, 'Two interviews on science and literature', in I. Calvino (trans. P. Creagh), *The Uses of Literature* (New York: Harvest, 1987), pp. 28–38, p. 36.

[8] For example, J. J. Bono, 'Science, discourse, and literature: the role/rule of metaphor in science', in S. Peterfreund, *Literature and Science: Theory and Practice* (Boston: Northeastern University, 1990), pp. 59–89.

[9] For example, B. Clarke and L. Dalrymple Henderson (eds), *From Energy to Information: Representation in Science and Technology, Art, and Literature* (Stanford, CA: Stanford University Press, 2002).

[10] W. C. Dimock and P. Wald, 'Literature and science: cultural forms, conceptual exchanges', 74 *American Literature*, no. 4, 2002, pp. 705–14.

[11] M. de Montaigne (trans. J. Florio), *Essays* (London: Blount, [1580] 1603), pp. 196–7.

[12] The caption is taken from Seneca (trans. J. W. Basore), *Moral Essays*, vol. 3, *De beneficiis*, II, 17 (Cambridge, MA: Harvard University Press, 1975), pp. 82–3. For the evolution of the notion of persona, from theatrical mask to legal personhood, see H. Arendt, *On Revolution* (Harmondsworth: Penguin Books, [1963] 1976) pp. 106–7.

Embodied Code

As a prohibition against putting pressure upon a suspect, the right not to incriminate oneself refers to the deference in law to the defendant as a party in criminal proceedings, when it comes to respecting human dignity, viewed as the combination of both free will and physical and mental integrity. As a legal right, it is indissolubly connected to the rule of law in a democratic society in the protection that it guarantees against unlawful intrusions into people's lives. Currently, however, it seems to be under pressure, given modern technologies being put to forensic use. In Greek and Roman antiquity, the entrails of animals were thought to speak the truth about what had happened in the past or would happen in the near future; the flight of birds helped the Roman *augur* and *auspex* predict the future. For those of Christian denomination, the evidence of things not seen could be based on faith, as Hebrews (*New Testament* (AV), 11:1) has it. Ironically, given the Enlightenment abolition of physical torture, it does not matter anymore today if a defendant invokes his right to remain silent, because we have the technological means to force his body to talk. At the same time, jurists must be cautious when they judge what forensic sciences offer in terms of evidence: how is one to read the findings, how to translate these according to the requirements of a specific evidentiary setting?

The first embodied forensic standard for criminal investigation was the introduction of fingerprint techniques in the nineteenth century. Since the discovery in 1953 of the double helix of deoxyribonucleic acid, DNA for short, technological developments have drastically augmented its forensic possibilities.[13] At the same time, the meaning of genomic information has taken different shapes. The order of the four bases A (adenine), T (thymine), C (cytosine), and G (guanine) as the way in which genomic information is inscribed in the DNA molecule can be compared to the order of letters in words. Any change in the genetic lettering has an impact on the functioning of the human body, much in the same way that a different combination of letters leads to semantic difference: for instance, bard does not mean the same as drab. As a method of identification, and, especially a means of eliminating people as suspects, DNA fingerprinting (note the term) was developed in the 1980s. Today, computerised databanks of DNA samples are used in the evidentiary setting in criminal cases, and in various projects aimed at exonerating those falsely accused. It is important to note that there is no such thing

---

[13] See J. D. Watson (ed. G. Stent), *The Double Helix: A Personal Account of the Discovery of the Structure of DNA* (London: Weidenfeld and Nicolson, 1981).

as *the* DNA profile, because it is an autosomal profile with fifteen different DNA characteristics, with a name per characteristic and a way of denoting the variables for the same characteristic, all internationally standardised. These variable areas are called *loci*, and they are admirably suited to distinguish between individuals, because 98% of our DNA does not encode, or codify, any hereditary traits, and it varies greatly from one person to another.

Given the overarching topic of this book, I do not aim to exhaust the whole range of forensic uses of biotechnology, not least because my training was not in genetics. However, some examples can help illustrate the issues that the literary work discussed below invite us to consider. Firstly, consider the field of medicine. Today, variations in DNA that underlie specific diseases can be identified. Gene therapy experiments are being done for various life-threatening diseases, so that hereditary components of diseases can be targeted, and treatment can become more precise. The bad thing is that such research of the *idem* can also be held against a person. What if you know that you are genetically predisposed to diabetes and you are prone to overeating? The legal and ethical component enters the fray when it comes to laying the blame on someone in, for example, the context of health and life insurance – and remember that the concepts underlying insurance used to be collectivity and solidarity – even though laws have been implemented in many countries to protect against discrimination on the grounds of genetic heritage.

Secondly, there are aspects of race and gender to consider. DNA can help ascertain to which section of the population a suspect belongs in terms of race. While this may help exonerate the individual, it contains a huge risk of bias. In family law, a focus on equality does not preclude race issues,[14] or gender issues in, for example, paternity suits. To complicate matters, it should be noted with respect to recent developments in transgenderism, that in France 'sexe psychologique', or individual gender identity, was classified as a mental illness until 2010, recalling the nineteenth-century use of the concept of personality disease.[15] Therefore, what if law is unable to do justice to one's experience of *ipseity*, as well as of *idem* identity when this does not correspond with what it says on one's birth certificate? Furthermore, what are the implications of advanced genetic techniques such as the modification of DNA sequences called CRISPR (Clustered Regularly Interspaced Palindromic Repeats) that from a critical, juridical-historical perspective also

[14] For example, *Johnson v. Calvert*, 5 Cal. 4th 84, 851 P.2d 776 (1993), the case of a black surrogate mother who tried to keep the child she had gestated for a white man and his Filipino wife because it looked white.

[15] See D. Salas, *Le Courage de Juger* (Paris: Bayard, 2014), p. 58.

bring to mind the risk of unsavoury eugenics, and the violation of human rights? In asylum law, the risk of discrimination looms large as well, because of what forensic biotechnology accomplishes. DNA tests help make decisions about family reunions. Bone scans ascertain a migrant's age. Biometrical data distinguish between migrants on the basis of race, skin colour and ethnic background, so that the question regarding the veracity of the narrative of the traumatic reason for the asylum seeker to flee his or her country in the first place is pushed into the background.[16] The use of the iris scan at international airports may be helpful for the hurried traveller, but its drawback is the invasion of individual privacy. The areas of contention are intensified by contemporary threats of global terrorism that obviously need to be taken most seriously, not least because of the political trend to want to reduce these, whatever the cost in terms of legal principles. In short, the proliferation of technological inventions facilitating forensic applications implies the juridical invasion of the body.

Who are You? What is Man?

The complications concerning DNA technology sit uneasily with what I would call the DNA of the rule of law in democratic societies: legality, separation of powers, rights, and fair trial. The principle of legality restricts the scope of the use of DNA findings. But when these are legitimised by saying that this is a passive rather than an active form of self-incrimination that does not violate the right to fair trial because it rests on the premise that this information exists independent of the individual's free will, this aspect is precisely the point. Surely there is irony in the CSI opening tune, 'Who are you?', especially since erroneous forensic identifications have already begun to dampen the enthusiasm with respect to the value of forensic technologies.[17] On the meta level, therefore, the question remains as to how law itself is affected by technology. What if neither the legislative nor the judicial branch can estimate the full implications of technological developments, or, worse, are unduly influenced by vested commercial interests? The whole system of checks and balances will become a charade, and the citizen will suffer the consequences. Abuse of authority and arbitrary rule loom large. Worst of all, we may not even notice. Furthermore, if it is not 100% certain who and what one is, how does that affect one's social, political, and human rights? Can new constructs – products of technological commodification – be

---

[16] For example, *Salah Sheekh versus The Netherlands*, European Court of Human Rights 11 January 2007, no. 1948/04, AB 2007/76.

[17] See M. J. Saks and J. J. Koehler, 'The coming paradigm shift in forensic identification science', *Science*, 5 August 2005, pp. 892–5.

endowed with rights that presume legal personhood? Can democracy in its current forms 'survive genetic engineering'?[18] This is not only to suggest that modern technology seriously challenges law's DNA; concepts such as equality, liberty, and fraternity are also increasingly put under pressure. Access to an impartial tribunal may prove to be an empty shell if judicial *phronèsis* in matters technological falls short. Uncertainties on this plane may also hamper people's ability to narrate themselves. In short, the global challenges on the plane of governance with regard to genetic (com)modification are not restricted merely to technical possibilities.

Before I turn to Houellebecq's *Atomised*, which focuses on one aspect of biotechnology – namely, the possibility of humans being cloned into immortality[19] – I want to draw attention to our cognitive ambiguity with respect to cloning in relation to *ipseity* and personhood. This ambiguity shows in our adamic naming of cloned animals. Years ago, we gave the bull Herman and the lamb Dolly names rather than numbers, to suggest their individual authenticity.[20] The question of authenticity and legal personhood is taken up in Kazuo Ishiguro's dystopian novel *Never Let Me Go*.[21] It asks what makes a human being, and portrays a picture of the consequences of uninformed farming of human clones for their organs. Thus, it asks us to examine *ipse* and *idem* identities by showing that biotechnology outpaces the persona. In the novel, clones supposedly have souls, but what are they? Can they be holders of rights? Not if they are natural men, slaves. However, on the assumption that all human bodies capable of independent integrated functioning as biological organisms are persons, the answer would be affirmative. A human person denotes a thing in the sense of an individual that occupies space and exists for a period of time, with a certain amount of self-sufficiency, and a form of identity. In short, an *idem* as much as an *ipse*. To be a person in law, does one then have to have subjective consciousness? Does one have to be emotive, or morally cognizant? Or rather, must a person be a human being as we think we know ourselves? Self-consciousness characterises *ipseity*. If we

[18] G. J. Annas, *American Bioethics: Crossing Human Rights and Health Law Boundaries* (Oxford: Oxford University Press, 2005), p. 37.

[19] For a cautionary tale on immortality, see Hawthorne's short story 'Dr Heidegger's Experiment', in N. Hawthorne, *Twice-Told Tales* (Philadelphia: David Mackay, [1837 and 1842] 1889), available at <http://www.gutenberg.org/files/13707/13707-h/13707-h.htm> [last accessed 19 January 2018].

[20] See also the last line of H. James, 'The Madonna of the Future' (1879), 'Cats and monkeys, monkeys and cats – all human life is here', available at <https://ebooks.adelaide.edu.au/j/james/henry/madonna_of_the_future/> [last accessed 21 December 2017].

[21] K. Ishiguro, *Never Let Me Go* (London: Faber and Faber, 2005). See also Fay Weldon's novel *The Cloning of Joanna May* (Glasgow: Fontana, 1989).

look at the criteria commonly attributed to human persons, Ishiguro's clones fill the bill. But legal personhood requires agency, so we end up in an aporia because clones cannot set their own life goals. They have no property in their own persons of the kind that John Locke in his *Second Treatise of Government* claimed for ordinary humans.

Legal personhood is indeed a construct, a fiction, but the quest for self-knowledge does not evaporate. Are we persons, minds or human animals? Are we material objects in which persons are embedded, or are we, as sociology would often have it, collective representations embedded in bodily materials? The very idea that personhood is assigned to selected bodies draws attention to the liminality of personhood, to its boundaries. And when it comes to organ donation – or harvesting, as in Ishiguro's novel – are we tenants or owners of our bodies? Will the body remain a material object *per se*, or will it also develop a parallel, a virtual-digital representation, as discussed in Chapter 13? More importantly, in what way is our self-conception influenced by technology? If we are supposedly enhanced by technological possibilities, what does this mean for our identity?[22] Who am I if I am determined in my choices to act by a variety of causes?[23] Or rather, is there an I that I can reflect on, and, if so, who is she? Technological developments have not helped us advance to any extent on the subject of the Cartesian duality of mind and matter. Philosophically, the problem of whether the legal subject still absorbs the human person does not disappear when law and technology opt for the predominance of one over the other for practical purposes. Terminologically, there is irony in the fact that the DNA *loci* challenge law's *loci* or *topoi* in the rhetorical sense as the special places where arguments may be found,[24] for the simple reason that *loci* are not infallible. They can become obstacles, when proved ill-matched to an argument. From law as a human practice, the disenchantment of the world – noted in Chapter 3 – demands legitimacy. Law finds its legitimacy in its genetic structure of legality, legislation, democracy, rights and fair trial at the level of the individual case. But there is one problem: legitimacy can be achieved only in the disenchanted world itself, precisely because law is man-made.

---

[22] See J. Finnis, '"The thing I am": personal identity in Aquinas and Shakespeare', in E. Frankel Paul et al. (eds), *Personal Identity* (Cambridge: Cambridge University Press, 2005), pp. 250–82.

[23] See D. DeGrazia, *Human Identity and Bioethics* (Cambridge: Cambridge University Press, 2005).

[24] See Aristotle (trans. J.H. Freese), *The Art of Rhetoric* (Cambridge, MA, and London: Harvard University Press, 2006). The seminal text on the *topoi* in law is T. Viehweg, *Topik und Jurisprudenz* (Munich: Beck, 1954).

That is why humans must inform science, and not the other way around, even if this is the easy way when we do not fully grasp the consequences of technology.

This is absolutely not to reject innovation and progress, or to advocate a kind of prelapsarian perspective on technology, but to caution against a Bouvardian attitude. An uninformed use of technological findings, especially in our contemporary, interconnected, or overlapping information networks, can have grave consequences. The influx of technology in law, more specifically genetic and robotic technology, results in exponential changes. With the traditional ontological constraints of religious eschatologies removed in our post-modern era, what, then, can or should be the reaction of law to the novel technological limitations on what has long been deemed the sovereignty of the human will? Can law keep pace with the acceleration of biotechnical innovations, or have we by now reached the edges of the juridical as we know it? The technological de-composition of the body forces us to rethink – by asking, 'What is Man?' – both the notion of the legal fiction of the subject and the humanities as instruments of self-exploration.

Michel Houellebecq's novel *Atomised* painfully illustrates our inability to read well the book of nature and man. It deals with profound scientific and technological developments of the kind that affect law. As such, its explanatory literary situation challenges us to think about the growing disjunction between principles of law. In the story of the protagonist Michel and his brother Bruno, the topic of the *ipse* and *idem* returns.

Michel Houellebecq's *Atomised*: Two Readings

Reading genetics

It is not until the Epilogue of Michel Houellebecq's *Atomised* that we understand that the story told by the narrator is a flashback, and that the year is 2079.[25] By then, the human beings who re-created life by cloning species into immortality have been wiped away. We learn that the protagonist Michel Djerzinski's work in molecular biology was successfully brought to its logical conclusion. On the premise that once the genome would be completely decoded, humanity would be in complete control of its evolution, Michel had dedicated his life improving on existing genetic codes and creating new ones. The consequence of his work was that

---

[25] The edition used is M. Houellebecq (trans. F. Wynne), *Atomised* (London: William Heinemann, [*Les Particules élémentaires* 1999] 2000). Hereinafter (A + page number). The title of the American edition is *The Elementary Particles*.

any genetic code, however complex, could be noted in a standard, structurally stable form, isolated from any mutations. This meant that every cell
contained within it the possibility of being perfectly copied. Every animal
species, however highly evolved, could be transformed into a similar species, reproduced by cloning and therefore immortal. (A 370)

Initially, this met with fierce opposition from traditional humanists and
religious people of different denominations, because the creation of a new
human, asexual species did away with cherished notions of freedom and dignity. In the end, however, Michel's successor and later biographer, Frédéric
Hubczejak, obtained UNESCO funding for the project that he initiated
after Michel's disappearance on 27 March 2009, on the principle that 'THE
REVOLUTION WILL NOT BE MENTAL BUT GENETIC' (A 377). In
2029, the first of a new intelligent species came into existence as a result of
the phenomenon of 'metaphysical mutations – that is to say radical, global
transformations in the values to which the majority subscribe' (A 4). The rise
of Christianity was the first example of such a metaphysical mutation; the rise
of modern science was the second; and Michel's work on genetics heralded
the third. Its eschatology starts to unfold when his studies of physics cause
him to realise that 'once biologists were forced to confront the reality of the
atom, the very basis of modern biology would be blown away' (A 19), and
that he will bring about a major paradigm shift.

The story of his scientific quest is also told in flashback. At the start of
the novel, we learn that, at the age of forty, Michel leaves a successful post as
head of a department for research in molecular biology. His farewell party is
a complete disaster. When he returns home, the canary, his sole companion,
has died. Michel takes three sleeping pills, and 'So ended his first night of
freedom' (A 14). With this cynical comment, the scene is set. The unfolding
of the stories of the lives of Michel and his half-brother Bruno shows the
importance of the influence of human, hereditary building blocks. The boys'
mother had married one of the first medical doctors who understood the uses
of bodily enhancements in the form of plastic surgery, and he had made a
career of it. In 1956, Bruno was born, and in 1958 he was sent to his maternal
grandmother in Algeria when his mother was pregnant with Michel, fathered
by another man. Michel, born in 1958, was rescued from his mother's neglect
and raised in the French countryside by his paternal grandmother. From an
early moment, Michel realised that nature's elementary particles could have
been totally different from what they actually are, and that everything is the
result of random events.

Throughout the novel, this idea is subtly worked out on the level of the
boys' lives. They, too, are elementary particles, and small changes have caused

huge differences, while at the same time their lives have remarkable parallels as well, especially when it comes to their inability to develop meaningful relationships with others generally, and with women specifically. Bruno's involvement with Annick ends in her suicide; his marriage to Anne and his role as a father to his son Victor are failures. Is it fate or genetic predisposition that he meets Christiane, a professor of natural science who is as critical as Michel when it comes to the uses of sexuality? Their happiness does not last long. Christiane is diagnosed with a severe illness. And when she realises that she will be confined to a wheelchair for the rest of her life, and with Bruno not being a very caring man, she commits suicide. As irony would have it, the parallelism in the two brothers' lives comes to its natural conclusion when Annabelle, Michel's love, has to undergo an abortion because she is diagnosed with uterine cancer. After the operation, she, too, commits suicide.

Are the half-brothers' emotional and relational restrictions caused by the fact that they share the same mother? Are matters indeed random, and yet genetically predisposed? The boys attend the same school, unaware of each other's existence. They meet once, and at school. From 1974 onwards, their lives go in different directions. Bruno opts for Kafka and masturbation. Michel turns to science, and uses the notion of a 'consistent Griffiths' history'- that is, a coherent narrative constructed from quantum information – to get a grip on life and *ipseity*, because

> As a being you are self-aware, and this consciousness allows you to hypothesise that the story you've created from a given set of memories is a *consistent history*, justified by a consistent narrative voice. As a unique individual having existed for a particular period and been subjected to an ontology of objects and properties, you can assert this with absolute certainty, and so automatically assume that it is a Griffiths' history. You make this hypothesis about real life, rather than the memories of dreams. (A 75–6, italics in the original)

Throughout the novel, we repeatedly read about the year 1974? Why? Is it because 1974 was the year in which the very idea of genetic manipulation became reality when it was found that *Agrobacterium tumefaciences* as a guest organism transmitted a small part of DNA from a plasmide to his host, and so proved that is was possible to enter a gene from the one organism into the genome of another?

Michel finds a place to satisfy his intellectual curiosity in the physics research faculty dedicated to the study of elementary particles. He wonders about the anomalous situation that the universe is made up of about one hundred elements, while as a matter of principle an infinite number of combinations is possible:

When we think about the present, we veer wildly between the belief in chance and the evidence in favour of determinism. When we think about the past, however, it seems obvious that everything happened in the way that it was intended. (A 215)

As far as volition is concerned, Michel 'realised that belief in the notions of reason and of free will, which are the natural foundations of democracy, probably resulted from a confusion between the concepts of freedom and unpredictability' (A 270). Such questions trouble and motivate Michel's purely intellectual existence, and they trigger his academic output. In 2002, he writes his first extensive work, *The Topology of Meiosis*, which tolls the death knell for the fiction of individual existence. A positivist reading of recent developments, in a manner August Comte would have approved of, will save the day, because 'Only an ontology of states was capable of restoring the practical possibility of human relationships', since

> in the ontology of states, the particles are indiscernible, and can be limited to an observable number. The only entities which can be identified and named in such an ontology are wave functions, and, using them, state vectors – from which arose the analogous concept of redefining fraternity, sympathy, and love. (A 360)

To us, as readers who are born rather than constructed, this is a bleak picture as far as human perceptions and experiences of reality are concerned. Although Michel has been unable to enter into a love relationship with Annabelle, he nevertheless emphasises the possibility of love in his own work. This has a cynical ring to it when, as readers, we understand that Michel's scientific goal to end sexual reproduction finds its counterpart in Annabelle's suicide after her reproductive capacity has gone,

> Djerzinski's great leap was not his rejection of the idea of personal freedom (a concept which had already been much devalued in his time, and which everyone agreed, at least tacitly, could not form the basis for any kind of human progress but in the fact that he was able, through somewhat risky interpretations of the postulates of quantum mechanics, to restore the possibility of love . . . though he had not known love himself, through Annabelle, Djerzinski had succeeded in forming an image of it . . . His work, he knew, was done. (A 363)

Michel's scientific contribution of physical immortality gives mankind more insight into the working of time, and, in a way reminiscent of Immanuel Kant's theory of the *schemata*, or categories of human thought used to grasp the reality around us, Michel, after seeing the illuminations of *The Book of Kells*, claims that natural forms are human forms.

In 2009, Michel's theory is proved. All scientists agree that 'the practical consequences of this were dizzying . . . every cell contained within it the possibility of being perfectly copied' (A 370). There is also criticism, of course, especially when Hubczejak proceeds on the road paved by Djerzinski. One objection is that sexual difference is central to human identity, and that suppression of such difference by means of cloning would end the possibility of uniqueness of the human *idem* identity at this level. One has only to consider contemporary debate on transgenderism to realise the importance of Houellebecq's narrative. The even more fundamental criticism in the narrative is that the existence of a species carrying the same genetic code implies that human individuality will disappear for good. The perversity as far as solving crimes by means of genetic technology is concerned is, obviously, that this door is slammed shut once we no longer have our unique genetic codes. To Hubczejak, however, the disappearance of the notion of human personality is not at all problematic.

The narrator points to one major mistake that Hubczejak made, and that is his positivist, literal reading of Djerzinski. It leads him to a 'gross misinterpretation of the philosophical subtleties of the project, and even his inability to recognize philosophical subtleties in general, in no way hampered or even delayed its implementation' (A 376). For those of us in the humanities, this positivist attitude with its subsequent instrumentalism strikes a final blow in stating that the concomitant effect is that 'The global ridicule inspired by the works of Foucault, Lacan, Derrida and Deleuze, after decades of reverence, far from leaving the field clear for new ideas, simply heaped contempt on all those who were active in "human sciences"' (A 376). From a disciplinary perspective as well, the novel points to the continued importance of the question in law and the humanities: What is Man?[26] So ends my first reading of *Atomised*.

Technè *and* poièsis

Michel's struggle with human relations is emblematic of the problem underlying his and Hubczejak's scientific quest. In 1998, the Council of Europe and, before that, in 1997 the European Parliament, declared that cloning is

---

[26] Or, as Marilynne Robinson asked with respect to the humanities, 'What are we doing here?', *The New York Review of Books*, 9 November 2017, pp. 28, 35–6, arguing that in contemporary literary studies over the last few decades, a utilitarian hostility has replaced the earlier 'animating spirit of humanism' that, as Robinson suggests, we need in order to understand the world, and, where necessary, to counterbalance instrumentalism.

an instrumentalisation of human beings that offends human dignity. One of the major problems regarding the forensic use of biotechnology was thereby succinctly pinpointed as well: namely, that of using people and their various body parts as instruments to arrive at a supposedly greater goal.[27] This is the result of what I consider a conflation of science and technology. Science is dedicated to theoretical knowledge, and technology is dedicated to its application. For the likes of Hubczejak, this distinction has evaporated: if it can be done, it will be done. Houellebecq is therefore right in having his narrator speak of Hubczejak's lack of attention to the possible philosophical issues involved. So we will do well to fill the void and turn to philosophy to ask, 'What is technology?'

From Heidegger, as noted in Chapter 10, we inherited the idea that language usage is in itself a selective interpretation, with the roads not taken always lingering in the background. The social dimension of dialogue does not save us from the risk of reification that is connected to conceptualisation. Here, I suggest, is the root of the problem that we face in forensic applications of biotechnology. Ever since we first created tools to fend off wild animals, we are *homo faber*. Nevertheless, we tend to underestimate the consequences of our uninformed application of technology in forensic settings. Therefore, for whatever reason, we all too often do not realise what is deliberately left out, or what is not incorporated. In the sense that technological possibilities are augmented beyond the traditional scope of human progress, and, moreover, at a high speed, we run the constant risk of being trapped in our conceptual frameworks, and of being ill-prepared for changes in perspective, either for good or for bad. Therefore, from a point of view of legal epistemology, this suggests that we need to provide another perspective. Here as well, the build- ing blocks of a humanistic jurisprudence advocated in Part II are admirably suited.

Furthermore, we can learn important lessons from Heidegger's phenom- enological distinction between *technè* and technology, both in the original and the contemporary sense of the terms. On the basis of this first distinction, Heidegger distinguishes between two views on technology that he claims we should consider in their interrelation: firstly, technology as a means to an end, and, secondly, technology as a human activity. It is exactly this distinction, I suggest, that is mistakenly pushed into the background. We have focused

---

[27] See the 'Explanatory Report to the Additional Protocol to the Convention on Human Rights and Biomedicine on the Prohibition of Cloning Human Beings' (1998) available at <https://rm.coe.int/16800ccde9> [last accessed 23 December 2017]. See also D. Gurnham, 'The mysteries of human dignity and the brave new world of human cloning', 14 *Social & Legal Studies*, no. 2, 2005, pp. 197–212.

on implementing technological innovations in a forensic setting by means of legal rules, with rights and guarantees included as much as possible, without reflecting enough on the *quidditas* of technology itself.

In 'The question concerning technology', Heidegger turns to the Greek roots of the term technology, with *technikon* stemming from *technè*. He starts with a methodological caveat from which I derive the subtitle of this chapter: 'Questioning builds a way . . . The way is a way of thinking.'[28] This is especially pertinent, given the predilection in the legal discussion about technology not to distinguish between what it is and what it does, and to refrain from combining such questions with the discussion on the most appropriate legal methodology to be adhered to. Or, in Heideggerian terms, between the essence of what a thing is, on the one hand, and its instrumental uses, on the other. Modern technology is a case in point. It has long been considered only in terms of human progress, while today we suffer the consequences in the form of juridical-ethical issues thrust upon us as we become more keenly sensitive to technology's darker side effects. Or, as Heidegger claims,

> Technology is not equivalent to the essence of technology . . . the essence of technology is by no means anything technological . . . But we are delivered over to it in the worst possible way when we regard it as something neutral; for this conception of it . . . makes us utterly blind to the essence of technology. (QCT 4)

For forensic biotechnology, the question will therefore be not only, 'What is its end?', but also 'How does an instrumental conception affect law and us?' This is so, because Heidegger cautions us about the side effect that 'The will to mastery becomes all the more urgent the more technology threatens to slip from human control' (QCT 5). If 'the correct instrumental definition of technology still does not show us technology's essence', we should probe the reciprocal relation between instrumentality and causality.

In order to show what causality means for the instrumentality of technology, Heidegger turns to the classical, philosophical view on causality that makes a distinction between four types of causes: (1) the *causa materialis*, the material out of which something is made; (2) the *causa formalis*, the shape into which that material enters; (3) the *causa finalis*, the purpose for which that something is made; and (4) the *causa efficiens*, the cause that brings about the finished thing. Therefore, gold or platinum, for example, can be made into a ring rather than, say, an Olympic medal or a diamond-studded

---

[28] M. Heidegger, 'The question concerning technology', in M. Heidegger (trans. W. Lovitt), *The Question Concerning Technology and Other Essays* (New York: Harper & Row, [1954] 1977), pp. 3–35, p. 3. Hereinafter (QCT + page number). Diacritics as used in the original.

platinum skull. Hence, its purpose differs depending on its form. Obviously, this affects who will be its maker (e.g., a unknown goldsmith or Damien Hirst). Our mistake, according to Heidegger, has been to collapse the distinctions between these four causes, and to view the *causa efficiens* as the standard for all causality, disregarding, more specifically, the question regarding the purpose. In short, ours is the attitude of 'if it can be done, it will be done'. Originally, however, each cause had its specific function to contribute to technology. Without the gold, no ring; and the ring's image or *eidos* – rather than the gold being made into something else – has consequences for its purpose and use. And it is the maker's work that brings about the finished product.

Here, the notion of human activity comes in. The maker does all this by means of his *logos*, carefully considering what he is going to bring into being, and what it is that will be revealed out of the specific material. Translated to the issue of biotechnology, we might say that the danger of the dominance of instrumentality is that we do not consider carefully enough what is brought into being.[29] Heidegger claims that we will fail to see what instrumentality really is if we keep thinking in terms of causality in terms of effecting.

For the clarification of this problem, he returns to the reciprocal relation between the four causes. Each in their own way, they occasion something; they call forth in the sense that they enable that which is not yet present to become present. The term for this event is *poiēsis*, a bringing forth (*Her-vor-bringen*) as defined in Plato's dialogue 'Symposium'. 'Bringing forth' means that something that was hitherto concealed is revealed: that is, the Greek concept of *alētheia*, the Roman *veritas*, and our truth in the sense of the correctness of an idea. Because the four modes of occasioning are gathered together within the very concept of 'bringing forth', clarifying their interrelation will provide insight into the essence of technology.

In a phenomenological manner, asking with regard to the Greek stem of *technikon* as that which belongs to *technē*, Heidegger returns to the question of what technology means. He points out that '*technē* is the name not only for the activities and skills of the craftsman, but also for the arts of the mind and the fine arts. *Technē* belongs to bringing-forth, to *poiēsis*' (QCT 13). The second point is that 'From earliest times until Plato the word *technē* is linked with the word *epistēmē*. Both words are names for knowing in the widest sense' (QCT 13). And knowing is opening up, revealing. It is important to note here that Heidegger says 'until Plato', because it is Plato whom we

---

[29] For the root of *logos* in *legein*, – that is, gathering as revealing a thing – see M. Heidegger (trans. G. Fried and R. Polt), *Introduction to Metaphysics* (New Haven and London: Yale University Press, [1935] 2000), pp. 180–1.

may thank for the schism of what was originally thought of as a unity, that of knowing that and knowing how – a schism that Aristotle, as noted in Chapter 6, fiercely rejected – and its consequences as far as the division and methodological strife between academic disciplines is concerned, as noted in Chapter 3.

Accepting the premise that *technē* is revealing brings us to the heart of the matter. It implies that if we make the mistake of thinking of technology purely as production and application, we disregard the way in which the four modes of causality work together to reveal the truth of technology. Of course, one might respond that this was all very well for the Greeks in their time, but it does not apply to modern technology, based as it is on the natural sciences. With Heidegger, however, I suggest that this does not exempt us from asking how technology deploys the findings of the natural sciences. An exclusive focus on one aspect of causality and a reductive view on the human activity of *poiēsis* as 'making' leads to the mistake of looking upon technology only as production: that is, as an object 'at hand' (QCT 17), disregarding the need to bring forth the correctness of the idea, the truth. This also affects humans in that they can – and will be – objectified, while they think that they are the makers in charge. This illusion, in turn, gives rise to one final delusion: 'It seems as though man everywhere and always encounters only himself . . . *In truth, however, precisely nowhere does man today any longer encounter himself, i.e., his essence*' (QCT 27, italics in the original). The result of modern technology as we have come to use it is that we ourselves have been reduced to being only at hand, objects that stand reserved for purposes of further ordering, in law and elsewhere. Applied to forensic DNA technology, Heidegger's point would be that such reduction of the human being to an object up for grabs, ordered by law and plundered for bodily materials, runs the severe risk of compromising traditionally respected legal values. Therefore, it is necessary to remain critical with regard to the question of whether technology should be put to use for the simple reason that it is available.

This is why we should challenge what is held before our eyes as the inevitable effect of technology. To nourish this capability, Heidegger advised that we (re)turn to the arts, for it is there that we can find inspiration for our current task of accomplishing the revealing of the 'what' of technology in the form of a methodology for reflection. Heidegger proved prophetic when he wrote,

> because the essence of technology is nothing technological, essential reflection upon technology and decisive confrontation with it must happen in a realm that is, on the one hand, akin to the essence of technology and, on the other, fundamentally different from it. Such a realm is art. But certainly

only if reflection on art, for its part, does not shut its eyes to the constellation of truth after which we are *questioning*. (QTC 35)

The divorce by modern science of *physis* from *technē* and *poiēsis* has as its
consequence that *nomos* as ordinance and code has become predominant in
law. This divorce also results in a proclivity to accept at face value what is
held before us as technology, and to reduce our ethical thought on the subject
to a discussion of the current mores, rather than to place the moral side of
humanity in the foreground. To keep questioning technology, and to realise
that its language is a specific perspective, albeit a forceful one, we need the
humanities to stem the tide of instrumentalism, as Heidegger reiterated in
connection to the risk of the supremacy of cybernetics as another example of
disenchantment.[30]

Acting as one person

The importance of biological sources of human identity *per se* needs no questioning, but when it comes to answering the question of our authenticity, its
discourse will benefit if we return to that other source of the self, literature,
using our imagination to determine our actions. Not least because science
divorced from morality will lead to the production of monsters, literally and
figuratively. Learning to face the consequences of human agency in law and
technology, and establishing a legal and moral relationship to the selves that
we are – a normative understanding – is too important to leave only to technology and scientific discourse to decide. To me, this would include a return
to a discussion of morality in the original sense before it came to be polluted
by an exclusively rule-bound model of reasoning, a return to a reflection
on man as a moral being. Moral, that is, in the sense of the human ethos of
searching for, and analysing values.[31] To Charles Taylor, this means that we
should look for alternative framings of technology to preserve the ability to
narrate ourselves and others.[32]

A more disruptive reading of the ending of *Atomised* is therefore called
for, because it would seem that Hubczejak as Michel Djerzinski's biographer
misreads his subject's contribution to science and humanity, in that as the
diehard of positivist science that he himself is, he accepts on the surface of it
the critical connection between Michel's ideas. Michel accepts as irrefutable
the position that, because of quantum mechanics, 'Man no longer needed

---

[30] M. Heidegger, 'Only a God can save us', XX *Philosophy Today*, no. 4, 1976, pp. 267–85.
[31] See also J. Gardner, *On Moral Fiction* (New York: Basic Books, 1978).
[32] C. Taylor, *The Ethics of Authenticity* (Cambridge, MA: Harvard University Press, 1991),
    pp. 106–7.

God nor the idea of an underlying reality' (A 359), for the very reason
that

> in experiments, it is possible to get a group of observers to agree on rea-
> sonable intersubjectivity; these experiments are linked by theories, which
> should, as far as possible, be succinct and which must, by definition, be
> refutable. This is a perceived world, a world of feelings, a human world.
> (A 360)

He does ask himself, however, whether 'the need to find meaning [is] simply
a childish defect of the human mind' (A 360). Nonetheless, Hubczejak also
mentions that the decisive moment in the evolution of Djerzinski's ideas was
when he first saw *The Book of Kells*, the study of which prompted scientific
intuitions that in retrospect – remember the year is 2079 – proved correct.
A childish defect? That Houellebecq has Hubczejak derail in positivism of a
kind that Flaubert's Bouvard and Pécuchet would have approved of is the
ironic twist that sows the seed of doubt at the end of the novel. Hubczejak is
the prime example of the effect of the third metaphysical mutation, a global
transformation in the values to which the majority subscribes in Djerzinski's
terms, combined with an absolute belief in what Djerzinski told about a
'consistent Griffiths' history'. What the literal reader Hubczejak lacks is what
Anthony Cunningham calls 'reading for life', an activity comparable to *phronèsis* as the recognition of what must be done and to act upon it, both also
being acts of self-exploration.[33] For this reason, Houellebecq's depictions of
Bruno and Michel's lives and feelings should be read for what they hide as
much as for what they reveal.

In other words, literature is no mere counterproposal to law and
science, no mere critique, but a dissenting opinion connected as it is to
law via the perspective of cases and narratives as the *locus* for a reflection on, and, if necessary, opposition to the language of science and
technology when that is incorporated instrumentally into law. If what
the engineers of the human body create is as yet unbelievable, given our
current, conceptual legal universe, and if they threaten to take over, or
erase our moral discourse, then scholars in *Law and the Humanities* will
do well to take up their tasks as engineers of the human soul – not as the
propagandists of indoctrination as Joseph Stalin would have the Russian
poets but as *poietai*, the makers who ask the awkward questions. If the
project of the invention of the human, for which Harold Bloom credited

---

[33] A. Cunningham, *The Heart of What Matters: The Role for Literature in Moral Philosophy*
(Berkeley: University of California Press, 2001).

Shakespeare,[34] is still in full swing, our ongoing concern and task should then be to question the stories in science and technology which are told to us, and which we ourselves tell to others. So ends my second reading of *Atomised*.

---

[34] H. Bloom, *Shakespeare: The Invention of the Human* (London: Fourth Estate, 1999).

13

Control, Alt, Delete?
Information Technology and the Human

New Kids on the Law Block?

'Control, Alt, Delete, username, password' is what we do automatically, every day, and without further thought, in order to gain access to the digital world. Failure to comply? Access denied! New information and communication technologies permeate our lives to such an extent that we take them for granted. Given the perspective that guides this book, I am interested in how, as recipients and users of new technologies not of our own design, our perceptions of the world and our epistemological assumptions are influenced. If Alberto Manguel was right when he proposed that 'a culture is defined by what it can name',[1] what does that mean for the (re)invention of the human, and what are its effects on law?

Would Shakespeare, fond as he was of twin images, recognise a digital representation of the human of the kind described as 'Digital-Me', a device as of yet a fantasy beyond contemporary 'smart' home devices, but a very serious one. It hints at what mobile communication and data mining can accomplish together: a human's digital replica as a kind of personal assistant, impersonating its busy owner and programmed to perform his or her simpler tasks; in doing so, it takes its owner's decisions independently, as if it were he or she, and it also 'knows' when to 'switch on' the real human.[2] In order to continue the discussion of questions pertaining to a humanistic view of technology, this chapter starts by highlighting, however briefly, significant developments in digital and/or smart technologies in the legal environment.[3] It does so,

---

[1] A. Manguel, *A Reader on Reading* (New Haven and London: Yale University Press, 2010), p. 204.

[2] This example derives from B. van den Berg, 'Ambient Intelligence: Wat, wie en . . . waarom?', *Computerrecht*, 2010, no. 6, p. 171.

[3] This chapter is informed by L. Floridi (ed.), *The Blackwell Guide to the Philosophy of Computing and Information* (Malden, MA: Blackwell Publishing, 2004); L. Floridi (ed.), *The Online Manifesto – Being Human in a Hyperconnected Era* (Dordrecht: Springer, 2014), available at

because the task of philosophy is not to make life easy, but, as in Chapter 12, to ask awkward questions, specifically of the kind that judicial *phronèsis* needs in order to be able to develop. The rest of this chapter is dedicated to the issues concerning individual authenticity and privacy, raised in, and by, Juli Zeh's dystopian novel *The Method*.

Contemporary legal-philosophical views on profiling, government surveillance, data mining, or, generally, artificial intelligence (AI) and ambient intelligence (AmI) as interrelated technological visions are the new kids on the law block, so to speak. As computational models of human behaviour and/or cognitive processes, processes of profiling and/or data mining – aimed at discovering correlations of data of groups or one individuated subject – use algorithms to arrive at results in the form of predictions about human behaviour.[4] And that could include the assessment of the behaviour of unsuspected citizens in order to search for potentially criminal acts: for example, social security fraud. Prominent in the descriptions and analyses of these models is the way in which aspects of volition are dealt with. Inasmuch as the neurosciences have forced us to rethink the concepts of volitional impairment and the determination of criminal responsibility, the workings of AI and AmI are excellent examples of José Saramago's suggestion that

> if we persist in stating that we are the ones who make our decisions, then we would have to begin to explain, to discern, to distinguish, who it is in us who made the decision and who subsequently carried it out, impossible operations by anyone's standards. Strictly speaking, we do not make decisions, decisions make us.[5]

If the data subject is targeted without being aware of it, and acts on that by showing a certain kind of behaviour, is this to be called an exercise of his

<https://link.springer.com/book/10.1007%2F978-3-319-04093-6> [last accessed 10 June 2016]; M. Hildebrandt, *Smart Technologies and the End(s) of Law: Novel Entanglements of Law and Technology* (Cheltenham and Northampton, MA: Edward Elgar Publishing, 2015); K. N. Hayles, *How We Think: Digital Media and Contemporary Technogenesis* (Chicago: University of Chicago Press, 2012); M. Hildebrandt and S. Gutwirth (eds), *Profiling the European Citizen: Cross-Disciplinary Perspectives* (Dordrecht: Springer, 2008).

4 For a working definition of profiling, see M. Hildebrandt, 'Defining profiling: a new type of knowledge?', in M. Hildebrandt and S. Gutwirth, *Profiling the European Citizen*, p. 19. For data mining, see S. van der Hof and C. Prins, 'Personalisation and its influence on identities, behaviour and social values', in M. Hildebrandt and S. Gutwirth, *Profiling the European Citizen*, pp. 111–24, p. 111. The EU General Data Protection Regulation (GDPR), May 2018, has as its aim to harmonise data privacy (available at <https://www.eugdpr.org/> [last accessed 29 January 2018]).

5 J. Saramago (trans. M. J. Costa), *All the Names* (New York: Harcourt Inc., [1997] 1999), p. 28.

or her free will? Does the subject in this way show his or her preferences? The same goes when we think of uses of AmI applied to, for example, the concept of contract. If the intelligent application enters into a legally binding obligation independently of its human user, whose risk is it when things go wrong? To give but one example: what if such a system, when the user gives the order to do so, buys the necessary medication for its user from a third party, within the limits set prior to the contract, implying the user's conscious consent? Suppose that the wrong medication is delivered? Whose risk is that? What does this mean for the concept of consideration?[6] This goes beyond the electronic identifications and the digital signatures that already form the basis of the digital economy. Even if we allow for the fact that humans act out of habit most of the time, and so the question of volition does not always turn up consciously, the point remains that (in)voluntary participation is immediately connected to a model of thought that has individual autonomy at its heart, the methodological individualism connected to the quest for certainty, as noted in Chapter 3.

Our articulation of reality as we perceive it by means of language is the result of a process of selective interpretation on the basis of the perspective we take. James Boyd White has consistently voiced the related argument that any form of speech is a form of translation that has deficiencies and exuberances, translation being the art 'of confronting unbridgeable discontinuities between texts, between languages, and between people'.[7] As users of technologies, we are dependent on the information they provide, so how are we to recognise reductions of meaning if we cannot adequately size up the full range of options available to start with? This has consequences for law as well if we follow White's proposal that law is a culture of argument that addresses questions of values and community. Van der Hof and Prins argue that the problem is that 'the use and "value" of personal data cannot be separated from the specifics of the context (social, economic and institutional settings) within which these data are collected and used'.[8] Therefore, our being unconscious of the fact that we leave a digital trail with practically every move – including the unconscious generation of clickstream data when we visit the worldwide web – shows that 'the real problem is *how* personal data are processed, in what context and towards what

---

[6] See J. Linnemann and J. Schmaal, 'Intelligent contracteren', *Computerrecht*, 2010, pp. 297–302.

[7] J. B. White, *Justice as Translation* (Chicago: University of Chicago Press, 1990), p. 257.

[8] Van der Hof and Prins, 'Personalisation', p. 112; see also, p. 118, 'protection of personal data . . . assumes the capability to know and to control the way in which our identities are constructed and used'.

end'.[9] In other words, the data controller in the guise of the Heideggerian maker is in control.

Furthermore, the question is how to create a public awareness of the fact that all too often our attitude towards technological innovations is casual, if not downright careless, if we consider what appears on Facebook and other social media. We readily give away information without considering the consequences we may suffer, as many have already found out to their considerable disadvantage; for example, those who engaged in sexting and fell victim to blackmailing. Paradoxically, while new technologies have opened cyberspace for us, the agora in the sense of the public debate has not grown in size.[10] Nevertheless, public debate is essential in order to be informed about and to reflect on the possible hazards of new technologies. The consequences of misinformation on the juridical-political level of human equality are not to be underestimated. How can one decide at all about what or what not to do under the circumstance that the self as data subject has become objectified as a designed product standing reserved for further ordering by even more sophisticated technologies?

While I fully agree with those scholars who focus on the effects of AI and AmI on concepts of individual privacy, autonomy and control or discrimination,[11] I also suggest that we think more in terms of the unsettling possibility that someone else is going to decide everything for us, state ideology writ large with or without populistic tendencies. Why? Because we are all too easily lulled into complacency when the services rendered by AmI aim at presenting the least inconvenience while providing maximum benefits. The 'behavioural turn' with respect to the average customer's habits is efficient. Let us be honest, who does not consider the recommendations any website offers on the basis of one's recent purchases, or what other customers have bought? Do you install all the apps that make you an ideal customer? At the end of the day, it is all a matter of good reading: of human behaviour, including human interaction, and of hidden premises and codes, overt and covert, by means of which these are governed, if only because of the dialectical connection between human behaviour and technology, with each new development necessitating an infinite regress of new forms of protection and disclosure. I suggest that we resist the unspoken presupposition behind technology's anticipation regarding its user, at least as far as design is con-

---

[9] Van der Hof and Prins, 'Personalisation', p. 117.

[10] Cf. W. J. Mitchell, *City of Bits: Space, Place, and the Infobahn* (Cambridge, MA: MIT Press, [1995] 2000), p. 176.

[11] See also M. Hildebrandt, 'Legal and technological normativity: more (or less) than twin sisters', 12 *Techné*, no. 3, 2008, pp. 169–83.

cerned, precisely because, paradoxically, the average human is still the target taken as the measure of things. If technology regulates human behaviour by nudging us to act in specific ways,[12] do we fully recognise this, and, in law more specifically, do we reflect enough on the consequences with an ethics of responsibility towards both the institution and the people whose lives and affairs it orders?

The above topics, especially when viewed as privacy issues in a digital age, can also be connected to Ricoeur's methodological distinction between one's *ipse* identity and *idem* identity. Hildebrandt has argued that what also matters in the context of new technologies is Ricoeur's call to see oneself as another, and to do so literally in order to be aware of how smart environments perceive us.[13] In other words, in order to understand my own actions, I have to be aware of how others, humans or machines, understand them. To me, this is the classical hermeneutic challenge of figuring out what the underlying question was when one confronts the text or action that is the answer. So whose free will is it anyway? The basic question behind new technologies is not 'so what?' but 'what if?' Big AI businesses have already been forum shopping over the past few decades when looking for places to establish their companies. Ireland, for example, became highly in demand when, as a result of the financial crisis after 2008, its Data Protection Authority consisted of a team so small that it could not possibly oversee everything. If contemporary technological developments are out of line with our more traditional ways of thinking about the human being's values and behaviour, the risk of Orwellian doublethink about technological applications threatens when decisions are made with an eye on future use only, rather than on present infractions of principles and values. And while *i-Government* may not yet be designed by an evil genius, we cannot deny the fact that information spreads like an inkblot and function creep is a real risk.[14] Brave New World has an ironic ring to it, for what if function creep is the default, and 'delete' – in the definition given by Viktor Mayer-Schönberg: namely, the virtue of forgetting and the right to being forgotten in the digital age – is not?[15] In this event, the disruption

---

[12] R. H. Thaler and C. R. Sunstein, *Nudge: Improving Decisions about Health, Wealth and Happiness* (New Haven: Yale University Press, 2008).

[13] M. Hildebrandt, 'Profiling and the identity of the European citizen', in M. Hildebrandt and S. Gutwirth, *Profiling the European Citizen*, pp. 303–26, p. 312.

[14] V. Böhre, *Happy Landings*, 2010, a study on the biometrical passport ordered by the *Scientific Council for Government Policy*, available at <www.wrr.nl> [last accessed 24 December 2017]; C. Prins et al., *i-Government* (Amsterdam: Amsterdam University Press, 2011).

[15] V. Mayer-Schönberg, *Delete: The Virtue of Forgetting in the Digital Age* (Princeton: Princeton University Press, 2009).

of the individual's freedom as far as life choices are concerned is a reality we have to reckon with.

Technological Reproductions

To ask how we confer legitimacy on new technologies, we can take as our starting point that technological as well as legal narratives are narratives legitimating a specific kind of knowledge, and that these narratives have their own concurrent strategies of inclusion and exclusion. What we need most, then, is linguistic awareness in technological environments. We need the kinds of expertise that help define both the dominant narratives and the lost, or repressed, narratives, to reflect on them in order to preclude repeating old mistakes. Put differently, now that the design choices of new technologies are all too often made without us, their users, and we have to be content with what is on offer, including its regulation by law, here as well we could turn to fiction because of its metaphorical potential, and read literary works as unorthodox jurisprudential texts on technological issues. If technology changes our identities in the sense of the perceptions of who we are, and, in doing so, develops its discursive idiosyncrasies, we should question the discursive *loci* of AI and AmI.

For a subject as consequential as law, including the concept of the rule of law, the reaffirmation or reinvention of the human in the sense of the legal persona is called for, precisely because there are scenarios dark enough to deserve our further consideration. In 'The work of art in the age of mechanical reproduction', Walter Benjamin contrasts the notion of the presence of the original work of art as a condition for authenticity with the consequence of technical reproduction that 'can put the copy of the original into situations which would be out of reach for the original itself'; that is to say, the reproduction detaches what is reproduced from its traditional domain.[16] The process of mass production has social significance, Benjamin claimed, and history proved him right. Yet, simultaneously, mass production is destructive when it results in a loss of the cultural value of the original. Subsequently, loss of uniqueness means loss of autonomy, as well as the genesis of a new way of looking at the thing, a 'revealing' in Heideggerian terms that is perfectly illustrated in art by Andy Warhol's *Campbell's Soup Cans* (1962). If technology affects our perceptions of who we are, then, as a result, changes in technology – looked upon as a cultural product – will lead to changes in the ways we perceive the world. On the one hand, this

---

[16] W. Benjamin, 'The work of art in the age of mechanical reproduction', in W. Benjamin (trans. H. Zorn), *Illuminations* (London: Pimlico, 1999), pp. 211–43, p. 214.

process may be a liberation of what is perceived as an outdated way of doing things, as the demise of the fax machine illustrates. On the other hand, when applied to law as it deals with the effects of technology, reproduction – for example, of sensitive information pertaining to individual privacy in biometrical data – when embraced as beneficial *per se*, may introduce a form of what may, at best, be called a societally disconnected aesthetics of the legal and the political, the history of which has shown that it engenders an instrumental attitude and entails the risk of totalitarian dominance. The work of the legal theorist of National Socialism, Carl Schmitt, is a case in point.

What Benjamin argued with respect to art in the age of mechanical reproduction goes for the human in relation to new AI and AmI technologies. We should therefore be wary of technologies when these are viewed only in terms of epistemological determinism, and of literal engineers of human souls, especially in an age of increasing populism, because contemporary technologies are influential on a far larger scale and at a far greater speed than before. This necessitates new legal norms to be enacted to help form new interrelations between the human and his artefacts, and between human beings inside and outside law.

In the context of technological influences on law, the quest after our identity and, with it, the quest after self-knowledge – to reiterate the point – does not evaporate. The questions concerning the fictions of the self in relation to personhood remain the same. Will 'Digital-Me', for example, be granted consciousness, and, if so, will that be the key to its personhood and to its capability to assert its existence and its possible dominance over the original 'me'? New technologies are still as undecided as they are undecidable from a legal point of view, despite all cybersecurity legislation. Therefore, law's attempts at codification of new norms suffer the consequences. The Faustian epistemological question remains centre stage with regard to the limits of human knowledge and the related ethical as well as the juridical-political question of whether or not it is justified to introduce new technological endeavours when we cannot fully size up the possible risks. As with biotechnology, the question of whether the legal subject still absorbs the human person remains acute. This is another reason to probe AI- and AmI-related narratives. With this in mind, I turn to literature in order to illustrate how particular concepts of law and legality operating in the author-jurist-philosopher Juli Zeh's novel *The Method* as a part of the human condition in a control society can help clarify some aspects of the interrelation between law and technology that deserve our close attention.

Dichterjurist Juli Zeh

My choice is also inspired by the fact that Juli Zeh is an author who is fully committed to the public cause.[17] She not only contributes to the debate on important societal issues, such as election campaigns, Wikipedia, and Linux open-source development,[18] but she does so on a regular basis, in interviews and by taking legal action, concerned as she is about the current rise of the control society. An example is that, on 28 January 2008, Zeh lodged a complaint with the German Federal Constitutional Court (BverfG) against the German government because of new legislation introducing the biometrical passport.[19] In an interview with the Dutch newspaper *Trouw*,[20] Zeh voiced concern that her complaint would be filed in the Court's office of European affairs. If so, the complaint would not stand a chance because, in Zeh's view, the European Union stretches the limits when it comes to security. The complaint would be better off filed in the office for home affairs, because the German government, owing to the horrors of the Nazi past, is reluctant to collect its citizens' personal data.

Why this kind of involvement? Because Zeh firmly believes that

> literature *per se* has a social and, in the broadest sense of the word, political function . . . [it] bears the responsibility to close the gaps that are exposed through journalism's attempt to present a supposedly 'objective' – and therefore distorted – picture of the world.[21]

Zeh wants the literary text to inspire conscious reflection and subsequent action in her reader, and to serve as an antidote to the numbing influence of modern media with their predominant format of the soap opera, the one-liner, the soundbite, the cliffhanger and other superficial ways of info-tainment. Her belief in the political function of literature in contradistinction to forms of journalism informed by ideology – with or without alternative facts and/or manipulated images – also puts her firmly in the tradition of literary realism. This is the background against which Zeh urges us to think

---

[17] See P. Herminghouse, 'The young author as public intellectual: the case of Juli Zeh', in K. Gerstenberger and P. Herminghouse (eds), *German Literature in a New Century: Trends, Traditions, Transitions, Transformations* (New York: Berghahn Books, 2008), pp. 268–84, p. 268.

[18] J. Zeh, 'Es werde Linux', *Die Zeit*, 30 March 2006, p. 39.

[19] Zeh's complaint is accessible at <http://zelos.zeit.de/2008/06/Verfassungsbeschwerde28012008.pdf> [last accessed 1 June 2016].

[20] A. Verbij, 'Interview Juli Zeh', *Trouw*, 4 September 2008, available at <https://www.trouw.nl/home/heerseres-over-recht-en-moraal~ab690a8e/> [last accessed 27 January 2018].

[21] Herminghouse, 'The young author', p. 277.

about the topic of freedom. To her, we are no longer free if we become 'transparent'. Surveillance mechanisms are everywhere, and we are nudged towards decisions by both manufacturers and government institutions. The persistent, fundamental dilemma is this: how can we can defend the value of any new system rooted in new technologies, while at the same time we are in the process of abolishing the value of freedom?[22] Significantly, in the street where Orwell used to live in London, 27b Canonbury Square, the nightmare described in *Nineteen Eighty-Four* has become reality with thirty-two CCTV cameras. In the German context, Zeh points to the phenomenon of the *Online-Durchsuchung*, a secret intervention by the state in a private person's personal computer; it obtained its legal basis on 1 January 2009 but was applied before that date.[23] What matters to Zeh is what free will actually means if one's identity, in the sense of the 'I' that one thinks one is, changes due to the influence of all kinds of persuaders, hidden or not.[24] Here is a direct connection, I suggest, to Ricoeur's distinction of the *ipse* and *idem*. And, if we consider the current flipside of the surveillance argument – namely, the question concerning Internet censorship by Facebook and Twitter themselves, such as in Germany on the basis of the *Netzwerkdurchsetzungsgezetz* – the contested law of 1 January 2018 requiring commercial organisations exploiting social media to remove hate speech and comparable utterances – that is to say, what does this mean for the individual's freedom of speech and other human rights? The balance between freedom and protection is very hard to strike and is extremely delicate.

The interplay between reality and possibility, one that Zeh had already devoted attention to in an earlier novel, *Gaming Instinct*, connects the Aristotelian mimetic idea of literature to the theme of veracity of the narrative that is presented. This chimes with the view on narrativity and with the notion that the just needs the equitable, as discussed in Part II of this book. To Zeh, law consists of codes that, in turn, consist of words that can have multiple meanings. She claims that the written rule should always be scrutinised critically because it applies to an infinite number of factual cases that are

---

[22] I. Trojanow and J. Zeh, *Angriff auf die Freiheit* (Munich: Carl Hanser, 2009), pp. 14 and 58.

[23] Ibid. p. 131. See also the decision of the BverfG, 27 February 2008, 1 BvR 370/07, available at <http://www.bundesverfassungsgericht.de/EN/Homepage/home_node.html> [last accessed 29 January 2018], that the individual's right to personality encompasses the right to the guarantee of the confidentiality of information technology systems, but that the state does not encroach on fundamental rights when it obtains information publicly accessible on the Internet.

[24] M. Kauffmann, 'Juli Zeh "das Projekt Aufklärung ist nicht zu Ende"', *Wiener Zeitung*, 27 February 2009, pp. 7–8.

themselves single happenings. Against the background of the traditions that Zeh is heiress to, all taken together, *The Method* merits our discursive attention as a special *Pitavalgeschichte* of a contemporary *Dichterjurist* (as noted in Chapter 2).[25] Zeh locates herself in the field of *Law and Literature* when she writes that, given the ancient bond between literature and legal rhetoric, it should come as no surprise that jurists-rhetoricians were often also writers of prose.[26]

The Method's narrative is a philosophical debate on individual freedom and responsibility. In it, we read about a state's obsessive, omnipresent health concerns and unprecedented form of health care, which together produce an inescapable ideology, with devastating consequences for its citizens. Having appropriated the responsibility for the physical wellbeing of the people to which everything else is subordinated, the state takes all the measures necessary to reach its goal. What is camouflaged as prevention of illness, however, turns out to be harmful to privacy and free will. As Zeh argued by way of example, nobody in his right mind would hand over his car key when asked in the street to do so by a total stranger who promises to return the car. However, practically everybody provides his or her e-mail address when so asked on a website by the company behind it, and is not concerned that it is resold to third parties.[27]

Control, Alt and/or Delete?

The novel opens with the preface to Heinrich Kramer's book dedicated to promote the state's ideology and policy, *Health as the Principle of State Legitimacy*.[28] This Health Principle is not only pervasive in all strata of society; it is also a doctrine with a Hobbesian twist in the sense that the individual – methodological individualism being the starting point – is thought of as having subjected himself to the Health Principle for the purpose of forming a society – the society that guarantees the individual's health – and as totalitarian in that once the *pactum subjectionis* is signed, the state's health rather than that of the individual is what matters most. All the healthy bodies together

[25] See H. Müller-Dietz, 'Literarische Verarbeitung von Recht in Gegenwartsromanen', in F. Stürmer and P. Meier (eds), *Recht Populär, populärkulturelle Rechtsdarstellungen in aktuellen Texten und Medien* (Baden-Baden: Nomos, 2016), pp. 37–59, p. 39. Other contemporary German *Dichterjuristen* are Bernhard Schlink and Ferdinand von Schirach.

[26] J. Zeh, *Alles auf dem Rasen, kein Roman* (Munich: Btb Verlag, 2008), p. 115.

[27] B. Heijne, 'Interview Juli Zeh', *NRC-Handelsblad*, 23 December 2010, pp. 8–9.

[28] J. Zeh (trans. S.-A. Spencer), *The Method* (London: Vintage, 2014). Hereinafter (TM + page number). Where necessary, the reference is to *Corpus Delicti, ein Prozess* (Frankfurt am Main: Schöffling & Co., 2009). Hereinafter (CD + page number).

form the body politic, conjuring up the image on the frontispiece of Hobbes's *Leviathan*. Therefore, each breach of the contract is seen as treason.[29] If the individual is guaranteed a life free from illness and fear – with all the laws functioning in the manner of the nervous system of a healthy body – then any infraction, any violation of the law, is an attack on the organism itself. The process is pictured by means of a virus metaphor. Punishment must therefore be meted out immediately, as the protagonist Mia Holl, and her brother Moritz before her, discover when they seek to destroy their own bodies: by suicide in Moritz's case, and by allowing private grief over Moritz's death to take precedence over physical fitness in Mia's case. In this state, the body is everything.[30] Heinrich Kramer moves with the naturalness of someone who has access to all places, as we will soon find out. He is not only a well-known author and TV personality but also the *auctor intellectualis* and the personification of The Method, as the practical application of the doctrine is aptly termed. And it is 'In the Name of THE METHOD' that Mia Holl is tried for incitement against The Method, and sentenced to a state of suspended animation by freezing for an indeterminate period. How this came about is what the rest of the narrative teaches us.

The scene is set when the judge, a young woman named Sophie, and the public prosecutor Barker gather together with the attorney Rosentreter in a kind of administrative settlement of easy cases. Oddly, from a legal point of view at least, Heinrich Kramer is present as well (did Zeh choose his name as a subtle reference to the author of the *Malleus Maleficarum* [1487], the *Witches' Hammer*?). In each case, the picture of the suspect is projected on the wall. Later, we learn that this is possible because all citizens have a microchip under their skin, so that their every move is registered. Moritz, for example, is unhappy when the ID chip in his upper arm comes into contact with the sensors on the side of all roads (TM 81). Fiction?[31] Future or already present?

---

[29] As can be seen in the definition, 'Health is the optimisation of the individual for the optimal social good. Health is what we naturally desire for ourselves and is therefore the natural objective of society, politics and law' (TM 1–2). The original reads, 'Gesundheit führt über die Vollendung des Einzelnen' (CD 7). Therefore, I suggest that 'optimisation' is not the best translation, for that would be 'the completion of the individual' which, not incidentally, fits better the protagonist Mia Holl's fate.

[30] 'Der Körper is alles' [CD 158], a line left untranslated in the English edition. That the body is in the state's service reminds us of the Nazi slogan *Dein Volk ist Alles*: 'The body is a machine, a walking, talking, ingesting apparatus; its principal responsibility is to function without a hitch' (TM 70).

[31] See M. Cunningham, *Specimen Days* (London: Fourth Estate, 2005), p. 281, where the biomechanically constructed human Simon is secretly given a poetry chip by his maker Lowell for the purpose of instilling into him a sense of morality, or as Lowell confesses,

Think of the 2011 Locationgate affair, when Apple through what was called a software error was able to register the exact location of any iPhone. While Steve Jobs hastened to emphasise that Apple did not track its users, this did not exactly remove anxieties. The same goes for Prey, the programme that protects computers against theft. It is a very useful tool, but once you report your computer as missing, the Prey website shows all the relevant, privacy-sensitive data such as the computer's IP address, its location based on the mobile networks, and the use made of wi-fi. Surely there is irony in the term wireless fidelity. What is more, in 2017 a Swedish office block offered its users an RFID chip implanted in the hand to access the premises, and the US company Three Square Market announced the same.[32] So there is all the more reason to consider the lessons the novel holds before us.

Enter Mia Holl, a biologist whose crime consists of her having neglected her duty to report. She has failed to hand in the data on her sleep and nutrition. Nor has she sent in the results of her blood pressure and urine tests. What is worse, the curve of her sports performance, strictly monitored as well, shows a sudden drop. Consequently, she is invited to come to court for what is euphemistically called an explanatory conversation, like having a cup of tea at a police station. It is interesting to note that both criminal law and criminal procedure in this fictional state have familiar features and yet are at odds with law as we know it in Western Europe. This adds an effect of alienation, not least when the reader realises that quite a number of legal measures are applied indiscriminately to all citizens, including those not even under suspicion of having committed a crime. Merely contemplating criminal activity is not prohibited, or should we say not yet, when the legislation aimed at preventing acts of terrorism is brought to mind, and given that in many jurisdictions preparatory acts have already been codified as criminal offenses.[33] This is obviously not to diminish the justified and necessary search for potential terrorists, given the continued need to protect society against acts of terrorism, but it should incite us to careful consideration, on the

---

'I thought that if you were programmed with the work of great poets, you'd be better able to appreciate the consequences of your actions'.

[32] See BBC News, 28 July 2017, 'Office puts chips under staff's skin', available at <http://www.bbc.com/news/technology-31042477> [last accessed 4 August 2017]; A. Robertson, 'Wisconsin company will let employees use microchip implants to buy snacks and open door', *The Verge*, available at <https://www.theverge.com/2017/7/24/16019530/> [last accessed 4 August 2017]. The issue of transhumanism – people who deliberately implement embodied technological enhancements – is outside the scope of this book.

[33] See C. M. Pelser, 'Preparations to commit a crime', 4 *Utrecht Law Review*, no. 3, 2008, available at <https://www.utrechtlawreview.org/articles/10.18352/> [last accessed 24 December 2017].

one hand, of how, as jurists generally and judges specifically, to deal with the dialectic movement between facts and legal norms at the case level, as discussed in Chapter 6, in situations in which both facts and norms are disputed or unclear, and, on the other hand, of our democratic discourse on the immensely important societal issues that often divide us. In connection to the concept of the rule of law, Ferdinand von Schirach, for example, urges us to realise that it is not terrorism that destroys our societies, but we ourselves if we distance ourselves from the rule of law, because that is 'the only way for a state based on justice to manifest its resilience and integrity'.[34] That is why he claims that 'Democracy demands discourse', and his play *Terror* wants

> us to talk about how we want to live. Terrorism is the greatest challenge of our time; it is changing our lives, our society, our thinking. How we deal with it isn't just a legal question. It's an ethical-moral decision.[35]

In other words, the rule of law is too important to leave only to the IT specialists.

Mia holds Kramer responsible for Moritz's suicide after he had been charged with, and convicted of, the rape and murder of Sibylle Meiler, his blind date, whom he had found dead at the meeting place. Moritz's sperm was found inside her body. Since, according to The Method, 'DNA evidence is infallible. Infallibility is the bedrock of the Method' (TM 30), a conviction is a mere legal routine, even though Moritz had vehemently pleaded not guilty, and consistently argued, 'You are sacrificing me on the altar of your delusions' (TM 27) – a cry that a bystander will later on repeat when Mia is sentenced (TM 224).

Since Mia does not show signs of physical or social disturbance – the human psyche is obviously of no concern to The Method – her grief over Moritz's death is incomprehensible to the system. Mia therefore avoids showing any outward signs, hoping to fool the surveillance system by not using the toilet equipped with sensors so that it will not record any change in her gastric juices when, in despair, she has to vomit. Epistemological doubt is not an option, argues Kramer, but Mia points to the fact that any man-made rule is by definition fallible, as history shows when paradigm changes occur. Combining syllogistic reasoning and the confirmation bias, Kramer contends

---

[34] F. von Schirach, 'Keep going come what may', Speech on the occasion of the presentation of the M100 Sanssouci Media Award to Charlie Hebdo in 2015, in F. von Schirach (trans. D. Tushingham), *Terror* (London: Faber and Faber, [2016] 2017), pp. 95–104, p. 101.

[35] D. Baur (trans. J. Uhlaner), 'Interview with the author Ferdinand von Schirach: When the only heroes left are law and morality', Goethe Institute, October 2016, available at <https://www.goethe.de/en/kul/tut/gen/tup/20848876.html> [last accessed 29 September 2017].

that doubt leads to casuistic decisions: 'The fickle rule of the heart' (TM 31), based on emotion rather than reason. That Moritz has consistently pleaded his innocence in the face of overwhelming technical evidence is proof of his repudiating The Method. In order to investigate this methodologically unthinkable discrepancy between private and public interest, Kramer even wants to interview Mia for the paper *The Healthy Mind* (TM 34), a name that in the German original reads as *Gesunden Menschenverstand* (CD 42), which has an uncanny resemblance to *das gesundes Empfinden des Volkes* – that which the German national character was thought to favour – that National Socialist Germany enforced as the criterion for judicial decisions in 1935 in Article 2 of the then renewed Criminal Code. In a scene reminiscent of Kafka's Joseph K.'s arrest, two guards come to take Mia to a physical exam, after which she is taken to court to account for her offence against The Method. Judge Sophie, like Kramer before her, is unable to grasp the concept of private grief, which Mia explains is the cause of her wrongdoings. We can recognise the linguistic subversion of reality that comes with totalitarian systems, as noted in Chapter 1.

Furthermore, what the case of Mia Holl also painfully shows is that the equality of speakers – both a precondition and a product of a culture of argument aimed at bringing about justice – is sorely lacking, because the state's Method is the sole directive. If recognition of our common humanity, rather than exclusion on the basis of a lack of commitment to The Method, and equality before the law – including the availability of a common language with which to tell one's story and be heard – are no options, there is irony in the observation that law is a game that we all have to play along with if we look at this double meaning in the German word 'mitspielen' ('Law is a game and everyone plays a part', TM 65, 'Das Recht ist ein Spiel, bei dem alle mitspielen müssen', CD 74). And especially when the juridical-political ideal of around-the-clock observation, lack of privacy, control and prevention works to the detriment of the individual and her privacy. What is left of autonomy, of finding one's own destiny in life, of deliberately entering into civil bonds to form a state and a society? Mia finds that out soon enough: namely, when her preliminary hearing ends abruptly because, as her defence attorney Rosentreter points out, if 'the defendant becomes implicated in anti-Method activities, it puts the case on a different level, so to speak' (TM 65). If this is the good news, the state of exception cannot be far behind, especially if a crime against The Method is deemed an act of terrorism. A network of reactionary activists called People's Right to Illness, illness being a right that obviously cannot be recognised by a healthy mind according to the state, has drawn public attention. Wörmer, host of the talkshow *What We All Think*, interviews Kramer on the subject. To Kramer, these anti-Methodists are still committed to that gross error of Enlightenment thought, individual freedom, because they claim that the right to illness is the recognition that one is free. This, of course, is an act of terror against the state. So when Moritz thought of life as 'an offer that you can also refuse' (TM 38), that is to say only worth living if you are at liberty to opt for death, he deliberately chose to be an enemy of The Method. For 'Methodic' law, truth is a subjective matter; believing and knowing are interchangeable, so one should use one's common sense in borderline cases and decide what is true on an instrumental basis, rather than on the basis of validity and veracity.

Therefore, *The Method* may help us stay alert to possible outgrowths of information technologies. That is all the more necessary, because Kramer thinks in terms of establishing offender profiles of terrorists, and of the difficulties involved with that, also as far as linguistic change is concerned – Moritz being named a terrorist is a case in point. Ultimately, Mia is charged with abuse of toxic substances because she smoked a cigarette in the open air near the brook where she and Moritz used to go. When arrested, she is asked whom she was going to meet there. Her answer, reminiscent of Odysseus' reply to the Cyclops, 'No one' (TM 184), leads to a hilarious argument by the public prosecutor that surely this 'No one' is a pseudonym of a member of the People's Right to Illness: that is, proof of Mia's defiance of The Method. Rosentreter in the meantime has his own, parallel agenda for trying to trip The Method up: he has fallen in love with a woman who is literally out of his league because of 'Methodologically' determined, immunological incompatibilities that preclude their marrying and having children. Rosentreter finds out that Moritz had suffered from leukaemia in the old days, and had undergone a stem cell transplant. As a result, he took over his donor's blood group, immune system and DNA. Because Walter Hannemann was Moritz's donor, it was revealed that he had raped and killed Sibylle Meiler. This unexpected dénouement leads to Mia's release. But not for long. After having denounced Kramer's epistemology that the will to live encompasses a right to health that conflates with the justification of The Method, Mia is arrested again. She abandons her trust in the human body if that is no longer described in terms of flesh and blood but merely as the collective view on what a normal, healthy body is supposed to be. As a consequence, she denies the legitimacy of a form of law that depends for its success on the total control of its citizens. She abandons her trust in a science that rejects free will. Public opinion turns against The Method, with mass demonstrations as a result. Since all now think that Mia is innocent, even Wörmer voices a critique of The Method. He pays for it dearly, for in an Orwellian exercise of 'doublethink' – linguistic distortion is a recurrent theme in Zeh's novels – he ends up being identified as the terrorist behind

'No one'. Orwell's presaging dialogue has come true: '"Are you guilty?" said Winston. "Of course I'm guilty!" cried Parsons with a servile glance at the telescreen. "You don't think the Party would arrest an innocent man, do you?".'[36] Or as Hildebrandt writes, 'Evidently self-monitoring – even without advice – may engender self surveillance, self discipline and boil down to an enforcement even more stringent than enforcement embodied in the automatic intervention of the smart environment.'[37] Not suprisingly, Wörmer is used as a witness for the prosecution.

Mia does not relent: '"I stand for what you really think," she cries, "I stand for what we all think. I am the *corpus delicti*"' (TM 192–3). What to Mia was a statement made in private is public business in Kramer's worldview. Kramer demands the destruction of all infectious thoughts that cause the pollution of The Method. He goes to see Mia in jail and charges her with being responsible, should the Right to Illness kill innocent people (by then he has violated the attorney-client privilege by tapping Mia's confidential telephone conversations with her defence lawyer on the grounds that the use of emergency powers is justified against an enemy of The Method). When Mia refuses to plead guilty, Kramer brings food and beverages to her in her prison cell, thus obtaining her fingerprints, which are subsequently found on a tube of botulinum in her house: technical *idem* evidence of her terrorist goal of destroying society, destroying mankind. That settles the case, of course, but still Mia does not relent. Not even when Kramer suggests that 'In certain situations, in highly sensitive cases, when there is a Benthamite threat to the greater good, a degree of backsliding has been known to occur. In such situations, the system may revert to somewhat *medieval* methods' (TM 206, italics in the original). Mia replies, 'The Middle Ages is not a historical period; the Middle Ages is the name of human nature' (TM 207). Or should we say that the Hobbesian state of nature with the *bellum omnium contra omnes* is a mindset that has never really left us? Unfortunately, examples abound in current global politics.

In a final act of defiance, Mia takes the needle that Rosentreter has smuggled into her cell, thrusts it into her arm, takes out the chip that identifies her, and gives it to Kramer as a token of remembrance, '"Take it. It's me"' (TM 217). In this celebration of the eucharist of transparency – if we recall the Christian liturgical phrase *Hic est corpus meum*, this is my body – the chip coincides with the human being, and Mia's code is cracked. For her crimes, this offender by conviction who is prepared to die for her cause

---

[36] G. Orwell, *Nineteen Eighty-Four* (London: Book Club Associates, [1949] 1967), p. 239.

[37] M. Hildebrandt, 'Legal and technological normativity', p. 175.

should not, however, get the supreme punishment, says Kramer. Then she would obviously be satisfied, for it would mean that she is respected as a free human being: 'The punishment honours the criminal!' (TM 222), as Musil's character Moosbrugger found out to his disappointment, as did Kafka's unnamed soldier in 'In the Penal Colony' to his horror, because it was literally inscribed on his body. Mia is sentenced to a state of suspended animation by freezing, a '*Kaltstellen*' as it says in German (CD 260), literally and figuratively: elimination from society by freezing. In contradistinction to the demands of fair trial, the decision was written before the trial even started. Furthermore, there is no separation of powers. The judge is also the executioner. When, at the very last moment, the prosecutor enters the room and tells Mia that the President of the Method Council has pardoned her – for fear of her becoming a martyr – and she will be sent to a resocialisation camp instead, she refuses to believe that she is saved. She demands that she be kept there. Only when Kramer has the last laugh and urges her to leave now that she is a free woman, she realises that she, the game and everything is over. Control, alter(nate), and delete? Does Mia end in oblivion, or is she destroyed? Does she choose her own fate, or is she conditioned, like Kafka's Joseph K.? If *The Method* shows us one thing, it is that Kafka was right when he wrote, 'The right perception of any matter and a misunderstanding of the same matter do not wholly exclude each other.'[38]

O Brave New World that Has Such People In't?

Zeh's nightmarish portrayal of the road to an ideological Wellville,[39] with its causal connection between the need for electronic surveillance and the prevention of illness, is all the more reason to think about what it means when one inadvertently or unintentionally becomes an outsider. In an interview on German TV, Zeh pointed out that one theme of *The Method* is that insurance companies hold people responsible for their own illnesses.[40] The argument is as old as the Bible's Book of Job: if misfortune happens to you, then surely you must have done something wrong. Mia Holl opts out for her own reasons. But what if you are excluded by the people in control of your embodied data? What then is left of the autonomous subject in the Kantian

---

[38] F. Kafka (trans. W. and E. Muir), *The Trial* (London: Penguin, 1978), pp. 238–9. Cf. Chapter 8, the text accompanying note 56.

[39] T. C. Boyle, *The Road to Wellville* (London: Granta Books, 1993), a hilarious narrative of Kellogg's cornflake-based totalitarian health system.

[40] J. Zeh, 'Interview with *Die Bananenrepublik*', 24 May 2011, available at <http://hdvidzpro. me/video/file/Juli-Zeh-bei-Erwin-Pelzig?id=-6DjHl3HWak> [last accessed 25 December 2017].

sense that law has long cherished?[41] Freedom is not a gift from the state to its citizens, it is a precondition for any thought about the state.[42] So those who consider their rights only when they are harmed entirely miss the point. In our communication era, information is the keyword. Being well informed implies being knowledgeable. This, in turn, implies the means to control. As Mitchell pointed out, 'control of code is power'.[43] And this is exactly why jurists need to think through the consequences of AI and AmI, and act proactively rather than retroactively.[44] What happens to Mia Holl is not just a fictional, or, at most, a future nightmare. It is a clear and present danger. Therefore, from a humanistic point of view, the fact that we are built from living cells as much as from data, and equipped not only with a body but also with a mind, favours a reading of *The Method* as a call to arms to resist an instrumental use of humans.

To Zeh, the greatest human problem is that we do not know when to stop when we have produced something good. She points to the work of the Austrian artist-writer Bernhard Kathan, whose *Schöne neue Kuhstallwelt*'s main argument I read as a metaphor for AmI.[45] The title translates as 'beautiful new cowshed world'. Its basic idea is that through new technologies dairy farming has completely changed. The cows move about freely, yet – like the human being in Jean-Jacques Rousseau's famous opening of *The Social Contract*, born free, but everywhere in chains – they are completely managed. The doors of the cowshed open by means of the cow's electronic identification. The feeder is programmed to know what to feed each individual cow. The cow's milking time is recognised by its movements. The result is a very efficient form of herd management that is applicable also to hospitals, homes for the elderly, prisons and universities, governed as they are by intricate codes of their own design. It is a model of power and control, of Foucauldian discipline and punishment. In the world of AI and AmI, we exchange freedom for the coercion to have to choose what others have decided is on offer. Like the cows, we are the consumers of our own Hobbesian subjection. In the same way that the architecture of the cowshed constitutes the cow's freedom to act, modern technologies organise the lives of humans by destinations

---

[41] H. Müller-Dietz, 'Zur negatieven Utopie von Recht und Staat', *JZ* 2, 2011, pp. 85–95.

[42] Trojanow and Zeh, *Angriff*, pp. 15–16.

[43] Mitchell, *City of Bits*, p. 112.

[44] See J. Titcomb, 'AI is the biggest risk we face as a civilisation, Elon Musk says', on Musk advocating a proactive approach in legislation, *The Telegraph*, 17 July 2017, available at <http://www.telegraph.co.uk/technology/2017/07/17/ai-biggest-risk-face-civilisation-elon-musk-says/> [last accessed 25 December 2017].

[45] B. Kathan, *Schöne neue Kuhstallwelt* (Berlin: Martin Schmitz, 2009).

made by third parties.[46] Both animals and humans are thus commodified. Traditional creatures become transparent, whereas technology dresses in a cloak of opacity. The cows constantly produce data by means of the machines they are hooked up to, while at the same time they are objects of descriptions by others, as are we by big businesses. In Aldous Huxley's *Brave New World*, humans are forced into a new form of slavery. They do not recognise it as such, because they like the situation that they are in.[47] When, with a variation on the old Kantian dilemma, the question of how to insist on the authority of science while preserving the autonomy of law returns with a vengeance, Kafka's doorkeeper may have been replaced by electronic devices, but the other question remains the same: What if the door does not open? Mia Holl's experience illustrates what Deleuze meant when he claimed that 'The digital language of control is made up of codes indicating whether access to some information should be allowed or denied'.[48] Human beings become the sum of their 'dividual' parts, used depending on the needs felt by the user. Marketing is the new instrument of social control, and Deleuze was proved right by the sales of successive generations of smart phones, tablets and what have you, and by the fact that electronic tagging is used as a control mechanism. This new system of domination is dangerous, because it leaves us in the dark as to who decides that sometimes the door does not open.

As a consequence, law and legal systems seem to vacillate between traditional, deeply ingrained principles and the unconditional acceptance of the new by means of *ad hoc* decisions: namely, uninformed applications of technology in, and for, law. Data Protection Acts may be wonderful legal devices, but do they protect data or humans? In this context, Heidegger's 'Question concerning technology', noted in Chapter 12, is valuable as well. If technology slips from human control, power is the only thing left. For that reason, we must not be epistemologically and methodologically naive, and accept that as a result of modern technology we have been reduced to 'being at hand' or 'on hold' only, objects that stand reserved for purposes of further ordering by others.[49] This is what Mia Holl experiences when she realises that she has internalised the system to such a degree that she tells her guards that they should not think that she failed to comply intentionally. To reiterate the argument made in Chapter 12, we should not accept at face value what is

---

[46] Kathan, *Kuhstallwelt*, pp. 26 and 269.

[47] Kathan, *Kuhstallwelt*, p. 251.

[48] G. Deleuze, 'Postscript on control societies', in G. Deleuze, *Negotiations 1970–1990* (New York: Columbia University Press, 1995), pp. 177–82, p. 319.

[49] For what being on file means in the legal context, see C. Vismann (trans. G. Winthrop-Young), *Files, Law and Media Technology* (Stanford, CA: Stanford University Press, 2008).

held before us as technology. Science as well 'must always be on its guard lest it mistake its own linguistic conventions for objective laws'.[50] Therefore, we should ask what the new technologies' scripts, stock stories, plot holes, and so forth are, as a reminder of the importance of attention to language and narrative, precisely because of the humanist Erasmus's working definition of knowledge: 'In principle, knowledge as a whole seems to be of two kinds, of things and of words.'[51] Attention to the linguistic pitfalls and peculiarities of any technological discourse remains called for.

On the one hand, technological developments have made the human the nodal point of relations and connections in a global network. As a result, new and exciting forms facilitating our being connected develop at a far larger scale than has ever been experienced in human history. On the other hand, we should question both the belief regarding individual autonomy behind the choices we make when entering this global network and the effect on the human of our going global in this way. I was particularly struck when, a couple of years ago, one of my students – a Frenchman in the international students' exchange programme – told me that he lamented the fact that, when he wanted to talk to a fellow student who lived in the same building, he sent an email or text message instead of going to his or her room. That is to say, he recognised the effects of his behaviour on human relations, the risk of loneliness and alienation they entailed, and yet he found it difficult to discontinue this behaviour. I do not offer this example and the argument of this chapter to renew the Luddite manifesto. I suggest that it is an unsimple truth that new technologies affect the constitution of the human self, both as *ipse* and *idem*. If we are to continue the conversation on the human in law, intersubjectivity in the form of interdisciplinary research is inescapable.[52] Inspired by Ghirlandaio's enigmatic picture, Chapter 12 asked *Sua cuique persona*, to each his own person and mask? Zeh's example of suspended animation by freezing combined with what I have read on comparable technologies already promoted to preserve the human body after death inspires me to offer another picture by way of conclusion: namely, that of the *Baker of Eeklo*,

[50] I. Calvino, 'Two interviews on science and literature', in I. Calvino (trans. P. Creagh), *The Uses of Literature* (New York: Harvest, 1987), p. 45.

[51] Desiderius Erasmus, *On the Method of Study, de ratione studii ac legendi interpretandique auctores* (trans. and annot. by B. McGregor, ed. C.R. Thompson), in *Collected Works of Erasmus: Literary and Educational Writings 2: de copia/de ratione studii* (Toronto, Buffalo and London: University of Toronto Press, 1978), p. 666.

[52] See N. Carr, *The Shallows: What the Internet is Doing to Our Brains* (New York and London: W. W. Norton & Co., 2010), p. 16, 'What's stored in the individual mind . . . is more than "the representation of distinctive personhood", that constitutes the self . . . It's also "the crux of cultural transmission".'

a *topos* found in seventeenth-century Dutch and Flemish iconography.[53] If one was not happy with one's *persona*, one could go to the baker of Eeklo, where one's head was removed and replaced by a newly baked one in order to start a new life. There was, of course, a risk of failure, and some ended up with more, or less, than they had bargained for. The moral of the story was that one should be satisfied with the identity one has, the person that one is. To me, it offers another sobering thought as well, in that it suggests that we should keep our legal heads when human freedom and privacy are concerned. Precisely because the algorithm in new technologies is comparable to the syllogism in terms of its language view of representation, we should avoid becoming the new Bouvards and Pécuchets.

---

[53] See the copy after C. van Dalem, *The Baker of Eeklo*, Collection of the Rijksmuseum, Amsterdam, available at <https://www.rijksmuseum.nl/en/collection/> [last accessed 29 January 2018].

Coda

My argument in this book is that a literary turn of mind together with the building blocks from philosophical hermeneutics help form a solid basis for the development of the essential capability of jurists to truly judge from experience: that is, to learn about the lives and experiences of others, and to act on what one learns, while at the same time to cherish an attitude of self-reflection in order to gain self-knowledge. Whatever the global, political, or technological developments, I am convinced that judging from experience is, and remains, the crucial, professional methodology and *habitus*. Without it, legal instrumentalism is bound to take over, and, when that happens, the rule of law does not stand a chance of survival. For the judge more specifically, the privilege of being appointed to decide about other people's lives comes with a huge responsibility. It is the judge who mediates between the world of the rule of law in democratic societies and the lives of their citizens. In this mediation lies her duty. She mediates while understanding that she is fulfilling her duties in an imperfect world in a state of flux. In this understanding lies her challenge.

Bibliography

Abbott, A., *The System of Professions: An Essay on the Division of Expert Labor* (Chicago and London: University of Chicago Press, 1988).

Abrahams, F., 'Achterberg', *NRC Handelsblad*, 21 November 2002, <https://www.nrc.nl/nieuws/2002/11/21/achterberg-7615090-a880063> [last accessed 4 December 2017].

Achterberg, G., *Blauwzuur* (The Hague: Bert Bakker, 1969).

Achterberg, G. (trans. J. S. Holmes), 'Epitaph', *Hommage aan Gerrit Achterberg*, 125 *De Gids*, no. 1, 1962 [1941], p. 166.

Aeschylus, *Eumenides* (*Oresteia* part 3), in H. W. Smyth (trans.), *Aeschylus in Two Volumes*, vol. II (Cambridge, MA, and London: Harvard University Press, 1971).

Albert, H., *Traktat über kritische Vernunft* (Tübingen: Mohr Siebeck, 1975).

Albert, H., *Traktat über rationale Praxis* (Tübingen: Mohr Siebeck, 1978).

Amsterdam, A. G. and J. S. Bruner, *Minding the Law* (Cambridge, MA: Harvard University Press, 2000).

Andersson, G., 'Is there a narrative method of text analysis and interpretation?', in G. Rossholm and C. Johansson (eds), *Disputable Core Concepts of Narrative Theory* (Berlin: Peter Lang, 2012), pp. 279–305.

Annas, G. J., *American Bioethics: Crossing Human Rights and Health Law Boundaries* (Oxford: Oxford University Press, 2005).

Aquinas, T., *Summa Theologica,* vol. 1 (Westminster, MD: Christian Classics, 1948).

Arendt, H., *On Revolution* (Harmondsworth: Penguin Books, [1963] 1976).

Arendt, H., *The Life of the Mind* (New York, Harcourt: 1981).

Aristodemou, M., *Law and Literature: Journeys from Her to Eternity* (Oxford: Oxford University Press, 2000).

Aristotle (trans. W. D. Ross), *Metaphysics* (Oxford: Oxford University Press, 1958).

Aristotle (trans. H, Rackham and ed. J. Henderson), *Nicomachean Ethics* (Cambridge, MA and London: Harvard University Press, [1926] 2003).

Aristotle (trans. S. Halliwell), *Poetics* (Cambridge, MA, and London: Harvard University Press, 1999).

Aristotle (trans. J. H. Freese), *The Art of Rhetoric* (Cambridge, MA, and London: Harvard University Press, 2006).

Aristotle (trans. B. Jowett [1895]), *The Politics*, I.ii,1253a, available at <http://classics.mit.edu/Aristotle/politics.html> [last accessed 13 January 2015].

Arntzen, H., 'Sprache und sprechen in Musils "Mann ohne Eigenschaften"', *Duitse Kroniek*, 1976, pp. 69–83.

Augsberg, I., 'Reading law: on law as a textual phenomenon', 22 *Law & Literature*, no. 3, 2010, pp. 369–93.

Austin, J. L. (eds J. O. Urmson and M. Sbisà), *How To Do Things With Words* (Oxford: Oxford University Press, [1962] 1976).

Bacon, F., *The Advancement of Learning* (Oxford: Clarendon Press, [1605] 1876).

Bal, M., 'Legal lust: literary litigations', 15 *Australian Feminist Law Journal*, 2001, pp. 1–22.

Bal, M., 'Scared to death', in M. Bal and I. E. Boer (eds), *The Point of Theory: Practices of Cultural Analysis* (Amsterdam: Amsterdam University Press, 1994), pp. 32–47.

Baldwin, C., 'Who needs facts, when you've got narrative? The case of P, C & S vs United Kingdom', 18 *International Journal for the Semiotics of Law*, 2005, pp. 217–41.

Balkin, J. M., 'Ideology as cultural software', 16 *Cardozo Law Review*, 1995, pp. 1221–33.

Barfield, O., 'Poetic diction and legal fiction', in O. Barfield, *The Rediscovery of Meaning and Other Essays* (Middletown, CT: Wesleyan University Press, 1977), pp. 44–64.

Barker, P., *Regeneration* (Harmondsworth: Penguin, 1992).

Baron, J. B., 'The rhetoric of law and literature: a skeptical view', 26 *Cardozo Law Review*, 2005, pp. 2273–81.

Barnes, B., *Flaubert's Parrot* (London: Pan Books, 1985).

Baur, D. (trans. J. Uhlaner), 'Interview with the author Ferdinand von Schirach: When the only heroes left are law and morality', Goethe Institute, October 2016, available at <https://www.goethe.de/en/kul/tut/gen/tup/20848876.html> [last accessed 29 September 2017].

Bayer, T. I., 'Vico's principle of senus communis and forensic eloquence', 83 *Chicago-Kent Law Review*, 2008, pp. 1131–55.

Bayle, P., *Dictionnaire historique et philosophique*, Tome II (Amsterdam: Compagnie des Libraires, 1734).

Bellah, R. N., *Habits of the Heart* (Berkeley: University of California Press, 1985).

Belleau, M. C., R. Johnson and V. Bouchard, 'Faces of judicial anger: answering the call', 1 *EJLS* no. 2 special issue 'Judging Judges', 2007, pp. 1–41, available at <http://www.ejls.eu/issue/2> [last accessed 2 May 2015].

Benjamin, W., 'The work of art in the age of mechanical reproduction', in W. Benjamin (trans. H. Zorn), *Illuminations* (London: Pimlico, 1999), pp. 211–43.

Ben-Yishai, A., *Common Precedents: The Presentness of the Past in Victorian Law and Fiction* (Oxford: Oxford University Press, 2013).

Berg, B. van den, 'Ambient intelligence: wat, wie en . . . waarom?', *Computerrecht*, 2010, no. 6, p. 171.

Berger, B. L., 'On the Book of Job, justice, and the precariousness of the criminal law', 4 *Law, Culture and the Humanities*, 2008, pp. 98–118.

Bergh, G. C. J. J. van den, '*Ius commune*: a history with a future?', in B. de Witte and C. Forder (eds), *The Common Law of Europe and the Future of Legal Education* (Deventer: Kluwer, 1992).

Berlin, I., *Vico and Herder, Two Studies in the History of Ideas* (London: Hogarth Press, 1976).

Berman, H. J., *Law and Revolution: The Formation of the Western Legal Tradition* (Cambridge, MA, and London: Harvard University Press, 1983).

Bex, F., *Arguments, Stories, and Criminal Evidence* (Dordrecht: Springer, 2011).

Biet, C., *La Jeu de la Valeur et de la Droit: droit et littérature sous l'Ancien Régime* (Honoré: Paris, 2001).

Biet, C. 'L'empire du droit, les jeux de la littérature', *Europe, revue littéraire mensuelle*, 2002, pp. 7–22.

Biet, C., 'Judicial fiction and literary fiction: the example of the factum', 20 *Law & Literature*, no. 3, 2008, pp. 403–22.

Bjerre, C. S., 'Mental capacity as metaphor', 18 *International Journal for the Semiotics of Law*, 2005, pp. 101–40.

Blaauw, M. (ed.), 'Introduction: epistemological contextualism', 69 *Grazer Philosophische Studien: Internationale Zeitschrift für analytische Philosophie*, 2005, pp. i–xvi.

Bloch, R. H., *Medieval French Literature and Law* (Berkeley: University of California Press, 1977).

Bloom, H., *Shakespeare: The Invention of the Human* (London: Fourth Estate, 1999).

Böhre, V., *Happy Landings*, 2010, a study on the biometrical passport ordered by the *Scientific Council for Government Policy*, available at <www.wrr.nl> [last accessed 24 December 2017].

Bond, C. D., '"We, the judges": the legalized subject and narratives of adjudication in reality television', 81 *UMKC Law Review*, 2012, pp. 1–60.

Bono, J. J., 'Science, discourse, and literature: the role/rule of metaphor in science', in S. S. Peterfreund (ed.), *Literature and Science, Theory and Practice* (Boston: Northeastern University Press, 1990), pp. 59–89.

Bordewijk, F. (trans. E. M. Prince), *Character: A Novel of Father and Son* (New York: New Amsterdam Books, [1938] 1990).

Bouhaïk-Gironès, M., *La Basoche et le théâtre comique: identité sociale, pratiques et culture des clercs de justice (Paris 1420–1550)* (Brussels: De Boeck, 2004).

Boyce, P. (ed. and trans.), *But This Land Has No End, Selected Poems of Gerrit Achterberg* (Lantzville, BC: Oolichan Books, 1989).

Boyle, T. C., *The Road to Wellville* (London: Granta Books, 1993).

Brennan, Jun., W. J., 'Reason, passion, and "The Progress of the Law" ', 10 *Cardozo Law Review*, 1988, pp. 3–23.

Brink, H. M. van den, 'De gratie voor Gerrit A.', *Vrij Nederland*, 30 November 2002, p. 59.

Brod, M. (ed.), *Briefe, 1902–1924*, available at <http://homepage.univie.ac.at/werner.haas/1903/br03-002.htm> [last accessed 10 September 2017].

Brooks, P., *Reading for the Plot* (Cambridge, MA: Harvard University Press, 1984).

Brooks, P., 'The law as narrative and rhetoric', in P. Brooks and P. Gewirtz (eds), *Law's Stories, Narrative and Rhetoric in the Law* (New Haven and London: Yale University Press, 1996), pp. 14–22.

Brooks, P., *Troubling Confessions: Speaking Guilt in Law and Literature* (Chicago: University of Chicago Press, 2000).

Brooks, P., 'Narrative in and of the law', in J. Phelan and P. J. Rabinowitz. (eds), *A Companion to Narrative Theory* (Oxford: Blackwell, 2005, pp. 415–26).

Brooks, P., 'Narrative transactions – Does the law need a narratology?' 18 *Yale Journal of Law & Humanities*, no. 1, 2006, pp. 1–38.

Brooks, P., *Enigmas of Identity* (Princeton: Princeton University Press, 2011).

Brooks, P., '*Scott v. Harris*: the Supreme Court's reality effect', 29 *Law & Literature*, no. 1, 2017, pp. 143–9.

Brooks, P., 'Retrospective prophecies: legal narrative constructions', in E. S. Anker and B. Meyler (eds), *New Directions in Law and Literature* (Oxford: Oxford University Press, 2017), pp. 92–108.

Brown, F., *Flaubert: A Biography* (New York: Little, Brown and Company, 2006).

Bruijn, P. G. de, *Gerrit Achterberg. Gedichten* (The Hague: Constantijn Huygens Institute, 2000).

Bruner, E. M., 'Ethnography as narrative', in V. W. Turner and E. M. Bruner (eds), *The Anthropology of Experience* (Urbana: University of Illinois Press, 1986).

Bruner Murrow, G. and R. W. Murrow, 'A biosemiotic *body* of law: the neurobiology of justice', 26 *International Journal for the Semiotics of Law*, 2013, pp. 275–314.

Bruner, J., 'The narrative construction of reality', 18 *Critical Inquiry*, 1991, pp. 1–21.

Bruner, J., *Making Stories* (Cambridge, MA, Harvard University Press, 2002).

Burke, P., *Cultural Hybridity* (Cambridge: Polity Press, 2010).

Callinan, I. D. F., 'Stories in advocacy and in decisions, the narrative compels the result', 12 *Texas Weslyan Law Review*, 2005, pp. 319–30.

Calvino, I. (trans. P. Creagh), *The Uses of Literature* (New York: Harvest, 1987).

Čapek, K. (trans. P. Selver and N. Playfair), *R.U.R* (Mineola, NY: Dover Pub. Inc., [1920] 2001).

Cardozo, B. N., *The Nature of the Judicial Process* (New Haven: Yale University Press, 1921).

Cardozo, B. N., *The Growth of the Law* (New Haven: Yale University Press, 1924).

Cardozo, B. N., 'Law and literature', *Yale Review*, 1925, pp. 489–507.

Carpi, D. and J. Gaakeer (eds), *Liminal Discourses, Subliminal Tensions in Law and Literature* (Berlin: De Gruyter, 2013).

Carr, N., *The Shallows: What the Internet is Doing to Our Brains* (New York and London: W. W. Norton & Co., 2010).

Chestek, K. D., 'Judging by the numbers: an empirical study of the power of story', *Journal of the Association of Legal Writing Directors*, 2010, pp. 1–35.

Chroust, A.-H., (trans.), *Aristotle: Protrepticus, a Reconstruction* (Notre Dame, IN: University of Notre Dame Press, 1964).

Chroust, A.-H., *The Rise of the Legal Profession in America* (Norman: University of Oklahoma Press, 1965).

Cicero (trans. H. Rackham), *De Finibus Bonorum et Malorum* (Cambridge, MA: Harvard University Press and London: Heinemann, [1914] 1967).

Cicero (trans. W. Miller), *De Officiis* (London: Heinemann, 1968).

Clarke, B. and L. Dalrymple Henderson (eds), *From Energy to Information: Representation in Science and Technology, Art, and Literature* (Stanford, CA: Stanford University Press, 2002).

Clarke, J., 'When he read', *The Juried Heart* (New York: Pleasure Boat, 2015), p. 21.

Coetzee, J. M., 'On the edge of revelation', on Robert Musil's *Five Women*, 33 *The New York Review of Books*, no. 20, 18 December 1986.

Coetzee, J. M., *Disgrace* (London: Vintage/Random House, 2000).

Coetzee, J. M., *Diary of a Bad Year* (New York: Viking, 2008).

Coing, H., *Die ursprüngliche Einheit der europäischen Rechtswissenschaft* (Wiesbaden: F. Steiner, 1968).

Cole, D., *The Torture Memos. Rationalizing the Unthinkable* (Oxford: Oneworld Publications, 2009).

Coleridge, S. T. (eds J. Engell and W. Jackson Bate), *Biographia Literaria*, in *The Collected Works of Samuel Taylor Coleridge*, vol. 1. (Princeton: Princeton University Press, 1983).

Colmjon, G. van, 'Letter en Geest', *Trouw*, 16 November 2002, pp. 37–8.

Condillac, *Essai sur l'origine des connaissances humaines* (Amsterdam: Pierre Mortier, 1746).

Corino, K., *Robert Musil, eine Biographie* (Reinbek: Rowohlt Verlag, 2003).

Cover, R., *Justice Accused, Antislavery and the Judicial Process* (New Haven and London: Yale University Press, 1975).

Cover, R., '*Nomos* and Narrative', 97 *Harvard Law Review*, 1983, pp. 4–68.

Cover, R., 'Violence and the word', 95 *Yale Law Journal*, 1986, pp. 1601–29.

Culler, J., 'What's the point?', in M. Bal and I. E. Boer (eds), *The Point of Theory: Practices of Cultural Analysis* (Amsterdam: Amsterdam University Press, 1994), pp. 13–17.

Cunningham, A., *The Heart of What Matters: The Role for Literature in Moral Philosophy* (Berkeley: University of California Press, 2001).

Cunningham, M., *Specimen Days* (London: Fourth Estate, 2005).

Currie, G., *Narratives & Narrators: a Philosophy of Stories* (Oxford: Oxford University Press, 2010).

Dagan, H. and R. Kreitner, 'The Interdisciplinary Party', 1 *Critical Analysis of Law*, no. 1, 2014, pp. 23–31.

Damaška, M. R., 'The competing visions of fairness: the basic choice for international criminal tribunals', 36 *North Carolina Journal of International Law and Commercial Regulation*, no. 2, 2011, pp. 365–87.

Danziger, K., 'Historical psychology of persons: categories and practice', in J. Martin and M. H. Bickhard (eds), *The Psychology of Personhood, Philosophical, Historical, Social-Developmental, and Narrative Perspectives* (Cambridge: Cambridge University Press, 2013).

Darbyshire, P., *Sitting in Judgment: The Working Lives of Judges* (Oxford and Portland, OR: Hart Publishing, 2011).

DeGrazia, D., *Human Identity and Bioethics* (Cambridge: Cambridge University Press, 2005).

Deleuze, G., 'Postscript on control societies', in G. Deleuze, *Negotiations 1970–1990* (New York: Columbia University Press, 1995), pp. 177–82.

Del Mar, M. and W. Twining (eds), *Legal Fictions in Theory and Practice* (Cham, Switzerland: Springer International Publishing, 2015).

Desai, K., *The Inheritance of Loss* (Harmondsworth: Penguin Books, [2006] 2007).

DeSanctis, C. H., 'Narrative reasoning and analogy: the untold story', 9 *Legal Communication and Rhetoric: JALWD*, 2012, pp. 149–71.

Devey, J. (ed.), *The Physical and Metaphysical Works of Lord Bacon, including The Advancement of Learning and Novum Organum* (London: George Bell and Sons, [1605; 1620] 1901).

Dimock, W. C. and P. Wald, 'Literature and science: cultural forms, conceptual exchanges', 74 *American Literature*, no. 4, 2002, pp. 705–14.

Dodsley, R. (ed.), *A Collection of Poems* (London: R. & J. Dodsley, 1755).

Dolin, K., *A Critical Introduction to Law and Literature* (Cambridge: Cambridge University Press, 2007).

Douzinas, C., 'A humanities of resistance: fragments for a legal history of humanity', in A. Sarat, L. M. Anderson and C. O. Frank (eds), *Law and the Humanities. An Introduction* (Cambridge: Cambridge University Press, 2010), pp. 49–72.

Durkheim, E., *The Division of Labor in Society* (New York: The Free Press, [1893] 1984).

Dworkin, R., *Justice in Robes* (Cambridge, MA, and London: Belknap Press, 2006).

Eagleton, T., *The Event of Literature* (New Haven: Yale University Press, 2012).

Edelman, B., 'La fabulation juridique', 41 *Droits*, 2005, pp. 199–217.

Eden, K., *Poetic and Legal Fiction in the Aristotelian Tradition* (Princeton: Princeton University Press, 1986).

Eliot, T. S., 'East Coker', *The Complete Poems of T.S. Eliot* (London: Guild Publishing/ Faber and Faber, 1986).

Engisch, K., *Logische Studien zur Gesetzanwendung* (Heidelberg: Winter, [1943] 1963).

Erasmus, Desiderius (trans. and annot. B. McGregor, ed. C. R. Thompson), *On the Method of Study, de ratione studii ac legendi interpretandique auctores*, in *Collected Works of Erasmus, Literary and Educational Writings 2: de copia/de ratione studii* (Toronto, Buffalo and London: University of Toronto Press, 1978).

Evans, G. R., *Law and Theology in the Middle Ages* (London: Routledge, 2002).

Fagundes, D., 'What we talk about when we talk about persons: the language of a legal fiction', 114 *Harvard Law Review*, 2001, pp. 1745–68.

Ferguson, R., 'The judicial opinion as literary genre', 2 *Yale Journal of Law & the Humanities*, 1990, pp. 201–7.

Festinger, L., *A Theory of Cognitive Dissonance* (Stanford, CA: Stanford University Press, 1957).

Finnis, J., '"The thing I am": personal identity in Aquinas and Shakespeare', in E. Frankel Paul, F. D. Miller, Jun. and J. Paul (eds), *Personal Identity* (Cambridge: Cambridge University Press, 2005), pp. 250–82.

Fisher, W. R. and R. A. Filloy, 'Argument in drama and literature: an exploration', in J. R. Cox and C. A. Willard (eds), *Advances in Argumentation Theory and Research* (Carbondale, IL: Southern Illinois University Press, 1982), pp. 343–62.

Fisher, W. R., 'Narration as a human communication paradigm: the case of the public moral argument', 51 *Communications Monographs*, 1984, pp. 1–22.

Fisher, W. R., 'The narrative paradigm: an elaboration', 52 *Communications Monographs*, 1985, pp. 347–67.

Flaubert, G. (trans. A. J. Kreilsheimer), *Bouvard and Pécuchet* (Harmondsworth: Penguin Books, [1881] 1978).

Flaubert, G. (trans. E. Borger), *Bouvard en Pécuchet* (Amsterdam: De Arbeiderspers, [1881] 1988).

Flaubert, G., *Bouvard et Pécuchet* (Paris: Livre de Poche, [1881] 1947).

Flaubert, G., *Bouvard et Pécuchet* (Paris: Point du Jour, [1881] 1947).

Flaubert, G., *Correspondance*, vols I–IV, J. Bruneau (ed.), vol. V, J. Bruneau and Y. Leclerc (eds) (Paris: Gallimard, Bibliothèque de la Pléiade, 1992–2007).

Flaubert, G. (trans. E. Borger), *Haat is een deugd, een keuze uit de correspondentie* (Amsterdam: De Arbeiderspers, 2009).

Floridi, L. (ed.), *The Blackwell Guide to the Philosophy of Computing and Information* (Malden, MA: Blackwell Publishing, 2004).

Floridi, L. (ed.), *The Online Manifesto – Being Human in a Hyperconnected Era* (Dordrecht: Springer, 2014).

Fludernik, M., 'Histories of narrative theory (II): from structuralism to the present', in J. Phelan and P. J. Rabinowitz (eds), *A Companion to Narrative Theory* (Oxford: Blackwell, 2005), pp. 38–58.

Fludernik, M. and G. Olson, 'Introduction', in G. Olson (ed.), *Current Trends in Narratology* (Berlin: De Gruyter, 2011), pp. 1–33.

Fludernik, M., 'A narratology of law? Narratives in legal discourse', 1 *Critical Analysis of Law*, no. 1, 2014, pp. 87–109, available at <http://cal.library.utoronto.ca/> [last accessed 2 January 2017].

Foqué, R. and A.C. 't Hart, *Instrumentaliteit en rechtsbescherming* (Arnhem: Gouda Quint, 1990).

Frank, A. W., *Letting Stories Breathe: A Socio-Narratology* (Chicago: University of Chicago Press, 2010).

Fricker, M., *Epistemic Injustice: Power and the Ethics of Knowing* (Oxford: Oxford University Press, 2007).

Fuller, L. L., *Legal Fictions* (Stanford, CA: Stanford University Press, 1967).

Gaakeer, J., 'Scraping the judge's conscience', *Pólemos*, no. 2, 2008, pp. 193–214.

Gaakeer, J., 'Interview with James Boyd White', 105 *Michigan Law Review*, 2007, pp. 1403–19.

Gaakeer, J., 'The art to find the mind's construction in the face: Lombroso's criminal anthropology and literature: the example of Zola, Dostoevsky, and Tolstoy', 26 *Cardozo Law Review*, no. 6, 2004, pp. 2345–77.

Gadamer, H.-G. (trans. N. Walker, ed. R. Bernasconi), *The Relevance of the Beautiful and Other Essays* (Cambridge: Cambridge University Press, 1986).

Gadamer, H.-G., *Truth and Method* (London: Stagbooks, 2001).

Garapon, A. and D. Salas, *Les nouvelles sorcières de Salem, leçons d'Outreau* (Paris: Seuil, 2006).

Gardam, J., *Old Filth* (London: Abacus, [2004] 2014).

Gardner, J., *On Moral Fiction* (New York: Basic Books, 1978).

Geertz, C., *The Interpretation of Cultures* (New York: Basic Books, 1973).

Geertz, C., *Local Knowledge* (New York: Basic Books, 1983).

Genette, G., 'Discours du récit', in G. Genette, *Figures III* (Paris: Seuil, 1972), pp. 67–282.

Gerber, E., 'Stephen Breyer on intellectual influences', available at <https://fivebooks.com/best-books/stephen-breyer-on-intellectual-influences/> [last accessed 12 January 2018].

Gilovich, T., *How We Know What Isn't So: The Fallibility of Human Reason in Everyday Life* (New York: Free Press, 1993).

Goddard Bergin, T. and M. H. Fisch (trans. and eds) *The New Science of Giambattista Vico* (Ithaca and London: Cornell University Press, [3rd edition 1744] 1986).

Gombrich, E. H., *Symbolic Images* (Oxford: Phaidon Press, 1972).

Goodrich, P., *Legal Discourse: Studies in Linguistics, Rhetoric, and Legal Analysis* (New York: St Martin's Press, 1987).

Goodrich, P., 'Screening law', 21 *Law & Literature*, no. 1, 2009, pp. 1–23.

Gould, S. J., *The Hedgehog, the Fox, and the Magister's Pox, Mending the gap between science and the humanities* (New York: Harmony Books, 2003).

Govers, A. J., 'Gerrit Achterberg en de psychiatrie', *Bzzlletin*, no. 79, October 1980, pp. 29–38.

Grassi, E., *Rhetoric as Philosophy: The Humanist Tradition* (University Park and London: The Pennsylvania State University Press, 1980).

Grassi, E., *Vico and Humanism: Essays on Vico, Heidegger, and Rhetoric* (New York: Peter Lang, 1990).

Gratian, *Decretum*, in E. L. Richter and E. Friedberg (eds), *Corpus Iuris Canonici* (Leipzig: Tauchnitz, [1140] 1879–81).

Greimas, A.-J. and E. Landowski, 'Analyse sémiotique d'un discours juridique', *Sémiotique et Sciences Sociales* (Paris: Seuil, 1976).

Greimas, A.-J. and J. Courtès, *Sémiotique, Dictionnaire raisonné de la théorie du langage* (Paris: Hachette, 1979).

Grimm, J., 'Von der Poesie im Recht', *Zeitschrift für geschichtliche Rechtswissenschaft*, in J. Grimm, 6 *Kleinere Schriften* (Hildesheim: Olms, [1816] 1965).

Grossfeld, B. and E. J. Eberle, 'Patterns of order in comparative law: discovering and decoding invisible powers', 38 *Texas International Law Journal*, 2003, pp. 291–316.

Grotius, H., *De Iure Belli ac Pacis* (Leyden: E. J. Brill, [1625] 1939).

Grotius, H. (trans. and ed. J. Waszink), *The Antiquity of the Batavian Republic* (Assen: Van Gorcum, 2000).

Gurnham, D., 'The mysteries of human dignity and the brave new world of human cloning', 14 *Social & Legal Studies*, 2005, no. 2, pp. 197–212.

Habermas, J., 'Philosophy and science as literature?', in J. Habermas (trans. W. M. Hohengarten), *Postmetaphysical Thinking: Philosophical Essays* (Cambridge, MA: MIT Press, 1992).

Hake, E. (ed. D. E. C. Yale), *Epieikeia, a Dialogue on Equity in Three Parts* (New Haven: Yale University Press, [1597] 1953).

Haldar, P., 'Law and the evidential image', 4 *Law, Culture and the Humanities*, 2008, pp. 139–55.

Haldar, P., 'The articles of law: renaissance theories of evidence and the poetic life of facts', 10 *Law and Humanities*, no. 2, 2016, pp. 281–99.

Halliwell, S., *Aristotle's Poetics* (London: Duckworth, 1986).

Halliwell, S., 'Diegesis-mimesis', in P. Hühn, J. Pier, W. Schmid and J. Schönert (eds), *The Living Handbook of Narratology* (Hamburg: Hamburg University), available at <http://www.lhn.uni-hamburg.de/article/diegesis-mimesis> [last accessed 20 January 2017].

Hamon, A. F. A., *Vrije wil, misdaad en toerekenbaarheid* (Amsterdam: Buys, 1907).

Hart, A. C. 't, *Strafrecht en Beleid, essays* (Zwolle and Louvain: W. E. J. Tjeenk Willink and ACCO, 1983).

Hawthorne, N., 'Dr Heidegger's Experiment', in *Twice-Told Tales* (Philadelphia: David Mackay, [1837 and 1842] 1889), available at <http://www.gutenberg.org/files/13707/13707-h/13707-h.htm> [last accessed 19 January 2018].

Hayles, K. N., *How We Think: Digital Media and Contemporary Technogenesis* (Chicago: University of Chicago Press, 2012).

Hazeu, W., *Gerrit Achterberg* (Amsterdam: Arbeiderspers, 1988).

Heald, P. J. (ed.), *Literature and Legal Problem Solving* (Durham, NC: Carolina Academic Press, 1998).

Hegel, G. W. F., *Grundlinien der Philosophie des Rechts* (Hamburg: Felix Meiser, 1967).

Hegel, G. W. F. (ed. A. W. Wood and trans. H. B. Nisbet), *Elements of the Philosophy of Right* (Cambridge: Cambridge University Press, 2003).

Heidegger, M., 'The question concerning technology', in M. Heidegger (trans. W. Lovitt), *The Question Concerning Technology and Other Essays* (New York: Harper & Row, [1954] 1977), pp. 3–35.

Heidegger, M., 'Only a God can save us', XX *Philosophy Today*, 1976, no. 4, pp. 267–85.

Heidegger, M. (trans. G. Fried and R. Polt), *Introduction to Metaphysics* (New Haven: Yale University Press, [1935] 2000).

Heijne, B., 'Interview Juli Zeh', *NRC-Handelsblad*, 23 December 2010, pp. 8–9.

Helenius, T., '"As if" and the surplus of being in Ricoeur's Poetics', 3 *Ricoeur Studies*, no. 2, 2012, pp. 149–70.

Herder, J. G. (ed. W. Flemmer), *Schriften, eine Auswahl aus dem Gesamtwerk* (München:Wilhelm Goldmann Verlag, 1960).

Herder, J. G., 'Die Sprache überhaupt', *Fragmente über die neuere deutsche Literatur* (1766–7), in J. G. Herder (ed. W. Pross), *Werke, Band I Herder und Sturm und Drang 1764–1774, erste Sammlung, zweite völlig umgearbeite Ausgabe* (Munich: Carl Hanser Verlag, [1768] 1984).

Herman, D., 'Histories of narrative theory (I): a genealogy of early developments', in J. Phelan and P. J. Rabinowitz (eds), *A Companion to Narrative Theory* (Oxford: Blackwell Publishing, 2005, pp. 19–35).

Herman, D., 'Narrative as cognitive instrument', in D. Herman, M. Jahn and M.-L. Ryan (eds), *Routledge Encyclopedia of Narrative Theory* (Abingdon and New York: Routledge, 2008), pp. 349–50.

Herman, D., 'Cognitive narratology', in P. Hühn, J. Pier, W. Schmid and Jörg Schönert (eds), *Handbook of Narratology* (Berlin: De Gruyter, 2009), pp. 30–43.

Herminghouse, P., 'The young author as public intellectual: the case of Juli Zeh', in K. Gerstenberger and P. Herminghouse (eds), *German Literature in a New Century: Trends, Traditions, Transitions, Transformations* (New York: Berghahn Books, 2008), pp. 268–84.

Herz, R., 'Anatomy of a judge', 9 *Law and Humanities*, 2015, pp. 123–35.

Hildebrandt, M., 'Legal and technological normativity: more (or less) than twin sisters', 12 *Techné*, no. 3, 2008, pp. 169–83.

Hildebrandt, M., *Smart Technologies and the End(s) of Law: Novel Entanglements of Law and Technology* (Cheltenham and Northampton, MA: Edward Elgar Publishing, 2015).

Hildebrandt, M. and S. Gutwirth (eds), *Profiling the European Citizen: Cross-Disciplinary Perspectives* (Dordrecht: Springer, 2008).

Hobbes, T., *Leviathan* (London: J. M. Dent and Sons, Everyman's Library, [1651] 1987).

Hochschild, A. R., *The Managed Heart: Commercialization of Human Feeling* (Berkeley: University of California Press, 1983).

Hof, S. van der, and C. Prins, 'Personalisation and its influence on identities, behaviour and social values', in M. Hildebrandt and S. Gutwirth, *Profiling the European Citizen*, pp. 111–24.

Hogan, P. C., *Affective Narratology: The Emotional Structure of Stories* (Lincoln, NB, and London: University of Nebraska Press, 2011).

Hogan, P. C., *What Literature Teaches Us About Emotion* (Cambridge: Cambridge University Press, 2011).

Holdheim, W. W., *Der Justizirrtum als literarische Problematik* (Berlin: De Gruyter, 1969).

Holmes, O. W., Jun., 'Review Langdell casebook', 14 *American Law Review*, 1880, pp. 233–5.

Houellebecq, M. (trans. F. Wynne), *Atomised* (London: William Heinemann, [*Les Particules élémentaires* 1999] 2000).

Howarth, D., *Law as Engineering: Thinking about what Lawyers Do* (Cheltenham and Northampton, MA: Edward Elgar, 2013).

Hutson, L., *The Invention of Suspicion: Law and Mimesis in Shakespeare and Renaissance Drama* (Oxford: Oxford University Press, 2007).

Hutson, L., '"Lively evidence": legal inquiry and the *evidentia* of Shakespeare drama', in B. Cormack, M. C. Nussbaum and R. Strier (eds), *Shakespeare and the Law: A Conversation among Disciplines and Professions* (Chicago and London: University of Chicago Press, 2013), pp. 72–97.

Hutson, L., 'Proof and probability: law, imagination, and the forms of things unknown', in E. S. Anker and B. Meyler (eds), *New Directions in Law and Literature* (Oxford: Oxford University Press, 2017), pp. 144–59.

Ihering, R. von (trans. C. L. Levy), *In the Heaven for Legal Concepts: A Fantasy*, 58 *Temple Law Quarterly*, [1884] 1985, pp. 799–842.

Ihering, R. von (trans. I. Husik), *Der Zweck im Recht*, 3 vols., 1877–84, *Law as a Means to an End* (Boston: The Boston Book Co., 1913).

IJsseling, S., *Rhetoric and Philosophy in Conflict* (The Hague: Nijhoff, 1976).

Ishiguro, K., *Never Let Me Go* (London: Faber and Faber, 2005).

Iversen, S., 'Narratives in rhetorical discourse', in P. Hühn, J. Pier, W. Schmid and J. Schönert (eds), *The Living Handbook of Narratology* (Hamburg: Hamburg University), available at <http://www.lhn.uni-hamburg.de/article/narratives-rhetorical-discourse> [last accessed 10 December 2016].

Jackson, B., *Law, Fact and Narrative Coherence* (Liverpool: Deborah Charles Publications, 1988).

James, H., 'The Madonna of the Future' (1879), 'Cats and monkeys, monkeys and cats – all human life is here', available at <https://ebooks.adelaide.edu.au/j/james/henry/madonna_of_the_future/> [last accessed 21 December 2017].

James, H., *The Portrait of a Lady* (Harmondsworth: Penguin, [1881] 1976).

James, H., *In the Cage* (London: Martin Secker, [1919] 2005).

Janik, A. and S. Toulmin, *Wittgenstein's Vienna* (New York: Simon and Schuster, 1973).

Jannidis, F., 'Character', in P. Hühn, J. Pier, W. Schmid and J. Schönert (eds), *The Living Handbook of Narratology* (Hamburg: Hamburg University), available at <http://www.lhn.uni-hamburg.de/article/character> [last accessed 16 February 2016].

Judson, P. M., *The Habsburg Empire: A New History* (Cambridge, MA, and London: Belknap Press of Harvard University Press, 2016).

Jurecic A., 'Empathy and the critic', 74 *College English*, no. 1, 2011, pp. 10–27.

Kafka, F. (trans. W. and E. Muir), *The Trial* (London: Penguin, 1978).

Kafka, K., Letter to Oskar Pollak, dated Sunday 8 November 1903, in M. Brod (ed.), *Briefe, 1902–1924*, available at <http://homepage.univie.ac.at/werner.haas/1903/br03-002.htm> [last accessed 10 September 2017].

Kagan, J., *The Three Cultures, Natural Sciences, Social Sciences and the Humanities in the 21st Century: Revisiting C. P. Snow* (Cambridge: Cambridge University Press, 2009).

Kathan, B., *Schöne neue Kuhstallwelt* (Berlin: Martin Schmitz, 2009).

Kauffmann, M., 'Juli Zeh "das Projekt Aufklärung ist nicht zu Ende"', *Wiener Zeitung*, 27 February 2009, pp. 7–8.

Keats, J., 'Letter of 21 December 1817 to his brothers George and Thomas', in M. H. Abrams, S. Greenblatt, C. T. Christ, A. David, B. K. Lewalski, L. Lipking, G. M. Logan, D. S. Lynch, K. E. Maus, J. Noggle, J. Ramazani, C. Robson, J. Simpson, J. Stallworthy and J. Stillinger (eds), *The Norton Anthology of English Literature* (New York: W. W. W. Norton & Co., 1974) vol. 2, p. 705.

Keen, S., 'Narrative empathy', in P. Hühn, J. Pier, W. Schmid and J. Schönert (eds), *The Living Handbook of Narratology* (Hamburg: Hamburg University), http://www.lhn.uni-hamburg.de/article/narrative-empathy [last accessed 4 April 2016].

Kelley, D. R., *The Human Measure, Social Thought in the Western Legal Tradition* (Cambridge, MA: Harvard University Press, 1990).

Kelly, J. M., *A Short History of Western Legal Theory* (Oxford: Clarendon Press, 1992).

Kermode, F., *The Genesis of Secrecy* (Cambridge, MA: Harvard University Press, 1979).

Kertzer, J., 'Time's desire: literature and the temporality of justice', 5 *Law, Culture and the Humanities*, 2009, pp. 266–87.

Kertzer, J., *Poetic Justice and Legal Fictions* (Cambridge: Cambridge University Press, 2010).

Kiernan-Johnson, D. H., 'A shift to narrativity', 9 *Legal Communication and Rhetoric: JALWD*, 2012, pp. 81–98.

King, P. K., *Dawn Poetry in the Netherlands* (Amsterdam: Athenaeum, Polak and Van Gennep, 1971).

Klemperer, V. (trans. M. Brady), *The Language of the Third Reich, LTI- Lingua Tertii Imperii: A Philologist's Notebook* (London and New Brunswick, NJ: The Athlone Press, [1957] 2000).

Kronman, A. T., *Education's End: Why Our Colleges and Universities Have Given Up On the Meaning of Life* (New Haven and London: Yale University Press, 2007).

Kronman A. T., *The Lost Lawyer: Failing Ideals of the Legal Profession* (Cambridge, MA: Harvard University Press, 1993).

Kuhn, T. S., *The Structure of Scientific Revolutions* (Chicago: University of Chicago Press, 1962).

Kukkonen, K., 'Plot', in P. Hühn. J. Pier, W. Schmid and J. Schönert (eds), *The Living Handbook of Narratology* (Hamburg: Hamburg University), available at <http://www.lhn.uni-hamburg.de/article/plot> [last accessed 12 December 2016].

Künzel, C., '"Aus einem Bette aufgestanden", Anmerkungen zum "Verhältnis" zwischen Recht und Literatur', in G. Hofmann (ed.), *Figures of Law: Studies in the Interference of Law and Literature* (Tübingen and Basel: A. Francke Verlag, 2007), pp. 115–32.

LaCapra, D., *Madame Bovary on Trial* (Ithaca and London: Cornell University Press, 1982).

Ladenson, E., *Dirt for Art's Sake* (Ithaca and London: Cornell University Press, 2007).

Langdell, C. C., 'Introduction' to *A Selection of Cases on the Law of Contracts*, in A. E. Sutherland, *The Law at Harvard* (Cambridge, MA: Harvard University Press, 1967).

Lakoff, G., 'The contemporary theory of metaphor', in A. Ortony (ed.), *Metaphor and Thought* (Cambridge: Cambridge University Press, 1993), pp. 202–51.

Lakoff, G. and M. Johnson, *Metaphors We Live By* (Chicago: University of Chicago Press, 1980).

Larenz, K. F., *Methodenlehre der Rechtswissenschaft* (Berlin: Springer, [1960] 1991).

Latour, B., *We Have Never Been Modern* (Hempel Hempstead: Harvester Wheatsheaf, 1993).

Leavis, F. R., *Two Cultures? The Significance of C. P. Snow* (London: Chatto and Windus, 1962).

Lessig, L., *Code version 2.0* (New York: Basic Books, 2006).

Levinas, E., (trans. A. Lingis), *Totality and Infinity* (Pittsburgh: Duquesne University Press, [1961] 1969).

Levinas, E. (trans. M. B. Smith and B. Harshav), *On Thinking-of-the-Other: Entre Nous* (London: The Athlone Press, [1991] 1998), pp. 186–7.

Lieblich, A. and R. Josselson, 'Identity and narrative as root metaphor of personhood', in J. Martin and M. H. Bickhard (eds), *The Psychology of Personhood: Philosophical, Historical, Social-Developmental, and Narrative Perspectives* (Cambridge: Cambridge University Press, 2013), pp. 203–22.

Linnemann, J. and J. Schmaal, 'Intelligent contracteren', *Computerrecht*, 2010, pp. 297–302.

Littell, J. (trans. C. Mandell), *The Kindly Ones* (London: Vintage, 2010).

Loemker, L. E. (ed.), *G. W. Leibniz, Philosophical Papers and Letters* (Dordrecht and Boston: D. Reidel Publishing, 1976).

Luhmann, N., *Ausdifferenzierung des Rechts: Beiträge zur Rechtssoziologie und Rechtstheorie* (Frankfurt am Main: Suhrkamp, 1981).

MacIntyre, A., *After Virtue: A Study in Moral Theory* (Notre Dame: University of Notre Dame Press, 1981).

Maine, H., *Ancient Law: Its Connection with the Early History of Society and its Relation to Modern Ideas* (Oxford: Oxford University Press, [1861] 1950).

Manderson, D., 'Modernism and the critique of law and literature', 35 *The Australian Feminist Law Journal*, 2011, pp. 105–23.

Manguel, A., *A Reader on Reading* (New Haven and London: Yale University Press, 2010).

Maroney, T., 'Law and emotion: a proposed taxonomy of an emerging field', *30 Law and Human Behavior*, no. 2, 2006, pp. 119–42.

Maroney, T., 'Emotional regulation and judicial behavior', 90 *California Law Review*, 2011, pp. 1481–551.

Maroney, T., 'The persistent cultural script of judicial dispassion', 99 *California Law Review* 2011, pp. 629–81.

Martín Alcoff, L., 'Sotomayor's reasoning', 48 *The Southern Journal of Philosophy*, no. 1, 2010, pp. 122–38.

Mauger, M., '"Observe how parts with parts unite/In one harmonious rule of right": William Blackstone's Verses on the Laws of England', 6 *Law and Humanities*, no. 2, 2012, pp. 179–96.

Mayer-Schönberg, V., *Delete: The Virtue of Forgetting in the Digital Age* (Princeton: Princeton University Press, 2009).

McArdle, A., 'Using a narrative lens to understand empathy and how it matters in judging', 9 *Legal Communication & Rhetoric: JALWD*, 2012, pp. 173–206.

McEwan, I., *The Children Act* (London: Jonathan Cape, 2014).

Meister, J.-C., 'Narratology', in P. Hühn, J. Pier, W. Schmid and J. Schönert (eds), *Handbook of Narratology* (Berlin: De Gruyter, 2009), pp. 329–50.

Merz, E. and J. Yovel, 'Court room narrative', in D. Herman, M. Jahn and M.-L. Ryan (eds), *Routledge Encyclopedia of Narrative Theory* (Abingdon and New York: Routledge, 2008), pp. 86–8.

Meuter, N., 'Narration in various disciplines', in P. Hühn, J. Pier, W. Schmid and J. Schönert (eds), *Handbook of Narratology* (Berlin: De Gruyter, 2009), pp. 242–62.

Michelon, C., 'Practical wisdom in legal decision-making', in A. Amaya and H. Hock Lai (eds), *Law, Virtue and Justice* (Oxford and Portland, OR: Hart Publishing, 2013), pp. 29–49.

Minda, G., *Postmodern Legal Movements: Law and Jurisprudence at Century's End* (New York and London: New York University Press, 1995).

Minow, M. L., 'Identities', 3 *Yale Journal of Law & the Humanities*, no. 1, 1991, pp. 97–130.

Minow, M. L. and E. V. Spelman, 'Passion for justice', 10 *Cardozo Law Review*, 1988, pp. 37–76.

Mitchell, D., *number9dream* (London: Sceptre, 2001).

Mitchell, W. J., *City of Bits: Space, Place, and the Infobahn* (Cambridge, MA: MIT Press, [1995] 2000).

Montaigne, M. de (trans. J. Florio), *Essays* (London: Blount, [1580] 1603).

Montaigne, M. de (trans. and ed. M. A. Screech), *The Complete Essays* (Harmondsworth: Penguin, [1580] 1991).

Mooij, A., 'Kant on criminal law and psychiatry', 21 *International Journal of Law and Psychiatry*, no. 4, 1998, pp. 335–41.

Mootz, F. J. III, 'Foreword to the Symposium on Philosophical Hermeneutics and Critical Legal Theory', 76 *Chicago-Kent Law Review*, no. 2, 2000, pp. 719–30.

Mootz, F. J. III, 'Law among the sight lovers', 75 *New York Law School Law Review*, 2012, pp. 61–74.

Moran, R., 'Seeing and believing: metaphor, image, and force', 16 *Critical Inquiry*, 1989, pp. 87–112.

Morawetz, T., 'Empathy and judgment', 8 *Yale Journal of Law & the Humanities*, no. 2, 1996, pp. 517–53.

Müller-Dietz, H., 'Literarische Verarbeitung von Recht in Gegenwartsromanen', in F. Stürmer and P. Meier (eds), *Recht Populär, populärkulturelle Rechtsdarstellungen in aktuellen Texten und Medien* (Baden-Baden: Nomos, 2016), pp. 37–59.

Müller-Dietz, H. 'Zur negativen Utopie von Recht und Staat', *JZ* 2, 2011, pp. 85–95.

Multatuli (trans. R. Edwards), *Max Havelaar, or the Coffee Auctions of the Dutch Trading Company* (Harmondsworth: Penguin Books, [1860] 1987).

Musil, R. (trans. S. Wilkins and B. Pike), *The Man without Qualities* (London: Picador, [1930–3] 1997).

Nickerson, R. S., 'Confirmation bias: a ubiquitous phenomenon in many guises', 2 *Review of General Psychology*, 1998, pp. 175–220.

Niederhoff, B., 'Focalization', in Peter Hühn, J. Pier, W. Schmid and J. Schönert (eds), *The Living Handbook of Narratology* (Hamburg: Hamburg University), available at <http://www.lhn.uni-hamburg.de/article/narration-various-disciplines> [last accessed 16 September 2017].

Nonet, P., and P. Selznick, *Law and Society in Transition: Toward Responsive Law* (New York: Harper and Row, 1978).

Noonan, J. T., *Persons and Masks of the Law* (Berkeley: University Of California Press, [1976] 2002).

Norrie, A., *Law and the Beautiful Soul* (London: GlassHouse Press, 2005).

Norton, R. E., *Herder's Aesthetics and the European Enlightenment* (Ithaca and London: Cornell University Press, 1991).

Nünning, A. and M. Basseler, 'Literary studies as a form of "life science": the knowledge of literature', in G. Olson and A. Nünning (eds), *New Theories, Models and Methods in Literary and Cultural Studies* (Trier: WVT, 2013), pp. 189–212.

Nussbaum, M. C., *The Fragility of Goodness* (Cambridge: Cambridge University Press, 1986).

Nussbaum, M. C., *Love's Knowledge* (Oxford: Oxford University Press, 1990).

Nussbaum, M. C., *Poetic Justice* (Boston: Beacon Press, 1995).

Nussbaum, M. C., 'Emotion in the language of judging', 70 *St. John's Law Review*, no. 1, 1996, pp. 23–30.

Nussbaum, M. C., *Cultivating Humanity: A Classical Defense of Reform in Liberal Education* (Cambridge, MA, and London: Harvard University Press, 1997).

Nussbaum, M. C., *Frontiers of Justice* (Cambridge, MA: Harvard University Press, 2007).

Nussbaum, M. C., *Not for Profit: Why Democracy Needs the Humanities* (Princeton: Princeton University Press, 2010).

Nussbaum, M. C., *Creating Capabilities: The Human Development Approach* (Cambridge, MA: Harvard University Press, 2011).

Olivier, P. J. J., *Legal Fictions in Practice and Legal Science* (Rotterdam: Rotterdam University Press, 1975).

O'Loughlin, M. (ed. and trans.), *Hidden Weddings, Selected Poems Gerrit Achterberg* (Dublin: Raven Arts Press, 1987).

Olson, G., 'De-Americanizing law-and-literature narratives: opening up the story', 22 *Law & Literature*, 2010, pp. 338–64.

Olson, G., 'Law is not turgid and literature not soft and fleshy: gendering and heteronormativity in law and literature scholarship', 36 *The Australian Feminist Law Journal*, 2012, pp. 65–86.

Olson, G., *Criminals as Animals from Shakespeare to Lombroso* (Berlin: De Gruyter, 2013).

Olson, G., 'Intersections of gender and legal culture in two women judge shows: *Judge Judy* and *Richterin Barbara Salesch*', in H. Petersen, J. M. Lorenzo Villaverde and I. Lund-Andersen (eds), *Contemporary Gender Relations and Changes in Legal Cultures* (Copenhagen: DJØF, 2013).

Olson, G., 'Futures of law and literature: a preliminary overview from a culturalist perspective', in C. Hiebaum, S. Knaller and D. Pichler (eds), *Recht und Literatur in Zwischenraum/Law and Literature in-between* (Bielefeld: Transcript, 2015), pp. 37–69.

Olson, G., 'The turn to passion: has law and literature become law and affect?', 28 *Law & Literature*, no. 3, 2016, pp. 335–53.

Orwell, G., *Nineteen Eighty-Four* (London: Book Club Associates, [1949] 1967).

Ostermann, E., 'Das Wildgewordene Subjekt. Christian Moosbrugger und die Imagination des Wilden in Musils *Mann Ohne Eigenschaften*', *Neophilologus*, 2005, pp. 605–23.

Papke, D. R., 'From flat to round: changing portrayals of the judge in American popular culture', 31 *The Journal of the Legal Profession*, 2007, pp. 127–51.

Paskey, S., 'The law is made of stories: erasing the false dichotomy between stories and legal rules', 11 *Legal Communication & Rhetoric: JALWD*, 2014, pp. 51–82.

Pavlakos, G., 'Normative knowledge and the nature of law', in S. Coyle and G. Pavlakos (eds), *Jurisprudence or Legal Science?* (Oxford and Portland, OR: Hart Publishing, 2005), pp. 89–126.

Pavlakos G. and S. Coyle, 'Introduction', in S. Coyle and G. Pavlakos (eds), *Jurisprudence or Legal Science? A Debate about the Nature of Legal Theory* (Oxford and Portland, OR: Hart, 2005), pp. 1–13.

Payne, P., 'Musil erforscht den Geist eines anderen Menschen – zum Porträt Moosbruggers im Mann ohne Eigenschaften', *Literatur und Kritik*, 1976, pp. 389–404.

Pech, T., *Conter le Crime: droit et littérature sous la Contre-Réforme* (Paris: Champion Slatkine, 2001).

Pelser, C. M., 'Preparations to commit a crime', 4 *Utrecht Law Review*, no. 3, 2008, available at <https://www.utrechtlawreview.org/articles/10.18352/> [last accessed 24 December 2017].

Peters, J. S., 'Legal performance good and bad', 4 *Law, Culture and the Humanities*, no. 2, 2008, pp. 179–200.

Peters, J. S., 'Law as performance: historical interpretation, objects, lexicons, and other methodological problems', in E. S. Anker and B. Meyler (eds), *New Directions in Law and Literature* (Oxford: Oxford University Press, 2017), pp. 193–209.

Phelan, J., 'Narrative ethics', in P. Hühn, J. Pier, W. Schmid and J. Schönert (eds), *The Living Handbook of Narratology* (Hamburg: Hamburg University), available at <http://www.lhn.uni-hamburg.de/article/narrative-ethics> [last accessed 2 December 2016].

Phelps, T., 'Narratives of disobedience', 40 *Journal of Legal Education*, 1990, pp. 133–43.

Pieroth, B., *Recht und Literatur, von Friedrich Schiller bis Martin Walser* (Munich: C. H. Beck, 2015).

Plato (trans. R. E. Allen), *The Dialogues of Plato*, vol. II (New Haven and London: Yale University Press, 1991).

Porsdam, H., *From Civil to Human Rights, Dialogues on Law and Humanities in the United States and Europe* (Northampton: Edward Elgar, 2009).

Posner, R. A., 'The ethical significance of free choice', 99 *Harvard Law Review*, 1986, pp. 1431–48.

Posner, R. A., *Law and Literature: A Misunderstood Relation* (Cambridge, MA: Harvard University Press, 1988 [rev. eds 1998 and 2009]).

Post, R. (ed.), *Law and the Order of Culture* (Berkeley: University of California Press, 1991).

Pound, R., *The Lawyer from Antiquity to Modern Times* (St Paul: West Publishing Co., 1953).

Prins, C., D. Broeders, H. Griffioen, A. -G. Keizer and E. Keymolen, *i-Government* (Amsterdam: Amsterdam University Press, 2011).

Propp, V., *Morphology of the Folktale* (Research Center: Indiana University, [1928] 1958).

Queneau, R. (trans. B. Wright), *Exercises in Style [Exercises de stile*, 1947] (Richmond: Oneworld Classics, 2009).

Quintilian, *Institutio oratoria* (Cambridge, MA: Harvard University Press, 1996).

Radbruch, G., *Kleines Rechts-Brevier* (Göttingen: Vandenhoeck & Ruprecht, 1954).

Radbruch, G. (eds E. Wolf and H. P. Schneider), *Rechtsphilosophie* (Stuttgart: K. F. Köhler Verlag, [1914, rev. 1932] 1973).

Ralph, A. E., 'Not the same old story: using narrative theory to understand and overcome the plausibility pleading standard', 26 *Yale Journal of Law & the Humanities*, no. 1, 2014, pp. 1–57.

Rayar, L., S. Wadsworth, M. Cheung, H. Lensing and G. van den Heuvel (trans.), *The American Series of Foreign Penal Codes: The Dutch Penal Code* (Littleton: Fred Rothman & Co., 1997).

Reagan, C. E., *Paul Ricoeur: His Life and His Work* (Chicago: University of Chicago Press, 1996).

Reich, C., 'Toward the humanistic study of law', 74 *Yale Law Journal*, 1965, pp. 1402–8.

Reichman, A., 'Law, literature, and empathy: between withholding and reserving judgment', 56 *Journal of Legal Education*, no. 2, 2006, pp. 296–319.

Reichman, R., 'Law's affective tickets', in E. S. Anker and B. Meyler (eds), *New Directions in Law and Literature* (Oxford: Oxford University Press, 2017), pp. 109–22.

Reiss, H., 'Musil and the writer's task in the age of science and technology', in L. Huber and J. J. White (eds), *Musil in Focus* (London: Institute of Germanic Studies, 1982), pp. 41–53.

Rhee, W., 'Law and practice', 9 *Legal Communication & Rhetoric: JALWD*, 2012, pp. 273–313.

Ricoeur, P., 'The metaphorical process as cognition, imagination, and feeling', *Critical Inquiry*, 1978, pp. 143–59.

Ricoeur, P., 'Narrative time', *Critical Inquiry*, 1980, pp. 167–90.

Ricoeur, P. (trans. and ed. J. B. Thompson), *Hermeneutics and the Human Sciences* (Cambridge: Cambridge University Press, 1981).

Ricoeur, P. (trans. R. Czerny, K. Mclaughlin and J. Costello), *The Rule of Metaphor: Multidisciplinary Studies in the Creation of Meaning in Language* (London: Routledge, [1975] 1986).

Ricoeur, P., 'Life: a story in search of a narrator' in M. C. Doeser and J. N. Kraaij (eds), *Facts and Values* (Dordrecht and Boston: Martinus Nijhoff Publishers, 1987).

Ricoeur, P. (trans. K. McLaughlin and D. Pellauer), *Time and Narrative* (Chicago: University of Chicago Press, 1984 (vol. 1), 1985 (vol. 2), 1988 (vol. 3)).

Ricoeur, P. (trans. K. Blamey and J. B. Thompson), *From Text to Action: Essays in Hermeneutics, II* (Evanston, IL: Northwestern University Press, 1991).

Ricoeur, P. (trans. K. Blamey), *Oneself as Another* (Chicago and London: University of Chicago Press, [1990] 1992).

Ricoeur, P. (trans. D. Pellauer), *The Just* (Chicago: Chicago University Press, [1995] 2000).

P. Ricoeur (trans. D. Pellauer), *The Course of Recognition* (Cambridge, MA: Harvard University Press, 2005).

Ricoeur, P. (trans. D. Pellauer), *Reflections on the Just* (Chicago and London: University of Chicago Press, [2001] 2007).

Rideout, J. C., 'Penumbral thinking revisited: metaphor in legal argumentation', 7 *Journal of the Association of Legal Writing Directors*, 2010, pp. 155–91.

Riffaterre, M., *Fictional Truth* (Baltimore: Johns Hopkins University Press, 1990).

Roach Anleu, S. and K. Mack, 'Magistrates' everyday work and emotional labour', 32 *Journal of Law and Society*, no. 4, 2005, pp. 590–614.

Robinson, M., 'What are we doing here?', *The New York Review of Books*, 9 November 2017.

Robinson, O. F., T. D. Fergus and W. M. Gordon, *European Legal History, Sources and Institutions* (Butterworths: London, 1994).

Robson, P. and J. L. Schulz (eds), *A Transnational Study of Law and Justice on TV* (Oxford and Portland, OR: 2016).

Robson, R. and J. R. Elkins, 'A conversation', 29 *Legal Studies Forum*, 2005, pp. 145–72.

Rosen, J., 'Sentimental journey: the emotional jurisprudence of Harry Blackmun', *The New Republic*, 2 May 1994.

Ross, L. and C. A. Anderson, 'Shortcomings in the attribution process: on the origins and maintenance of erroneous social assessments', in D. Kahneman, P. Slovic and A. Tversky (eds), *Judgment Under Uncertainty: Heuristics and Biases* (Cambridge: Cambridge University Press, 1982), pp. 129–52.

Ryan, M.-L., *Possible Worlds, Artifical Intelligence, and Narrative Theory* (Bloomington: University of Indiana Press, 1991).

Ryan, M.-L., 'Cheap plot tricks, plot holes, and narrative design', 17 *Narrative*, no. 1, January 2009, pp. 56–75.

Ryle, G., 'Knowing how and knowing that', 46 *Proceedings of the Aristotelian Society*, 1945, pp. 1–16.

Saks, M. J. and J. J. Koehler, 'The coming paradigm shift in forensic identification science', *Science*, 5 August 2005, pp. 892–5.

Salas, D., *Le Courage de Juger* (Paris: Bayard, 2014).

Samuel, G., *A Short Introduction to the Common Law* (Cheltenham: Edward Elgar, 2013).

Samuel, G., 'Equity and legal reasoning', 11 *Pólemos*, no. 1, 2017, pp. 41–53.

Saramago, J. (trans. M. J. Costa), *All the Names* (New York: Harcourt Inc., [1997] 1999).

Sarat, A. and T. R. Kearns (eds), *Law in the Domains of Culture* (Ann Arbor: University of Michigan Press, 1998).

Sarat, A. and J. Simon, 'Beyond legal realism?: Cultural analysis, cultural studies, and the situation of legal scholarship', 13 *Yale Journal of Law & the Humanities*, 2001, pp. 3–32.

Sartre, J.-P., *Qu'est-ce que la littérature?* (Paris: Gallimard, 1948).

Saussure, F. de (trans. W. Baskin, eds P. Meisel and H. Saussy), *Course in General Linguistics* (New York: Columbia University Press, [1916] 2011).

Savigny, F. C. von (trans. A. Hayward), *Of the Vocation of our Age for Legislation and Jurisprudence* (New York: Argo, [1815] 1975).

Scarry, E., 'Speech acts in criminal cases', in P. Brooks and P. Gewirtz (eds), *Law's Stories: Narrative and Rhetoric in the Law* (New Haven and London: Yale University Press, 1996), pp. 165–74.

Schernus, W., 'Narratology in the mirror of codifying texts', in G. Olson (ed.), *Current Trends in Narratology* (Berlin: De Gruyter, 2011), pp. 277–96.

Schirach, F. von (trans. D. Tushingham), *Terror* (London: Faber and Faber, [2016] 2017).

Schlag, P., 'The dedifferentiation problem', 42 *Continental Philosophy Review*, 2009, pp. 35–62.

Schmeiser, S. R., 'The ungovernable citizen: psychopathy, sexuality, and the rise of medico-legal reasoning', 20 *Yale Journal of Law & the Humanities*, no. 2, 2008, pp. 163–240.

Schneck, P., *Rhetoric and Evidence, Legal Conflict and Literary Representation in U.S. American Culture* (Berlin: De Gruyter, 2011).

Scholten, P., *General Method of Private Law*, vol. 1, ch. 1 of *Mr. C. Asser's Manual for the Practice of Dutch Civil Law* (Amsterdam: Digital Paul Scholten Project, [1931] 2014), available at <http://www.paulscholten.eu/research/article/english/> [last accessed 1 April 2016].

Schön, D. A., *The Reflective Practitioner* (New York: Basic Books, 1983).

Schönert, J., 'Author', in P. Hühn, J. Pier, W. Schmid and J. Schönert (eds), *Handbook of Narratology* (Berlin: De Gruyter, 2009), pp. 1–13.

Schorske, C., *Fin-de-siècle Vienna: Politics and Culture* (New York: Knopf, 1980).

Scott, W., *Guy Mannering* (London and New York: Dent and Dutton, [1815] 1954).

Semprun, J. (trans. L. Coverdale), *Literature or Life* (New York: Viking, 1997).

Seneca (trans. J. W. Basore), *Moral Essays*, vol. 3, *De beneficiis*, II, 17 (Cambridge, MA: Harvard University Press, 1975).

Sette Lopes, M., 'Clarice Lispector and forgiveness: incidences and coincidences', in M. P. (ed.), *Dossier Law and Literature, Discussion on Purposes and Method* (Italian Society for Law and Literature, 2010), pp. 43–63, available at <http://www.lawandliterature.org/> [last accessed 2 January 2015].

Shapiro, B., 'The concept "fact": legal origins and cultural diffusion', 26 *Albion*, 1994, pp. 227–52.

Shelley, P. B., 'A defence of poetry', published posthumously 1840, available at <https://www.saylor.org/site/wp-content/uploads/2011/01/A-Defense-of-Poetry.pdf> [last accessed 4 December 2017].

Sheppard, C.-A., *The Law of Languages in Canada: Studies of the Royal Commission on Bilingualism and Biculturalism*, no. 11 (Ottawa: Information Canada, Queens Printer, 1971).

Sherwin, R. K., 'Law frames: historical truth and narrative necessity in a criminal case', 47 *Stanford Law Review*, 1994, pp. 39–83.

Sherwin, R. K., 'A manifesto for visual legal realism', 40 *Loyola of Los Angeles Law Review*, 2007, pp. 539–791.

Sherwin, R. K., 'Law, metaphysics, and the new iconoclasm', 11 *Law Text Culture*, 2007, pp. 70–105.

Slaughter, J. R., *Human Rights Inc.: The World Novel, Narrative Form, and International Law* (New York: Fordham University Press, 2007).

Sloterdijk, P., *Falls Europa erwacht* (Suhrkamp: Frankfurt am Main, 2002).

Snow, C. P., *The Two Cultures* (Cambridge: Cambridge University Press, [1959] 1993).

Snyder, T., 'Foreword', in T. Judt and T. Snyder, *Thinking the Twentieth Century* (London: William Heinemann, 2012).

Soar, D., 'Short cuts', *London Review of Books*, 30 June 2011, p. 22.

Spivack, C., 'Ways of reading', 22 *Law & Literature*, no. 3, 2010, pp. 491–507.

Steegmuller, F. (trans. and ed.), *The Letters of Gustave Flaubert*, vols I–II, 1830–80 (Basingstoke and Oxford: Picador, 2001).

Stein, E. (trans. W. Stein), *On the Problem of Empathy. The Collected Works of Edith Stein*, vol. 3 (Washington, DC: ICS Publications, 1989).

Stein, P., *Roman Law in European History* (Cambridge: Cambridge University Press 1999).

Stein, P. and J. Shand, *Legal Values in Western Society* (Edinburgh: Edinburgh University Press, 1974).

Stern, S., 'Legal and literary fictions', in E. Anker and B. Meyler (eds), *New Directions in Law and Literature* (Oxford: Oxford University Press, 2017), pp. 313–26.

Stevens, W., 'Two or three ideas', in W. Stevens, *Opus Posthumous* (New York: Knopf, 1989).

Stone Peters, J., 'Law, literature, and the vanishing real: on the future of an interdisciplinary illusion', 120 *PMLA*, no. 2, 2005, pp. 442–53.

Surdukowski, J., 'Is poetry a war crime? Reckoning for Radovan Karadzic the poet-warrior', 26 *Michigan Journal of International Law*, 2000, pp. 673–99.

Swift, J. (eds P. Dixon and J. Chalker), *Gulliver's Travels* (Harmondsworth: Penguin, [1726] 1977).

Szasz, T., '"Diagnosing" behavior: cui bono?', XXV *Legal Studies Forum*, 2001, pp. 505–17.

Tavris, C. and E. Anderson, *Mistakes Were Made (but not by me): Why We Justify Foolish Beliefs, Bad Decisions, and Hurtful Actions* (Harcourt: Orlando, 2007).

Taylor, C., *The Ethics of Authenticity* (Cambridge, MA: Harvard University Press, 1991).

Thaler, R. H. and C. R. Sunstein, *Nudge, Improving Decisions about Health, Wealth and Happiness* (New Haven: Yale University Press, 2008).

Thibodeau, P. H. and L. Boroditsky, 'Metaphors We Think With: The Role of Metaphor in Reasoning', available at <http://www.plosone.org/article/info:doi/10.1371/journal.pone.0016782> [last accessed 1 March 2015].

Thiher, A., *Fiction Refracts Science: Modernist Writers from Proust to Borges* (Columbia: University of Missouri Press, 2005).

Tissaw, M. A., 'The person concept and the ontology of persons', in J. Martin and M. H. Bickhard (eds), *The Psychology of Personhood: Philosophical, Historical,*

Social-Developmental, and Narrative Perspectives (Cambridge: Cambridge University Press, 2013), pp. 19–39.

Todorov, T., *Grammaire du Décaméron* (Paris and The Hague: Mouton, 1969).

Tokko, R. (pseud. of L. Dexheimer), *Das Automatenzeitalter* (Berlin: Shayol Verlag, [1930] 2004).

Toulmin, S., *Cosmopolis: The Hidden Agenda of Modernity* (New York: The Free Press, 1990).

Toulmin, S., *Return to Reason* (Cambridge, MA: Harvard University Press, 2001).

Treffers, F., 'Ik breng met u geen woorden meer te weeg', 9 *Maandblad Geestelijke volksgezondheid*, 2003, p. 839.

Treffers, F. and D. Bos, 'De loopbaan van Gerrit Achterberg in de psychiatrie', 9 *Maandblad Geestelijke volksgezondheid*, 2003, pp. 804–36.

Trojanow, I. and J. Zeh, *Angriff auf die Freiheit* (Munich: Carl Hanser, 2009).

Troyat, H., *Flaubert* (Paris: Flammarion, 1988).

Vaihinger, H. (trans. C. K. Ogden), *The Philosophy of As-if* (London: Routledge and Kegan Paul, 1924).

Vermeule, B., *Why Do We Care About Literary Characters?* (Baltimore: Johns Hopkins University Press, 2010).

Vico, G., *On the Heroic Mind*, in G. Tagliacozzo, M. Mooney and D. P. Verene (eds), *Vico and Contemporary Thought* (London: MacMillan Press, 1980).

Vico, G. (trans. E Gianturco), *On the Study Methods of Our Time* (Ithaca and London: Cornell University Press, 1990).

Viehweg, T., *Topik und Jurisprudenz* (Munich: Beck, 1954).

Vink, J., 'Spiegelingen, Gerrit Achterberg psychiatrisch bezien', 9 *Maandblad Geestelijke volksgezondheid*, 2003, pp. 767–82.

Vismann, C. (trans. G. Winthrop-Young), *Files, Law and Media Technology* (Stanford, CA: Stanford University Press, 2008).

Vismann, C., 'Die unhintergehbare theatrale Dimension des Gerichts', in C. Vismann, *Medien der Rechtsprechung* (Frankfurt am Main: S. Fischer Verlag, 2011, pp. 19–37).

Vismann, C., 'Image and law – a troubled relationship', in C. Vismann (eds M. Krajewski and F. Steinhauer), *Das Recht und Seine Mittel* (Frankfurt: S. Fischer, 2012), pp. 417–27.

Voltaire (eds J. Benda and R. Naves), *Dictionnaire historique et philosophique* (Paris: Garnier, [1744] 1961).

Wagenaar, W. A., P. J. van Koppen and H. F. M. Crombag, *Anchored Narratives: The Psychology of Criminal Evidence* (Harvester Wheatsheaf: St Martin's Press, 1993).

Wall, G. (trans. and ed.), *Gustave Flaubert, Selected Letters* (Harmondsworth: Penguin, 1979).

Walters, M. D., 'Legal humanism and law-as-integrity', 67 *Cambridge Law Journal*, 2008, pp. 352–75.

Walton, K. L., *Mimesis as Make-Believe* (Cambridge, MA: Harvard University Press, 1990).

Wan, M., 'Fetishistic reading, intertextual reading: law, literature and androgyny in the *Madame Bovary* trial', 2 *Law and Humanities*, no. 2, 2008, pp. 233–54.

Watson, J. D. (ed. G. Stent), *The Double Helix: A Personal Account of the Discovery of the Structure of DNA* (London: Weidenfeld and Nicolson, 1981).

Watt, G., *Equity Stirring: The Story of Justice beyond Law* (Oxford and Portland, OR: Hart Publishing, 2009).

Weber, M., 'Science as a vocation', in P. Lassman, I. Velody and H. Martins (eds), *Max Weber's Science as a Vocation* (London: Unwin Hyman, 1989).

Weisberg, R. H., *The Failure of the Word: The Protagonist as Lawyer in Modern Fiction* (New Haven: Yale University Press, 1984).

Weisberg, R. 'The law-literature enterprise', 1 *Yale Journal of Law & the Humanities*, 1988, pp. 1–67.

Weldon, F., *The Cloning of Joanna May* (Glasgow: Fontana, 1989).

Weresh, M. H., 'Morality, trust, and illusion: ethos as relationship', 9 *Legal Communication & Rhetoric: JALWD*, 2012, pp. 229–72.

West, R., 'Submission, choice and ethics', 99 *Harvard Law Review*, 1986, pp. 1449–56.

West, R., 'The anti-empathic turn', in J. E. Fleming (ed.), *Passions and Emotions. Nomos, LIII* (New York: New York University Press, 2012, pp. 243–88.

Westen, D., P. S. Blagov, K. Harenski, C. Kilts and S. Hamann, 'The neural basis of motivated reasoning: an fMRI study of emotional constraints on political judgment during the U.S. presidential election of 2004', 18 *Journal of Cognitive Neuroscience*, 2006, pp. 1947–58.

White, J. B., *The Legal Imagination. Studies in the Nature of Legal Thought and Expression* (Boston: Little, Brown and Company, 1973).

White, J. B., *When Words Lose Their Meaning, Constitutions and Reconstitutions of Language, Character, and Community* (Chicago: University of Chicago Press, 1984).

White, J. B., *Heracles' Bow* (Madison: University of Wisconsin Press, 1985).

White, J. B., 'Law and literature: no manifesto', 39 *Mercer Law Review*, 1988, pp. 739–51.

White, J. B., *Justice as Translation* (Chicago: University of Chicago Press, 1990).

White, J. B., *Living Speech, Resisting the Empire of Force* (Princeton and Oxford: Princeton University Press, 2006).

White, J. B., 'Establishing relations between law and other forms of thought and language', 1 *Erasmus Law Review*, no. 3, 2008, available at <https://www.eras muslawreview.nl> [last accessed 1 November 2017].

Wiersma, S. (ed. and trans.), *A Tourist Does Golgotha and other Poemas by Gerrit Achterberg* (Grand Rapids: Being Publications, 1972).

Wigmore, J. H., 'A list of legal novels', 2 *Illinois Law Review*, 1908, pp. 574–93.

Wigmore, J. H., 'A list of one hundred legal novels', 17 *Illinois Law Review*, 1922, pp. 26–41.

Williams, M., 'Socio-legal studies and the humanities – law, interdisciplinarity and integrity', 5 *International Journal of Law in Context*, no. 3, 2009, pp. 243–61

Williams, R., 'Culture is ordinary', in R. Williams, *Resources of Hope: Culture, Democracy, Socialism* (London: Verso, [1958] 1989), pp. 3–14.

Wilson, P. H., *The Holy Roman Empire, A Thousand years of Europe's History* (London: Allen Lane, 2016).

Wistrand, S., 'Time for departure? The principle of minimal departure – a critical examination', in G. Rossholm and C. Johansson (eds), *Disputable Core Concepts of Narrative Theory* (Berlin: Peter Lang, 2012), pp. 15–44.

Witteveen, W. J., 'Seeing Rhetoric as Law as Literature', in R. Kevelson (ed.),

Conscience, Consensus, & Crossroads in Law (New York: Peter Lang, 1995), pp. 387–402.

Wittgenstein, L. (trans. G. E. M. Anscombe), *Philosophical Investigations* (Oxford: Oxford University Press, 1953).

Wittgenstein, L. (trans. D. F. Pears and B. F. McGuiness), *Tractatus Logico-Philosophicus* (London, Routledge, [1922] 1961).

Wolf, W., 'Narratology and media(lity): the transmedial expansion of a literary discipline and possible consequences', in G. Olson (ed.), *Current Trends in Narratology* (Berlin: De Gruyter, 2011), pp. 145–80.

Wood, M., *Literature and the Taste of Knowledge* (Cambridge: Cambridge University Press, 2005).

Yoshino, K., 'The city and the poet', 114 *Yale Law Journal*, 2005, pp. 1835–96.

Zamyatin, Y., *We* (New York: Dutton, [1921] 1924).

Zartaloudis, T., 'Ars inventio, poetic laws: law and literature – the and', 29 *Cardozo Law Review*, 2008, pp. 2431–59.

Zeh, J., 'Es werde Linux', *Die Zeit*, 30 March 2006, p. 39.

Zeh, J., *Alles auf dem Rasen, kein Roman* (Munich: Btb Verlag, 2008).

Zeh, J., *Corpus Delicti, ein Prozess* (Frankfurt am Main: Schöffling &Co., 2009).

Zeh, J., 'Interview with *Die Bananenrepublik*', 24 May 2011, available at <http://hdvidzpro.me/video/file/Juli-Zeh-bei-Erwin-Pelzig?id=-6DjHl3HWak> [last accessed 25 December 2017].

Zeh, J. (trans. S.-A. Spencer), *The Method* (London: Vintage, 2014).

Zijderveld, A. C., *On Clichés: The Supersedure of Meaning by Function in Modernity* (London: Routledge, 1979), p. 20.

Cases

Belgium

Court of Cassation, Belgium, 3 May 2011, N292_3.5.11, available at <https://justitie.belgium.be/sites/default/files/downloads/AC%202011%2005.pdf>.

European Court of Human Rights

Johnston and others v. Ireland, European Court of Human Rights 18 December 1986, Application no. 9697/82.

Keegan v. Ireland, European Court of Human Rights 26 May 1994, Application no. 16969/90.

Kyprianou v. Cyprus, European Court of Human Rights 15 December 2005, Application no. 73797/01.

Salah Sheekh versus The Netherlands, European Court of Human Rights 11 January 2007, Application no. 1948/04, *AB* 2007/76.

Krumpholz v. Austria, European Court of Human Rights 18 March 2010, Application no. 13201/05.

England

Miller v. Jackson ([1977] 1QB 966).

Re A: Letter to a Young Person, [2017] EWFC48 (26 July 2017).

Germany

Bundesverfassungsgericht 27 February 2008, 1 BvR 370/07, available at <http://www.bundesverfassungsgericht.de/EN/Homepage/home_node.html> [last accessed 29 January 2018].

The Netherlands

Hoge Raad (Dutch Supreme Court) 21 April 1998, ECLI:NL:HR:1998:ZD1026.
Hoge Raad 25 januari 2005, ECLI:NL:HR:2005:AS1872.
Hoge Raad 31 January 2012, ECLI:NL:HR:2012:BQ9251.
Hoge Raad 12 March 2013, ECLI:NL:HR:2013:BZ2653.
Hoge Raad 26 November 2013, ECLI:NL:HR:2013:1431.
Rechtbank Limburg 21 November 2014, ECLI:NL:RBLIM:2014:10041.

USA

SUPREME COURT
Lochner v. New York, 198 U.S. 45 (1905).
Muller v. Oregon, 208 U.S. 412 (1908).
Buck v. Bell, 274 U.S. 200 (1927).
Jacobellis v. Ohio, 378 U.S. 184 (1964).
Miranda v. Arizona, 384 U.S. 435 (1966).
Bumper v. North Carolina, 391 U.S. 543 (1968)
DeShaney v. Winnebago County Department of Social Services, 489 U.S. 189 (1989).
Johnson v. Calvert, 5 Cal. 4th 84, 851 P.2d 776 (1993).

FEDERAL COURT
United States v. Amy, 24 F.Cas. 792 (1859).

STATE COURT
Riggs v. Palmer, 115 N.Y. 506, 22 N. E. 188 (1889).
Hynes v. New York Central Railroad Co., 231 N.Y. 229, 131 N.E. 898 (1921).
Palsgraf v. Long Island Railroad Company, 248 N.Y. 339, 162 N.E. 99 (1928).

Newspaper items and/or internet items

BBC News, 28 July 2017, 'Office puts chips under staff's skin', available at <http://www.bbc.com/news/technology-31042477> [last accessed 4 August 2017].
The Guardian, Friday, 5 September 2014, available at <http://www.theguardian.com/books/2014/sep/05/ian-mcewan-law-versus-religious-belief> [last accessed 26 November 2016].
Titcomb, J., 'AI is the biggest risk we face as a civilisation, Elon Musk says', on Musk advocating a proactive approach in legislation, *The Telegraph*, 17 July 2017, available at <http://www.telegraph.co.uk/technology/2017/07/17/ai-biggest-risk-face-civilisation-elon-musk-says/> [last accessed 25 December 2017].
Robertson, A., 'Wisconsin company will let employees use microchip implants to buy snacks and open door', *The Verge*, available at <https://www.theverge.com/2017/7/24/16019530/> [last accessed 4 August 2017].
Verbij, A., 'Interview Juli Zeh', *Trouw*, 4 September 2008, available at <https://www.trouw.nl/home/heerseres-over-recht-en-moraal~ab690a8e/> [last accessed 27 January 2018].

Picture reference

Dalem, C. van, *The Baker of Eeklo*, Collection of the Rijksmuseum, Amsterdam, available at <https://www.rijksmuseum.nl/en/collection/> [last accessed 29 January 2018].

Reports

'Explanatory Report to the Additional Protocol to the Convention on Human Rights and Biomedicine on the Prohibition of Cloning Human Beings' (1998) available at <https://rm.coe.int/16800ccde9> [last accessed 23 December 2017].

Recommendation CM/REC (2010)12 of the Committee of Ministers to Member States on Judges: independence, efficiency and responsibilities, a European Code adopted on 17 November 2010 by the Committee of Ministers.

The *ENCJ* (European Network of Councils for the Judiciary) *Working Group Judicial Ethics Report 2009–2010. Judicial Ethics: Principles, Values and Qualities*, adopted in 2010 by the ENCJ General Assembly.

Speech

Clinton, H., Speech at the National Urban League meeting held at Ford Lauderdale, Florida, 31 July 2015, CNN Newsreel 31 July 2015.

Index